INTEREST GROUPS IN SOVIET POLITICS

Published for the
Centre for Russian and East European Studies,
University of Toronto

A list of other Centre publications appears
at the back of this book

Interest Groups in Soviet Politics

EDITED BY H. GORDON SKILLING

AND FRANKLYN GRIFFITHS

PRINCETON UNIVERSITY PRESS

PRINCETON, NEW JERSEY 1971

This book has been composed in Linotype Times Roman

Printed in the United States of America by
Princeton University Press

PREFACE

THIS volume originated with a hypothesis concerning the presence and the importance of group conflict in communist political systems and the value of an "interest group" approach in the study of Soviet politics. Since the editors' viewpoints underwent a process of development and change during the gestation of the book, it may be useful at the outset to indicate the successive stages of their thinking. The original hypothesis was set forth by Gordon Skilling in a paper delivered at the annual meeting of the Canadian Political Science Association in Vancouver, B.C. in June 1965, and was subsequently embodied in an article published in *World Politics* in April 1966, which is included, in somewhat shorter form, at the beginning of this book. It soon became evident that the notion of employing the concept of interest groups in the study of communist politics was a controversial one and deserved to be put to the test of further research. In 1966-1967, while jointly conducting undergraduate and graduate courses on the interest group theme, the editors conceived the idea of preparing a symposium on the subject, and began to select contributors with specialized knowledge of particular groups in the Soviet System. Although there was no desire to force them into a Procrustean bed, Skilling, with valuable help from his co-editor, prepared a preliminary analysis of the topic which appears—largely in its original form—as the second chapter of this book.

From 1967 to 1969 the editors had opportunities to test and develop their ideas in discussions with many colleagues, who made suggestive and valuable comments. Special appreciation is expressed to Professors Ronald Manzer and Hugh Whalen, both then at Toronto (the latter now at Memorial University, Newfoundland), and to our graduate students, in particular Richard Day (now a faculty member at Toronto), for their helpful criticism. Useful comments were made in correspondence by Kenneth Jowitt, University of California (Berkeley), and by Grey Hodnett, York University, Toronto. With the assistance of a grant from The Canada Council, a conference of the contributors was held at Massey College, University of Toronto, in January 1968. Others who participated were Professors Alexander Dallin (Columbia), Alfred Meyer (Michigan), Jeremy Azrael (Chicago), Nicholas De Witt (Indiana), Grey Hodnett (York), and Harold Swayze (Washington). Later

Gordon Skilling conducted seminars on the theme of Soviet group politics in Great Britain, at London and Glasgow Universities; and in North America, at the Universities of Toronto, Columbia, Michigan, and California (Berkeley). He gave papers on the same topic at the Sixth World Conference on International Politics in Berlin in September 1967, and at the workshop on Comparative Communist Studies in Palo Alto during the summer of 1968. Franklyn Griffiths elaborated an alternate approach which was presented in a paper to the Canadian Political Association at its annual meeting in June 1968, in Calgary, and at the Columbia University Seminar on Communism in October 1969.

The reaction to the group approach among Western scholars was not uniform, as will be indicated in the concluding chapter. This was also true of the response in Communist countries. In a brief comment in *Literaturnaya gazeta* (November 1967, p. 9), a reporter wrote: "On the basis of the latest 'theory of groups,' a certain Gordon Skilling of Toronto (Canada) has discovered that 'the party in the USSR is being transformed into a mediator (!) between conflicting interests.' " This discovery, it was said, had the advantage of not requiring knowledge of Soviet realities, but could be constructed "out of whole cloth"(*sobstvennogo paltsa*). Discussions with Soviet scholars during a visit in 1966 revealed a more receptive attitude and indeed a general acceptance of the usefulness of analysing the Soviet political scene in terms of interest groups and group conflict. Although emphasis was placed on the organized mass associations and on the consultative role of specialists, some were ready to admit the importance of more informal group action. Conversations in Czechoslovakia in 1967, 1968, and 1969 indicated that many Czech and Slovak scholars were prepared to recognize the conflict of interest groups and political tendencies as an integral part of communist politics.

These discussions were helpful in clarifying the issues and in suggesting lines of future research. Griffiths came to the conclusion that an interest group approach which was derived from, even though it did not closely follow, David Truman's analytical scheme, was open to serious question. He preferred to employ a method of analysis derived in part from the originator of group theory, namely Arthur Bentley, and centering on the concept of "tendencies of articulation." His viewpoint is embodied in one of the final essays of this book. The other editor, although recognizing the validity of some of Griffiths' critique and the usefulness of his alternative approach, remained convinced of the value of an interest group analysis, and is solely responsible for the concluding chapter. Although the contributors all accepted some version of the concept of interest groups, they interpreted it differently and employed it in their research in varying ways.

The volume in its final form does not, therefore, fully confirm nor entirely negate the original hypothesis about the role of interest groups in Soviet politics. Nor does it provide a uniform set of ideas on the subject nor an integrated array of methods for employing the group concept. It has admittedly not answered all the questions raised at the outset nor eliminated conceptual ambiguities in the term "interest group." Its chief value may be in setting forth a variety of approaches to this subject and thus stimulating continued thought and research. It also provides a Soviet component for the further development of interest group theory and may thus make some contribution to comparative politics generally.

A word of warm thanks is due to those who contributed to the preparation of the volume in its final form: to Sally Skilling, for editorial assistance and for compiling the index; to Ahnna Lowry, for secretarial and administrative work; to Elizabeth Stone, Irene Kenyon, and again, Ahnna Lowry, for typing the manuscript; to Sergei Kononoff, for checking the transliteration from Russian, and to Mrs. William Hanle and Miss Lalor Cadley, of Princeton University Press, for preparing the manuscript for publication. Special appreciation goes to The Canada Council for its generous financial support.

July 1970
Toronto

H. Gordon Skilling
Franklyn Griffiths

NOTE: Transliteration of Russian words follows the style used by the Current Digest of the Soviet Press.

CONTENTS

INTEREST GROUPS IN SOVIET POLITICS

CHAPTER I ~ BY H. GORDON SKILLING

Interest Groups and Communist Politics:* An Introduction

THE IDEA that interest groups may play a significant role in communist politics has, until recently, not been seriously entertained either by Western political scientists or by Soviet legal specialists. The concept of "totalitarianism" that dominated the analysis of communism in the West seemed to preclude the possibility that interest groups could challenge or affect the single ruling party as the fount of all power. The uniqueness of a totalitarian system was deemed to lie in the very totality of its political power, excluding, as it were by definition, any area of autonomous behavior by groups other than the state or party, and still more, preventing serious influence by them on the process of decision-making. Marxist theorists, starting from different presuppositions, assumed that the single ruling party, the organization of the working class, best knew the "real" interests of the people as a whole and denied the possibility of fundamental conflicts of interest within the working class, or between it and associated classes such as the peasantry. Within the ruling party itself, groups or factions opposing the leadership were not admitted in theory or permitted in practice.[1]

Although there was no general agreement on the meaning of totalitarianism, and the term was rejected out of hand by communist scholars, it was common in the West to treat it as a phenomenon unique in world history, sharply distinguished not only from Western democratic soci-

* This is a shortened version of an article of the same title originally published in *World Politics*, xviii, No. 3 (April 1966), 435-451. Reprinted also in Roy C. Macridis and Bernard E. Brown (eds.), *Comparative Politics, Notes and Readings* (3rd edn., Homewood, 1968) and in Frederic J. Fleron, Jr. (ed.), *Communist Studies and the Social Sciences: Essays on Methodology and Empirical Theory* (Chicago, 1969).

[1] See, for instance, *Osnovy marksizma-leninizma* (Moscow, 1959), pp. 352-354. Cf. Frederick C. Barghoorn, "Soviet Political Doctrine and the Problem of Opposition," *Bucknell Review*, xii (May 1964), 11ff.

3

eties but also from traditional authoritarian regimes.[2] It was usually accepted that totalitarianism entailed the widest possible extension of state power over society, thus tending to annihilate all boundaries between state and society, and destroying any associations or groups intermediate between the individual and the state.[3] Zbigniew Brzezinski and Carl Friedrich, in a book published in 1956, established a syndrome of indispensable elements, and argued that the system involved an unavoidable compulsion on the part of the ruling movement to absorb or destroy all social groups obstructing its complete control of society.[4] This line of thought assumed a totally organized or totally administered society, a mass community in which the individual was alone and helpless.[5]

Yet even the most vigorous protagonists of the totalitarian model admitted the existence of "islands of separateness," such as the family or religion,[6] and others wrote of the "limits" on totalitarian power set by the ability of the individual to resist the pressures put upon him.[7] Even more destructive of totalitarian uniqueness was the suggestion, advanced by N. S. Timasheff, of a "democratic-totalitarian" continuum

[2] See the symposium *Totalitarianism*, ed. by Carl J. Friedrich (Cambridge, Mass., 1954; later edition, New York, 1964), for a wide array of views. Citations are to the later edition. Note in particular Friedrich's "The Unique Character of Totalitarian Society," pp. 47ff.

[3] *Ibid.*, N. S. Timasheff, p. 39; Waldemar Gurian, pp. 125-126; Alex Inkeles, pp. 93-95, 99-101. See also Bertram D. Wolfe, "The Durability of Soviet Totalitarianism," a paper given in 1957, and reprinted in Inkeles and Kent Geiger (eds.), *Soviet Society: A Book of Readings* (Boston, 1961), pp. 648-659; and the comment by Daniel Bell, *ibid.*, pp. 49-50. Ralf Dahrendorf, in his *Class and Class Conflict in Industrial Society* (Stanford, 1959), denied the existence of "oppositional interest groups" or "conflict groups" in a totalitarian society (p. 186).

[4] *Totalitarianism*, pp. 52-53, and Friedrich and Brzezinski, *Totalitarian Dictatorship and Autocracy* (Cambridge, Mass., 1956), pp. 9-10. The five essential features were an official ideology, a single mass party, a monopoly of control of all means of armed combat, a monopoly of control of mass communication, and terroristic police control. See also the article by Brzezinski, "The Nature of the Soviet System," *Slavic Review*, xx (October 1961), 353.

The Friedrich-Brzezinski book was revised by Friedrich and later published under the same title (2nd ed., Cambridge, Mass., 1965). The original thesis concerning the nature of totalitarianism was, in the main, unchanged.

[5] Compare later articles in the same spirit by Allen Kassof, "The Administered Society: Totalitarianism Without Terror," *World Politics*, xvi (July 1964), 558ff.; and by T. H. Rigby, "Traditional, Market, and Organizational Societies and the USSR," *ibid.*, 539ff.

[6] Friedrich and Brzezinski, *op.cit.*, pp. 239-289.

[7] David Riesman, "Some Observations on the Limits of Totalitarian Power," *Antioch Review*, xxii (June 1952), 155-68, reprinted in Riesman's *Individualism Reconsidered* (Glencoe, 1954), Chap. 25.

4

involving an infinite gradation of differing degrees of totalitarianism and democracy.[8] A specialist on Eastern Europe, Andrew Gyorgy, denied that the communist states of that area were, at the time of writing, fully totalitarian, and suggested they were instead "partialitarian," thus implying the self-contradictory notion of a "relative," or nontotal, totalitarianism.[9]

The totalitarian concept also often implied a certain changelessness in the nature of communist politics.[10] Even after the death of Stalin, the likelihood of a decline of totalitarianism was doubted by some; if anything, it was argued by Friedrich and Brzezinski, communist societies would probably become *more*, not *less*, totalitarian.[11] Some scholars, however, forecast the possibility that existing totalitarian societies might "mellow," or be "undermined" by their own features, thus opening up the perspective of nontotalitarian communist systems as theoretically conceivable.[12] Barrington Moore, in his *Terror and Progress USSR: Some Sources of Change and Stability in the Soviet Dictatorship*, discussed several future alternatives, including nontotalitarian ones, and calculated the balance of social forces that might produce new political conditions.[13] Writing some years later, Alex Inkeles and Raymond Bauer argued that Soviet society was the product of the interplay of two elements: its distinctive totalitarian character and the pattern of an industrial society which it shared with others.[14] The latter had modified

[8] *Totalitarianism*, p. 43. Openly doubting the usefulness of the term "totalitarianism," Robert C. Tucker wrote of a sequence of different political systems in Russia since 1917. See his comment on Brzezinski's "Nature of the Soviet System," *Slavic Review*, xx (October 1961), 379-380.

[9] *Totalitarianism*, pp. 381ff., esp. n. 2.

[10] The most extreme version of this view is given by Bertram Wolfe in the paper cited in n. 3, above.

[11] Friedrich and Brzezinski, *op.cit.*, p. 300; Brzezinski, "Totalitarianism and Rationality," *American Political Science Review*, L (September 1956), 761.

[12] See in *Totalitarianism*, George F. Kennan, pp. 31-32, 34, 83; Paul Kecskemeti, p. 379; Karl W. Deutsch, pp. 317-318, 320-321, 331ff. Deutsch wrote of a "steady drift to a peripheralization and pluralization of the centers of decision."

[13] (Cambridge, Mass., 1954). Isaac Deutscher also predicted a change in Soviet society as a result of industrialization, which, in his view, had undermined Stalinism and had stimulated democratic aspirations. See his *Russia: What Next?* (London, 1953).

[14] See the final chapter of their book *The Soviet Citizen: Daily Life in a Totalitarian Society* (Cambridge, Mass., 1961): "Trying to read the future of Soviet development solely on the basis of the distinctive characteristics of Soviet totalitarianism without taking account of the changes in the Soviet industrial social structure and in the Soviet people is like trying to understand a story when the pages have been torn in half, lengthwise, and you have only the left halves to read" (pp. 383-384).

5

the former, producing changes similar to those in other industrial societies. Deliberate actions already taken to improve the system had made it "less totalitarian" and reflected "the mellowing, even to some extent, the 'liberalization' of Soviet society."[15]

Paradoxically, the wide-ranging reevaluation of comparative politics which was conducted during the past several decades largely ignored the Soviet system. No doubt the use of the totalitarian concept, reinforced by the pressures of the cold war, produced a propensity to think in black-and-white terms about Soviet and Western politics and tended to obscure the differences within the so-called totalitarian category as well as the common features of all political systems, the Soviet included.[16] A gulf opened up between two developing subdisciplines, comparative politics and communist political studies, each pursuing its own course largely unaware of, or at least unaffected by, the other's efforts.[17] Needless to say, the comparative analysis conducted by David Easton, Gabriel Almond, and others was intended to be applicable to all types of state, including the communist.[18] Nonetheless, the search for a new theory of politics was based largely on materials and concepts derived from the study of American and other Western democratic institutions, enriched by postwar research and theoretical speculation concerning non-Western or developing societies. No serious effort was made to test empirically concepts derived from these political experiences by applying them to communist states; still less was any attempt made to derive from Soviet political life concepts that might be useful in interpreting other systems. In the course of disquisitions on the comparative approach, there were only random remarks referring to Soviet and com-

[15] See the criticisms of the "totalitarian model" in Siegfried Jenkner, "On the Application of Integration and Conflict Models in Research on Communist Social and Ruling Systems," *Modern World* (Köln and Berlin), III (1963-1964), 117-127; and in A. J. Groth, "The 'Isms' in Totalitarianism," *American Political Science Review*, LVII (December 1964), 888-901.

[16] This paraphrases a comment made by Gabriel Almond in an unpublished address at a meeting of the Conference on Soviet and Communist Studies of the American Political Science Association, September 10, 1964.

[17] See my article "Soviet and Communist Politics: A Comparative Approach," *Journal of Politics*, XXII (1960), 300-313. This was reprinted in Frederic J. Fleron, Jr. (ed.), *op.cit.*

[18] See David Easton, *The Political System* (New York, 1953); Gabriel Almond and James S. Coleman (eds.), *The Politics of the Developing Areas* (Princeton, 1960); and the substantial literature cited in Roy C. Macridis and Bernard E. Brown (eds.), *Comparative Politics: Notes and Readings* (Homewood, 1961; rev. ed., 1964; 3rd ed., 1968). See also Harry Eckstein's introduction to Eckstein and David E. Apter (eds.), *Comparative Politics: A Reader* (London, 1963), pp. 3-32.

munist politics, and occasional warnings against a polarization of analysis of the totalitarian and democratic extremes.[19]

On the other hand, a generally applicable concept such as that of the "elite" was sometimes used as an instrument for the study of Soviet politics.[20] Moreover several books, such as those of Sigmund Neumann and Maurice Duverger on political parties, and of Henry W. Ehrmann on interest groups, embraced the communist systems in a general comparative treatment.[21] In both Neumann and Duverger, however, the bulk of the analysis was devoted to two-party and multi-party systems, and the one-party system was treated as a thing apart, sharply differentiated from the others and hardly comparable with them in function or organization.[22] On the other hand, Professor Djordjević, in his contribution to the 1958 conference proceedings edited by Ehrmann, recognized the value of the comparative approach for the study of interest groups in both communist and noncommunist systems, and applied the group concept to Yugoslavia in an original manner (to be discussed more fully later in this chapter). His ideas were not, however, seriously incorporated in the general thinking of the conference.[23] In all these cases,

[19] For example, Almond and Coleman (eds.), op.cit., p. 49. They themselves used the totalitarian concept, with, however, some suggestive reservations (pp. 40-41). See also Almond's article "Comparative Political Systems," *Journal of Politics*, XVIII (1956), 391-409.

[20] John Armstrong, in *The Soviet Bureaucratic Elite* (New York, 1959), wrote of the conflict and diversity beneath the monolithic surface of Soviet politics (pp. 28, 30). See also Merle Fainsod, *How Russia Is Ruled* (2nd ed., Cambridge, Mass., 1963), pp. 36-37, 417-420, on the struggle of elites in Soviet bureaucratic politics. On elites, see also Raymond Bauer, Alex Inkeles, and Clyde Kluckhohn, *How the Soviet System Works* (Cambridge, Mass., 1956); and David Granick, *The Red Executive* (New York, 1960).

[21] Sigmund Neumann (ed.), *Modern Political Parties* (Chicago, 1955), esp. the editor's essay, "Towards a Comparative Study of Political Parties," pp. 395-421; M. Duverger, *Les Partis politiques* (Paris, 1951), and in English, *Political Parties* (London and New York, 1954); Henry Ehrmann (ed.), *Interest Groups on Four Continents* (Pittsburgh, 1958), esp. the report by Jovan Djordjević, "Interest Groups and the Political System of Yugoslavia," pp. 197-228, and his later comment, pp. 292-294.

[22] Neumann at first described the one-party system as a contradiction in terms, since one can speak of a party only if more than one exists. He later compared it with other systems, but noted that in spite of apparent similarity of function, there was a fundamental difference in their actual nature, and the contrast between democracy and dictatorship was embodied in the types of party system. Neumann spoke, however, of a hidden multi-party system within the monolithic regime (*op.cit.*, p. 411). Duverger similarly counterposed sharply the single-party system and democracy, but noted that theoretically a single party might not be totalitarian, and that "the real opposition *might* exist within the party" (*op.cit.*, pp. 261, 276ff., 393, 413).

[23] Ehrmann (ed.), *op.cit.*, pp. 198, 227, 292-294. Only two of the participants,

then, the traditional dichotomy between communist and other political systems remained largely unbridged, and the general lack of more systematic comparative analysis was pointed up still more sharply.

The model of communist politics implicit in most Western analysis seemed, strangely enough, to be exclusively concerned with "outputs," i.e., the imposition of binding decisions, and to be entirely lacking in the "inputs" regarded by Easton as an essential element of every political system.[24] Unlike all other systems, the Soviet was often depicted as one in which struggles over ideas and interests, or conflicts of rival groups, were absent. Issues requiring decisions were raised not by society or social groups but presumably by the party, or better, by its topmost leaders, without regard for the values and interests of other entities. The monolithic party was regarded as the only interest group, not itself differentiated in its thinking or behavior. Almond and Coleman, however, offered the suggestive thought that the articulation and aggregation of interests characteristic of all systems took place within a totalitarian party, largely latently, through the interplay of interest groups and factions.[25]

Western scholars were not fully prepared for the extraordinary changes that occurred in the Soviet political system after Stalin's death, and for the increasing diversity among the communist countries. Many continued to use the term "totalitarian" while the facts of communist society were rendering it less and less helpful for satisfactory analysis. The evidence steadily mounted that the Soviet system was far from being "conflictless" and that behind the façade of the monolithic party a genuine struggle was taking place among rival groups.[26] Carl Linden

---

Gunnar Heckscher and Gabriel Almond, commented on his view (p. 302). Both urged the need for the study of interest groups in communist countries.

[24] "An Approach to the Analysis of Political Systems," *World Politics*, ix (April 1957), 383-400.

[25] *Op.cit.*, pp. 40-41.

[26] There is an interesting confrontation of views in T. H. Rigby and L. G. Churchward, *Policy-Making in the USSR, 1953-1961: Two Views* (Melbourne, 1962). On the post-Stalin succession struggle the literature is too extensive to list, but the following may be cited as representative: Myron Rush, *The Rise of Khrushchev* (Washington, D.C., 1958); Robert Conquest, *Power and Policy in the U.S.S.R.* (London, 1961); Roger Pethybridge, *A Key to Soviet Politics* (London, 1962). See also the discussions in successive issues of *Problems of Communism* cited below in nn. 27, 31. Cf. the earlier articles under the common title "The Soviet Leadership: Trends and Portents," by Richard Lowenthal and Robert Conquest respectively, *ibid.*, ix, No. 4 (July-August 1960), 1-7, 7-11. On the struggle for power before and after Khrushchev's fall, see Rush, *Political*

spoke of a "continuing battle between powerful and entrenched elements in the party's higher echelons," and referred to these as "constraints built into the Soviet system of power," limiting the complete freedom of the top leaders.[27] The conflict was sometimes interpreted as a mere personal struggle for power, largely divorced from questions of policy or ideology, or from the interests of social groups, and involving a conflict between the main institutions of power, namely the party apparatus, the state bureaucracy, the army, and the police.[28] In other studies, however, the struggle was linked with major issues of public policy and was related to more narrowly defined groups, such as the central or peripheral party organizations; the *apparatchiki* and state bureaucrats; central and local economic management; conservative, liberal, and centrist factions; the intelligentsia and its various sectors; special interests such as heavy industry, agriculture, or arms production; the nationalities; and so on.[29] Robert Conquest listed the "pressures"—including the peasantry, intellectuals, and national minorities—under which the struggle for power occurred, and the "institutional elements" involved, such as the various organs of party and government, and the army, police, and managers. Although he did not assign great influence to these groups, he viewed the power of Khrushchev as somewhat limited and not necessarily complete and final.[30] T. H. Rigby, although insisting on the supreme power of the top leader, noted the foci of conflict, which he listed under twelve headings, including not only the conflicts obviously related to the struggle for power but also those between different sections

---

Succession in the USSR (New York, 1965); and Conquest, *Russia After Khrushchev* (New York, 1965).

[27] "Khrushchev and the Party Battle," *Problems of Communism*, XII, No. 5 (September-October 1963), 27-35; also Linden's comment, *ibid.*, No. 6 (November-December 1963), 56-58. His view was strongly commended by Robert C. Tucker and Wolfgang Leonhard in letters, *ibid.*, 59-61, 61-64. See also Tucker's letter, *ibid.*, XIII, No. 3 (May-June 1964), 88.

[28] Pethybridge (*op.cit.*, pp. 17ff.) in his discussion of the 1957 crisis defined "pressure groups" as "influential bodies of men within and without the Presidium and the Central Committee whose composite power makes them a force to be reckoned with in Soviet politics." He distinguished two major groups—the party apparatus and the government bureaucracy—and two minor groups—the economic elite and the army—and, under Stalin, a further major group—the police.

[29] V. V. Aspaturian, in his analysis of Soviet foreign policy in Roy C. Macridis (ed.), *Foreign Policy in World Politics* (Englewood Cliffs, 1958), wrote of the competing interest groups or elites, including the party apparatus; the government bureaucracy; the economic managers and technicians; the cultural, professional, and scientific intelligentsia; the police; and the armed forces (pp. 169-175). He, however, referred to groups as mere "formless clusters of vested interests."

[30] Conquest, *Power and Policy*, pp. 18ff., 29ff., 48.

of the bureaucracy; between informal groupings of officials; between areas and occupational groups; between and within the groups purveying values in the arts and sciences, and even in ideology; and between the masses and the regime.[31]

Under Khrushchev a new element, in the form of a greatly expanded participation in decision-making by experts and specialists in their respective fields, made itself evident. In an increasingly vigorous debate on public policy, certain specialized elite groups were able to express their views and interests and to exert some influence on the ultimate decisions in areas such as education, military strategy, industrial management, legal reform, science, art, and literature. In some cases initial proposals were substantially altered as a result of the discussions.[32] The cultural, professional, and scientific intelligentsia thus emerged as one of the main pressure groups affecting public policy.[33] It was increasingly difficult to accept Conquest's flat assertion that Soviet politics was quite unlike Western politics because there was "no mechanism in the U.S.S.R. for social forces to express themselves."[34] The various sectors of the intelligentsia exerted their influence through their institutes and associations, and through newspapers, scholarly journals, and special confer-

[31] Rigby's rejoinder to Linden, *Problems of Communism*, XII, No. 5 (September-October 1963), 36ff. See his "How Strong is the Leader?" *ibid.*, XI (September-October 1962), 1-8. Barghoorn dealt extensively with the play of social forces in Soviet politics, and referred to the limited degree of pluralism and group action that was emerging. He explicitly denied the existence of organized interest groups comparable to those in the West. See his chapter on the USSR in Lucian W. Pye and Sidney Verba (eds.), *Political Culture and Political Development* (Princeton, 1965), pp. 450-511.

[32] The expanded public discussion and the increasing role of experts were noted by Churchward who quoted a Soviet source that between 1953 and 1956 some 20 conferences, involving some 30,000 persons, took place. See Rigby and Churchward, *op.cit.*, pp. 30, 39-40, 42, and n. 35. See also the article by Jenkner (cited in n. 15, above) and, on the role of the intelligentsia in East Germany, Ernst Richert, *Macht ohne Mandat* (Köln and Opladen, 1963), esp. pp. 281-289.

[33] This was acknowledged by Aspaturian, in Macridis (ed.), *Foreign Policy*, pp. 170-171. See also his analysis of Soviet politics in Macridis and Robert E. Ward (eds.), *Modern Political Systems: Europe* (Englewood Cliffs, 1963), pp. 526-527. Bauer, Inkeles, and Kluckhohn argued that a large proportion of the intelligentsia were not members of the "political elite" and were "apolitical." Somewhat contradictorily the intelligentsia were said to have "a good deal of power," but not to "have much power" in current decisions (*op.cit.*, pp. 157, 175-176). John Hazard discussed the growing influence of the intellectuals in *The Soviet System of Government* (Chicago, 1957), pp. 29-31. See also Barghoorn, in Pye and Verba (eds.), *op.cit.*, pp. 486-490, 508-510.

[34] "After the Fall: Some Lessons," *Problems of Communism*, XIV, No. 1 (January-February 1965), 18.

10

ences, and in varying ways expressed the needs and interests of broader segments of the population.

Individual case studies provided much data that might be used for further generalization concerning the role of these groups. Among the jurists, for instance, there was substantial freedom of discussion and sharp cleavages of opinion, which had considerable impact on legal reforms.[35] On questions of planning and management there were deep-seated differences among the economists, and among managers, officials, and engineers, between the extreme centralizers and others less centralist in attitude.[36] Among writers and artists, a vigorous struggle between liberals and conservatives occurred, with an embryonic public opinion emerging, and some success was occasionally registered in limiting the party's policy of restricting freedom of expression.[37] Discussion among educators exercised a definite influence on Khrushchev's educational reforms.[38] Scientists, although they were said not to have an impact on major policy, were important as "lobbyists," and the leadership was responsive to their argumentation.[39] The military were divided among themselves; they differed with the political leadership on military strategy and sought to affect decisions on other matters of public policy affecting them.[40]

The study of political power in the United States and the U.S.S.R.

[35] See Harold J. Berman, "The Struggle of Soviet Jurists against a Return to Stalinist Terror," *Slavic Review*, XXII, No. 2 (June 1963), 314-320, and his *Justice in the USSR* (rev. ed., New York, 1963), esp. p. 80; A.J.C. Campbell, "The Legal Scene: Proceduralists and Paternalists," *Survey*, No. 57 (October 1965), pp. 56-66.

[36] Leon Smolinski and Peter Wiles, "The Soviet Planning Pendulum," *Problems of Communism*, XII, No. 6 (November-December 1963), 21-33; Alec Nove, "The Liberman Proposals," *Survey*, No. 47 (April 1963), pp. 112-118. See also Smolinski, "Khrushchevism Without Khrushchev," *Problems of Communism*, XIV, No. 3 (May-June 1965), 42-44.

[37] See Priscilla Johnson, "The Regime and the Intellectuals: A Window on Party Politics," supplement, *Problems of Communism*, XII, No. 4 (July-August 1963), xxvii, and her book *Khrushchev and the Arts: The Politics of Soviet Culture, 1962-1964* (Cambridge, Mass., 1965). Cf. Vera S. Dunham, "Insights from Soviet Literature," *Journal of Conflict Resolution*, XVIII (December 1964), 386-410.

[38] Barghoorn, in Pye and Verba (eds.), *op.cit.*, p. 488.

[39] Nicholas De Witt, "The Politics of Soviet Science," unpubl. paper given at the American Political Science Association, September 7, 1962.

[40] See the articles by Thomas W. Wolfe and M. P. Gallagher in *Problems of Communism*, XIII, No. 3 (May-June 1964), 44-52, 53-62; Wolfe, "Problems of Soviet Defense Policy Under the New Regime," *Slavic Review*, XXIV, No. 2 (June 1965), 175-188, and Wolfe, *Soviet Strategy at the Crossroads* (Cambridge, Mass., 1964).

11

published in 1964 by Brzezinski and Huntington was a major break-through in comparative analysis.[41] In this work the authors dealt extensively with the role of interest groups, including "social forces" (aspirations of workers, peasants, and so on) impinging on Soviet politicians and creating the main issues of politics; "specific interest groups" (intellectuals, scientists, or minorities); and "policy groups" (the military, heavy and light industry managers, agricultural managers, and state bureaucrats) which participated in the formation of policy. Like most of the other specialists cited, however, they continued to regard conflict as taking place mainly at the peak of the Soviet political pyramid, with only the top party echelons making policy, and the other groups not enjoying much autonomy or influence. It was, however, increasingly evident that a totalitarian concept which excluded group interest and conflict was no longer an appropriate means of analyzing Soviet politics, and that a more systematic study of the reality of group politics was overdue.[42]

In the communist states of Eastern Europe there was even clearer indication of the growing importance of groups in the political process.[43] This was acknowledged by some communist theorists. Professor Djordjević expressed the opinion that groups were inevitable features of every system, communist as well as noncommunist, although they manifested themselves in different ways. The recognition of these groups was hampered, he said, by absolutist and totalitarian ideologies, idealistic or legalistic theories of the state, and, in communist countries, by "Stalinist dogmatism." "Modern society is a dynamic body, complicated and diversified in its structure, full of conflicting and even antagonistic interests. Consequently, the political affirmation, the role and influence of different interest groups, are the general tendency of human society."[44]

[41] *Political Power: USA/USSR* (New York, 1964), esp. pp. 195-198. See my review article "Soviet and American Politics: The Dialectic of Opposites," *Canadian Journal of Economics and Political Science*, XXXI (May 1965), 273-280. The word "totalitarianism" was not listed in the index and was deliberately not used in the book.

[42] See esp. Tucker on "The Conflict Model" in *Problems of Communism*, XII, No. 6 (November-December 1963), 59-61. Cf. Sidney I. Ploss, *Conflict and Decision-Making in Soviet Russia. A Case Study of Agricultural Policy, 1953-1963* (Princeton, 1965). The author concluded that there was "a genuinely oligarchic procedure for policy-making, and its most outstanding feature is conflict" (p. 283).

[43] See my book *Government and Politics in Communist East Europe* (New York, 1966), esp. Chap. 11.

[44] Ehrmann (ed.), *op.cit.*, esp. pp. 292-294.

A Slovak theorist, Michal Lakatoš, writing in the legal journal *Právny obzor*, argued that socialist society was characterized not merely by differences of class, but also by conflicts "evoked by the intra-class social differentiation of our society, i.e., by interest groups." These he termed "the real basis of the structure of the social and political system." The role of such groups in politics had been neglected in Europe until the late fifties, he said, both by bourgeois political science, with its emphasis on the individual and the state, and by Marxist scholars, with their exclusive concern with social classes. A scientific study of politics required, he said, an investigation of "the interests of people in the entire complicated structure of socialist society, and especially group interests."[45]

There can be no doubt that communist society, in spite of its monolithic appearance and the claims of homogeneity made by its supporters, is in fact as complex and stratified as any other, and is divided into social classes[46] and into other categories distinguished by factors such as nationality or religion. Each group has its own values and interests, and each its sharp internal differences, and all are inescapably involved in conflict with other groups. The novelty of the views expressed by both Djordjević and Lakatoš lay in their recognition, in the words of the former, that socialist society *is* "complex and heterogeneous." "In the

[45] "K niektorym problémom štruktúry našej politickej sústavy ("On Some Problems of the Structure of Our Political System"), *Právny obzor* (Bratislava), No. 1 (1965), pp. 26-36. Cf. his orthodox class analysis in an article published less than two years earlier, "K otázce vývoje sociálně politické základny socialistického státu v ČSSR" ("On the Question of the Development of the Social and Political Basis of the Socialist State in the ČSSR"), *ibid.*, No. 7 (1963), pp. 385-394. In his later article Lakatoš referred to the work of Arthur Bentley on interest groups and cited also the study by Stanislaw Ehrlich, *Grupy nacisku w strukturze politycznej kapitalizmu* (Pressure Groups in the Political Structure of Capitalism) (Warsaw, 1962), in Polish. See the review of the latter by W. Wesolowski in *Polish Perspectives*, VII (January 1964), 78-80. A revised version of Ehrlich's book was published under the title *Wladza i interesy* (Power and Interests) (Warsaw, 1967). Lakatoš elaborated his views in a book written in 1964 but published later, *Občan, právo a demokracie* (The Citizen, Law and Democracy) (Prague, 1966), pp. 13-19, 98-108, 133-140.

An important study by the Czech economist O. Šik, *Ekonomika, zájmy, politika* (Economics, Interests, and Politics) (Prague, 1962), in Czech, also published in Russian as *Ekonomika, interesy, politika* (Moscow, 1964), noted the importance of non-economic as well as economic needs and interests and referred to national as well as class interests.

[46] See Inkeles, "Myth and Reality of Social Classes," reprinted from an article originally published in *American Sociological Review*, XV (1950), in Inkeles and Geiger (eds.), *op.cit.*, pp. 558-573. See also his fuller study, with Bauer, *The Soviet Citizen*, esp. Chap. 13, "Social Class Cleavage."

sociological sense, society is a mosaic of larger and smaller, and highly different, interest groups." Djordjević referred also to amorphous groupings—ethnic, local, or regional in character— which might seek precedence over the national interest; the clashing of specialized interests, such as consumers and producers; and other influences such as those of "a backward environment," "bureaucratic and authoritarian groups," and "personal notions of individuals."[47]

Lakatoš wrote of the conflict between the interests of society as a whole and of individuals and groups, and recognized that these were not mere vestiges of capitalism. In a list not meant to be exhaustive he suggested the following criteria of social differentiation: relationship to the means of production (state sector, cooperative sector, or small production); division of labor (industry, agriculture, intellectual, or physical work); level of income; participation in the direction of society (communists, nonparty persons, or organizers of production); ethnic affiliation; territorial divisions (different administrative entities); biological character (men and women); and so on. He referred to "inner conflicts which existed between society as the proprietor and interests of groups and individuals," and which called forth "a whole series of conflicting relations in economics and in the social-political sphere," and cited the especially deep conflicts over the distribution of income.[48]

More relevant for political analysis than such broad groupings of a sociological character are organized political groups that claim to express the interests of the broad groupings and to exert pressure on government for their implementation. Djordjević defined three categories of such groups in Yugoslavia: (a) those participating directly in the process of governing (such as economic organizations and social institutions); (b) those holding "strategic positions" in the political system (such as the League of Communists); and (c) those representing the special interests of citizens (such as unions or churches). He recognized that these might have their own selfish interests and might also seek to impose their views on the social forces they were supposed

---

[47] Ehrmann (ed.), *op.cit.*, pp. 203, 210, 212-213, 222.

[48] Lakatoš, "On Some Problems," pp. 29-31. Some support for this approach was forthcoming in the Soviet Union in an article by V. Shubkin, "O konkretnykh issledovaniakh sotsialnykh protsesov," *Kommunist*, No. 3 (February 1965), pp. 48-57, which referred to the complexity of society and the need to study not only classes, but also definite groups within classes, "the differences among which were conditioned not by forms of ownership of the means of production, but by factors such as profession, level of training, education, and extent of income" (pp. 49, 51).

to represent. There might also be conflicts of interest between the leaders of such groups and their members, or between their central and local organizations. Djordjević saw in the development of a public opinion favorable to "the general interest" the major safeguard of a correct relation between "rightful" and "selfish" group interests. The direct participation of many groups in the governing process (their "institutionalization") was regarded as a unique and valuable feature of the Yugoslav system. In similar vein Lakatoš expressed the opinion that groups might one-sidedly pursue their own interests, at the expense of the general interest, or might, unless closely connected with the social forces they represented, fail to express real group interests and become mere arms of the state. An indispensable part of socialist democracy, in his view, were "interest groups, the institutional expression of group interests"; to them, "as an integrating element, the guidance of society must be adapted."

In speaking of interest organizations Lakatoš had in mind mainly the societal or mass associations that exist in all communist countries; the trade-unions, youth leagues, women's committees, and a host of other bodies in specialized fields, such as the unions of writers and journalists. Known in Stalin's times as "transmission belts," they were regarded as the means of transmitting policy *to* the groups rather than as sources originating it, and had in fact no share in the shaping of public policy. Power was, in any case, concentrated in their higher echelons, so that each organization tended to stand not for the special interests of its members, or of a broader social group such as the workers or writers, but rather for a general "public" interest as conceived by the party and its spokesmen within the organization.[49]

In the context of group conflict, the necessity arose of "sublimating" or "integrating" the competing interests and arriving at a decision that ostensibly represented the public or general interest. "The social interest in our society," wrote Lakatoš, "can be democratically formed only by the integration of group interests; in the process of this integration, the interest groups protect their own economic and other social interests; this is in no way altered by the fact that everything appears on the surface as a unity of interests." The main burden of responsibility for this

---

[49] Cf. the later article by Lakatoš, "Dvadsat rokov budovania socialistickej demokracie" ("Twenty Years of Building Socialist Democracy"), *Právny obzor,* No. 5 (1965), pp. 265-274, in which he spoke of the mass associations as exerting pressure, on behalf of interest groups, on the party and government organizations that resolved conflicts between group and general social interests.

15

task fell to the groups holding "a strategic position," to use Djordjević's term (borrowed from David Truman), which he identified in Yugoslavia with the League of Communists and the Socialist Alliance.[50] Although it was not expressly stated, the function of these strategic groups was presumably to cultivate the public interest, and to subordinate to it special and partial interests. Lakatoš developed the same theme at greater length, referring at one point to the state as "an active organ capable of coordinating these interest conflicts, and under the pressure of these group interests, of forming a general social interest." The task was shared, in his opinion, with the societal organizations, and with the Communist Party, all of which bore some of the responsibility for resolving the conflicts of class, group, and individual interests. "The party as the leading and directing political force fulfills its function by resolving intra-class and inter-class interests."[51]

In the words of a Western commentator, the party was "an arena in which the various Soviet elites make known their demands on one another, articulate their special interests, and try to impose their desires as the unified will of society as a whole."[52] It was no longer seen as completely monolithic, but as a "conglomeration of interests."[53] Since it already possessed power, it did not need to be concerned with what is often the most important function of parties elsewhere, the acquisition of power. Nonetheless, within every communist party there was a hidden struggle for power, a subterranean rivalry over policy and the public interest, sometimes bursting into the open in purge and counterpurge. In the absence of an effective representative body, and also of independent and competing parties, the single party had to fill many roles performed in other systems by various institutions and, above all, to

[50] Ehrmann (ed.), op.cit., p. 205.

[51] Lakatoš, "On Some Problems," pp. 34-35. Herbert Marcuse, in his Soviet Marxism (New York, 1958), wrote of the competing special interests in Soviet society, even within the party, and of the role of the bureaucracy in representing "the social interest over and above individual interests," and the "real" interest as distinct from the immediate interests of the people (pp. 107-119).

[52] Aspaturian, in Macridis and Ward (eds.), op.cit., pp. 492-494, 526. He did not admit the possibility of an "accommodation" of interests, but spoke only of an "imposition" or of "mutual elimination." Ploss, in his "Soviet Politics Since the Fall of Khrushchev," Foreign Policy Research Institute Series, mimeographed (Philadelphia, 1965), rejected the abstraction of a cohesive Soviet leadership and argued that the leadership "frames its policies with need (sic) to compromise and adjust between diverse groups and their interests in society" (p. 12).

[53] Aspaturian, in Macridis (ed.), op.cit., p. 170. Cf. Barghoorn on intra-party differences, in Pye and Verba (eds.), op.cit., pp. 468-470, 510.

16

serve as a broker of competing group interests.[54] In the post-Stalin era, with the circle of decision-making widening and public discussion less restricted, the party chiefs increasingly had to give attention to forming a consensus among competing policy groups, specialist elites, differing viewpoints within the party, professional and other associations, and broader amorphous social groupings.

A new version of communist politics slowly began to emerge as a result of the changes that had occurred since Stalin's death and the shifting perspectives of both Western and communist analysts. The concept of a totalitarian system, in which a single party, itself free of internal conflict, imposes its will on society, and on all social groups, was challenged by an approach that took account of the conflicting groups that exert an influence on the making of policy by the party. This could not be described as genuine pluralism; it appeared rather to be a kind of imperfect monism in which, of the many elements involved, one—the party—was more powerful than all others but was not omnipotent. It might be called a "pluralism of elites," or to borrow Robert Dahl's expressive term, a "polyarchical" system, but oligarchical rather than democratic in character.[55] As in all systems, the final product—policy—was highly political, reflecting conflicting forces and interests within the structure of the single party, of the national communist society, and, to an increasing extent, of the communist world as a whole.[56]

[54] The computer approach to comparative politics by Arthur A. Banks and Robert B. Textor, *A Cross-Polity Survey* (Cambridge, Mass., 1963), is weak in its analysis of Eastern European communist states with reference to interests. It assumed that "interest articulation" by associational groups and nonassociational groups, or by several political parties, was limited or negligible, and was significant only through institutional groups (the single party). "Interest aggregation" by the legislature was "negligible," and, for the executive was "unascertained." The role of the single party in interest articulation and aggregation was also said to be not ascertainable (pp. 89ff.).

[55] *Preface to Democratic Theory* (Chicago, 1963), p. 63. See Barghoorn's speculations on the growth of elite influence and incipient pluralism, in Pye and Verba (eds.), *op.cit.*, pp. 507-510. Cf. the discussion of the continuance of traditional elites under Nazism and Fascism, in Groth, "The 'Isms.' "

[56] Z. Mlynář, a Czech scholar, discussed at length the relations of individual and group interests with the general social interest, and the role of the party, the trade-unions, the representative bodies, and the technical experts in achieving a reconciliation of these conflicting interests. See his "Problemy politicheskovo rukovodstva i novaya ekonomicheskaya sistema" *Problemy mira i sotsializma*, No. 12 (December 1965), pp. 90-99, also available in English, "Problems of Political Leadership and the New Economic System," *World Marxist Review*, VIII (December 1965), 58-64. Mlynář had already developed this argument in his

17

book, *Stát a člověk* (The State and Man) (Prague, 1964), pp. 32-69. In this scholarly study he treated "pressure groups" or "interest groups" as important components of the political system (pp. 38, 46), urged that the societal organizations become real "interest organizations" (p. 62), and described the party as a "special social organism" which represented and defended the interests of the whole society and resolved interest conflicts in harmony with this general interest (pp. 66-67).

Groups in Soviet Politics
Some Hypotheses

IT IS THE central assumption of this volume that in the seventeen years since Stalin's death the Soviet political system has been passing through a period of transition, characterized among other things by the increased activity of political interest groups and the presence of group conflict. Although decision-making in its final stage still remains in the hands of a relatively small group of leaders at the top of the party hierarchy, there has been, it is assumed, a broadening of group participation in the crucial preliminary stages of policy deliberation and in the subsequent phase of implementation. These aspects of policy-making have been called by some specialists in comparative politics the "articulation" and "aggregation" of group interests, and "rule-application."[1] It is the purpose of this volume to probe more deeply into these important phases of the Soviet political process by examining a series of selected interest groups and their operations primarily at the national level.

Earlier studies of the Soviet political system, as we have noted in the introductory chapter, identified it as a totalitarian dictatorship and largely ignored or denied the existence of conflict, which is normally regarded as a central feature of all politics. Stressing the hierarchical nature of political control and the penetration of the whole of society by state and party, the traditional view tended to deny the existence of autonomous and intermediate associations between state and society, and to recognize group conflict only in the form of factional struggles among the top leaders and, in a limited degree, of bureaucratic competition among the organs of administrative power such as the military, police, party, and state. When an alternate model of Soviet politics, describing conflict

---

[1] Gabriel A. Almond and James Coleman (eds.), *The Politics of the Developing Areas* (Princeton, 1960), pp. 33ff., and Almond and G. Bingham Powell, Jr., *Comparative Politics: A Developmental Approach* (Boston and Toronto, 1966), Chaps. IV and V.

19

as a crucial feature of the system, developed,[2] attention was concentrated, in the main, on the top-level struggle over power and policy among the leaders, rather than on the activity of other groupings at the middle and upper levels of Soviet society.[3] The analysis of this factional conflict tended to be highly speculative, based on esoteric sources of information, and frequently identified leaders and factions with various social groups and institutions, or with particular policies, on somewhat tenuous grounds.[4] Moreover it was often assumed, without much evidence, that the "party apparatus," or the "state bureaucracy" constituted single interest groups with more or less homogeneous attitudes on public issues.[5] This overlooked the fact that various other groups were intervening with increasing frequency in the political process. If such groups *were* mentioned, their importance was usually minimized.[6] The analysis tended also to treat such groups as mere objects of manipulation by the top leaders and factions, and to discount the possibility of autonomous action by them.[7]

[2] See in particular Carl Linden, *Khrushchev and the Soviet Leadership, 1957-1964* (Baltimore, 1966), Introduction and esp. pp. 20, 218, and Sidney I. Ploss, *Conflict and Decision-Making in Soviet Russia. A Case Study of Agricultural Policy, 1953-1963* (Princeton, 1965), Introduction and Conclusions. Cf. Frederick C. Barghoorn, *Politics in the USSR* (Boston and Toronto, 1966), p. 222, and Robert Conquest, *Power and Policy in the U.S.S.R.* (London, 1961), pp. 11-12. See Chap. 1 above, pp. 8-10.

[3] In addition to the Books by Linden, Ploss, and Conquest, see Myron Rush, *Political Succession in the USSR* (New York and London, 1965), esp. pp. 154, 163, 189; Robert Conquest, *Russia After Khrushchev* (New York, 1965); and Howard R. Swearer, *The Politics of Succession in the USSR* (Boston, 1964). See also pp. 35-36, below, in this chapter. A later book of this kind is Michel Tatu, *Power in the Kremlin, From Khrushchev to Kosygin* (New York, 1968), originally published in French, *Le Pouvoir en URSS* (Paris, 1967). Although Tatu describes his book as a study in Kremlinology, he discusses certain contending groups or "lobbies," as he terms them, in the post-Khrushchev period. These include in particular the powerful groups of *apparatchiki* and economic administrators or managers, as well as the army, the police, and the "steel-eaters" lobby (pp. 429ff.).

[4] See for instance Aspaturian's analysis of groups favoring and opposing a relaxation of tensions in R. Barry Farrell (ed.), *Approaches to Comparative and International Politics* (Evanston, 1966), pp. 212-287.

[5] See the discussion of the interest group approach in T. H. Rigby, "Crypto-Politics," *Survey*, No. 50 (January 1964), pp. 183-194. See also his article, "The Extent and Limits of Authority (A Rejoinder)," *Problems of Communism*, XII, No. 5 (September-October 1963), 36-41.

[6] Alfred Meyer, in *The Soviet Political System* (New York, 1965) recognized the existence of interest groups but warned against exaggerating their role (pp. 48, 234-235, 259-260, 468-473). Cf. Marshall Shulman, *Beyond the Cold War* (New Haven, 1966), pp. 40ff.

[7] Z. Brzezinski and S. P. Huntington, *Political Power: USA/USSR* (New York, 1964), pp. 196-197; Shulman, *op.cit.*, p. 40.

Several scholars, notably Barghoorn, Aspaturian, and Brzezinski, paid more attention to the role of interest groups at the levels below the pinnacle, and in varying degrees tried to relate them to the conflict at the apex of the Soviet system.[8] This widened the range of observed political activity in the USSR to include many groups previously neglected and strengthened our conviction that further study of these phenomena was justified. Although we did not fully share the views of the scholars cited, we recognized the importance of these initial contributions to the study of what was a virtually uncharted wilderness and resolved to pursue further preliminary explorations of this territory. We were fully conscious of the difficulty of the task, in part because of the general problem of using the interest group concept as a tool of analysis of Soviet society, and in part because of the special obstacles in the way of identifying groups and group interests in a highly controlled society such as the Soviet. This chapter was written to suggest a number of tentative hypotheses concerning the nature of interest groups in the Soviet setting and the forms and methods of their action.

The Interest Group Approach

To avoid misunderstanding, it should be stated at once that this is not an attempt arbitrarily to apply to the Soviet system interest group theories which have been developed in the West in the past sixty years.[9] In fact it can be said without much fear of contradiction that no general group theory has yet emerged which is suitable for use in all

[8] See especially Barghoorn, *op.cit.*, Chaps. II and VII, particularly pp. 223-242. Cf. V. V. Aspaturian, "Social Structure and Political Power in the Soviet System" (unpublished paper delivered at the American Political Science Association, 1963); his chapter on the Soviet Union, in Roy C. Macridis and Robert E. Ward (eds.), *Modern Political Systems: Europe* (Englewood Cliffs, 1963); his chapter in Farrell (ed.), *op.cit.*, esp. pp. 256-283; Brzezinski and Huntington, *op.cit.*, esp. Chap. 4. See also Brzezinski, "The Soviet Political System: Transformation or Degeneration?" *Problems of Communism*, xv, No. 1 (January-February 1966), 9, n. 18. A suggestive, although impressionistic, survey of interest groups was sketched out by Isaac Deutscher, "Moscow: The Quiet Men, 1. Constellations of Lobbies," *The Nation*, cc, No. 14 (April 5, 1965), 352-357.

[9] See especially David B. Truman, *The Governmental Process, Political Interests and Public Opinion* (New York, 1951), and Earl Latham, "The Group Theory of Politics: Notes for a Theory," *American Political Science Review*, XLIII (June 1952), 376-397, reprinted largely unchanged in his book, *The Group Basis of Politics* (Ithaca, 1952), Chap. 1 (later references are to the article). See also Arthur F. Bentley, *The Process of Government* (Evanston, 1949). For a further review of the literature, see H. Zeigler, *Interest Groups in American Society* (Englewood Cliffs, 1964), Chap. 1, and Mancur Olson, *The Logic of Collective Action* (Cambridge, Mass., 1965), Chap. v.

countries.[10] In the voluminous literature that has appeared on this subject since the revival of Arthur Bentley's group approach in the early fifties, it was forcefully argued that group theory is deficient if it neglects the political culture and the institutional setting in which group activity occurs,[11] and that an approach which reflects too closely the special features of American society and politics may not be applicable to other political systems.[12] Moreover, purportedly "universal" group theories were vitiated by their concentration, until recently, on Western democratic systems and pressure group activity characteristic of them, and by their almost total neglect of communist systems.[13] Even the more broadly conceived concepts of interest articulation and aggregation suggested by Almond and Coleman were based primarily on the experiences of the developing areas and gave only limited attention to the communist states. Nonetheless these authors recognized the usefulness of an interest group approach in the analysis of communist societies. Later versions of this viewpoint, more universal in scope, were hampered by the use of a totalitarian model which dealt with group conflict in communist countries ambiguously and tended to treat it as peripheral.[14]

[10] Note for instance the comments of Samuel J. Eldersveld, in Henry W. Ehrmann (ed.), *Interest Groups on Four Continents* (Pittsburgh, 1958), pp. 178-179, and of Joseph LaPalombara, in Harry Eckstein and David E. Apter (eds.), *Comparative Politics: A Reader* (New York, 1963), p. 422. Other general critiques are available in Eckstein's introduction to Part VI of Eckstein and Apter (eds.), *ibid.*, pp. 389-397; P. Odegard, "A Group Basis of Politics; a New Name for an Old Myth," *Western Political Quarterly*, XI, No. 3 (September 1958), 689-703; Charles B. Hagan, "The Group in a Political Science," in Roland A. Young (ed.), *Approaches to the Study of Politics* (Evanston, 1958); P. Monypenny, "Political Science and the Study of Groups," *Western Political Quarterly*, VII, No. 2 (June 1954), 183-201; Stanley Rothman, "Systematic Political Theory: Observations on the Group Approach," *American Political Science Review*, LIV, No. 1 (March 1960), 15-33. See the cogent critique by Theodore J. Lowi, "American Business, Public Policy, Case Studies, and Political Theory," *World Politics*, XVI, No. 4 (July 1964), 677-715.

[11] See in particular, Roy C. Macridis, "Interest Groups in Comparative Analysis," *Journal of Politics*, XXIII, No. 1 (February 1961), 25-45.

[12] Joseph LaPalombara in Eckstein and Apter (eds.), *op.cit.*, pp. 421-422; Jean Meynaud, "Les groupes d'intérêt et l'administration en France," *Revue française de science politique*, VII, No. 3 (July-September 1957), 573-574.

[13] A significant early exception was the contribution by Jovan Djordjević to Ehrmann (ed.), *op.cit.*, pp. 197-228.

[14] Almond and Powell, *op.cit.* There is some inconsistency between the recognition of some degree of pluralism and group autonomy in the brief section dealing with the Soviet Union (pp. 272, 275-278) and the denial of autonomous group activities in the many references to totalitarian systems throughout the book (e.g., pp. 47, 79, 312). But see above, Chap. 1, pp. 6-7 and n. 19.

In spite of serious doubts and reservations concerning Bentley-Truman group theories, many scholars recognized that the interest group concept, provided it was suitably adapted to the concrete conditions of a given society and supplemented by other analytic concepts, was a useful instrument of analysis.[15] In Oliver Garceau's words, the group approach was "a way to talk about and analyze the political process."[16] Although often regarded with suspicion both in European and American political theory, the group idea had a long pedigree in the history of political thought.[17] In the past fifteen years in particular the group approach has been the subject of intense discussion and has been employed as an effective tool of research on many political systems. It has directed the attention of the researcher to hitherto neglected aspects of political systems and especially to "real forces" which are sometimes hidden behind formal structures but nonetheless profoundly affect the latter's operations.[18] It has often raised crucial questions which were relevant and offered insights which were suggestive for further research.[19]

The application of the group concept to political behavior in the USSR, it should be stressed, does not necessarily involve an interpretation of Soviet politics solely in terms of interest groups and group conflict. None of the authors cited earlier takes this viewpoint, nor does this volume. The group approach, however, sensitizes the observer to a realm of political activity that has gone almost unnoticed and thus facilitates our understanding of Soviet and other communist systems in the course of their development. Although we do not expect to present a full and complete analysis of the dynamics of Soviet policy-making, we may, by focusing attention on the structure and role of interest groups, be able to perceive more accurately the nature of this process, in particular in the stages before and after the formal making of decisions by the topmost leaders. In so doing, our analysis may point up some of the weaknesses of contemporary interest group theory and thus eventually contribute to a more solidly based general theory of group politics.

[15] Note for instance the opinions of critics such as Macridis, Meynaud, Monypenny, Rothman, and LaPalombara in the works cited above.

[16] Oliver Garceau, "Interest Group Theory in Political Research," *The Annals of the American Academy of Political and Social Science*, CCCXIX (September 1958), 105.

[17] For a historical review, see Earl Latham, *op.cit.*, and Stanislaw Ehrlich, "Les 'groupes de pression' et la structure politique du capitalisme," *Revue française de science politique*, XIII, No. 1 (March 1963), 25-43.

[18] Eckstein, in Eckstein and Apter (eds.), *op.cit.*, p. 393.

[19] *Ibid.*, p. 394. Cf. Truman's list of questions for research, *op.cit.*, p. 65.

23

Political Interest Groups Classified

It should be clearly stated at the outset that we are focusing our attention not on all groups, and all forms of group action, but only on "political interest groups," as we shall define them. Paraphrasing David Truman, we shall consider as a political interest group an aggregate of persons who possess certain common characteristics and share certain attitudes on public issues, and who adopt distinct positions on these issues and make definite claims on those in authority.[20] For reasons to be more fully explained later, we are deliberately excluding from detailed analysis *both* the broad social groups into which Soviet society, like every other, is divided, and the leadership factions which bear the main responsibility for the final making of formal decisions. We are concentrating on a relatively small circle of elite groups, at what might be called the upper and middle levels of the Soviet social structure, that are active politically in the sense that they are able to express attitudes, and to make demands, concerning matters of public policy.[21] This does not imply, be it noted, that these groups, any more than their counterparts in other societies, are always successful in achieving their goals. It does, nonetheless, assume that they have means, however inadequate, of giving voice to their attitudes and claims.

Specifically, the political groups under discussion in this volume include what we shall call "occupational groups" and "opinion groups." "Occupational groups" include (a) certain "intellectual" groups, whose task is primarily research or creative work, for instance, writers, economists, lawyers, and natural scientists, and (b) certain groups which we shall call "official" or "bureaucratic" and which occupy key positions in the power structure, namely, party *apparatchiki*, state bureaucrats and managers, police officials, and the military. It is recognized that some officials may also be intellectuals in training and in the nature of their work, and that some intellectuals may occupy official positions. The classification, therefore, does not represent a sharp division but is employed as a tool of analysis.

[20] *Ibid.*, pp. 33, 37.
[21] The term "elite group" is used here to designate a group whose members have special training, enjoy a higher social and economic status than the mass of the population, and in some cases occupy official positions in the government and party hierarchy. The "elite group" may be regarded as roughly equivalent to the "intermediate participants," the term used by Professor Griffiths below (Chap. 10). Where the term "political elite" is used, it refers to the policy-makers at the highest level of the party and government.

It is taken as an initial hypothesis that each one of these broad occupational categories (intellectual or official) *may* have certain common interests, for instance, all managers, in a high level of remuneration, or all the military, in professional autonomy, and *may* press upon the top rulers demands consonant with these interests. On the other hand, the occupational aggregates are also likely to be divided in their attitudes on certain public issues, the military on military strategy, the economists on economic reform, or the writers on literary policy. It is, therefore, assumed that within the occupational categories (both official and nonofficial) just mentioned, certain "opinion groups" such as "liberal writers," "centralist economists," or "conservative military," *may* be identified. The members of such a group share, it is assumed, a common viewpoint on specific public policies, usually in sharp conflict with that held by other members of the same occupation. In view of the presumption that such opinion groups may be more unified in their views and more active in their defense than the whole of the occupational category to which they also belong, we are deliberately refraining from identifying them as subgroups.

We recognize that in strict logic *all* political groups are "opinion groups," in the sense of having "attitudes" of their own, and also that broader "opinion groups," linking together persons from several occupations, may also exist. In the latter sense, an opinion group would be simply an aggregate of persons of like mind, having no common occupational identification, say "liberals or centralists," a classification which would be too loose and diffuse to be employed easily in analysis. For the sake of convenience, and in the absence of a more meaningful terminology, we are, therefore, somewhat arbitrarily reserving the term "opinion groups" to denote those persons, within a given occupation, who have a distinguishable viewpoint of their own. Only empirical research will reveal whether the attitudes shared by all members of a given occupation, or those held by only a sector of the occupation, are more significant, and whether therefore "occupational" or "opinion" groups are more relevant in Soviet policy-making.

Each of the two principal categories of groups, the "occupational" and the "opinion," may be further broken down into a complex web of subgroups, reflecting divergent aspects of occupational affiliation or different nuances of outlook. Scientists, for example, might be classified according to various criteria: institutional affiliation (Academy of Sciences, universities, other institutions); regional level of activity (all-

25

union, union-republic, provincial or local); official or nonofficial employment (party *apparat*, government department or nonofficial institutions); geographical location of employment (Leningrad, Moscow, Novosibirsk); scientific field (biology, geography, etc.); function (pure scientists, technologists, governmental administrators); rank or position (full or corresponding member of the Academy of Sciences, or research employee), and so on. In each case, it would be a matter of research to determine whether and in what degree the institutional, regional, or other subgroup possesses distinctive views of its own, and whether and in what degree it shares common attitudes with other subgroups in the broader category of scientists. It would also have to be investigated how far each subgroup was divided ideologically into opinion groups with differing political attitudes and policy demands.

Each opinion group may also be analyzed as a complex network of subgroups, exhibiting a wide spectrum of views. For instance, among writers, it may be possible not only to distinguish "liberals" and "conservatives," but also to make narrower distinctions within these categories, with differing degrees of liberalism or conservatism. Moreover, opinion groups, within the military for example, may be based not on a liberal-conservative dichotomy, but on other criteria such as differing views of war strategy.

Earl Latham described group relations in the USA in terms not entirely unapplicable to the Soviet situation, referring to "a moving multitude of human clusters, a consociation of groups . . . an intersecting series of social organisms, adhering, interpenetrating, overlapping—a single universe of groups which combine, break, federate and form constellations and coalitions of power in a flux of restless alterations."[22] Allowing for the greater restrictions on group activity in the Soviet Union, there exists a similar complicated patchwork of intersecting and overlapping groups. These may in turn form complex group alliances, which give each other mutual support in defense of common interests. There may be, for instance, alliances of differing professional or bureaucratic groups, based on a common regional (e.g., Leningrad) or ethnic (e.g., Ukrainian) interest, or a common functional interest (e.g., agricultural). A kind of military-industrial complex allying the military, heavy industry, and the party *apparat*, may perhaps be identified.[23] Within several intellectual and official groups, there may be opinion

[22] Latham, *op.cit.*, p. 396.
[23] Shulman, *op.cit.*, p. 43, and Aspaturian in Farrell (ed.), *op.cit.*, pp. 261 *et seq.*

groups which cut across occupational lines and link together, say, the liberal writers, artists, scientists, and lawyers in a common front on one or more issues.[24] Brzezinski has proposed a scheme for analyzing the spectrum of opinion in Soviet politics ranging from the systemic left (radical reformists) to the systemic right (reactionaries), and including in the mainstream the left, centrist, and right.[25] Empirical research may reveal whether particular occupational categories as a whole can be identified with certain opinions (e.g., *apparatchiki* as "conservatives," or writers as "liberals"), or whether such categories are normally divided into rival opinion groups.[26]

Some Problems of Definition

In our analysis we are using the concept "interest group," in spite of the ambiguity surrounding both the words "interest" and "group," in part to conform to general practice, and in part for want of a satisfactory alternative. In its most limited and neutral form, the term "interest" may refer merely to a concern about a particular sphere of policy-formation. In this sense, each group will normally have an interest primarily related to a particular sphere or subject, such as the writers in literary matters or the army officers in military affairs. Some groups will have a wider concern with many fields of public policy, although subgroups will have a more restricted interest. Without denying the utility of such a usage, we are employing the concept of "interest" in a more precise and limited sense, to refer to an expressed attitude on the matter of concern, and to an articulated claim for some kind of public action in this respect. A more accurate way of expressing our meaning would be to use the designation "demand" group.[27] From time to time

[24] See, for example, the letter to the Central Committee, in 1966, opposing the rehabilitation of Stalin, which was signed by leading writers, scientists, and artists (*New York Times*, March 21, 1966). *Ad hoc* alliances are sometimes formed on matters of lesser importance. For instance, a protest concerning the danger of contaminating Lake Baikal through industrial waste was published in *Komsomolskaya pravda*, signed by leading scientists, an artist, a novelist, and other public figures (*ibid.*, May 13, 1966). Similar protests have been reported on such matters as the projected route of the Moscow Metro extension, or the building of the Hotel Rossia on Red Square (*ibid.*, August 25, 1965, and January 4, 1967).

[25] "The Soviet Political System," p. 10. Barghoorn referred to a liberal-conservative continuum (*op.cit.*, pp. 180-181), with certain occupational groups tending as a whole to one or other extreme.

[26] Wolfgang Leonhard, "Notes on an Agonizing Diagnosis," *Problems of Communism*, xv, No. 4 (July-August 1966), 36-37.

[27] Note that Almond and Powell equate articulation with "demands for polit-

we shall, however, employ another term—"political group"—as an abbreviation to be equated with "political interest group."

Nor are we using the term "interest" as though it were necessarily "self-regarding" or "selfish."[28] Whether the "interest" involved is a "selfish" one or a more general concern for the "public interest" is a matter for investigation in each case and cannot be assumed a priori. In some cases, the interests *may* be "selfish," for example, relating to an interest of all writers in higer compensation or status, or of "liberal" writers in greater creative freedom. In other cases, especially in the case of opinion groups, the interest may be a broader public interest, either general (the acceleration of de-Stalinization) or specific (the correction of a particular legal injustice). As in all countries, the separation of the "selfish" from the "public" interest is difficult, the professed public interest often concealing a more selfish one, and the selfish aim often being identified by its advocates as a public interest. Moreover, even by articulating "selfish" interests, groups may in some circumstances be indirectly benefitting the community as a whole.

In employing in effect Truman's definition of political interest groups, we are not necessarily accepting many of his assumptions about the nature of groups and their activity. We do not, for example, assume that the attitudes of an individual member of a social or occupational category are always determined by his belonging to that aggregate, or that all persons in a specific social category necessarily act together as a political interest group. We are focusing our attention, not on the "shared characteristics" of a particular social group, but on the actual "common attitudes" and "claims" of the politically active group.

To put it another way, three levels of "groupness" may be distinguished. A group may be marked by certain distinctive characteris-

---

ical action," *op.cit.*, pp. 73, 224. An interest group is defined as a group of individuals linked by bonds of concern or advantage and aware of these bonds (p. 75).

W.J.M. Mackenzie similarly suggests, as synonyms for "interest," "wants," or "needs," or "purposes." See his "Pressure Groups: The 'Conceptual Framework,'" *Political Studies*, III, No. 3 (October 1955), 249.

[28] Traditional group theory in the West has, of course, focused on groups supposedly reflecting a "selfish" social or occupational interest, such as trade-unions or farm organizations. See for instance Truman, *op.cit.*, pp. 98ff.; Zeigler, *op.cit.*, pp. 30, 226-227; Olson, *op.cit.*, pp. 159-160. Ideological groups, seeking "a nontangible interest" have been dealt with, but more as an exception than the normal case. See Zeigler, *op.cit.*, pp. 226-227. Zeigler, however, argued that "opposing concepts of the national welfare" was the heart of politics (p. 25).

tics, for instance, that all members are Ukrainians, or peasants, lawyers or writers, obkom secretaries or managers. Such a "categoric" group may or may not possess similar attitudes on matters relating to their group or on public issues in general. Certain common attitudes *may* be present, held either by all or the overwhelming majority of the group, or by a distinct section. The members of such an "attitudinal" group may not, however, have an opportunity to express their views collectively, except in the most informal way, still less to make a specific claim on the public authorities for action corresponding to their attitude. Therefore, it does not constitute a political interest group in our meaning of the term. It is only when a common attitude, associated with, but not identical to, a common characteristic, leads to an expressed common claim that a "political interest group" may be said to exist.[29]

The functions of political groups in the Soviet setting are, it may be assumed, dual in nature. On the one hand, the groups which are formed in the upper sections of society may directly articulate their own special interests or their distinctive attitudes. On the other hand, these groups may be regarded as occupying a position between society and the decision-makers, reducing the innumerable raw demands arising from society as a whole to more definite claims for action. In this sense even the official groups, such as the party and state bureaucracies, share with the nonofficial groups a role in mediating between the rule-makers and society and in influencing the ultimate allocations of value. Political interest groups may thus render an important service by directing attention to the needs of social groups that might otherwise go unnoticed and by encouraging actions which benefit these groups. They may also perform a disservice by pressing on the authorities narrow group interests or policy attitudes harmful to the general interest.

Internal Politics of Political Groups

A striking feature of political interest groups in the Soviet Union is that normally they are not formally organized, but are more often loose groupings of like-minded or like-interested persons. Western group theory, especially in the form developed by Almond and others, has

---

[29] This does not imply a complete identity of views or exclude substantial differences, but it does assume a certain consensus. In addition there are varying degrees of explicitness in the making of claims, as will be noted later.

recognized the importance of unorganized or "informal" groups, especially in primitive or developing societies, and has referred to them as "non-associational" groups.[30] On the whole, however, the emphasis has been placed on the highly organized "associational" groups ("pressure groups"), such as trade-unions, farm organizations, or professional groups.[31] Almond has regarded as a central feature of political development the formation of specialized structures for the articulation and aggregation of interests.[32]

The paradox of the Soviet situation is that loose associations of individuals are more likely to be active exponents of common attitudes than organized groups, and more likely also to assert demands for government or party action. In fact, such groups may come into existence because organized groups, such as the Union of Writers, do not perform these functions adequately.[33] The more highly organized groups, such as trade-unions, or the Komsomol, we assume, express only in a limited degree distinctive interests of their own or of the social groups which they are supposed to represent.[34] Although an interest group is not usually able to set up a formal organization of its own, it may work within a legitimate, officially established organization, if one exists, and seek to use it to defend distinctive group interests. A whole occupational group, such as the writers, or a segment of it, may, for instance, express their views in the meetings and journals of the Union of Writers. In the same way, an interest group may be able to express its interests within official institutions, as, for instance, the professional interests of all scientists through the Academy of Sciences, or the views of likeminded persons, say, the conservative army officers, through military journals. In Almond's terminology, such a group might be called an "institutional" group working in and through an institution established primarily for other purposes.[35] In all these circumstances, the winning of key organizational positions, such as the editorship of a journal or a post in an executive organ, assumes great importance, and the compe-

[30] Almond and Powell, op.cit., p. 76.

[31] See the works by Zeigler and Olson. Cf. Ralf Dahrendorf, *Class and Class Conflict in Industrial Society* (Stanford, 1959), pp. 180, 238.

[32] Almond and Powell, op.cit., pp. 106ff.

[33] This reverses the conclusion of Olson that groups are usually organized because the members are unable to fulfill their desires in unorganized fashion (op.cit., p. 20). A similar proposition was advanced by Almond and Powell, op.cit., pp. 77-78. Olson, however, noted that small and unorganized groups may be more likely to seek common interests and to win group support than the large organized groups.

[34] See below, in this chapter.   [35] Almond and Powell, op.cit., p. 77.

tition for such offices may sometimes assume certain democratic features in the form of genuine elections.

The high incidence of informal group behavior in the Soviet Union raises a special question as to whether interaction among members is a prerequisite for group existence—a problem whose solution is not eased by the obscurity of Western interest group theory on this point. David Truman argued the need for frequent interaction of members as a precondition for the existence of a group, and yet laid stress on the role of "potential groups" where interaction is fragmentary at best.[36] In the Soviet Union, where group activity is often characterized by minimal formal interaction of members, the term "informal group" or "interest grouping" might, strictly speaking, be more appropriate.[37] Occasionally, for instance, a group, especially an "opinion group," will be constituted by spontaneous and parallel actions by outstanding individuals, perhaps expressed merely in articles or speeches similar in vein. This comes close to saying, in Bentleyan terms, that a political interest group is simply "any mass of human activity tending in a common political direction."[38] A political group might therefore be considered as an identity of political attitudes and activity, with or without a high degree of interaction. Usually, however, even in the Soviet context, group members will presumably be, to some extent, conscious of belonging to a common group and will be aware of the activities of fellow members. It is assumed, therefore, that in most cases a political interest group is characterized by a certain degree of interaction of its members,

[36] Truman, op.cit., pp. 23-24, 34-35, and passim. Cf. Dahrendorf's concept of "quasi-group" (op.cit., pp. 180, 237-238).

[37] It has been suggested that the concept of "reference group" might be useful in this connection, since, it is assumed, no interaction is involved in such a group. However, in Western usage, the term "reference group" is applied both to groups where interaction is present and where it is absent. Robert A. Feldmesser, who employed this concept to analyze both tsarist and Soviet society, used it to refer to a group of individuals sharing distinctive views and shaping their behavior in accordance with them, thus implying a high degree of interaction. His conclusion was that such groups cannot be said to exist in a totalitarian society such as Soviet Russia. See his "Social Classes and Political Structure" in Cyril E. Black (ed.), The Transformation of Russian Society (Cambridge, Mass., 1960).

[38] Paraphrased by Eckstein and Apter (eds.), op.cit., p. 381. An advocate of Bentley's views, Charles B. Hagan, argued that there is "a mass of activity" pro and con on every issue and that the group consists of "those activities of individuals which support or oppose the matter at issue" (Young [ed.], op.cit., p. 34). Cf. Monypenny, who referred to a group as "a statistical class identified by activity with an apparently common political objective, independently of any observable activity between members of the group" (op.cit., p. 187). Cf. Griffiths' chapter below.

31

although not necessarily in the formalized patterns often assumed by Western group theory, and with less frequency and intensity.[39]

In the absence of even a minimum degree of organization in the shape of associations or formalized procedures, or of a high degree of interaction among members, the membership of the group is difficult to identify with accuracy, and the boundary lines between groups are tenuous and indistinct. Group consciousness may sometimes be marginal, and group cohesion minimal. In the case of occupational groups, especially of an institutional type, there is somewhat greater definiteness of group membership, but members may, as we have seen, be scattered in many places and agencies and may form subgroups whose particular interests are not easily distinguished. In opinion groups, members may move from one group to another at different times and on different issues, so that the boundaries of groups may be constantly shifting. In occupational groups, too, persons may over time move from one to another, for instance from the party *apparat* to the civil service, from a professional institute to a government agency, from a party or Komsomol post to the police, or from one branch of the party *apparat* or the state bureaucracy to another. At any one time, too, an individual may belong to several groups, with differing degrees of loyalty to each of them. Needless to say, even in the most formal Western interest groups, similar features are often present, and a formal organization does not exclude differences within the group, informal associations, and shifting allegiances.[40]

In view of the often fluid and amorphous character of the Soviet political group, its internal configuration is not easy to analyze and will differ from case to case. Within the group there is likely to be a hierarchy of power and influence, extending from those who are included in the official system of power, through different levels of authority, to those who are "rank and file" members. A few influential individuals, for instance prominent writers or scientists, may take on the main responsibility of speaking and acting for the group, without, however, having any claim to be genuinely representative.[41] Other group mem-

---

[39] Zeigler (*op.cit.*, pp. 31-32) regarded formalized patterns of interaction as essential features of a "purposive," as distinct from a "categoric" group. Cf. Truman, *op.cit.*, p. 24. A somewhat similar viewpoint was expressed by Earl Latham (*op.cit.*, p. 384, n. 17), who wrote that the indispensable ingredient of "groupness" was "consciousness of common interest and active assistance, mutually sustained, to advance and promote this interest."

[40] Monypenny, *op.cit.*, pp. 188-191.

[41] Cf. the idea of the "active minority," in Truman, *op.cit.*, p. 139.

bers may have little or no voice even though they may share these attitudes and to some extent back up the main spokesmen by their own actions. In some cases, there may be conflict between rival spokesmen, and a cleavage of opinion within the group as a whole, and there may be few, if any, formal procedures for reaching a consensus, still less a definite majority viewpoint. In all these respects, Soviet groups resemble pressure groups, whether organized or unorganized, in other societies, but have their own peculiar features resulting from their unique setting.

Groups in Strategic Location

Group theory, as it developed in the West, from Bentley and Truman on, tended to emphasize or to treat exclusively the so-called private associations or pressure groups, such as trade-unions or farm organizations.[42] Very early, however, Earl Latham pointed out that within the official governmental structure group conflict is intense and continuous, sometimes between official agencies and sometimes between informal groups within such agencies. Latham argued that all groups, whether official or unofficial, belong to the same group universe and can be analyzed from the point of view of their common attitudes and demands.[43] True, there is a difference in degree of authority, or "officiality," in Latham's term, but the so-called private groups have their own internal system of "government" and possess power and influence, sometimes even greater than that of official groups.

In the Soviet context, where the making of final decisions rests largely in the hands of a very small group of leaders at the apex of the system, there seems all the less reason to exclude group conflict at the next lower tier, i.e., at the higher levels of the party and state structures. Certain official groups such as party *apparatchiki*, state bureaucrats, managers, security police, and the military, who possess, in varying degrees, official authority, may have their own occupational group interests or their own views of the general public interest, and may press these on the ultimate decision-makers. Within these power-holding groups, as in the case of nonofficial groups, there may also be rival and conflicting viewpoints on public policy, reflecting regional or func-

[42] See works cited by Truman, Olson, Zeigler, etc.

[43] Latham, *op.cit.*, pp. 382-383, 389-396. Truman, although stressing private organizations, referred to groups in legislatures, in government departments, and courts (e.g., *op.cit.*, pp. 343-346, 453-457, 484-487, 513). Bentley also discussed groups within the government (*op.cit.*, pp. 260, 290, 300, 358, 360, 398).

tional considerations, or ideological criteria. Moreover, the intellectual groups often straddle the line between those who hold offices endowed with official powers and those who have influence without office. Some economists, for instance, work for government departments or in party institutions; others are employed in the Academy of Sciences, the universities, or individual factories. In some nonpublic organizations, such as the Union of Writers or the Academy of Sciences, certain functionaries enjoy a good deal of semi-official power, much greater than that of the rank and file, and sometimes equal to those with formal authority in government or party. Moreover, certain so-called official groups, such as the military or the managers, may consist of, or include in their ranks, highly trained professional persons with specialized knowledge. Increasingly, too, both party and state have enlisted the services of experts from the scholarly world in advisory capacities, thus bringing them closer to "officiality" and smudging the boundary between official and nonofficial groups.

This is not to say, of course, that official and nonofficial groups will not differ in their character and make-up, in the style and pattern of their action, and above all, in their relative power. Some groups, which are close to the strategic locus of decision-making, are often consulted and may be able to exert serious influence on decisions; others, outside the inner circle, possess less influence. We might, alternatively classify them as "in-groups" or "out-groups," or "strategic" and "nonstrategic" groups. Nonofficial professional groups, however, because of their technical expertise, their indispensability to the ruling circles, and their access to influential media of communication, may possess substantial influence. Empirical research might determine how power and influence are distributed between the official and unofficial groups, and among groups in general. It may also provide evidence as to the sources of group power: to what extent is it derived from the possession of the means of coercion? To what extent does it depend on the holding of public office? To what extent is it based on special skills and access to certain media of communication? To what extent is it related to the personal prestige of group spokesmen?[44]

[44] Boris Meissner made a useful distinction between those groups whose power rests on "positions held," and those whose power rests on "functions performed" and particularly on specialized knowledge. See his "Totalitarian Rule and Social Change," *Problems of Communism*, xv, No. 6 (November-December 1966), 58.

Conflict among Leaders

We do not propose to deal extensively in this volume with another aspect of group conflict, namely the struggles among the top leaders and their closest associates and followers. Many Western scholars emphasize the fact that behind the totalitarian façade a bitter conflict for personal power has often raged, especially during periods of unstable leadership, such as the crisis of succession, but even in times of apparent stability, such as the height of power of Stalin or Khrushchev. It has been recognized that this struggle for power is frequently linked with controversies over policy, and has been an expression of the conflict of broader social groups, as individual leaders or factions identified themselves with such groups and sought to articulate their interests (e.g., Khrushchev with the farmers, Beria with the nationalities, Malenkov with the consumers).[45] Analysis of group conflict at the top level has sometimes assumed that certain leaders, identified with key institutions such as the party, state, army, or police, have used these institutions as the sources or bases of their power and have adopted positions reflecting the peculiar interests of these institutions.[46] Groups based on regional affiliations, such as the Ukraine, Moscow, or Leningrad, or on close personal associations with individual leaders, have sometimes been assumed. A conflict between conservatives and reformers among the top leadership has also been described by several authors.[47]

Leadership conflict of this kind will undoubtedly remain an important aspect of Soviet politics and will provide the framework within which other forms of group conflict will take place. Leadership factions will continue to perform significant functions of articulating and amalgamating the interests of social and political groups. This type of group conflict is not given separate consideration in this volume, however, in part because it has already received ample attention in Western scholarship. An even more important consideration is that such leadership groups or factions are themselves responsible for the actual making

[45] Cf. Linden, *op.cit.*, p. 7, and Ploss, *op.cit.*, pp. 19-23. See especially Barghoorn's treatment of the relationship of interest groups and leadership factions (*op.cit.*, Chap. VII). See above, Chap. 1, pp. 8-10 and in this chapter p. 19-20.

[46] See especially Rush, *op.cit.*, pp. 152-164; Conquest, *Power and Policy*, pp. 37ff.

[47] Linden, *op.cit.*, p. 6; Conquest, *Power and Policy*, pp. 26-28; Barghoorn, *op.cit.*, pp. 216-219, 243; Ploss, *op.cit.*, pp. 279-280.

of policy and are not mere vehicles for the expression of limited group interests. Individual leaders or factions may in some cases express the interests of broad social or political groups and may themselves be members of such entities. To the extent that such factional groups pursue special political interests of their own, these relate primarily to the attainment of power. The intellectual and official groups on which we are focusing attention may often become involved in the top-level power struggle and may be greatly affected by the outcome of that struggle. They are, however, primarily interested not in attaining power but in seeking to influence the policy pursued by the power-holders.[48]

The Role of Social Groups

Soviet society is, of course, heterogeneous, and social groups may be identified in the form not merely of classes, but also of intra-class and cross-class groupings.[49] These include, for instance, the workers and peasants, and many subgroups of these classes; the intelligentsia, also with many subcategories; regional, national, or religious groupings; groups based on age or sex (e.g., the youth, or women); on income, status differences, and rural or urban residence. These broader social categories which Bentley referred to as "fundamental" or "underlying" groups,[50] may possess shared values or interests and may make implicit demands on the authorities. It is also likely that there will be wide divergencies of attitude within such groups and no uniform consciousness of identity of interests. These broad social categories and their interests are politically relevant in the sense that their needs and wants are in some degree taken into account and articulated by political leaders, increasingly so in the post-Stalin period. We exclude them from direct consideration in this volume because they lack, more than the

[48] A similar distinction has often been made in group theory between interest groups and political parties, since the former seek not to "become the government," as do parties, but to "realize aspirations through governmental decision-making" (Eckstein in Eckstein and Apter [eds.], op.cit., p. 412). Cf. S. Finer and others, ibid., pp. 235-237; Zeigler, op.cit., p. 30.

[49] Certain Western scholars have made analyses of the social profile of the USSR and its political relevance. See especially Barghoorn, op.cit., Chap. II, and Aspaturian in his works already cited. Cf. Leopold Labedz, "Sociology and Social Change," Survey, No. 60 (July 1966), pp. 18-39; Boris Meissner, op.cit., pp. 56-61. For communist analyses see Djordjević and Lakatoš, cited in Chap. 1, above, and Ehrlich, op.cit.

[50] Bentley, op.cit., pp. 209, 441-446, 460-462.

36

higher elite groups, a high degree of mutual awareness and interaction, and have at present much less effective means to express their interests explicitly and to press them upon those responsible for policy-making.[51]

Certain important groups, such as the peasants, find themselves in somewhat the same position as, say, the consumers in a Western democracy, possessing no formal association for pressing their demands on the government. Even where mass societal organizations do exist, as in the case of the industrial workers, or the youth, these associations are in the main not able autonomously to express or defend the interests of the social categories concerned. They are designed rather to transmit the party's conception of the "real" group interest, or more often, the national or party interest to which the group interest is to be subordinated or sacrificed.[52] The intelligentsia has not been able to conduct political activity as a whole class or stratum; it can act only through groups representing the occupational interests or opinions of particular segments. Nationalities, despite the existence of official institutions both in the republics and in the central government, can articulate their interests through them only in a limited way and must otherwise resort to more informal channels, such as literary works, for the expression of national concerns. Religious groups are even less able to defend their special interests, although they have their own institutions, especially the churches for propagating their faith.

True, in the changed climate since Stalin's death, there is some evidence that the mass organizations, especially the trade-unions, sometimes provide a setting for the expression of a distinctive social group

[51] A similar viewpoint is expressed by Barghoorn, op.cit., pp. 71, 222, 255-257, and Aspaturian, "Social Structure and Political Power," pp. 10-13. See also Conquest, Power and Policy, p. 18; Brzezinski and Huntington, op.cit., pp. 296, 309, 329. Barghoorn's analysis is valuable in discussing the indirect political impact of the main social groups. This argument does not exclude the possibility of the defense of social group interests by "anomic" procedures (Almond and Powell, op.cit., p. 75), such as unofficial or illegal strikes, or the concentration of farmers' efforts on their private plots to the detriment of the collective farm.

[52] See Emily Clark Brown, Soviet Trade Unions and Labor Relations (Cambridge, Mass., 1966), esp. Chap. XI. Cf. her article, "Interests and Rights of Soviet Industrial Workers and the Resolution of Conflicts," Industrial and Labor Relations Review, Vol. 16, No. 2 (January 1963), pp. 254-278. Brown concluded that although the unions are expected to protect the interests of the workers more than in the past, they still function more as "arms of the government or party, carrying out policies established above, than as independent agencies representing the workers and their interests" (ibid., p. 277; cf. her book, pp. 80-85). They act "more like sections of a government department of labor than as independent trade union centres" (her article, p. 319).

interest.[53] Moreover, some of the political interest groups among the intelligentsia may articulate broader group interests, when, for instance, liberal writers express the interests of certain nationalities, or of the peasants, or of the intelligentsia as a whole.[54] As time goes on, other social groups may become better able to express their own group interests within existing organizations or even to form new associations for this purpose. To that extent they may be regarded as "latent" or "potential" interest groups, of which Truman has written, although not in the sense that there is anything inevitable about their future action and organization.[55] At present, however, these social groups have not been capable of expressing their interests through autonomous and overt political action in any way comparable to the intellectual and official interest groups under consideration here.

Strategies of Group Action

It is a commonplace of Western interest group analysis that the nature of group conflict and the style of group action are profoundly affected by the political culture of the particular society, especially by the structure of its political institutions.[56] In a system in which authority is strictly centralized, the means of communication under highly unified control, and the normal process of democratic discussion and free elections absent, group action will necessarily assume peculiar forms. In particular the pervasive character of party control means that the *apparatchiki* will penetrate other groups, for instance, the military and the writers, and seek to subordinate them to the interests of the *apparat*.[57]

As in other countries procedures of group activity change over time,

---

[53] This is particularly true at the factory and regional level of the trade-unions. At the national level, the trade-unions are consulted on labor legislation and even issue, with government or party, joint decrees, but it is difficult to determine whether and to what extent they express a distinctive workers' interest in this activity. See Brown, "Interests and Rights," pp. 258-259, 261ff., 277, and her book, pp. 139ff. For a controversy over the role of Soviet unions, see the article by Paul Barton in *Problems of Communism*, IX, No. 4 (July-August 1960), 18-27, and the ensuing discussion, *ibid.*, No. 6 (November-December 1960), 38-47. Cf. the symposium, "Soviet Workers: The Current Scene," *ibid.*, XIII, No. 1 (January-February 1964), esp. Jay B. Sorenson, "Problems and Prospects," p. 32.

[54] Certain writers have directed attention to economic difficulties on the collective farms (Solzhenitsyn), or to the continued existence of anti-semitism (Yevtushenko).

[55] Truman, *op.cit.*, pp. 34, 114-115, 511.

[56] Macridis (ed.), *op.cit.*, pp. 39ff.   [57] Barghoorn, *op.cit.*, p. 40

with goals and methods shifting as conditions alter.[58] Group action is different at present from what it was in the Stalin period, and will presumably continue to change in future. Group activity will also vary according to the type of group involved, especially as between official and nonofficial groups, and as between party and state groups. It will vary according to the level of the political system at which they are operating, i.e., whether at the top level, in Moscow, or at lower levels, in the union-republics or in cities, regions, and districts. Above all, group activity is likely to differ greatly according to the kind of issue involved, for instance, as between budgetary, literary, or military questions.[59]

In Western societies interest groups seek to vindicate their interests either by pressure upon those holding public office, or by securing representation directly in the organs of government. Pressure groups also strive to achieve their aims indirectly through efforts to influence public opinion. In interest group theory, therefore, much attention has been paid to the problem of "access" to the key points of authority and "channels" for expressing group views. Research has been conducted on the relationship of groups with legislative or representative bodies, executive agencies, courts, political parties, and public opinion.[60] It has been noted that the methods used by interest groups vary in particular countries in accordance with the differing roles of, say, legislature and executive and the special features of each of these organs.[61] It has also been understood that even where a definite framework of group action exists and certain procedures are accepted as legitimate, groups also resort to informal procedures, which often take place behind the scenes and are not therefore subject to full scholarly investigation. The studies of Almond, Coleman, and Powell have placed more stress on informal procedures (including, for instance, violence or personal connections),

[58] Cf. Zeigler, op.cit., pp. 73-81; Eldersveld in Ehrmann (ed.), op.cit., pp. 190-194.

[59] See below. Leiserson writes that "each area of public policy has its own aggregation of interest groups" (Ehrmann [ed.], op.cit., pp. 236, 283). See also Lowi, op.cit., pp. 688ff.

[60] See Truman, op.cit., and the individual studies in Ehrmann's book. Cf. Gabriel A. Almond, "A Comparative Study of Interest Groups and the Political Process," American Political Science Review, LII (March 1958), 270-282. For the USA, see V. O. Key, Jr., Politics, Parties and Pressure Groups (rev. ed., New York, 1966), pp. 130-150.

[61] Eckstein, "The Determinants of Pressure Group Politics," in Eckstein and Apter (eds.), op.cit., pp. 408ff. Cf. Meynaud and LaPalombara.

but have recognized the important role of the principal political institutions for rule-making, rule-applying, and rule-interpreting.[62]

Points of Access to Power

Soviet interest groups naturally seek to exert influence where the power of ultimate decision-making lies, namely on the party leaders in the Politburo. As we have noted, elite struggles at this topmost level often involve the interests of broader groups, mainly through the manipulation of certain social forces and social groups, or the articulation of their interests, by the individual leaders, but perhaps also by direct group pressure on the leaders.[63] These key points of authority are not, however, open to easy access, except by the more powerful elements of the party apparatus and state bureaucrats, both of which are strongly represented in the Politburo.[64] As we have already noted, the party and state officials may themselves constitute interest groups on their own account, sometimes pressing upon the topmost leaders a common "partisan" or "ministerial" interest, but also presenting an array of conflicting interests, representative of particular departments, or the distinct viewpoints of individual officeholders or opinion groups within the bureaucratic agencies. In spite of its apparently monistic character, Soviet decision-making is thus to some degree pluralistic, so that there are several points of access or channels of possible influence in the various departments of government and sections of the party *apparat*.[65]

It is not unnatural that other political interest groups will turn directly to these top bureaucratic agencies for the presentation of their special interests. Particular interests will have certain natural points of access to the state administration: the military group in the Ministry of Defense; the literary community in the Ministry of Culture; the judges and lawyers in the Ministry of Justice; the scientists in the State Committee for Science and Technology in the Council of Ministers; or managers and planners in Gosplan and in individual ministries and their particular departments. Similarly, the professional as well as the governmental

[62] Almond and Powell, *op.cit.*, pp. 81-85.

[63] Cf. Almond and Powell on "elite representation" (p. 83).

[64] Jerry Hough, "The Soviet Elite: I, Groups and Individuals," *Problems of Communism*, XVI, No. 1 (January-February 1967), 28-35.

[65] Cf. Eckstein on the pluralism of the apparently highly unitary British system of policy-making (Eckstein and Apter [eds.], *op.cit.*, p. 396). This is not to deny the striking contrast of both the British and the Soviet with the American system, with its multitude of "points of access" (Truman, *op.cit.*, p. 519).

groups may, each in its own sphere, deal with appropriate divisions of the party apparatus, for instance, the literary community with *Agitprop*, the military with the Military Department, and the scientific, legal, and economic professions with the relevant section. Although the main thrust of influence presumably moves from the bureaucratic agencies to the nonofficial professional groups, the latter, it may be assumed, attempt to penetrate or "colonize" the bureaucratic groups. These, in turn seek allies in other official agencies. Within the administrative structure there will likely be inter-departmental and inter-agency contacts and pressures, in a bureaucratic type of group conflict.[66] To a considerable extent the ability of a group to vindicate its special demands will presumably be enhanced if it achieves access to the bureaucratic groups and influences the attitudes of their members.

In view of the absence of a genuine representative or legislative system in the USSR, Soviet interest groups do not have much opportunity to function through the supposedly "representative" organs of the party or state. The Supreme Soviet, for instance, or the Party Congress or Central Committee, are so constituted that certain social and occupational groups receive representation. In the party organs, the *apparatchiki* and state bureaucrats predominate, although there is some limited representation of professional groups such as the military or the writers.[67] The Supreme Soviet is a more accurate microcosm of the whole nation, with representation of the broader social groups and the professional elites, as well as the state and party machines. In neither body, however, are the representatives selected by specific groups or authorized by the latter to express a group position. Moreover, none of these organs, so far as can be seen, has great influence on the determination of policy, and hence they are not likely to be important in the process of aggregating diverse group interests.

Nonetheless, the representative bodies may afford a modest means for articulating certain group interests. In the Central Committee members may voice differing opinions on subjects under debate and thus give expression to conflicting group interests. In plenary Soviet sessions

[66] See Meyer, *op.cit.*, pp. 230-235, 250-252, for an analysis of administrative politics. Cf. Merle Fainsod, *How Russia Is Ruled* (2nd ed., Cambridge, Mass., 1963), pp. 417-420.

[67] Barghoorn, *op.cit.*, p. 242. Cf. Hough, *ibid.*; Meissner, *op.cit.*, pp. 58-60; Aspaturian, "Social Structure and Political Power," pp. 15ff. See also Aspaturian's chapter in Macridis and Ward (eds.), *op.cit.*, pp. 494-502. On the dominance of the *apparatchiki*, see Barghoorn, *op.cit.*, Chap. VI, and Brzezinski and Huntington, *op.cit.*, pp. 153ff.

there may be expression of regional and functional interests by deputies. The increasing role being given to committees of the Soviet and the practice of bringing in experts in various fields (sometimes formalized in advisory committees) for consultation with the committees and with the Presidium of the Supreme Soviet, are drawing professional groups closer to the locus of decision-making, although not as authorized spokesmen of the groups to which they belong. The individual deputies of the Soviet are presumed to be channels through which citizens may raise complaints and requests, and they are expected to defend the interests of their constituents at the administrative level. It is difficult to know, however, whether membership in the Supreme Soviet or even in the Central Committee gives greater access to higher administrative authorities than would be available to persons who already enjoy a substantial status. Empirical research may determine whether these procedures, which now appear to be marginal in their effectiveness, are becoming more significant forms of group activity.

What we have been discussing so far may be considered the direct approach by interest groups to the official Soviet institutions, sometimes in accordance with constitutional provisions or practice, sometimes in consultative form as a result of request from authoritative quarters, and sometimes in the form of pressure on the authorities by groups or individuals. This type of "pressure" may be compared in some degree with the process of "lobbying" in other countries, but the main target, we have assumed, is not the legislative or representative bodies, but rather the administrative agencies of party and state, which in turn exert pressure on each other, and on the topmost leaders. By the nature of things, much of this pressure and counterpressure goes on behind the scenes, so that not much is known about it. It may be assumed that in the whole process the party *apparat* occupies a privileged position, since it has the crucial responsibility of articulating and amalgamating the interests of groups within itself and outside, in both the state and military sectors, and in the intellectual realms, and of preparing the ground for the actual making of policy at the leadership level.[68]

Media for Expressing Group Opinion

A more striking and uncommon form of group activity has developed outside the formal system of political authority and has employed un-

---

[68] Barghoorn, *op.cit.*, p. 39. Cf. Meyer, *op.cit.*, p. 110.

usual techniques and methods of operation. This has involved an indirect approach to the policy-makers through public debate on questions of literary policy, economic or legal reforms, or military strategy, and is designed to affect the general climate of opinion, especially among the relevant groups, on the issues under discussion. In a kind of surrogate for democracy of the more usual type, this debate takes place not on the floor of a parliament or congress, nor in electoral contests, but mainly in the conferences and the publications of professional and scholarly associations, and in the newspapers and magazines generally. Such discussions reach the public only in printed form, with appropriate emendations and omissions, which presumably reflect only in limited degree the sharpness of private debate. The evidence concerning this type of group conflict is chiefly to be found in the specialized publications of scholars (for instance, *Voprosy ekonomiki*); the literary magazines (*Novy mir, Oktyabr*, etc.); the professional newspapers of the military, the teachers, or the scientists; the general newspapers, such as *Pravda* and *Izvestia*; and the works published by scholars and creative writers. Letters to the newspapers and speeches on public occasions also play a significant role.

Although the party's monopoly of the media of communication and the normally one-directional nature of communications set severe limits on freedom of expression, this has not prevented sharp confrontations of conflicting opinions, sometimes quite openly, sometimes in veiled and Aesopian form. The differences must often be deduced by interpreting subtle shades of meaning or by reading between the lines. The regulated nature of the discussion, especially in its written form, suggests that the diversity of view is the result not merely of initiative from below by individuals, but also of decisions by persons in authority, who approve or perhaps sometimes sponsor certain lines of argument. Editors, publishers, *Agitprop* officials, even censors, and in some cases, political leaders, are thus involved in this interplay of group attitudes and interests. In this market place of ideas, there is neither a perfect monopoly by the party, nor entirely free competition, but an imperfect market reflecting pressures and counterpressures by groups of varying strength.

In this realm of group action much activity presumably takes place privately, e.g., in conversations among friends or associates, or in documents circulated secretly. An extremely important role is played by letters sent privately to government or party agencies, such as the

Presidium of the Supreme Soviet, or to the officers of the Central Committee; some of them become known in informed circles and are published abroad.[69] Like an iceberg, a large part of group opinion is concealed below the surface and yet may exert a significant influence on the course of events, on occasion lending strength and added confidence to public spokesmen. Moreover, in view of the lack of formal channels and of assured procedures, interest group expression tends to be sporadic and explosive, and to manifest itself sometimes in spontaneous or anomic fashion. Applause for Stalin at a meeting in the Kremlin addressed by Brezhnev, unplanned demonstrations outside a courthouse during a trial, or gatherings for the reading of poetry in Mayakovsky Square—these are but a few examples of activities that revealed a special depth of feeling or insistence on demands by certain groups.

The Role of Groups in Soviet Decision-Making

It remains a paradox that the formal structure of the Soviet system has remained unchanged since Stalin, with a single centralized party in command, controlling the representative institutions, the mass organizations, and the communications media. Although there is some willingness by party theorists to recognize the existence of varied and conflicting interests, Soviet doctrine still rejects the rights of autonomous groups to articulate interests distinct from those of the party, and still claims the exclusive right to aggregate, and even to articulate, the interests of all social groups.[70] In fact, however, the system is operating differently than it did under Stalin, in part as a result of increased activity by political groups which have attained a certain degree of autonomy of action. In that sense Soviet society has shown signs of at least an incipient pluralism.[71]

It should be made clear that public policy in the Soviet Union is *not* assumed to represent a nice balancing or equilibrium of more-or-

[69] For instance, the letter concerning the Daniel-Sinyavsky trial signed by 63 writers (*New York Times*, November 19, 1966). Other letters were referred to by Ilichev in his speech of December 17, 1962, to representatives of literature and art (*Pravda*, December 22, 1962).

[70] Barghoorn, *op.cit.*, pp. 13, 20-21.

[71] *Ibid.*, p. 42. In an interesting but somewhat ambiguous treatment, Shulman noted that there are groups with "varying degrees of influence" (*op.cit.*, p. 40), capable of affecting policy and exerting "upward pressures," but argued that the party has prevented them from becoming "political entities, with independent sources of political power" (pp. 42-43). The system, therefore, remains totalitarian, he argued, although in "a mature form" (pp. 38-39).

less equal contending groups, or that it is a kind of automatic product of a parallelogram of group forces.[72] The making of policy remains highly centralized and authoritarian, with great power resting in the hands of a few at the top, and with groups usually playing a secondary and subordinate role. Top Soviet leaders are often at one and the same time articulators and aggregators of group interests, as well as the final rule-makers, and may often be in a position to impose policies upon the groups rather than be forced by the groups to follow certain policies.[73] Nonetheless, a number of political groups exist and possess some means of giving expression to their interests and to conflicting views on public policy. Policy-making, accordingly, more and more takes place within a context of sharp group conflict. Political groups may interpose their own viewpoints, presenting alternative policies for consideration, and endorsing, criticizing, or sometimes resisting, the carrying out of policies already resolved upon. Although interest groups seldom possess constitutional or even practical sanctions to enforce their views on the topmost leaders, they may on occasion succeed in influencing the ultimate decision or in blocking its implementation. On the other hand, they may often be faced with the reality of unwelcome decisions made by the leaders.

[72] Cf. criticisms of the "cash register" theory of group politics in Garceau, *op.cit.*, p. 106; Latham, *op.cit.*, pp. 390-391.
[73] Almond and Powell, *op.cit.*, p. 99.

CHAPTER III ~ BY JERRY F. HOUGH

The Party *Apparatchiki**

AS SCHOLARS began to speak of the existence of interest groups in the Soviet Union, they have almost invariably pointed to the party *apparatchiki* as one of the key groups in the political process. Implicitly or explicitly, most would follow the lead of Zbigniew Brzezinski and Samuel Huntington in describing the *apparatchiki* as men with a "highly professionalized career pattern"—with loyalties "more exclusive" and a commitment "more intense" than Western politicians. In this view of the party apparatus, the commitment of party officials to the apparatus has important consequences for the apparatus as a group: "The organizational tradition and discipline of the Party inhibit the formation of a narrow, specialized outlook among the Presidium and Secretariat members. Like the cardinals on the Vatican Curia, they are predominantly professional politicians, sharing a common organizational outlook, common interests, and increasingly a common background."[1]

While this image of the party apparatus is often retained by those moving toward an interest group interpretation of Soviet politics, it is in fact far more the product of a different approach to the study of political systems—that concentrating on the nature of "the elite" in a given country. This is particularly true if one accepts Brzezinski's and Huntington's broad definition of the *apparatchiki*: not only full-time party officials, but also those who have passed through the party apparatus into governmental posts. The correct use of the interest group approach would suggest a quite different image of the party apparatus, one which would correspond much more closely to Soviet reality.

What then does an interest group approach to politics entail? What are its implications for the study of the party apparatus? There are, of

* I would like to thank Professor Denis Sullivan of Dartmouth College for much help and stimulation in the development of the line of analysis presented in this chapter.
[1] Z. Brzezinski and S. P. Huntington, *Political Power: USA/USSR* (New York, 1964), p. 163.

47

JERRY F. HOUGH

course, a number of different interest group theories and approaches, and many are of little relevance to the study of the Soviet Union. However, that presented by Arthur Bentley a half-century ago does embody some reasonably concrete propositions which can be used to illuminate the role of the party apparatus in the Soviet political system:

(1) Political life can never be fruitfully analyzed in terms of a striving for the national interest. In the words of Arthur Bentley, "On any political question which we could study . . . we should never be justified in treating the interests of the whole nation as decisive. There are always some parts of the nation to be found arrayed against other parts."[2]

(2) Political life can seldom be fruitfully analyzed in terms of the interests of a unified elite or unified classes. Indeed, Bentley, unlike many of his followers, cautioned against using such broad categories as "race, various economic interests, religion, or language." He asserted that "in practice we shall have to do mainly with much more specialized groupings than these."[3]

(3) Persons engaged in similar activities, particularly of an economic-professional nature, tend to have similar attitudes on key political issues. However, all men have a multiplicity of interests (or group memberships—to phrase the identical point in different language) which destroy the possibility of "hard and fast" groups and which involve each man in a complex set of crosscutting alliances with a variety of different persons.

(4) Every government, every policy, inevitably must reflect some interest or set of interests within society—or to put the same point in different words, some group or set of groups within society. While Bentley insisted that any stable government has to be somewhat responsive to the aspirations of broad groups in the population, he recognized that a government might provide "wretched mediation" to the various interests in society and might in practice be responsive to the interests of a relatively few. (He explicitly discussed the tsarist regime in these terms.)

(5) The most useful approach to the study of the political process is to look for the way in which interests clash and coalesce and to ascertain which interests are expressed in the policy that emerges. This is

[2] Arthur F. Bentley, *The Process of Government* (Chicago, 1908), p. 220.
[3] *Ibid.*, p. 207. See pp. 465-468 for Bentley's criticism of Marx's "hard and fast" classes.

48

true if we are analyzing the formation of specific policies within a country: "If a law is in question, we find that our statement of it in terms of the groups of men it affects—the group or set of groups directly insisting on it, those directly opposing it, and those more indirectly concerned in it—is much more complete than any statement in terms of self-interest, theories, or ideologies." It is also true if we are comparing entire political systems.[4]

Even if the five propositions only approximate the conclusions of the group approach—or, perhaps better, the interest approach—they still suggest a far different analysis of the party and the party apparatus than that customarily found in Western studies. Given the distribution of party members throughout the administrative hierarchy, Bentley would surely react to statements about "the party's point of view," "the party's goals," "the party's hierarchy of values," "the party's distrust of all officials"[5] in the same way that he reacted to talk about "the" national interest. If he was doubtful about an analysis focusing on broad occupational groups, he would be even more dubious about the "common interests" of 100,000-200,000 "politicians" working in all territorial units of the country, many in specialized positions with responsibility for one sector of economic life.[6]

Even if we were to discover that officials of the party apparatus hold certain interests in common, the group approach would deny the possibility that they share many common interests. A proponent of the Bentley approach would take for granted that Soviet politics features a broad and shifting variety of alliances, with any official of the apparatus being allied with some party officials on one issue in opposition

[4] *Ibid.*, pp. 204, 270, 300.

[5] These phrases are all taken from Alfred G. Meyer, *The Soviet Political System* (New York, 1965), pp. 238-243.

[6] Using a projection from the pre-war period, Fainsod places the size of the apparatus in the 150,000-200,000 range. Extrapolating a statistic given for Armenia in 1962, he arrives at a figure of approximately 100,000. Merle Fainsod, *How Russia Is Ruled* (2nd ed., Cambridge, Mass., 1963), pp. 206-207. On the basis of a number of references to the size of the apparatus of various city and district party committees, I find it difficult to arrive at a figure much beyond 100,000-125,000—unless one assumes most improbable sizes for the higher levels. Such a figure does not, however, include "technical" personnel—typists, stenographers, janitors, cleaning women, etc., who supplement the "responsible officials." It may well be that many of the Soviet claims of a reduction in the size of the apparatus are to be explained by an increase in the number of technical personnel. In the past, the instructors often performed such functions as typing reports, and an increase in the number of secretaries (in the American sense of the word) would permit a reduction in the number of instructors without a reduction in the activity of the party organ.

to a group containing other party officials, while being allied with other party officials on another issue, and so forth. If we examine the actual participation of party officials in the political process from this perspective, we find support for an image of the apparatus characterized by many sources of cleavage, which moreover are reflected in political behavior.

Potential Sources of Cleavage in the Party Apparatus

Even a cursory examination of the officials of the party apparatus reveals a number of potential sources of cleavage among them. In terms of their age distribution, for example, the officials of the lower levels of the apparatus are quite different from those in higher positions.

The significance of these patterns of age distribution is difficult to judge, but the quarter of a century range in Table 1 covers a wide variety of experience. Early political socialization, nature of education, participation in the Great Purge, involvement in World War II—these can be strikingly different for Soviet citizens born in 1910 and 1920, let alone in 1905 and 1930. For example, 95 percent of the RSFSR obkom first secretaries born after 1914 had graduated from a regular university or institute early in their career as compared with 44 percent of those born prior to that time.[7]

Another potential source of cleavage within the party apparatus is the considerable ethnic diversity among the party officials. The top officials of the Central Committee secretariat—the secretaries and the heads of the departments—have been almost exclusively Russians in recent years. Since the death of Kuusinen in 1964, none of the ten or eleven Central Committee secretaries has been a non-Russian. Of the seven nonsecretarial heads of department elected to the Supreme Soviet in 1966, all were Russians except for the head of the culture department—V. F. Shauro, a Belorussian. The background of other department heads suggests that one at most is non-Russian.[8]

---

[7] The biographies of the obkom first secretaries can be found in *Deputaty Verkhovnovo Soveta SSSR, Sedmoi sozyv* (Moscow, 1966) (henceforth *Deputaty*). For the date of college graduation, one must refer to the 1966 yearbook of the *Bolshaya sovetskaya entsiklopedia* (henceforth *Bol. sov. entsik.*), pp. 574-621. Unfortunately, the latter source includes only those obkom secretaries elected to the Central Committee or the Auditing Commission of the party. All obkom first secretaries in the RSFSR were named to these bodies, but the first secretaries in the other republics are represented less frequently.

[8] The biographies of all department heads were printed in *Bol. sov. entsik.*, 1966 yearbook, but this source does not list the nationality of these men. This

TABLE 1.

YEAR OF BIRTH OF PARTY OFFICIALS (IN PERCENTAGES), 1966-1967

Year of Birth	Cent. Comm. Secretaries and Dept. Heads	RSRSR[a]					
		Obkom First Sects.[b]	Obkom Second Sects.	Other Obkom Sects.	Obkom Dept. Heads	Gorkom First Sects.	Raikom First Sects.
Pre-1905	4	—	—	—	—	—	—
1905-1909	25	15	4	—	—	—	3
1910-1914	38	51	35	27	5	7	3
1915-1919	33	25	22	20	22	18	16
1920-1924	—	7	26	29	34	33	31
1925-1929	—	2	13	23	31	38	36
1930-	—	—	—	2	7	7	10
Average year of birth	1912	1914	1918	1920	1923	1923	1923
Total Number	24	55	23	56	82	62	92

[a] This table is limited to the RSFSR because the information about the other republics is too scattered for confidence about its reliability. However, the officials in the non-Russian areas appear to be somewhat younger. This is certainly true of the obkom first secretaries, the one category of officials on which complete information is available. The obkom first secretaries of the autonomous republics and oblasti of the RSFSR were born in 1915 on the average, those of the Ukrainian obkomy in 1916, those of the obkomy of other republics in 1919. The 5 obkom second secretaries of non-Russian oblasti on whom information is available were born in 1920 on the average, the 10 lower obkom secretaries in 1919, the 23 obkom department heads in 1924, the 29 gorkom first secretaries in 1924, the 40 raikom first secretaries in 1923.

[b] This column includes all the oblasti in the RSFSR, except for the autonomous republics and oblasti. The information is as of June 1966.

SOURCES: Information on the Central Committee officials and obkom first secretaries was drawn from biographies published in the 1966 yearbook of the *Bol. sov. entsik.*, pp. 574-621, and in *Deputaty Verkhovnovo Soveta SSSR, Sedmoi sozyv* (Moscow, 1966). Information on the lower officials was drawn primarily from lists of oblast deputies elected in 20 oblasti in February-March 1967. (The year of birth was included with the man's name and position.) The 20 oblasti do not include the giants of Moscow, Leningrad, and Sverdlovsk nor the small Siberian oblasti, but otherwise they constitute a fairly representative cross section of the RSFSR oblasti.

The Russian domination of the Central Committee secretariat does not, however, extend to the lower party apparatus. The officials at these levels reflect the ethnic diversity of the country. For example, of the 139 obkom first secretaries in the USSR in June 1966, 47 percent were

information is found in *Deputaty* (1966), but not all department heads are included in this volume.

Russians, 24 percent were Ukrainians, and the remaining 29 percent were divided among 24 nationalities. The ethnic differences among the obkom first secretaries were associated with significant differences in life-experiences.

TABLE 2.

BACKGROUND OF OBKOM FIRST SECRETARIES
OF DIFFERENT NATIONALITIES

	Percentage with Agricultural or Engineering Education	Percentage with Experience as Komsomol Officials[a]	Percentage with Experience as Teachers
Russians (Number = 66)	64	35	17
In largest oblasti[b]	82[c]	18	18
In large oblasti[b]	67[c]	40	13
In medium and small oblasti[b]	53[c]	41	18
Ukrainians (Number = 33)	64[c]	21	15
Other Nationalities (Number = 40)	32[c]	40	42

[a] This refers to Komsomol experience listed in biographical sources. Presumably most secretaries were reasonably active in the Komsomol while undergoing higher education.

[b] The "largest oblasti" are the 17 oblasti whose population permitted them 7 or more deputies in 1966. The "large oblasti" are the 15 with 5 or 6 deputies in 1966. The "medium and small oblasti" are the remaining 34.

[c] If we exclude the engineering and agricultural degrees received *after* the first secretary reached party or state posts at the oblast level, the percentages would be: All Russians: 55 percent; Russians in largest oblasti: 76 percent; Russians in large oblasti: 60 percent; Russians in medium and small oblasti: 41 percent; Ukrainians: 61 percent. Too little information is available about the date of graduation of the other first secretaries to permit any correction in the cited figure.

SOURCES: *Bol. sov. entsik.*, 1966 yearbook, pp. 574-621, and *Deputaty*.

The potential cleavages of greatest interest are those associated with the differentiated structure of the apparatus itself. A number of officials work in the Central Committee secretariat in Moscow, but most are scattered across the country. Some work in rural raikomy, others in industrialized centers. Some lead party organizations in cotton-growing areas in Uzbekistan, others head organizations in the Donbass coal region. Some work in the iron and steel centers in the Ukraine, while others work in the timbering-paper districts of Karelia.

Within any given party organization, the officials work within quite specialized subunits. By 1966 there were four Central Committee departments dealing with foreign policy questions and thirteen handling various internal policy spheres: administrative organs (working on law and order questions), agriculture, chemical industry, construction, culture, defense industry, heavy industry, light industry and food industry, machine-building industry, propaganda (working in part on the publishing industry), science and education, trade, financial, and planning organs, and transportation and communications.

The local party organs have also been organized along branch lines for the last two decades. Each republican central committee and obkom has had one secretary specializing (*vedayushchy*) on industrial questions, one on agricultural questions, and one on cultural-education questions. (The last-named official has had the title "secretary handling ideological work," but leadership of agitation-propaganda work forms only a relatively small part of his responsibility.) Under the supervision of the specialized secretaries have been a number of branch departments. A medium-sized obkom has had eight departments: administrative organs, agriculture, construction, industrial-transportation, light and food industry and trade, organizational-party work, propaganda-agitation, and science, colleges, and schools.

The differentiation in party structure has been accompanied by specialization in the career patterns of personnel. In the Central Committee secretariat, for example, the head of the agriculture department has long experience in agricultural administration (head of the Penza agriculture administration, RSFSR Deputy Minister of Agriculture, RSFSR Minister of Grain Products) and in party and soviet work in rural areas; the head of the heavy industry department is an engineer who has been a plant director for five years and chairman of the Chelyabinsk *sovnarkhoz* for two years; the head of the light industry and food industry department is a graduate of the Moscow Textile Institute and a former USSR Deputy Minister of the Textile Industry; the head of the transportation department is a graduate of the Leningrad Institute of Railroad Engineers with 22 years of administrative and scientific work in the railroad industry (including service as head of the Gorki railroad); the head of the chemical industry department is a graduate of the Moscow Institute of Chem-

53

ical Machine-building, who worked for a dozen years in the USSR Gosplan, rising to the post of deputy department head. The heads of the departments for the machine-building, defense, and construction industries had only lower level administrative experience in their respective industries before entering party work, but their careers in the party seem to have been quite specialized ones; the head of the science and education department is a graduate of the Academy of Social Sciences, a doctor of historical science, and a man with eight years' experience as director of the Moldavian Party School and five years' as deputy director for research at the Higher Party School.[9]

The specialization in career pattern within the Central Committee secretariat is not a post-Khrushchev innovation. Table 3 summarizes the educational background of 89 officials (heads of departments, deputy heads of departments, heads of sectors, and instructors) who have worked in the Central Committee secretariat at some time during the period since 1953. These 89 include all the Central Committee officials of this period whose published biography indicated the Central Committee department in which the man was employed.

There are also striking differences in the work experience of the officials of different Central Committee departments. Thus, 70 percent of the known officials of the agriculture department had at least five years' experience in administrative posts in agriculture prior to their appointment in the Central Committee secretariat. Similarly, two-thirds of the officials of the industrial department had at least that many years in engineering-administrative positions in industry or construction, and over 55 percent had at least a decade of such experience. One-half of the officials in the propaganda-agitation, culture, and science-education departments had worked for at least five years in editorial work or in teaching, 40 percent for at least ten years. The officials of the party organs department, on the other hand, generally had longer experience in the Komsomol or party organs. Only one-third of these men had five years' experience in industry, agriculture, *or* teaching positions; only 8 percent had ten years of such experience.

[9] The department heads are: agriculture, F. D. Kulakov; heavy industry, M. S. Solomentsev; light industry and food industry, P. K. Sizov; transportation and communications, K. S. Simonov; chemical industry, V. M. Bushuyev; machine-building, V. S. Frolov; defense industry, I. D. Serbin; construction, A. E. Biryu-kov; science and education, S. P. Trapeznikov. Their biographies can be found in *Bol. sov. entsik.*, 1966 yearbook, pp. 578, 580, 597, 611, 613, 615, 617.

TABLE 3.

EDUCATIONAL BACKGROUND OF CENTRAL COMMITTEE OFFICIALS
(IN PERCENTAGES)

Cent. Comm. Departments	University, Social Science, Peda-gogical	Engi-neering	Agric. Higher Educ.	Agric. Spec. Sec. Educ.	Higher Party School[a]	Other
Agriculture (Number = 17)	—	—	65[b]	24	6	6
Industry-Construction (Number = 18)	—	89[c]	—	—	6	6
Party Organs (Number = 24)	17	38	4	—	33	8
Propaganda-Culture (Number = 30)	67	7	—	—	10	17

[a] The only officials included in this column are those for whom the Higher Party School was the only higher education listed in the biography. A number of officials hold two degrees—one received from an institute relatively early in his career, one from the Higher Party School in mid-career.

[b] This figure includes two men who graduated from institutes for the mechanization of agriculture.

[c] This figure includes an architect with years of work in construction design and a graduate of the mechanics-mathematics division of Moscow University.

SOURCES: The biographies were gathered from a decade of yearbooks of the *Bol. sov. entsik.*, from the three volumes of *Deputaty*, and from a variety of Soviet newspapers. (Most of the latter biographies were obituaries.)

Systematic information about the specialized officials of the local party organs is more difficult to collect than that about officials of the Central Committee secretariat. Nevertheless, the evidence suggests that a similar differentiation in career pattern has also taken place at this level. If we examine the men selected as republican secretaries for industry in 1966, for example, we find that they normally had an engineering diploma and often had held such posts as republican minister or plant manager. The secretaries for agriculture usually were agronomists with administrative experience in agriculture (in four cases as republican minister). The ideological secretaries usually had been educated in a university or a pedagogical institute, and their work experience normally had been in the Komsomol, education, newspaper, and cultural realms.[10]

Specialization in career pattern has even become quite frequent among the obkom first secretaries. At the time of the last election to the Supreme Soviet (June 1966), 19 of the first secretaries in the 25 most industrialized oblasti in the RSFSR and the Ukraine had engineering training, 2 had a technical secondary education, 2 graduated from a physics-mathematics division of the university, and 1 was an economist. On the other hand, in the 25 most important agricultural oblasti in the RSFSR there were only 4 engineers among the first secretaries (and one of them had graduated from an institute for the mechanization of agriculture), while 13 of the first secretaries were agronomists.[11]

The early work experience of the first secretaries in the most industrialized and the most important agricultural oblasti was as disparate as their education. Of the 25 secretaries in the agricultural oblasti, 10 had held posts in governmental administration of agriculture at the level of MTS (Machine Tractor Station) director or higher, and another 8 had once been first secretary of a rural raikom and/or head of the agriculture department of an obkom. By contrast, none of the first secretaries in the 25 most industrialized oblasti had held administrative jobs in agriculture at the level of MTS director or higher. Only 4 had been first secretary of a rural raikom, and in two of these cases the raion contained considerable industry.

These aggregate statistics reflect the frequent practice of selecting obkom first secretaries from men whose background especially prepares them to supervise the major branch of the economy in their oblast. Thus,

[10] These secretaries were selected at the republican party congresses held in February and March 1966. More information on these officials can be found in Jerry F. Hough, *The Soviet Prefects* (Cambridge, Mass., 1969), p. 36.

[11] Information on regional industrial output is spotty, and the list of the most industrialized oblasti was compiled in the following manner. Since Soviet industry is overconcentrated in the larger cities, I took the 200 largest cities in the 1959 census and grouped them by oblasti. I assumed that the 25 oblasti with the most people concentrated in these 200 cities were the most industrialized. But since agriculture clearly overshadows industry in three of the regions near the bottom of the list (Altai krai, Bashkiria ASSR, and Omsk oblast, in each of which the rural population constituted over 60 percent of the total population), I replaced them with three oblasti which just failed to make the top 25, but which clearly occupied an important role in the country's industrial life—Ivanovo, Zaporozhye, and the Russified Karaganda in Kazakhstan.

The 25 most important agricultural oblasti are those with the largest rural population, excluding the autonomous republics and those oblasti already included among the most industrialized.

in 1966 the obkom first secretaries in Kemerovo (the center of the Kuzbass) and in Donetsk (the center of the Donbass) were the former heads of a coal combine and a coal trust respectively. The first secretary of the Kharkov obkom was an engineer with twenty years of lower administrative work in machine-building plants (up to the level of shop head) before becoming party secretary of the Kharkov Transportation Machinery Works. On the other hand, in Belgorod, Smolensk, and Orenburg (oblasti whose population was over two-thirds rural in 1959), we find obkom first secretaries who were once MTS directors with years of subsequent party and soviet work primarily oriented toward agriculture; in North Kazakhstan, Kustanai, and Semipalatinsk oblasti in the Virgin Lands we find agronomists who had been minister or deputy minister in the republican ministries supervising agriculture.

There are, of course, limitations to the degree of specialization possible among the obkom first secretaries. As Khrushchev correctly noted when he proposed the bifurcation of the party apparatus in 1962, all oblasti are developing increasingly complex economies. Moreover, the basic job of the first secretary is to be the prefect in his region—to make judgments about relative priorities when the interests, the plans, and the directives of the local representatives of the various ministries come into conflict with each other.[12] Because of the nature of their role, "there is not a [single] question in the economic, cultural, and public life of the district in which the party organ would not be interested."[13] Consequently, even a first secretary who is a specialist on the main branch of the economy in his area will continually have to make decisions on questions on which he has little expertise.

One attempt to solve this problem has been to place in charge of each party organization a team of secretaries with a variety of specialties. For example, a new obkom first secretary was named in Rostov oblast in the latter half of 1966. He was an agronomist who had worked in agricultural research and teaching until the age of forty-two and then in agriculturally oriented party and soviet work for six years. Surely it was not an accident that he was buttressed by a second secretary who was an ideological specialist, by an industrial secretary who was an industrial specialist (a former director of a defense industry plant), and by a gorkom first secretary in Rostov with long experience in construction

---

[12] See Hough, *op.cit.*, for an elaboration of this theme.
[13] E. I. Bugaev and B. M. Leibson, *Besedy ob ustave KPSS* (Moscow, 1962), p. 141.

administration and the education of construction engineers.[14] Presumably such a combination of specialized knowledge implies the type of team decision-making which Galbraith suggests is inevitable in very large-scale organizations.[15]

Another solution to the wide range of demands on an obkom first secretary is to move specialists into party work at an early age (in some cases drawing them from Komsomol work) and to let them "specialize" on the skills of the general coordinator by being advanced through general leadership posts in progressively larger and more complex territorial units. Of course, many obkom first secretaries already have such a career pattern, and nearly all of the first secretaries with a more specialized background have some generalized supervisory experience before rising to their current position.

However, we should recognize that even career patterns with years of generalized party and soviet work may be far more specialized than seems on the surface. Consider, for example, the following two biographies: Konstantin Pysin was born in 1910 and graduated from the Perm Agriculture Institute in 1935.[16] After six years of work as a zootechnician and as a teacher at the agricultural institute, he moved into party work, first as instructor, then as head of a department, then as secretary of the Perm obkom. (Because of his background, it is likely that he was head of the agriculture department and then secretary for agriculture.) In 1947 he was named chairman of the Perm oblispolkom and in 1949 chairman of the Altai oblispolkom. From 1955 to 1961 he was first secretary of the Altai kraikom.

Aleksandr Tokarev was born in 1921, served in the army during the war, and then in 1949 graduated from the Kuibyshev Institute of Construction Engineers.[17] Upon graduation he served as Komsomol secretary and then deputy party secretary at an oil refinery construction site. In 1951 he became secretary of a gorkom and in 1952 the gorkom first secretary in the city in which the construction site was located. From 1955 to 1958 he was head of the construction department of the Kuibyshev obkom and from 1958 to 1959 a secretary of the obkom. In 1959 he was named chairman of the Kuibyshev oblispolkom, in 1963 first secretary of

---

[14] The biography of the new first secretary, I. A. Bondarenko, is found in *Deputaty* (1966), p. 65. The biographies of the other secretaries were found in the oblast newspaper.

[15] Kenneth Galbraith, *The New Industrial State* (Boston, 1967), Chap. vi.

[16] *Deputaty* (1966), p. 372.   [17] *Ibid.*, p. 444.

the Kuibyshev industrial obkom, and in 1964 first secretary of the Kuibyshev obkom.

In many ways these two biographies might seem to be those of "typical" *apparatchiki*, and this is in fact the case. Yet they are the biographies of men with quite different experiences and quite different expertise. Pysin has the career pattern essentially of an agricultural specialist, Tokarev one essentially of an industrial-construction specialist. Both had ample preparation for the next post to which they were appointed—in Pysin's case First Deputy Minister, then Minister of Agriculture of the USSR, in Tokarev's case USSR Minister of Industrial Construction.

The type of generational, ethnic, educational, and occupational divisions which we have been examining need not, of course, be associated with policy differences among party officials. It is possible that some of the potential sources of division are not as politically important as commonly perceived interests and perspectives deriving from employment within the party apparatus. It is quite possible that men may perceive their interests in quite different ways than an outside observer would think likely or advantageous.

However, if we are to treat the party apparatus as a unified interest group in the political process, let us be fully aware of the assumptions we must accept. We must assume that the agriculture department and the defense industry department of the Central Committee (with their leaders of quite different backgrounds) have greater community of views and interests than do the agriculture department of the Central Committee and the Ministry of Agriculture. We must assume that the specialized local secretaries who have spent their lives in industrial, agricultural, and cultural-education work respectively, and who in the future will probably return to governmental work in their branch, function more as allies than as competitors in the policy sphere. We must assume that the former coal industry administrator who is obkom first secretary in the iron and coal oblast of Kemerovo has much the same set of perspectives on important political issues as the former agriculture administrator who is obkom first secretary in the flax oblast of Smolensk. We must assume that the construction engineer whose party and soviet work in urban areas apparently warranted his appointment as Minister of Industrial Construction has a set of interests and outlooks which are basically in common with the agronomist whose party and soviet work in rural regions earned him appointment as Minister of Agriculture.

59

The next two sections will examine the actual participation of the regional first secretaries and then the specialized officials of the party apparatus in the political process. They will explore the question: to what extent are the potential sources of cleavage reflected, in practice, in the political behavior of the party officials?

The Regional First Secretaries

Normally, when one thinks of the *apparatchik*, the first official that comes to mind is the regional first secretary—primarily the first secretary of the republican central committee and obkom (regional party committee) but also that of the gorkom (city committee) and the raikom (district committee). Like the French prefects, they are "the" representative of the center in each territorial unit, the men who must decide what the center would want done in circumstances not foreseen in central directives.

The primary responsibility of the prefect is to enforce central priorities, but both the Soviet press and Western observers have noted the "localism" often displayed in their activity. From the point of view of the group approach, however, this "localism" should be viewed not simply as a shortcoming in the work of the party officials, but as a major symptom of the group configuration of Soviet politics on certain issues, particularly those of an appropriations nature.[18]

Any person reading Soviet press reports about the local party organs will quickly notice that the party officials are not only supervising local governmental officials, but are also appealing for funds, supplies, and other types of support from party and state officials at higher territorial levels. Consider, for example, the speeches of the obkom first secretaries at the Twenty-third Party Congress in 1966. The first secretary of the Gorky obkom asked the Council of Ministers to support the specialization of the Gorky Auto Works and the development of a network of cooperating supplier-plants.[19] (In an earlier article in the republican newspaper, *Sovetskaya Rossia*, he had advocated that these plants be established within Gorky oblast.)[20] The first secretary of the Perm

---

[18] The next four pages of this paper summarize material found in Hough, *op.cit.*, Chap. XII.

[19] *XXIII Syezd Kommunisticheskoi Partii Sovetskovo Soyuza, 29 marta-8 aprelya 1966 goda, stenograficheskyy otchyot* (Moscow, 1966), I, 198-199.

[20] *Sovetskaya Rossia*, March 15, 1966.

obkom spoke out for the realization of the "centuries-old dream" of diverting part of the water of the Pechera and Vishera Rivers into the Kama and the Volga.[21] The first secretary of the Krasnoyarsk kraikom complained about the limited participation of the central research and design institutes in work associated with Siberian development, and he demanded improvement.[22] The first secretary of the Primorsk kraikom called for a rapid expansion both of the krai's coal-electricity energy base and of its acreage devoted to rice cultivation.[23] And so forth.

The public presentation of such claims and suggestions is not a new development in the Soviet Union, nor is it limited to the party congresses. Although public advocacy by party officials seems to be more frequent in the 1960's than it was in the last decade of Stalin's life, even in the past the local organs frequently expressed "to the ministries their ideas about the best way of using local reserves and possibilities."[24] Indeed, in this respect the speeches of the party secretaries at the Nineteenth Party Congress in 1952 are almost indistinguishable from those made by their counterparts fourteen years later.[25]

In advancing proposals to higher officials, the local party officials are usually acting not alone but in conjunction with local governmental, economic, and/or scientific institutions. Indeed, instead of initiating proposals themselves, they often can be found supporting the ideas and interests of these other institutions. In one typical example the director of the Dneprodzerzhinsk Metallurgy Works (one of the largest in the country) had been appealing to higher officials for funds to reconstruct the plant. "Why, new air heaters alone . . . would permit an increase in production of pig iron from each furnace by 27,000 tons a year and would achieve an annual economy of 400,000 rubles." The first secretary of the local gorkom wrote, "Of course, in such a situation the party gorkom had to harness itself in one team with the industrial administrators: to apply pressure, to push (*tolkat*), to solicit funds."[26]

This type of alliance, this "harnessing in one team" in the seeking of investment funds, is a completely normal feature of the Soviet admin-

---

[21] *XXIII Syezd*, I, 542. [22] *Ibid.*, 560. [23] *Ibid.*, 250-252.

[24] *Kommunist*, No. 1 (January 1958), p. 61.

[25] Leo Gruliow (ed.), *Current Soviet Policies* (New York, 1953). See, for example, pp. 145, 173, 174, 179, 198. Examples are cited in Hough, *op.cit.*, pp. 258-259.

[26] *Pravda Ukrainy*, October 28, 1965.

istrative scene. It is true that the development of new facilities complicates the lives of local officials, who might dream of avoiding capital investment in a search for the "peaceful life." However, they can never forget what Joseph Berliner called "the ratchet principle"—namely, the central practice of increasing the planned targets by a certain percentage every year.[27] The administrators know that next year's plan will be higher than this year's and that without new investment this plan will be extremely difficult to fulfill. Consequently, whatever difficulties will be created by the introduction of new equipment or the construction of new units or subunits, administrators must fight for them if they are to survive.[28] The local party secretaries, judged in large part on the basis of the economic performance of their region, have a similar interest in helping local administrators receive the funds and supplies they need. In addition, they undoubtedly observe many regional shortcomings which could be corrected, many local needs which could be satisfied, if only higher authorities could be persuaded to authorize the proper project.

For these reasons it is not surprising that in 1957 when the Minister of Machine-building wrote about the communications which he had received from the provincial party and economic organizations, he warned of their local bias: "Analysis shows that they are chiefly demanding money for supplementary capital construction or are asking us to assign them material and equipment. . . . It is difficult to recall even one case of a refusal of capital construction because of a better utilization of the capacity of the enterprises." The minister did not feel it necessary to distinguish between communications from party officials and those from industrial administrators.[29]

Of course, the community of interest between a local party organ and any particular enterprise or institution in the region cannot be complete. The party officials' responsibility for resolving day-to-day conflicts among the local enterprises and institutions means that they must repeatedly take actions which impinge upon the interests of one or another of the state institutions. However, when funds are being sought from

[27] Joseph Berliner, *Factory and Manager in the USSR* (Cambridge, Mass., 1957), pp. 78-79.
[28] Another factor which may be important is the practice of basing the salary scale of the manager and other officials upon the size of their enterprise. Expansion of a plant may result in it moving into the next higher category.
[29] *Pravda*, April 3, 1957.

62

outside, the conflicts of interest between the regional first secretaries and the state officials are held to a minimum, for normally the local party officials need not choose among the various requests for funds advanced by local administrators.

At the center there undoubtedly has been fierce competition for funds among officials of the different branches of the economy, but this competition usually does not extend into the provinces. Once the central organs decide on the allocation of funds among the various ministries, each ministry has the funds for its branch at its disposal. Even in realms supervised by the local soviets, the oblast and the city are not allocated funds which their officials can then subdivide among the claimants. For example, the city soviet is not allocated money for culture and education and then permitted (or forced) to choose between building a new high school and a new theater. Nor is it allocated money for city services and then permitted to choose between a new hospital and a new department store. Rather, it is the oblast health department (or health officials at a higher level) which has the resources for new hospitals, the oblast education department which has the resources for new schools, and so forth. The officials of the city soviet can (and must) seek both the new hospital and the new high school, and the city party officials have no difficulty in supporting both proposals.

When the regional first secretaries deal with enterprises subordinated directly to republican or all-union ministries (for example, industrial enterprises), they find it even easier to support the claims of nearly all local administrators. They can support the expansion both of the chemical plant *and* of the steel plant, both of the defense industry plant *and* the textile plant. Only when the area contains a number of enterprises turning out precisely the same product (perhaps, for example, in coal mining) is there likely to be any necessity for the party officials to act as a filter for the proposals rather than as a transmitter or supporter of them.

Indeed, the local party officials frequently may not even have to choose between types of appropriations for a given plant. Except on marginal matters, the plant director does not have the authority independently to determine the structure of investment within the plant. In particular, he is not faced with the necessity (or the possibility) of deciding to use a lump-sum ministerial appropriation for a new apartment house or new equipment. Ministerial funds for factory housing and new equipment come from different sources—in essence from different deputy ministers—and the plant manager can fight for both simultaneously. Therefore, the local party officials can also ally themselves with the managers on both appeals.

At the same time that the nature of the Soviet appropriations process reduces the conflicts between the first secretary and the other officials in his city or region, it magnifies the conflicts among the first secretaries of different cities and regions. The crucial fact about the advocacy role of the local party organs is that they are all engaged in it. With each organ suggesting projects or demanding more supplies and funds, the result (as in all bureaucratic situations) is that there cannot be enough funds to finance all proposals. Inevitably, the seeking of funds becomes a competitive process, and the regional first secretaries collectively find it quite impossible to serve as a unified force in this type of appropriations politics.

When one examines the role of the provincial officials in the appropriations process, the analogy which repeatedly comes to mind is the seeking of defense contracts in the United States. Just as the traditional American categories of "labor," "management," "Democrat," and "Republican" lose almost all real meaning in this process as the alliances center upon certain key companies and the communities in which they are located, so the categories of "party" and "state" have little relevance for understanding the Soviet appropriations process, at least once the basic rate of investment is decided. The major conflicts here involve a series of shifting groups comprising both party and state officials. In the struggle for a new hospital, a new steel plant, a new dam, there will be one group of state and party officials in one city or region struggling for a particular project, another group in another city or region struggling for another project or projects, and so forth.

The cleavages among the regional first secretaries on micro-appropriations questions are relatively easy to document. Nonetheless, to say that these men do not function as a unified group in the appropriations process is not necessarily to deny that they constitute a meaningful group in regard to other political issues. The question is: are there circumstances in which the regional first secretaries do, in fact, share a community of interest and do act as a unified interest group?

Few questions about the Soviet political system have produced more extensive and dogmatic discussion and less empirical investigation and careful thought than this one. In our assessment of the *apparatchiki*, we have failed in the past to make a distinction between their approach and attitude on questions involving the fundamentals of the political system and their position on the typical political conflict which does not challenge the system as they perceive it. When in doubt about the approach and behavior of the party officials on a particular question of internal policy, we have repeatedly assumed the rigidity and dogmatism which we find in communists in other settings.

Before speaking with confidence about the policy positions of the regional first secretaries, their approach to major questions, and the way they perceive their own interests, we need a series of thorough studies of developments in various policy realms over a ten-year period—studies set within the framework of a sound comparative knowledge of the phenomenon of bureaucratic politics and based upon a combination of content analysis, career pattern study, and interview techniques. At this stage it is a mistake to pretend to greater knowledge about the policy positions of the regional first secretaries than we actually have. Consequently, it seems to me more useful to point to conceptions about the party secretaries which are open to question and to suggest possibilities about their role which deserve detailed consideration in future studies. It is to this task that the rest of this section will be devoted.

Perhaps the basic political issue in the Soviet Union has been the priority to be given heavy industry, light industry, and agriculture; and on this question it seems fairly clear that there has been a good deal of cleavage among the regional first secretaries. The outlook of these officials on macro-appropriations questions often seems affected by the nature of their region and their own personal background. At the party congresses, for example, the first secretaries usually propose various investment projects for their region, and the type of project chosen for inclusion in their short speeches varies considerably from one secretary to another. It is by no means certain that the type of specific suggestions given priority in a secretary's speech corresponds to his position on overall investment priorities, but there are suggestive differences among first secretaries of different backgrounds.

At the Twenty-third Party Congress, for example, the speeches given by the republican and obkom first secretaries who were engineers are quite unlike those given by the first secretaries who were not engineers. In the speeches of the 5 first secretaries who were agronomists, 303 lines (as reported in the Stenographic Report)[30] were devoted to

---

[30] The agronomist first secretaries (and the volume and page on which their speech begins in *XXIII Syezd*) are: I. I. Bodyul (I, 417), A. V. Georgiyev (II, 75),

policy suggestions and investment demands related to agriculture, the rural sector, and agriculture-oriented industry (the agriculture machinery and food-processing industries), while 127 lines were devoted to suggestions with respect to industrial development (excluding the agriculture-oriented industries). Indeed, if we exclude the first secretary of the Ulyanovsk obkom, who devoted most of his speech to the reconstruction of Ulyanovsk in preparation for the 100th anniversary of Lenin's birth, the ratio would be 303 to 87. In the speeches of the 11 first secretaries who were engineers, we find only 69 lines devoted to agriculture-related suggestions (including the expansion of the industries connected with agriculture) as compared with 513 lines to suggestions about the industrial sector. The 17 secretaries with neither engineering nor agronomy degrees were more balanced in their treatment—339 lines to industry compared with 294 lines to agriculture. Among these 17 secretaries, however, the 3 who were leaders in one of the 25 most industrialized oblasti devoted 92 lines to industry and 17 to agriculture.

While the precise numbers of lines have limited significance, it is highly probable that the differences in the speeches reflect real cleavages among the first secretaries. The crucial question is, do these men have an institutional interest on macro-appropriations questions which transcends the pressures toward disunity among them? Or, at a minimum, is a particular set of appropriations priorities accepted by a clear enough majority to say that on balance the first secretaries constitute a meaningful interest group in this respect? If so, in which direction do their interests and attitudes point?

Unfortunately, several contrasting a priori arguments can be advanced on this question. On the one hand, the party's commitment to modernization and industrial development has surely attracted to it those men who are positively oriented to the urban sector, industrial growth, and the future. It might further be argued that the legitimacy of one-party rule ultimately rests upon a policy of rapid economic growth. For these reasons (as well as a possible dogmatic commitment to old ideological positions) the first secretaries might be said to share a set of attitudes

---

D. Rasulov (I, 272), A. A. Skochilov (I, 584), and N. F. Vasilyev (II, 143). The engineering first secretaries are A. F. Eshtokin (I, 572), K. I. Galanshin (I, 538), K. F. Katushov (I, 195), D. A. Kunayev (I, 148), K. K. Nikolayev (I, 332), N. N. Rodionov (I, 598), P. E. Shelest (I, 130), M. S. Solomentsev (I, 518), and V. S. Tolstikov (I, 140). The three other secretaries heading oblasti from among the 25 most industrialized are F. S. Goriachev (I, 157), F. A. Tabeyev (I, 505), and A. F. Vatchenko (I, 512).

which make them one of the major forces supporting the high-tempo development of heavy industry.

On the other hand, it might well be argued that the immediate interests of the first secretaries lead most of them to oppose the priority of heavy industry. For years the greatest danger for the obkom first secretaries has arisen from the agricultural sector, for the low priority assigned to agriculture has made plan fulfillment much more difficult in this realm than in industry. The many obkom secretaries who were driven to false reporting and who were removed prior to the Twenty-second Congress can scarcely have been comforted by the thought that the emphasis upon heavy industry makes the position of the party apparatus as a whole more secure. A second major threat to a first secretary has been that of a large demonstration by the local population. The 1959 demonstration in Temir-Tau, for example, resulted in the obkom first secretary being reduced to the level of shift head in a plant,[31] while the 1962 Novocherkassk demonstration led to the obkom leader being transferred to lower level diplomatic work until after Khrushchev's removal.[32] A reduction in the emphasis placed upon heavy industry might reduce both of these dangers for the first secretaries, at least in the short run.

The second set of arguments seems more convincing, at least if we limit the argument to recent years. Although the first secretaries certainly are not united on the heavy industry issue, I suspect that the most powerful concentration of political support for agricultural, rural expenditures in the Soviet Union comes from the rural raikom secretaries, from among the republican and obkom first secretaries of the less industrialized areas, and from the specialized secretaries for agricultural and possibly ideological-cultural questions. Moreover, the frequent demand by urban party officials for an increase in consumer goods production by heavy industry plants (and their frequent complaints that the heavy industry ministries are cutting back on such production) indicate at least some ambivalence on the heavy industry question even on their part.

Although many of the major issues in Soviet politics center on ap-

[31] This was P. N. Isayev. The demonstration occurred between the time of the election to the 1958 Supreme Soviet and the publication of the biographical directory of deputies. His biographical entry does not mention his various party positions. *Deputaty Verkhovnovo Soveta SSSR, Piatyi sozyv* (Moscow, 1959), p. 168.

[32] This was A. V. Basov. *Bol. sov. entsik.*, 1966 yearbook, p. 577.

propriations questions, there are, of course, other issues whose budgetary implications are at best indirect. Among these are the degree of economic reform in industry and agriculture and the degree of freedom to be permitted the intellectual. Included in the general question of the freedom for the intellectual are two further subsets of questions: the prerequisites of "law and order" and the structure of the decision-making process. It is on these questions more than on any others that the *apparatchik* has the reputation in the West of being a "conservative," a supporter of the *status quo*, even a "neo-Stalinist." In the words of Brzezinski and Huntington: "The engineering background of the Soviet apparatchik is supplemented by intense and continuing political training and many years of direct occupational experience in politics. Political experience and engineering background combine to give Soviet leaders a highly focused, direct, down-to-earth, problem-solving approach, without concern for legal niceties and with little tendency toward compromise solutions."[33] These images of the *apparatchik* probably have a good deal of truth in them, at least with respect to many party officials. However, they must not be accepted uncritically.

In the first place, it would be a major mistake to think of all regional first secretaries as men infused with an "ideological style," as men with a "rigid and closed set of rules of conduct spelled out by the ideology," as men "with little tendency toward compromise solutions."[34] The assignment of the role of the prefect to the local party organs has virtually required the first secretaries—even those of the Stalin period—to acquire a balancing, incremental perspective on many issues and to develop bargaining techniques. The first secretaries have had to compromise, to resolve conflicts among specialists in circumstances in which both sides in the dispute are "right" in terms of party policy and goals; they have had to learn the arts of persuasion and of mobilization of support in seeking funds from higher territorial levels and even in obtaining certain kinds of behavior from powerful local subordinates; they have had to learn how to permit and even require violation of the law and the plan in some circumstances while maintaining high "moral tone"

[33] *Op.cit.*, p. 146.

[34] The first two phrases about ideological style come from Gabriel A. Almond and G. Bingham Powell, Jr., *Comparative Politics: A Developmental Approach* (Boston and Toronto, 1966), pp. 60-61. Their discussion does not deal with the regional party secretaries, but rather with a type of political culture. The Soviet Union is, however, said to have such a political culture. See p. 312. The ideological-instrumental dichotomy is also analyzed in Brzezinski and Huntington, *op.cit.*, particularly pp. 71-76.

in the administrative apparatus. In short, as Brzezinski and Huntington recognize at one point, the first secretary must be "an expert in dealing simultaneously with a variety of issues and pressures, balancing one against another, attempting to resolve problems at the least cost to the greatest number of interests."[35]

Of course, to say that the party officials often are "rational, analytical, and empirical in their political action," that they often display "open, bargaining attitudes" and a "pragmatic, instrumental style,"[36] is not to deny that they may have quite rigid, ideologically conditioned views on *some* subjects. The combination of an instrumental, pragmatic approach on some questions and a dogmatic, rigid approach on others is quite normal—in fact, quite inevitable—in participants in all political systems. The problem is, on what questions are the first secretaries dogmatically agreed on the nature of the answers?

It is beyond the scope of this chapter—and beyond the knowledge of its author—to analyze the various policy positions of the first secretaries. One would certainly expect the overwhelming majority to take for granted the wisdom of governmental ownership and planning of industry and agriculture; the desirability of a political order which avoids the factional squabbling and "irresponsible" criticism of a multi-party system; the desirability (if perhaps not the absolute necessity) of writers and artists providing moral inspiration to the citizens and particularly to the youth; the need of "society" to protect itself against those malcontents who spread "malicious lies" about it; the need of the Soviet Union to protect itself against "American imperialism"; and the desirability of supporting those foreigners fighting against private-ownership social systems. On these types of questions the apparatus is presumably a unified interest group supporting major elements of the *status quo*.

This does not necessarily mean that all party officials dogmatically support all aspects of the existing policies in these spheres, or even that they are the most vigorous supporters of these policies. On all of the issues enumerated in the last paragraph, the position of the leading state and economic administrators is probably little different from that of the party secretaries, and on each issue (except perhaps that of for-

[35] *Ibid.*, p. 141.
[36] Again the phrases come from Almond and Powell, *Comparative Politics* [pp. 24, 61, 87], and were not used to describe party officials, but to epitomize the attitudes found in a culture with "full secularization."

69

eign policy) there are other subgroups within the elite who are likely to support the *status quo* more intensely than the first secretaries.

For example, the apparent rejection by the first secretaries of radical and rapid movement toward market socialism does not result, I think, from worry about the ideological respectability of profits, incentives, and so forth. Rather, it stems from their "membership" in two larger groups which also include the great majority of the important industrial administrators: first, the engineering-managerial personnel who have dominated Soviet industrial administration and much of the political system in recent decades—men whose training has not accustomed them to the idea of an "invisible hand" and whose position might be severely shaken in an economic system in which different skills (e.g., those of the economist) become more vital; second, the middle-aged, middle-class men who have achieved high status and economic comfort, but who may have an intense fear (perhaps reinforced by the Yugoslav experience) that market mechanisms produce inflation.

Within these major groups, the regional first secretaries may actually be among those most receptive to the initial steps in economic reform. The potential impact of the local organs upon economic decisions made within the region is much greater than on decisions made at higher territorial levels, and the devolution of authority (and particularly investment funds) to the plant level would significantly broaden the scope of action of party functionaries. For this reason it is not surprising that one of the most prevalent themes in articles by party officials on the economic reform has been criticism of the ministerial and financial personnel (those with most to lose in the reform) who restrict even those rights which the managers have already been granted.

In other major policy realms as well, the regional first secretaries are unlikely to be as dogmatic in their support of the *status quo* as the other major groups benefitting directly from it. On literary and artistic questions, the party officials—even those in ideological work—are probably far less intense in their opposition to experimentation in style than many of the leading officials of the writers' and artists' unions. A Komsomol official with whom I once talked expressed the exasperated belief that an all-out struggle against abstract art is not worth the bother— a feeling that I suspect is widely shared. Similarly, the opposition of functionaries to most types of sociological and economic research is likely to be less than that of the academic political economists. On questions of law and order, one would expect the party officials to be essentially "conservative" in their approach and not to show tolerance toward "agitators." Yet, even on this question many officials may be more receptive than other groups to the proposition that stability depends upon the correction of social evils and that the latter in turn requires a reasonably free flow of "responsible" criticism.

Of course, on many of the issues raised in the last paragraph there may be as little unity among the first secretaries as there is on appropriations questions. There may be "conservative" and "liberal" wings of the apparatus, with each position on an issue perhaps being strongly rooted among officials of particular backgrounds or areas. The first secretaries with the background of an industrial administrator (particularly those from heavy or defense industry) may tend to be conservative or even reactionary with respect to literary dissidence, market socialism, and a reduced priority for heavy industry; the younger first secretaries with a Komsomol background are, I suspect, often relatively "liberal" on these questions. Even if these suppositions are accurate, however, it is unlikely that knowledge of an official's "conservative" or "liberal" stand on one issue will reveal his position on all issues. It seems clear, for example, that the leaders of the Leningrad party organization have been quite reactionary in their relationships with literary dissidents, but that they have been most vigorous in their support for the development of concrete sociological investigation.[37]

Usually there is one question on which politicians can be expected to be quite conservative—the need to support the political structures in which they have learned to operate and which confer power and status upon them. Certainly, party officials are unlikely to lead the fight for a multi-party system and were undoubtedly prominent among those who were disturbed by the frequent reorganizations of the Khrushchev period, particularly by the bifurcation of the party apparatus.[38] Even on the question of the role and nature of the party apparatus, however, the regional first secretaries may not be completely united and rigid supporters of the organizational *status quo*. It is quite possible that many of these men might come—or already have come—to favor basic

[37] The leading place of Leningrad in Soviet sociology is mentioned in Frederick C. Barghoorn, *Politics in the USSR* (Boston and Toronto, 1966), p. 254. The Leningrad first secretary was also the most vociferous speaker in support of sociological research at the Twenty-third Congress, *XXIII Syezd*, I, 146-147.

[38] For example, the first secretary of the Estonian Central Committee asserted at the Twenty-third Congress, "We have experimented and reorganized too much [on structural questions]," and he received applause on this point. *XXIII Syezd*, I, 443.

71

changes in the mechanisms by which the General Secretary has exercised control over the apparatus. Considering that they were the major source of support for both Stalin and Khruschev in their rise to power, the first secretaries reaped fewer benefits than they might have expected. Even in the post-Stalin period, they found the authority of "their" *sovnarkhoz* quickly whittled away, and were themselves subjected to a large-scale purge in 1960-1961; the apparatus itself was torn asunder in 1962. They have even suffered the ignominy of being unable to hire good typists and stenographers because pay rates for these positions have been set lower than those in other institutions.[39]

If a coalition of leaders attempting to limit the power of the General Secretary struck upon the device of restricting his ability to remove key officials in the lower apparatus, this proposal might win considerable support among the local officials. The regional first secretaries might be made responsible to the local organization, or, once selected from above, they might be given immunity from removal by the General Secretary. Indeed, the latter development seems, in practice, to have taken place in the immediate post-Khrushchev period, for almost all republican and obkom first secretaries (at least those who were full members of the Central Committee) either retained their posts through 1968 or were given another job which normally would warrant Central Committee membership. If such a practice were instituted on a long-term basis, indeed, if there were any permanent limitation on the ability of the General Secretary to remove disloyal (or inefficient) party officials, it would constitute a radical transformation in the political system. Although the present tendency toward "respect for cadres" may be relatively short-lived, even the possibility that the regional first secretaries might support such an important change in the political system should remind us of the need to exercise care in generalizing about them.

The Specialized Officials of the Party Apparatus

Although Western scholars focus upon the regional first secretaries as the epitome of the *apparatchik*, the typical official, in numerical terms, is the employee of a specialized department of a party organ. With the exception of a few senior secretaries, all of the employees of

[39] *Partiinaya zhizn*, No. 22 (November 1965), p. 35.

the key Central Committee secretariat fit within this category. The Central Committee officials are probably of primary interest to a student of the Soviet political system, but because of the greater availability of information on the specialized officials of the local organs, we shall examine them first.

The practice of naming specialists to the apparatus has usually been attributed to a desire of the leadership to provide the first secretaries with the expert staff assistance which is necessary to control the specialists in the state and economic apparatus. This interpretation is unquestionably correct, but we should be careful about deducing the nature of these Soviet politicians from the original functions assigned to them. Like the first secretaries, they have also been assigned—or at least have assumed—the responsibility of supporting, of "pushing," and of fighting for investment projects relating to the branch of the economy they supervise. It is this responsibilty which is vital in determining their role in the policy-making process.

As we have seen, the first secretaries of local organs are active in advancing and supporting local development projects, but much of the working support for these projects is undoubtedly provided by the specialized secretary and department most directly involved. Since one of the normal techniques for developing support for a project is to speak out for it in a public speech or article, the extent of the participation of the specialized officials in the appropriations process may be readily discerned. In a speech at a republican party congress, a republican secretary for agriculture may "propose that the opening of the pastures on the Zaunguz plateau, in the southeastern and southwestern Kara-Kums, and in the Kara-Kum Canal zone be considered, [for, he asserted] this will open the gate to large-scale livestock raising in Tashauz oblast."[40] A deputy head of the industrial-transportation department of the Kazakhstan central committee may write an article in *Ekonomicheskaya gazeta*, complaining that the expansion of oil production in the new Mangyshlak field is being delayed by the failure of central authorities to make sufficient preparation for the transportation of the oil in 1968 and 1969, and he may end the article with the plea that action be taken.[41] An ideological secretary of the Bashkirya obkom may report that the drive for universal secondary education is gaining

[40] *Turkmenskaya iskra*, September 17, 1961.
[41] *Ekonomicheskaya gazeta*, No. 43 (October 1967), p. 15.

success, but that in the process is creating a serious shortage of ninth-grade teachers in the area. Consequently, he may call for the creation of a pedagogical institute in Ufa to solve this problem.[42]

The specialized party officials do not limit their support to specific local projects; they also publicly propose the appropriation of funds to benefit their branch on a nation-wide basis. Thus, in an article the head of the industrial-transportation department of the Krasnodar kraikom (together with the head of the Krasnodar Oil Prospecting Trust) asserted that recent successes in experimental drilling of deep oil wells in their region justified (indeed, made imperative) the mass production of the equipment necessary for this work.[43] In another article, the agricultural secretary of the Pskov obkom recognized that "Yes, we now receive more funds [for land reclamation] than before," but continued: "Often [the funds] do not have an impact because they are not invested in an integrated fashion. Let's say, the situation has become better with fertilizers, but there are few machines for applying them and only a small number of poorly equipped agro-chemical laboratories to consult with the kolkhozy and sovkhozy on how to apply the mineral fertilizers."[44] The Pskov secretary bluntly insisted, "If we want to intensify agricultural production in the Non-Black-Earth region on a modern level, then it is necessary first of all to create a durable production-technical base for land-reclamation and to improve the supplies situation."[45]

It is important to note that the "secretaries for ideological questions" also participate in this aspect of the appropriations process, and it is vital to understand the nature of their participation. As indicated earlier, the responsibilities of these secretaries are not limited to the supervision of propaganda and agitation and to the exercise of ideological control over the creative intelligentsia. They also have many down-to-earth responsibilities in the cultural-education realm. For example, the ideological functionaries may at times appeal publicly for an increase in the quantity and quality of film strips for the party's political education program. But their participation in the appropriations process is more vigorous on other questions.

A large portion of the time of the ideological officials must be devoted to the school system—and in considerable part to its financing

---

[42] *Sovetskaya Rossia*, June 22, 1966.

[43] *Ekonomicheskaya gazeta*, No. 46 (November 1967), p. 29.

[44] *Sovetskaya Rossia*, January 22, 1966.   [45] *Ibid.*

and supplying. We have already mentioned the ideological secretary of the Bashkirya obkom who fought for a new pedagogical institute. Even more frequently, the problem is to ensure that the various agencies responsible for elementary and secondary school funding and construction perform this task faithfully. Thus, the ideological secretary of the Krasnodar kraikom wrote an article in the newspaper of the Russian Republic criticizing the Ministry of Agriculture for creating a smaller, worse-equipped school network in the sovkhoz settlements than the kolkhozy were creating in the kolkhoz settlements.[46] He also pointed to the need to solve the "painful problem" of shortages of school furniture and laboratory equipment. The ideological secretary of the Penza obkom went further. He acknowledged that the present practice of financing school construction through the enterprises and kolkhozy resulted in sufficient funds for this purpose, but complained that the absence of centralized supplying of construction materials and equipment created great problems. "Construction materials and equipment have to be beat out with all truths and nontruths."[47]

Judging from their articles in the press, the ideological secretaries fully realize that shaping the citizens' attitudes requires more than exposing them to Marxism-Leninism and shielding them from "hostile" ideologies. In an article about the education of persons in their late teens, the ideological secretary of the Bashkirya obkom seemed quite sensitive to the importance of jobs for high school graduates and of meaningful training on their first jobs. While indicating that the obkom had been quite interested in ensuring that the local economic administrators hired and trained recent graduates, he stated that several policy changes were demanded at the national level. He proposed that the planning organs and ministries begin locating more plants in small and medium-sized cities to ease the difficulties of placement there. Moreover, he called upon the USSR State Committee for Labor and Wages to introduce a system of material incentives to reward foremen who assumed the responsibility of training high school graduates on their new jobs.[48]

Similarly, in an article dealing with the problems of developing a positive world-view among young people, the ideological secretary of the Uzbekistan central committee asserted that a lack of concern for young people on the part of some administrators seriously hampered this work. He demanded greater managerial sensitivity concerning the

---

[46] *Sovetskaya Rossia*, February 12, 1966.
[47] *Ibid.*, August 9, 1967.   [48] *Ibid.*, June 22, 1966.

need for adequate sports facilities and decent dormitories.[49] Two months prior to calling for better schools in the sovkhozy, the ideological secretary of the Krasnodar kraikom declared that production esthetics and city beautification were vital programs in shaping the cultural outlook of Soviet citizens. He insisted that they receive greater attention (and presumably funds).[50]

In appealing for funds, the specialized officials of a particular local party organ sometimes operate as a unified interest group. Since the funds for each branch are controlled by the respective ministries, the specialized officials can function together as a team, each attempting to obtain projects for the region by tapping a different set of central funds. There are, however, limits to the extent of the community of interests among the specialized officials of a particular organ.

In the first place, of course, some of their appeals go beyond a claim for a larger share of the branch's funds. It is one thing to call for the establishment of a local pedagogical institute; it is something else to call for a large-scale, integrated land-reclamation program. In the real world, it may be quite impossible to institute at the same time a large-scale expansion in the production of school furniture, in the development of new oil fields, in the land-reclamation program, and in the city beautification program. Consequently, when the specialized officials make appeals which have macro-appropriations implications, their interests come into sharp conflict with each other.

In the second place, even on micro-appropriations questions there can be a great difference in the intensity of the support which the bureau and the first secretary give to a project. It is one thing for the ideological secretary to write of the need for a pedagogical institute and even to gain the endorsement of the bureau and the first secretary for the project. It is quite a different matter if the first secretary places the institute at the top of his list of priority projects for the region and is willing to "bang the desk" when he visits the Central Committee secretariat and the Council of Ministers in Moscow. In attempting to win this type of support from the first secretary, the interests of the specialized officials may come into conflict in a fundamental way.

Finally, the last stages of the appropriations process—the "appropriations" of real men and materials for the construction of the project— produce further conflicts of interest among the specialized officials. To obtain appropriations in the sense of money authorizations is far easier

<hr/>

[49] *Izvestia*, November 17, 1965.   [50] *Ibid.*, December 21, 1965.

than to ensure the "mastering" (*osvoeniye*) of the funds. For example, a sovkhoz which I visited in 1967 had had no difficulty in obtaining the funds for a "palace of culture," but the project had remained uncompleted for several years. The raion authorities would not include it in the list of the priority projects to be built by the overburdened local construction trust. The problem is a typical one and becomes particularly great in those cases in which the allocation of supplies is not organized in a centralized fashion. It is on decisions about the priority to be given construction projects that the competition among the specialized officials may become most severe. In the Kazakhstan Party Congress of 1961 this competition came to the surface in a strong complaint by the republican secretary for industry: "For two years the plans for capital investment in housing, culture, education, public health, and communal construction have been overfulfilled. The plan for capital investment in agriculture has been overfulfilled by almost a billion rubles. However, we have far from mastered the funds allocated for the development of heavy industry and the construction industry."[51]

On these aspects of the appropriations process group conflict is far different from that suggested by those analyses which emphasize the conflict between the party and the state, the *apparatchik* and the manager, the ideologues and the intelligentsia. On these questions, the key groupings are usually formed along functional lines, as the party secretaries ally themselves with, and defend the interests of, state officials over whom at other times they exercise control. The obkom secretary for agriculture, the deputy chairman of the executive committee of the oblast soviet for agriculture, the head of the oblast agriculture administration (the direct subordinate of the ministry), and the head of the agriculture department of the party obkom are likely to be natural allies in a struggle with, for example, the obkom secretary for ideological questions, the deputy chairman of the executive committee of the oblast soviet for cultural-education questions, the head of the oblast education department, and the head of the science, higher education, and schools department of the obkom. For this reason, it was not surprising to hear a young and by no means doctrinaire director of an art museum exclaim in a 1967 conversation, "Where would we be without the party obkom?" In a conflict with the bank over funding, he had found the obkom (presumably first and foremost the ideological officials) the only effective source of local support.

[51] *Kazakhstanskaya pravda*, September 30, 1961.

Of course, on many issues the essential conflicts take place within the confines of one branch of the economy rather than between branches. Should priority be given to the development of heavy industry or light industry, to the development of the Virgin Lands or to the reclamation of the western lands? How much authority should be delegated from the ministry to the plant manager or the university rector? To what extent should experimentation be permitted within the theaters and the art galleries? At what stage should defense attorneys participate in criminal investigations? On these questions do the specialized officials have a different "party" perspective than their counterparts in the governmental and economic hierarchies?

To some extent these questions are answered by the very structure of the apparatus. Because a local party organ has only one secretary for industry, it is obvious that the policy positions of this official will not always coincide with those both of the heavy industry and the light industry administrators of the area. Similarly, since the administrative organs department oversees the activities of the police, the procuracy, the courts, and presumably the defense attorneys, its officials would find it impossible to reflect mechanically the views of all the men they supervise, regardless of their own wishes.

Although there is ample room for a distinct "party position" on many issues, it is not at all clear what that position is—or, indeed, whether one actually exists. Certainly there is little evidence that the specialized party officials, even the ideological ones, are always the spokesmen for the dogmatic, "ideological" position on a given issue. The specialized functionaries do not have the same range of coordinating responsibilities as the first secretaries, but they, too, must make a continuing series of hard choices among widely varying claims within their branch. They, too, must develop some of the politician's skills and behavior in their participation in the appropriation process. As the ideological officials fight "with all truths and nontruths" for materials and equipment for school construction and attempt to persuade local plant managers to improve sports facilities and to employ school dropouts, they are far more likely to develop into pragmatic politicians than mere "ideologues" preoccupied with the intricacies of Marxist philosophy.

In practice, the relation of the specialized officials and the state administrators varies considerably from one issue to another. In the cultural-education area, for example, the ideological officials may well be more dubious about the showing of foreign films than are the theater managers who are more immediately worried about fulfilling their attendance plan. Yet, as already indicated, most ideological officials are probably more willing to tolerate artistic innovation than many conservative writers, and more eager to encourage sociological research than many political economists.

To the extent that the specialized officials have an identifiable group position on intra-branch questions, it is likely that these positions are associated with the party organs' responsibility for regional coordination and political stability. The major difference between ideological officials and the educational administrators involves not, I suspect, the ideological content of the curriculum, but the education of potential dropouts. Most Soviet educators seem dedicated to a program designed for the college-bound; the ideological officials often seem more concerned with the dangers of idle teen-agers wandering the streets. The industrial party officials are probably more sensitive than the industrial administrators about the need to hire soon-to-be-drafted teen-agers, to improve working conditions at the factory, and to produce more small-scale consumers' goods out of scrap material.

A critical question is whether these hypotheses are valid so far as the specialized officials of the Central Committee secretariat are concerned. Do these officials take a "presidial perspective" on policy questions, or do their attitudes often correspond to those of the respective specialized officials of the local party organs and the administrators they supervise?[52]

Unfortunately, as all scholars concerned with the Soviet Union have found reason to lament, it is precisely when we turn to a discussion of the Central Committee apparatus that the problem of information becomes the most acute. Soviet newspapers seldom provide much information about the inner workings of the party organ to which they are directly subordinate, and the central press adheres to this rule even more closely than the local press. If we take an interest group approach, however, we begin with great skepticism about the likelihood of a common set of values within such an internally differentiated institution as the Central Committee secretariat—or, at least, a common set of values with respect to the typical "within-system" political conflicts of Soviet society. The limited information available indicates that this skepticism is justified.

Perhaps the surest indication of cleavage within the Central Committee secretariat is the nature of the job which its officials have been

[52] Brzezinski and Huntington, *op.cit.*, p. 199.

assigned. In particular, the responsibility for "verification of the fulfillment of party and state decisions" has important implications for the role of the secretariat in the policy process. Each party member is obligated by the party to "speak out against any actions which harm the party and the state and to inform the party organs, right up to the Central Committee, about them,"[53] and the party organs are obligated to investigate these complaints and to correct the situation reported. The Central Committee officials also are given the responsibility of seeking information on their own. For example, in 1962 the party secretary of the Minsk Automatic Lines Works reported, "Long in advance of the plenary session [of the Central Committee on leadership of industry] a representative of the Central Committee came to our plant. He asked what questions concerning the leadership of the economy and particularly industry agitated us, and he said that the Central Committee would like to know our opinion on these questions—the opinion of the party *aktiv* and the leaders and employees of the plant."[54]

In performing their information-collecting functions, the specialized party officials repeatedly learn of the need for more funds and supplies. When, for example, the officials of the agriculture department check on the fulfillment of the Central Committee decree on irrigation and land reclamation, they obviously are told privately what the Pskov secretary said in public: "Often [the funds] do not have an impact because they are not invested in an integrated fashion." They are told, "If we want to intensify agricultural production in the Non-Black-Earth region on a modern level, then we first of all must create a durable production-technical base for land-reclamation and must improve the supplies situation." As the top party leaders ask the specialized officials how the performance of their branch could be improved, the latter frequently must pass along the investment suggestions and demands of ministerial and lower party officials, and the information and suggestions emanating from each Central Committee department must to a considerable degree reflect the differences of opinion among these officials.

Party spokesmen continually emphasize that "verification of performance" entails the responsibility not only to report shortcomings, but also to see that they are removed. Western scholars have emphasized that this responsibility requires the specialized party officials to prod "their" ministry or ministries to use existing resources more

[53] Party Rules, Statute 2. *Pravda*, November 3, 1961.
[54] *Sovetskaya Belorussia*, November 21, 1962.

effectively, but it would be a mistake to focus exclusively upon the tensions built into the relationship of the ministries and the Central Committee secretariat. The very nature of their duties identifies the specialized party officials with the major goals assigned the ministries they supervise. It is inevitable, for example, that the head of the oil industry sector of the Central Committee's heavy industry department will adhere to the position he enunciated in *Ekonomicheskaya gazeta* in 1968: "It is very important to speed the introduction of new capacity in the oil industry. This means we must increase the known reserves, widen the scale of oil-well drilling, and perfect the exploitation of the deposits."[55]

Since significant increase in productivity in modern industry requires investment, it is also inevitable that party officials dedicated to the development of their branch must fight for the funds this requires. And so, the head of the oil industry sector raises his voice publicly for the "integrated automation and telemechanization of the production processes."[56] Similarly, the head of the agriculture department of the Central Committee can be found stating that the agricultural machinery plants must develop a wider assortment of machines to deal with the peculiarities of different zones of the country, while two Central Committee officials specializing in light industry demand an increase in the quantity and an improvement in the quality of machines producing shoes.[57]

In practice, it is highly probable that on fundamental appropriations questions each department usually works together with the relevant ministries as the combined representative of their branch. In the conflict which flared over the level of agricultural investment in the late 1950's, for example, Khrushchev has testified that the party and governmental officials specializing in agriculture functioned as allies:

At the end of 1959, at the December plenum of the Central Committee of the CPSU, our Party worked out new important measures in the agricultural realm. . . . I should tell you, when we prepared for this plenum, our agricultural organs—the departments of the Central Committee for the union republics and the RSFSR and the ministries of agriculture—worked out fairly broad proposals for the development of all branches of agriculture in the Soviet Union. We

[55] *Ekonomicheskaya gazeta*, No. 51 (December 1968), p. 8.
[56] *Ibid.*
[57] *Partiinaya zhizn*, No. 5 (March 1958), p. 14, and No. 19 (October 1958), pp. 45-48.

81

rejected these proposals. The Central Committee considers that the basic boundaries of the development of agriculture are well stated in the seven-year plan.[58]

It seems certain that the "metal-eaters" on the other side of the issue likewise included within their ranks both party officials (for example, the iron and steel sector of the heavy industry department) and governmental officials (for example, the Ministry of Ferrous Metallurgy). Such behavior seems almost certainly to be the norm rather than the exception.

On intra-branch questions there is less inherent reason to assume a community of interests and viewpoints between the officials of the Central Committee department and the ministerial officials they supervise. As Fainsod has pointed out, the basic rationale for the creation of a duplicate set of "ministries" in the Central Committee secretariat is to provide the party leadership with diversity in information and policy suggestions:

> By pitting the competitive hierarchies of administration, party, and secret police against each other at lower levels of the governmental structure, [the leadership] frees itself from exclusive dependence on any single channel of fact gathering and encourages rivalries among the various agencies to correct distortion and prevent concealment. In this fashion it mobilizes the cumulative resources which competition sometimes generates.[59]

If the overlapping of the party and state institutions is to serve this function, then one would expect the party leadership to take steps to ensure some diversity in viewpoint between them. It would be logical to appoint a Central Committee secretary for agriculture whose general policy views on agriculture are known to differ somewhat from those of the Minister of Agriculture.

Yet, despite the competition built into the secretariat-ministry relationship on intra-branch questions, there are a number of forces that tend to draw together the party and governmental officials dealing with a particular branch of the economy. There is frequent and intimate contact between such men, and common attitudes have ample opportunity to develop. The investigations carried out by the party officials bring

[58] N. S. Khrushchev, *Stroitelstvo kommunizma v SSSR i razvitiye selskovo khozyaistva* (Moscow, 1963), IV, 109.
[59] Fainsod, *op.cit.*, p. 341.

them into close contact with ministerial personnel, but the interaction often takes more prolonged and often more cooperative forms. In the past—and probably at the present—officials of the Central Committee staff attended meetings of the collegia of the ministries and presumably participated in their discussions. Moreover, officials of the Central Committee secretariat and the state institutions usually seem to work together in the drafting of major decisions. Normally *ad hoc* bodies ("commissions") are formed, composed of representatives of the interested Central Committee department or departments, ministries, and state committees, as well as experts from the academic and scientific community. A commission may produce a draft decision which the top policy-makers find unacceptable, as apparently was the case in the 1959 agricultural investment policy mentioned by Khrushchev; at other times it is probably more conscious of "political realities." Sometimes, particularly in a decision of the Secretariat alone, officials from the outside may be invited for long discussions on the draft. In the case of a 1957 decision on the historical journal, *Voprosy istorii*, for example, eight- to nine-hour discussions were held on two successive days, and the editors of the journal, the president and vice-president of the Academy of Sciences, and other representatives from the Academy of Sciences participated along with officials of the relevant Central Committee departments.[60]

In either case, however, the repeated give-and-take which this type of "legislative process" requires between party and state officials specializing on a given branch of the economy could be expected to push them toward a common definition of key problems and possible solutions for them. In the course of prolonged interaction with "their" state officials, the specialized functionaries may come to have a vision of the political world more similar to that of their counterparts in the government than to that of their nominal colleagues in other departments of the Central Committee. In fact, since the specialized party officials are usually drawn from those with administrative experience in their own field, these men may well have had a similar outlook before their appointment.

Of course, there are no institutions or groups of specialists without differences of opinion, and such differences surely exist between the officials of a Central Committee department and those whose work they oversee. Many policy differences must be essentially idiosyncratic in

[60] *Ibid.*, p. 339.

83

nature, but some undoubtedly reflect basic institutional differences. A department of the Central Committee, like that of a local party organ, has a broader set of responsibilities than any one ministry or state committee, and this inevitably prevents the development of a complete community of interests and views between a department and all the institutions it supervises. It should be noted, however, that the greater number of departments in the Central Committee secretariat reduces the number of state institutions within the jurisdiction of any one Central Committee department and, consequently, reduces the amount of conflict with the state apparatus. The head of the industrial-transportation department of a local party organ will inexorably come into conflict with some of the industrial administrators he supervises; however, it is at least within the realm of possibility that the head of the chemical industry department of the Central Committee and the Minister of the Chemical Industry might be in near-complete agreement. Because of the greater specialization within the Central Committee secretariat, one would tend to suspect that many of the department heads and particularly the sector heads often have a narrower perspective on a number of issues than do many specialized local party officials.

The crucial question, once again, is whether the officials of the Central Committee departments, more than those of the governmental agencies, are men with "an ideological form of political calculation and analysis" who act in accordance with a "rigid and closed . . . set of rules of conduct spelled out by the ideology."[61] As before, this is a difficult question to answer. The officials of the Central Committee departments seem to be guided by a willing or unwilling passion for anonymity, and their policy positions on intra-branch questions are seldom discernible.

The one piece of evidence that we have would by itself provide little reason to conclude that the officials of the Central Committee departments are as a whole more rigid than their counterparts in the ministries or state committees. When we look at year of birth and of party admission for the Central Committee department heads, the ministers, and the chairman of state committees who worked on internal policy questions in 1966,[62] we find that the department heads were on the

[61] Almond and Powell, *op.cit.*, pp. 61, 312.

[62] In the foreign policy realm two of the department heads were born and joined the party over a decade prior to the average department head specializing on internal policy questions. However, even the four foreign policy department heads (Iu. V. Andropov, A. S. Paniushkin, B. N. Ponomarev, and D. P. Shevly-

84

average five years younger (1914 *vs.* 1909) and joined the party four years later (1939 *vs.* 1935). In some cases the contrast was striking. The head of the transportation and communications department of the Central Committee (a man who was born in 1917 and joined the party in 1943) oversaw ministers of railroads, communication, and merchant marine whose year of birth averaged 1902 and whose year of party admission averaged 1922.[63] The head of the light industry and food industry department of the Central Committee (born 1916) joined the party in 1941—a year after the Minister of the Food Industry (born 1899) and the Minister of the Fish Industry (born 1905) had already become Peoples' Commissar for the branch of industry they still head.[64] The head of the agriculture department of the Central Committee was nine years younger than the Minister of Agriculture and seventeen years younger than the Chairman of the State Committee for Deliveries; the head of the construction department was eleven years younger than the average age of the construction administrators who sat on the Council of Ministers.[65] Eight of the eleven ministers and chairmen of state committees cited in these examples had reached the level of minister by 1955, five of them by 1948. None of the four Central Committee department heads had held their post for as many as five years. (Indeed, at the time of the Twenty-third Congress in the spring of 1966, over three-quarters of the department heads dealing with internal policy had tenure of under two years.)

Age alone is, of course, not a conclusive indication of attitude. But in the absence of other evidence, there seems to be no a priori reason to believe that the ministers just discussed have been the pragmatic, inno-

---

agin) on the average were born and joined the party a year earlier than the top four state officials handling foreign policy questions (A. A. Gromyko, V. V. Kuznetsov, N. S. Patolichev, and S. A. Skachkov). *Bol. sov. entsik.*, 1966 yearbook, pp. 575, 584, 597, 605, 607, 611, 619.

[63] The head of the transportation and communications department of the Central Committee was K. S. Simonov; the Minister of Railroads, B. P. Beshchev; the Minister of Communications, N. D. Psurtsev; and the Minister of the Merchant Marine, V. G. Bakayev. *Ibid.*, pp. 577, 578, 608, 611.

[64] The head of the light industry and food industry department of the Central Committee was P. K. Sizov; the Minister of the Food Industry was V. P. Zotov; and the Minister of the Fish Industry was A. A. Ishkov. *Ibid.*, pp. 589, 590, 611.

[65] The head of the agriculture department was F. D. Kulakov; the Minister of Agriculture was V. V. Matskevich; and the Chairman of the State Committee for Deliveries was L. R. Korniets. *Ibid.*, pp. 595, 597, 601. The head of the construction department was A. E. Biriukov, while the four construction administrators were I. A. Grishmanov, F. B. Yakubovsky, E. F. Kozhevnikov, and I. T. Novikov. *Ibid.*, pp. 578, 584, 593, 604, 621.

vative advocates of reform within their branch, while the younger department heads mentioned have been the hidebound opponents of change. Similarly, is the Furtseva (Minister of Culture) who joined the party in 1930 at the age of twenty likely to be less "ideological" in her approach than the Shauro (head of the culture department of the Central Committee) who joined the party in 1940 at the age of twenty-eight? Is the Stepakov (head of the propaganda department of the Central Committee) who first entered party work in 1944 after seven years of administrative work in industry and transportation necessarily more "ideological" than the Mikhailov (Chairman of the State Committee of the Press) who was first secretary of the All-Union Komsomol from 1938 to 1952? The honest answer to all these questions is—we really do not know. But again we can say that the scholar who hypothesizes a Central Committee secretariat united in an ideological approach and opposing a more pragmatic, rational state administration should be aware of the assumptions he is making. In practice we have too often compared the attitudes of the Central Committee official with those of the intellectual—and the dissident intellectual at that—or perhaps we have been too much impressed by the mere designation "party." If we compare the "ideological approach" of Central Committee officials with that of top governmental administrators, we may be forced to make a more complex analysis than is customary.

If we seek issues on which the Central Committee secretariat is likely to be a group with unified interests in opposition to those of another group within the elite, we find few such issues readily discernible. Like the specialized officials of the local party organs, the officials of the Central Committee departments are probably more immediately aware of the implications of policy for political stability than are many of the state officials, and this awareness may well have an impact on their attitudes similar to that hypothesized for local party officials.

Moreover, the very high rate of turnover among the department heads within a year of Khrushchev's removal (and a similarly high rate in 1953-1955) suggests that there may be a close personal relationship between the General Secretary and the department heads and that the latter may be more sensitive than the governmental officials to the implications of policy for the stability of the position of the party leader. The department heads may be fairly united in trying to defend the General Secretary's political position, and they may tend to close ranks when he is involved in a critical political conflict over a particular issue. Even in such a case, however, the department heads whose branches are threatened by the General Secretary's attitude surely emphasize to him the potential consequences of his position, and continue to attempt to produce one of those policy changes for which General Secretaries have been famous. When—as usually must be the case—the General Secretary tries to give himself flexibility by occupying a more centrist position, even the most loyal specialized party officials will be free to speak vigorously for "their" branch in intra-branch conflicts.

Paradoxically, the "within-system" issue on which the Central Committee officials may be most united is one which involves conflict with other parts of the party apparatus rather than with the ministerial officials. The Central Committee officials are located in the center; they work intimately with central state officials; they find it easier to influence policy in one nearby ministry than in fifteen scattered republics. Since the specialized officials may eventually decide that they could have a greater impact on events through the use of centrally controlled economic levers, there is little reason to expect them to be dedicated to the principle of decentralization of policy-making authority. Particularly, given the overwhelming Russian domination of the Central Committee secretariat, they are probably quite unsympathetic to the idea of moving in the direction of genuine federalism. On the other hand, the lower party officials, whatever their devotion to the principle of a centralized party and state, are surely pressing for more decentralization on specific questions. This is an important cleavage and is likely to become even more so with the passage of time.

Conclusion

The emphasis throughout this chapter has been placed upon the divisions within the party apparatus and upon the complexity of the role of its officials in the decision-making process. To the extent that this assessment is valid, it tends to lend support to many of the key propositions of the interest group approach presented in the opening pages of this chapter.

Beyond furnishing evidence that the phenomena emphasized by Bentley are present even in totalitarian regimes, does this study have any implications for comparative interest group theory? Does an examination of the party apparatus in the Soviet Union provide insights into the similarities and differences in the political processes of the Soviet Union and Western democracies?

On the surface at least, one sees striking differences between the interest group or groups described in this paper and those usually described in Western interest group studies. In the West, attention is concentrated on associational interest groups (e.g., the AMA or the AFL-CIO), which are autonomous vis-à-vis the government and able to provide "the average citizen with a large number of channels of access to the political elite."[66] But the persons discussed in this essay all occupy elite positions within the political machine itself. All have been appointed by the leaders on whom they make demands, and they may be removed by these leaders. Moreover, while associational groups may use a variety of techniques (including strikes, demonstrations, and so forth) to dramatize and elicit support for their demands, the party officials in the Soviet Union—particularly the Central Committee officials—are severely limited in what they can say publicly, and especially in how they can say it.

It has been argued that evidence of "subsystem autonomy" in a Western democracy and the lack of it in a totalitarian regime is a crucial distinction in defining the nature of the political systems:

A totalitarian system in a nominal sense has all the structures and subsystems of roles that exist in a democratic system, but rather than being autonomous, the interaction of these political substructures is hierarchically controlled. In conversion or process terms, the flow of inputs from the society is suppressed or strictly regulated. Consequently, we cannot speak of interest groups, media of communication, and political parties as constituting an autonomous political infrastructure. They are to be viewed more as mobilization structures contributing to the regulative, extractive, and symbolic capabilities than as substructures creating the basis for a responsive capability. . . .

This implies that *regardless* of the personal desires and ideological commitments of the political leaders, it will be very difficult for such systems to develop a broad responsive capability. We can predict that systems of this class will continue to show a limited range of responsiveness as long as subsystem autonomy remains low and differentiation high.[67]

[66] Almond and Powell, *op.cit.*, p. 169. This phrase was applied to "input" structures "such as interest groups and parties."

[67] *Ibid.*, pp. 312, 325.

This line of argument, however, gives rise to serious questions, particularly if one accepts Bentley's interest approach. Bentley, as we have seen, argued that a government must by its very nature be responsive to some interest or interests, but that in the nature of things it cannot be completely responsive to all interests. The crucial question, therefore, is: to whose interests is policy responsive?

It would certainly simplify the comparative study of political systems if we could assume that the elite members of the institutional groups which comprise "the gigantic bureaucracy-party organizational complex" in a country such as the Soviet Union represent essentially their own interests, and not those of the farmers, workers, and clerks whom they supervise. It would also be convenient if we could assume that through the presence of "numerous and autonomous associational groups, with access to political agencies through a variety of legitimate channels" "the institutional interests can be checked and combined with other interests."[68]

It is tempting to make such a priori assumptions—but highly dangerous. In the first place, it is by no means certain that institutional interest groups always represent the interests of the top administrators of the institution alone. In any country, as Almond and Powell point out, "elite representation may . . . serve as a channel for interest groups which have no other means of articulation. In the 1830's and 1840's in Great Britain certain aristocratic and middle-class members of Parliament took it upon themselves to articulate the interests of the working class. Their work on Committees of Inquiry and the like did much to promote the passage of factory and mines legislation."[69] When governmental and party officials specializing in agriculture appeal for additional machinery and fertilizer, when they call for a more effective incentive system to stimulate production, they represent some of the vital interests of the peasant. The subordination of nearly all rank and file Soviet citizens to some ministry or state committee provides all citizens with institutional leaders who have ample incentives to learn their grievances. These leaders know, to quote Almond and Powell, that "peasants on collective farms and workers in factories [can] bargain with their rates of output."[70]

In the second place, it is by no means certain that Western associational interest groups—particularly the large ones usually emphasized by scholars—should be viewed as "channels of access to the political elite

[68] *Ibid.*, p. 91.   [69] *Ibid.*, p. 84.   [70] *Ibid.*, p. 278.

[through which] . . . the citizen can easily voice his demands."[71] Mancur Olson has correctly asserted that membership in large associational groups in the United States usually results from compulsion or from tangible benefits other than interest representation.[72] His analysis would lead one to expect few membership challenges to the group leadership— even if the interest representation is considered inadequate. Or, at least, one would expect major challenges only when there is a level of dissatisfaction which would be readily discernible in any political system.

Olson's argument tends to be supported by the empirical work of a leading American specialist on the subject, the late V. O. Key, Jr. At the end of a lifetime of study, Key concluded that "to a considerable degree the work of the spokesmen of private groups, both large and small, proceeds without extensive involvement of either the membership or a wider public."[73] He depicted interest group leaders less as the representatives of autonomous groups than as members of a common political elite—a "leadership echelon." At times he found it possible to speak of this echelon in the singular, attaching great importance to "the motives that actuate the leadership echelon, the values that it holds, . . . the rules of the political game to which it adheres, . . . the expectations which it entertains about its own status in society, and perhaps . . . some of the objective circumstances, both material and institutional, in which it functions."[74] Key even hypothesized that "the pluralistic interaction among leadership echelons may occur, and may be tolerable, precisely because leadership clusters can command only a relatively small following among the masses."[75]

Charles Lindblom has interpreted the activity of associational interest groups in a similar manner, contending that "interest-group leaders will be listened to with respect not because they wield power but because they are perceived to be representatives of interests entitled (by the accepted norms of rules governing the few activists) to be heard and to be accorded consideration." He continues: "The big engine of interest-group participation in the play of power . . . is persuasion. . . . Interest-groups are highly-skilled practitioners of partisan analysis; it is per-

[71] *Ibid.*, p. 169.

[72] Mancur Olson, *The Logic of Collective Action* (Cambridge, Mass., 1965), pp. 5-16, 132-167.

[73] V. O. Key, Jr., *Public Opinion and American Democracy* (New York, 1967), p. 530.

[74] *Ibid.*, p. 537.   [75] *Ibid.*, p. 530, n. 9.

haps their main source of influence or power. . . . Their educational or persuasive work is typically more restricted . . . to showing the proximate policy maker how a policy desired by the interest-group squares with the policy-maker's philosophy, values, or principles."[76] Lindblom did not hesitate to point up the obvious implication of this interpretation: "If . . . their powers are largely those of partisan analysis, then, great as they are, they are nevertheless constrained by the fundamental values of . . . proximate policy-makers to whom they appeal."[77]

On an observational level, the Western interest groups described by Key and Lindblom and the Soviet groups described in this essay have many more similarities than suggested in a book such as Almond's and Powell's *Comparative Politics*. In both countries members of the political elite claim to speak for broader groups within society. In both countries these avowed elite representatives of interests advance their case largely through persuasion, as argued in the passage quoted above. Even the fact that the elite representatives of interests in the Soviet Union are administratively responsible to the top political leaders conceivably may make them little less "autonomous" than are the appointed leaders of military establishments throughout the world.

Thus, the questions to which we must return are: for whom *do* the specialized elites in a country speak? To what extent do they serve as channels through which all significant interests in society can be equitably represented in the political process? And, of course, ultimately we face the question which Bentley raised with respect to a despotic ruler (and also a democracy)—which interests "are most directly represented through him, . . . which almost seem not to be represented through him at all, or to be represented to a different degree or in a different manner"?[78] It is these questions—particularly the last one—which we must answer before we can say anything meaningful about the "responsiveness" of different political systems.

Unfortunately, a study of an interest group such as the party apparatus or even of the multitude of groups of which different party officials are members does little to answer the questions raised in the last paragraph. The interest group approach really suggests that we study not only the interest groups themselves, but also the relationship

---

[76] Charles E. Lindblom, *The Policy-Making Process* (Englewood Cliffs, 1968), pp. 64-65.
[77] *Ibid.*, p. 68.   [78] Bentley, *op.cit.*, p. 270.

among them. If we are to compare how interests are represented in different political systems, we may have to take seriously Lasswell's definition of politics and begin to explore the question—who, in fact, does get what in different political systems? It is this type of exploration that will be necessary before we can make a definite judgment about the role of the party *apparatchiki* as an interest group in Soviet society.

The Security Police

Introduction

THE activities of political organizations, or of the political systems in the contexts of which these institutions function, may be better understood if data can be examined in a comparative frame that sharpens perception of similarities, and differences. The Committee of State Security (KGB) and the Ministry of Internal Affairs (MVD) in the USSR, and the Federal Bureau of Investigation (FBI) and the Central Intelligence Agency (CIA), in the USA, for example, are similar in important respects but the scope, methods, and impact of their operations differ as widely as do the political systems that these agencies serve. Both sets of agencies perform political security functions. Within the broad category of interest groups, both fit into the subcategory of bureaucratic, nonassociational groups. LaPalombara's definition of interest group as "any aggregation of interacting individuals who manifest conscious desires concerning the authoritative allocation of values"[1] seems to be applicable to them. However, neither could very easily be squeezed into the same subcategory as, let us say, an informal Soviet grouping of "liberal" writers, or an *ad hoc* American associational interest group, such as Scientists and Engineers for McCarthy. In terms of areas of jurisdiction and organizational structure, the CIA and FBI and, the KGB and the MVD, which perform in the Soviet system a range of functions as broad as the above-mentioned United States agencies—plus, it seems, functions corresponding to those of the Secret Service, the National Security Agency, and probably some other related organizations—could be very roughly compared with each other and with other bureaucratic-institutional agencies in the USSR, the United States, or other countries. However, no United States federal agencies have ever performed the function of exploiting vast masses of forced labor as in Stalin's labor camp system, administered by the MVD.

[1] Joseph LaPalombara, *Interest Groups in Italian Politics* (Princeton, 1964), p. 18.

Intelligence, security, police, and law enforcement agencies of all modern societies have much in common, but they vary greatly in respect to attributes of jurisdiction, structure, and function. They differ also in their style of operations, which reflects or is associated with the distinctive patterns of organization that distinguish pluralistic democracies from either traditional monarchies or oligarchies, or from the Soviet-type "unified hegemony," to use the terminology suggested by Robert A. Dahl. The fact that roughly similar functions, or, to be more accurate, sets of functions, are performed differently in different types of social and political systems is obvious, but needs to be stressed early in this essay. There is a certain danger that scholars may be so beguiled by the "interest group approach" as to lose sight of the broad systemic differences which distinguish Soviet from "Western" politics. Such a blurring of distinctions could be particularly misleading if it obscured the differences between a "political police" of the Soviet type, and corresponding agencies in countries where their jurisdiction and operations are much more precisely defined or circumscribed by law, the constitutional order, and traditional norms.

Interest group theory was, after all, developed primarily by American scholars to facilitate the understanding of a system which permits and, within broad limits, facilitates, the ready access of individuals and groups to the political process, in varied situations and on terms and conditions determined by rules and customs which constrain both officials and ordinary citizens. These rules are made, in the Western "polyarchies," by legislative bodies the membership of which is determined by reasonably competitive elections. Both the rules and their application are subject to a great deal of free and critical, if not always rational, public discussion. The norms of democratic political culture, and to a relatively high degree its practices, hold that the welfare of the citizenry is fostered when a multiplicity of individuals and groups competitively press for fulfillment of their special interests, within a framework of generally accepted rules; in a communist dictatorship, at least in its Soviet variant, the attempt is made to eliminate the very concept of any "interest," other than the general public or community interest, as selfish and evil.

To be sure, the Leninist doctrine, which is still the official creed of the Soviet Union, and in which citizens, particularly officials, are intensively indoctrinated, reluctantly admits that a variety of group and individual perspectives and even conflicting or clashing preferences and outlooks, reflecting "survivals of the past" and the persistence of socio-economic division of labor, exist, but it is maintained that such differences will eventually give way to wholehearted and united support of society's collective goals, as interpreted by the CPSU leaders. This conception may be regarded as an utopian vision sincerely believed in, or as a propaganda myth by which party, police, and other officials justify their status and privileges. Doubtless it has served, and even today continues to serve, for various members of Soviet society, these and other purposes. It is well to keep it in mind as we attempt to apply interest group analysis to the set of political control agencies discussed in this chapter.

Attention is focused primarily, but not exclusively, on the description and analysis of the roles, status, activities, and, insofar as it can be known, the impact upon Soviet political and social life of the Committee of State Security, or KGB, which has been since 1954 the official designation of the inner core of an ensemble of intelligence and counterintelligence, surveillance, detection, detention, and punitive organizations, the executive personnel of which are selected by the CPSU leadership. This system of agencies was known first as the Cheka and then successively as the GPU, OGPU, NKVD, NKGB, MVD, MGB, MOOP, and since 1954 and 1962 respectively, as the KGB and MVD.[2] It should be noted that this system has also performed and still performs important economic functions, including industrial operations employing convict labor, the latter on a reduced scale since Stalin's death. Before the death of Stalin, the political weight of the "punitive organs," as the dictator chose to refer to the security services and police agencies, was far greater than it has been since his passing. During the heyday of his dictatorship, from the early or mid-1930's until March 1953, the police agencies were clearly the mightiest force,

[2] The Cheka, founded in 1917, was renamed State Political Administration (GPU) in 1922 (after 1924, OGPU), and became in 1934 the People's Commissariat of Internal Affairs (NKVD). This agency in turn was eventually divided, in 1943, into the NKVD and the People's Commissariat of State Security (NKGB), both of which became, in 1946, with the replacement of the term "commissariat" with that of "ministry," the MVD and the MGB. United again as the MVD in 1953, they were separated a year later, this time under the name MVD and the Committee of State Security (KGB). In 1960 the MVD was replaced by ministries of the same name in each of the republics, which were in 1962 renamed Ministries of Protection of Public Order (MOOP). In 1966, these were in turn replaced by a USSR ministry of this name (MOOP), which resumed its original title MVD in 1968. The KGB has retained the same designation since its formation in 1954. See Merle Fainsod, *How Russia Is Ruled* (2nd ed., Cambridge, Mass., 1963), Chap. 13 for details.

after Stalin and his immediate entourage, in Soviet life, superior even to the party itself.[3]

Even today the interlocking network of security and police agencies may perhaps still be regarded as an element of the Soviet bureaucracy second in influence and impact on society only to the decision-making and control structures of the ruling communist party. Probably, in the post-Stalin period, the police and security agencies have had less political power and influence than the numerically much larger regular Soviet armed forces. Even if this generalization is correct in terms of the total influence of the organizations involved, it still seems almost certain that man for man, the officers of the KGB dispose of more political influence than their counterparts in the Soviet army, navy, and air forces.

This writer ventures to forecast that the power and influence of the police and security agencies in the USSR will diminish, perhaps, very slowly and gradually, but possibly with suddenness and swiftness. The process will probably proceed in fits and starts. This admittedly speculative forecast is based in part on projection into the future of trends observable since the death of Stalin. However, it rests mainly upon the belief that the internal and external factors which impelled and

[3] Merle Fainsod in his *Smolensk Under Soviet Rule* (Cambridge, Mass., 1958) presents, esp. in Chap. 8, convincing evidence, based on archival data captured by the United States army from the German armed forces, of the superordination of the police, in an important political-administrative unit, even over the provincial party leadership. The best general descriptive account of Stalin's police agencies is probably the study by Robert Slusser and Simon Wolin, *The Soviet Secret Police* (New York, 1957). See also James Bunyan, *The Origins of Forced Labor in the Soviet State* (Baltimore, 1967); Elsa Bernaut and Melville J. Ruggles, *Collective Leadership and the Political Police in the Soviet Union*, Rand Corp., RM-1674, Santa Monica, Cal., 1956; Barrington Moore, Jr., *Terror and Progress* (Cambridge, Mass., 1954); Merle Fainsod, *How Russia Is Ruled*; and John A. Armstrong, *The Politics of Totalitarianism* (New York, 1961). Of the several works by defectors from the Soviet police, perhaps the most valuable is Peter Deriabin and Frank Gibney, *The Secret World* (Garden City, 1959). Also extraordinarily interesting, especially on the purges of 1936-1938, is Alexander Orlov, *The Secret History of Stalin's Crimes* (New York, 1953). An unusual contribution to our knowledge of the post-Stalin period, but one regarding the authenticity of which there is controversy, is *The Penkovskiy Papers* by Oleg Penkovskiy, with introduction by Frank Gibney (New York, 1965). See also David Dallin and Boris Nikolaevsky, *Forced Labor in Soviet Russia* (New Haven, 1947) and Otto Kirchheimer, *Political Justice* (Princeton, 1961). Eugenia Ginzburg, *Into the Whirlwind* (New York, 1967) gives a vivid, informative account of the experiences of an idealist communist woman in the toils of Stalin's interrogation, political prisoner, and camp agencies. Svetlana Allilueva in *Twenty Letters to a Friend* (New York, 1967) adds significant details to our knowledge of the political police as a state within the state.

assisted Lenin and Stalin in creating the massive instrument of coercion and deterrence known first as the Cheka and now as the KGB and MVD are of diminishing relevance. Despite world-wide rivalry with the United States, aggravated by tensions generated by Vietnam, the difficulties created for the Kremlin by the "Mao Tse-tung group"—attacked, interestingly enough by KGB head Yuri Andropov in his speech on the fiftieth anniversary of the security "organs"—and the incalculably difficult problems of the nuclear arms competition, today's Soviet rulers operate under very different circumstances than those that shaped the outlook of Lenin and Stalin. Soviet "socialism" has achieved a substantial degree of external and domestic acceptance, legitimacy, prestige, and prosperity. Memories of traumatic experiences of foreign invasion and "counterrevolutionary" threats, traditionally cited in justification of the maintenance of a powerful police establishment, are, perhaps, not a much more vivid memory in the minds of Soviet young people today than the great depression is in the perspectives of young Americans. As time passes, those memories will fade still further. At the same time, if security against "the restoration of capitalism" has increased, so has susceptibility to liberalizing pressures, both from the bourgeois West, from revisionist communism, especially in Eastern Europe, and from emerging trends in Soviet society itself. Perhaps the most important new factor in the internal environment of Soviet politics is the increasing sophistication of the Soviet economy and society, with its growing strata of highly trained, well-informed specialists, and an accompanying disfunctionality of crude police methods of rule. In this changing situation, loyal, but critical young Soviet intellectuals, no longer cut off from knowledge of developments in the West, pose new and perhaps unique challenges to the power of the KGB. Their dissent cannot be so easily equated with treason as it could in the not so distant past.

There are indeed some hopeful portents of change in the contemporary Soviet political scene. However, as Soviet intervention to suppress Czechoslovak "democratic socialism" has demonstrated, leaders who cherish authoritarian, centralist, and coercive methods of rule remain, for the present at least, far more powerful than those who would base public policy upon freedom of information and discussion and the uncoerced articulation of diverse individual and group preferences. Among those in the USSR determined to defend and if possible to enhance the "conquests of October," as Bolshevik achievements are

97

often referred to, the highly trained, heavily indoctrinated, and lavishly equipped "Chekists," or officers and men of the security services, have the most obvious and urgently perceived stake in the Soviet *status quo.*

The State Security Agencies

The security services, like the regular armed forces, were created by the CPSU; they are often described in party documents as "children" of the party. Both of these creatures of the party, however, have tended, at times, to wax so strong that much ingenuity has been devoted to making certain that they did not devour their masters. A persisting technique employed by the party leadership in its struggle for mastery—and indeed, perhaps, survival—has been the playing off of the police and the military against one another. At times, as during Khrushchev's struggle for the mantle of Stalin, recourse has been had to the help of the military in curbing the influence of the police. As a rule, however, the executive levels of the party bureaucracy have been in a kind of alliance with the security agencies against the pressures by the military for a role in national policy-making, or even in the application of military power to foreign policy, that might be regarded by the party leadership as a threat to its hegemony.

Thus the security agencies have been the ultimate guardians of party supremacy. They have also served as a special striking force, the elite corps of a political combat organization to which the Soviet Communist Party as a whole has often been likened. They constitute a part, but a very special and distinctive part, of the structure of political control, which is composed of the various segments of the party Bureaucracy, including the territorial network of executives, theoreticians, journalists, and indoctrination specialists.

It seems reasonable to assume that the men of state security and MVD share the same sentiments as other segments of the party—held, less intensely, perhaps throughout the bureaucracy as a whole—regarding the dangers posed to "socialism" by "imperialist" threats from without and ideological subversion from within. To be sure, even KGB opinion is presumably not monolithic, and there may well be stresses and strains generated by inconsistencies among some of the various objectives assigned by the Kremlin to the security agencies, or between KGB assignments and official Soviet policies. For example, there is evidence that the KGB—not unlike the FBI in the United States, and perhaps other Western security agencies—is unenthusiastic about the policy of cultural exchanges between the USSR and "bourgeois" states. It is possible that there are in the KGB cautious men who disapprove, at times, of particular Soviet foreign policies that they regard as involving excessively high risks, and such security officers may well be supported by likeminded officers of the regular armed forces.

Generally, however, it seems reasonable to assume that as members of important agencies of the total Soviet command and control system, the overwhelming majority of MVD and KGB personnel perceive their personal and collective interests to be closely bound to the fortunes of the Soviet system as a whole. In addition to a general sense of identity, fostered both by the regular political education experienced by all citizens, and particularly by elite cadres, and by what must be an acute sense that they might well be the prime targets of any successful revolution against the political order they have served loyally and harshly, the intelligence, coercion, and deterrence specialists have their own vested interests in the maintenance and growth of Soviet authority. The Kremlin, in order to assure the support and loyalty of these specialists, has granted them a considerable measure of autonomy and a share in the status and material values available in Soviet society that is second to none. This fact, of course, by stimulating the envy of other segments of the elite, not to mention the hostility of the "popular masses," and by increasing the positive attractiveness of a police career, heightens concern in the Chekists' ranks lest all be lost to "counterrevolutionary" enemies of the state. The structure of government, built by Lenin and Stalin and altered much less by Stalin's successors in basic structure than in the style and mood of its behavior, left powerful vested interests that can be counted upon, in spite of the emergence of countervailing forces, to struggle tenaciously and effectively in defense of their status, prerogatives, and privileges.

The morale of the Chekists, and at least some measure—impossible to evaluate—of general public acceptance of their role, are nourished not only by ideology and rational self-interest but also by the persistent influence of autocratic Russian political tradition. This tradition of stern, centralized rule, in which powerful secret political police agencies were relied upon to ferret out treason and subversion was already centuries old in Russia before Lenin's Bolsheviks seized power in 1917. The assumption that whatever security measures the political leadership chose to undertake were probably justifiable simply because the

99

FREDERICK C. BARGHOORN

authorities were the only persons capable of knowing what was best for the community, and that the Russian state was menaced by powerful, cunning enemies, seems to have been transmitted, at least partially intact, from tsars to commissars. To be sure, as the late David Dallin correctly noted, Soviet police practices were much more directly and powerfully influenced by the experiences of anti-tsarist revolutionaries in their struggle against the tsarist police than by borrowing from the despised tsarist tradition.[4] However, continuity in concepts and practices of public order was fostered by the fact that both victors and vanquished, in the long revolutionary struggle resolved by Bolshevik victory in 1917, shared, for the most part, the same central beliefs about the nature of political authority and the means by which it must protect itself against destruction at the hands of external or internal enemies. Among important similarities between the tsarist and Soviet political cultures, is the widely held conception of the central role of a system of powerful political police agencies as the guardian of community interests and of social cohesion.

Finally, although Marxism-Leninism may seem to the outside observer and to some Russians to be a system of thought irrelevant to the modern scientific age and one which is indeed increasingly regarded in the West as a rationalization of attitudes generated by experiences remote from present concerns, Leninism nevertheless remains an uniquely important legitimizing and orienting force in Soviet society. Assistance in maintaining its dominant position as the official political creed is one of the principal functions of the police agencies, especially of the KGB. Like other elements of the Soviet elite, the latter is pledged to preserve Leninism, which, under party guidance, it proclaims to be "scientific" truth, essential to the government of the USSR and destined, at least so KGB chief Yuri Andropov proclaimed, in his speech on the fiftieth anniversary of the secret police, in December 1967, to inherit the earth.

In the remainder of this essay a number of indicators of the role of the Soviet security agencies as an interest group will be examined. These include (1) statements by the top party executives, and their reflections in official documents and commentaries, defining the functions, structure, operations, tasks, and "image" of these agencies; (2) data on the access to, and membership of their leading personnel in, decision-making bodies and also their participation in high-level polit-

[4] David Dallin, *Soviet Espionage* (New Haven, 1955), Chap. 1.

100

ical activity; (3) surveillance, investigatory and other operational responsibilities which facilitate the functioning of the police agencies as a privileged arm of the national political executive; and (4) evidence on the degree to which the recruitment and training, especially the in-service training, of the KGB and related organizations facilitates or hinders their behavior as more-or-less autonomous sectors of the political process. Unfortunately, it will be necessary, because of problems of data, paucity of previous research, and insufficiency of space, to treat these topics selectively and incompletely. This incompleteness results only partly from the attempt to deal with vast subjects in brief compass. It also reflects the secrecy with which the agencies under consideration operate and its effects on the quality of the data available. Finally, it reflects the relative neglect of the Soviet police agencies in Western scholarly literature.

The Official Image of the Security Agencies

It has been observed that "The Soviet regime and its secret police came into existence almost simultaneously."[5] The Extraordinary Commission for Combating Counterrevolution and Sabotage, or Cheka, was established in December 1917, and immediately proclaimed the "red terror" against the "counterrevolutionary bourgeoisie and its agents."[6] Although there was some talk, for example by the Soviet leader, Grigori Zinoviev in 1918, to the effect that the Cheka, being an extraordinary institution, would soon "wither away," in fact it steadily became more powerful. However, the agencies which replaced it in, respectively, 1922, and 1924, the GPU (state political administration) and the OGPU (unified state political administration) were purposely given innocuous names.

The vast importance attributed by the authorities to the "punitive organs," even in the relatively uncoercive era of the 1920's, is indicated by the language used in describing the functions of the NKVD, or People's Commissariat of Internal Affairs, in an article in a Soviet

[5] Slusser and Wolin, op.cit., p. 3. See pp. 3-61 of this work for a detailed account of the evolution of the police agencies to 1956. The most important organizational and personnel developments since 1962 have been the establishment, by a decree of the USSR Supreme Soviet, dated July 26, 1966, of the Ministry of Protection of Public Order of the USSR, the appointment of N. A. Shchelokov as its head, the replacement of Vladimir Semichastny by Yuri Andropov as Chairman of the KGB, in 1967, and the revival of the MVD in 1968.

[6] I. I. Yevtikhiyev and V. A. Vlasov, Administrativnoye pravo SSSR, p. 185, quoting a statement made to a foreign labor delegation by Stalin.

encyclopedia published five years later. This early NKVD, originally an agency of the Cheka, is not to be confused with the NKVD which was established in 1934 as the successor of the OGPU. According to the article, the early NKVD coordinated the establishment and functioning of the soviets (councils) during the revolutionary struggle of 1917. Indeed, according to this authoritative compilation on Soviet statecraft, "the NKVD in the first period of its existence was the workshop in which were forged and hammered out the local organs of Soviet administration created by the October Revolution."[7] More generally, from the early 1920's, official doctrine asserted, as it has continued to do to the present, that the security agencies were instruments and executors of the will of the party and state leadership. Concurrently, the functionaries, in particular the commissioned officers, of these agencies acquired high professional status and increasingly a privileged position with respect to allocation of goods and services. They also secured not only immunity from control by the party organizations, except at a very high level, but greater ability to penetrate and to exercise surveillance and control over the entire party organization and over the membership as a whole, as well as increasing ability to determine the "life chances" of individual Soviet citizens.

The norms laid down by Stalin in the 1930's regarding party and state leadership and discipline, and the safeguarding of the party against treasonous infiltration by disguised class enemies, assigned exceptional honor and responsibility to the security services. The official image of the police agencies attained a hitherto unprecedented saliency during the *Yezhovshchina*, in 1937, when the "iron commissar" N. I. Yezhov acted as Stalin's right-hand man in eliminating the "band of counter-revolutionary terrorists, wreckers, spies and diversionists," as the dictator characterized former and present, actual and potential oppositionists.[8] Some features of Stalin's political doctrine, by which the privileged, albeit ultimately insecure, position of the security agencies were justified, especially the proposition that the "resistance of the last elements of the dying classes" to the dictatorship of the proletariat grew fiercer as the power of the Soviet state increased, were to be repudiated by his

---

[7] *Entsiklopedia gosudarstva i prava* (Moscow, 1927), II, 1115-1117.

[8] See, for example, reference to Stalin's statement in *Malaya sovetskaya entsiklopedia* (2nd ed., Moscow, 1938), II, col. 743. *Pravda*, May 4, June 21, and July 8, 13, 16, and 18, 1937, contained photographs of Yezhov, and the July 18 issue reported the award to him of the Order of Lenin.

successors.[9] However, some of the essential elements of Stalin's party and state doctrines, which were of course never effectively challenged during his lifetime, have survived his death.

Although the impact of the activities of the Chekists, as the security police cadres were and still are called, on the Soviet citizenry as a whole, was actually to increase considerably after the completion of the Great Purge, it should be noted that at no time did official publicity assign, either to the police organizations or to their chiefs, anything but a status subordinate to the highest level of national political leadership. Indeed, the official tenure, the reputation, and the physical existence of state security leaders and high officials were exceedingly insecure under Stalin. To a lesser but still striking degree this insecurity has characterized their situation in the post-Stalin era, although execution, imprisonment, and banishment have been, on the whole, replaced, in the case of unsuccessful or delinquent police officials, by demotion in rank, transfer to the provinces, or retirement on pension.

The only political police chief who is apparently fixed firmly in the Soviet ideological galaxy is Feliks Dzerzhinsky, the incorruptible, politically reliable, but cruel and fanatical founder of the Cheka whose name is associated with the practice and doctrine of strict police subordination to the party leadership. To be sure, his weak successor, Menzhinsky, is praised, but Menzhinsky's successor, Yagoda, was executed following his trial, together with Bukharin and other prominent "traitors," in 1938; Yezhov, picked by Stalin to eleminate Yagoda, was, together with thousands of top leaders and hundreds of thousands of ordinary citizens, quietly eased to an obscure fate in the same year. Eventually, an even more inglorious end was to befall the mighty Lavrenti Beria, after he had succeeded in narrowly escaping the destruction which Stalin was apparently planning for him and other lieutenants during the last months of the dictator's rule.

After the Great Purge, capricious and awful violence was replaced by permanent, one might say chronic, terror, efficiently, expertly, and professionally administered. The Kremlin's preoccupation with the military conduct of World War II brought to the Soviet people a measure of relief from surveillance and pressure, which, however, was

[9] For a criticism of this doctrine as the basis of "illegal repressions," see M. S. Strogovich, *Osnovnye voprosy sovetskoi sotsialisticheskoi zakonnosti* (Moscow, 1966), p. 139.

103

increasingly reapplied as the war moved to an end. The power and glory of the political police reached its peak during the period from early 1945 until the uncertain and menacing months preceding Stalin's death. By a decree of the Supreme Soviet dated July 9, 1945, the military title of Marshal of the Soviet Union was conferred upon the powerful Georgian, Beria. The issue of *Pravda* for July 11, 1945, in which this decree was published, featured on its front page a large, almost elegant photograph of him, wearing rimless glasses, dressed in his marshal's uniform, and bedecked with medals and star. The same issue contained other decrees, conferring ranks of colonel, general, lieutenant general, and major general on scores of other officers of the NKVD and its inner core, the NKGB (the security and police services had been divided into these two commissariats, in February 1943). Vsevolod Merkulov, Beria's second in command in the security machine, was raised to the rank of army general and his photograph was published directly beneath that of Beria. To be sure, even at his greatest power, Beria was overshadowed by Stalin.[10]

For a number of years both the top supervisory and leading personnel of the police agencies, and its rank and file, were to enjoy a stable preferential position vis-à-vis all other segments of Soviet society. They were to be Stalin's principal helpers, as long as he lived, in holding his subjects, high and low alike, in a state of awe-stricken submission to his will. Within this general framework, the security agencies performed many important specific services. For example, they helped to make it impossible for popular military leaders to coalesce into an interest group which might, potentially at least, have become a threat to Stalin's power or at least a check on his freedom of political action. They excised from the Soviet body politic persons who during the period of the wartime "coalition" had come to expect relaxation of controls and increased freedom of intellectual expression.

Beria, who attained a position of influence among Stalin's inner-circle inferior to none except perhaps that of Georgi Malenkov, remained in ultimate control of the police machine until about the

[10] An odd but significant indication of the honored image which Stalin permitted Beria and his subordinates to enjoy was furnished by the publication early in 1946 of two songs, entitled, respectively, "The Song of the Chekists" and "The Song about Marshal Beria," which were purchased by this writer in the leading music store of Moscow, on Gorky Street. According to the second of these songs, Beria was "warmed by Stalin's friendship." Both songs used the familiar imagery, which was retained after Stalin's death, of the Cheka as the sword and shield of the revolution.

end of 1951. Although he had been replaced as operational head of the MVD in 1946, his long-time associates held most of the key positions in the agency and he was a full member of the Politburo from 1946 until Stalin's death. In the early months following the dictator's demise, Beria, of course, was to make a bid for supreme power which ended disastrously for him and for many of his henchmen. Indeed, the 1953 and 1954 purges of Beria and his partners, and also of many lesser figures, might be described as the second decapitation of the secret police, the first having occurred in 1937 and 1938 when a majority of the veteran professional Chekists who had begun their careers under Dzerzhinsky were liquidated.[11]

In the post-Stalin period the official image of the security services has remained one of high honor and prestige. Of course, Khrushchev, both in his "secret speech" at the Twentieth Party Congress and in many more public statements, vigorously denounced the arbitrary and illegal actions of Stalin and many party and police officials. Even before the Twentieth Congress, the notorious "special board" by means of which the security police had been empowered to arrest, imprison, and exile, without formal judicial proceedings of any kind, persons suspected of anti-state activity or even persons regarded as potentially dangerous, was abolished. The campaign for "socialist legality" was to lead to the important legal reforms of 1958-1959 and subsequent years. There is no doubt that despite such actions as the treatment of Sinyavsky and Daniel, of Bukovsky, of Ginsburg, Galanskov, Dobrovolsky and Lashkova, and of many other young dissident intellectuals, the post-Stalin pattern has been one in which the KGB, although powerful and privileged, has ceased to be a law unto itself, or at least has been forced to temper its actions in the light of Soviet and world public opinion, including the opinion of relatively liberal Italian and other Western communist intellectuals.

However, Khrushchev and his successors took pains not to allow the prestige, morale, or powers of the security agencies to be seriously impaired. Party and police officials in effect asked the Soviet citizenry to believe that the security and law enforcement agencies, purged of Stalinist excesses and subordinated to the collective leadership of a

---

[11] For a vivid account of the 1937-1938 operations, see Orlov, *op.cit.*, esp. Chaps. 19 and 26. The purge of Beria's associates is dealt with by Armstrong, *op.cit.*, Chap. 18, and by Zbigniew Brzezinski, *The Permanent Purge* (Cambridge, Mass., 1956), Chap. 9.

revived Leninist party, rather than to one man, would spare and protect the innocent and would punish the guilty in accordance with both the letter and the spirit of the law.[12] Even at the de-Stalinizing Twentieth Congress, Khrushchev declared that the overwhelming majority of "Chekists" were honest, trustworthy officials, devoted to the "common cause." He characterized as harmful the mistrust which, he observed, had developed among "some comrades" in connection with the purging of a number of police officials.[13] Khrushchev also noted that the courts and the state security and law enforcement agencies had been replenished with new cadres. In his report to the Twenty-second Congress in 1961, Khrushchev asserted that, as long as "imperialist aggressors" existed, it was necessary for the USSR to perfect its armed forces and "the organs of state security."[14]

In the late Khrushchev and post-Khrushchev periods it became common practice for high-ranking state security and law enforcement officials to publish articles in the major Soviet newspapers and political journals. Typical of the statements contained in such articles is that by K. Nikitin, Deputy Minister of Protection of Public Order, according to which it was "necessary," from the first days of the revolution, to introduce the strictest revolutionary order, for which purpose "were established the organs of Soviet justice, the militia and state security."[15] In 1964 and 1965 the exploits of Soviet espionage agents Richard Sorge and Rudolph Abel were for the first time openly acknowledged and these men were fulsomely praised as national and international heroes. In recent years, an extensive literature on the history of the secret police, couched in carefully guarded terms, designed to conceal as much as it revealed, has developed.[16]

---

[12] It is interesting to note that Eugenia Ginzburg concluded her account of her victimization by the security police with an expression of joy that after the Twentieth and Twenty-first Party Congresses, "the great Leninist truths have again come into their own in our country and Party"! (Ginzburg, *op.cit.*, p. 416).

[13] *XX Syezd Kommunisticheskoi Partii Sovetskovo Soyuza, stenog. otchyot* (Moscow, 1956), I, 95.

[14] *XXII Syezd Kommunisticheskoi Partii Sovetskovo Soyuza stenog. otchyot* (Moscow, 1962), I, 25. This statement by Khrushchev was quoted by V. I. Kurlyandsky, *et al.*, *Osobo opasnye gosudarstvennye prestupleniya* (Moscow, 1963), p. 7.

[15] *Partiinaya zhizn*, No. 23 (December 1967), pp. 20-23.

[16] See Robert M. Slusser, "Recent Soviet Books on the History of the Secret Police," *Slavic Review*, XXIV, No. 1 (March 1965), 90-98; additional detail is contained in Frederick C. Barghoorn, *Politics in the USSR* (Boston and Toronto, 1966), Chap. IX.

A new post-Stalin peak of public acclaim for the KGB was reached in the celebration, in December 1967, of the fiftieth anniversary of the organs of state security. The CPSU Central Committee, jointly with the Presidium of the Supreme Soviet and the Council of Ministers, issued greetings hailing the "honor and glory of Soviet Chekists." KGB head Yuri Andropov gave a speech, which, as printed, filled almost a page in *Izvestia* and was delivered in the Kremlin Palace of Congresses, in the presence of Brezhnev, Podgorny, Kosygin, Suslov, and other top party leaders.[17]

As has so often been the case in matters involving the security agencies, the honorific publicity referred to above was not without elements of ambiguity. Although the KGB was honored, Andropov, still relatively fresh from his service on the party secretariat, heavily stressed party control, guidance, and indoctrination as the basic principles governing the work of the security machine. Important, in terms of reminding the KGB that the party was its master, was the fact that, a month before its anniversary, considerable fanfare was devoted to celebrating the fiftieth anniversary of its sister, and probably to some extent, rival agency, the MOOP, soon to be renamed the MVD. As in the case of the KGB, mention was made not only of the MOOP's crime detection and investigatory functions, but also of its "organs and troops."[18] In an interview with a special *Pravda* correspondent, N. A. Shchelokov, head of MOOP, referred to such of its capabilities, achievements, and activities as a big, growing educational network, the latest in scientific equipment, and a vigorous program of sociological research. It should be noted that not only MOOP and KGB, but also the personnel of Soviet courts and of the diplomatic service, were honored by official ceremonies and extensive publicity during the closing months of 1967. Andropov, in his KGB address, referred to the honors accorded to courts, militia, and KGB—though not to the Ministry of Foreign Affairs (Minindel), perhaps because of the propaganda sensitivities of any admission that KGB and Minindel might be interlinked—and noted that the army's turn to receive public praise would come in February, when Army Day would be celebrated. Of the 1967 cere-

[17] *Izvestia*, December 21, 1967. For three or four days, beginning about December 17, the central Soviet press featured laudatory historical and other items on the Cheka, KGB, etc. Among other points, the above issue of *Izvestia* reported that the ceremonies were attended by "heads of delegations of state security organs of socialist countries."

[18] *Pravda, Izvestia*, November 21, 1967.

monies, that accorded to the KGB certainly exceeded the others in duration, saliency, volume, and the status of major, organizing participants.

Andropov's statement embodied a systematic presentation of the official post-Khrushchev image of the functions and rationale of security police activities and will be summarized rather fully. Beginning with expressions of gratitude to the Central Committee and the Soviet government, Andropov noted that the former had indicated their high appreciation of the work of the "Chekists" by conferring orders and medals upon a large group of KGB officials. He devoted about a quarter of his address to a more-or-less standard history of the activities of the security agencies. In the section of his speech dealing with the early years of Soviet power, Andropov dwelt heavily upon achievements of the political police which had major international impact, such as the "liquidation" of the "counterrevolutionary organization" headed by the British representative in Russia, Bruce Lockhart. He was exceedingly vague with regard to the terrible years of the Great Purge in the 1930's and did not mention by name either Yezhov, Beria, or Stalin. He confined his treatment of this crucial era to the assertion that no small credit in preventing disorganization of the Soviet rear and undermining of the military capability of the USSR during World War II belonged to the organs of state security and their work in the years before the war. He had high praise for the exploits of the Soviet border guards in military operations during the war and for Chekist intelligence work.

Again without mentioning Beria, Abakumov, or others by name, Andropov referred to "that period when political adventurers in the leadership of the NKVD attempted to deflect the organs of state security from party control, to isolate them from the people, and to commit illegalities which did serious harm to the interests of our state, of the Soviet people and of the organs of state security themselves." He assured his listeners that the "distortions" which had for a time affected the work of the security organs had been fully corrected and that the security organs were working in close contact with the Soviet citizenry as a whole, and under the close and beneficial supervision of the Communist Party. The party had made certain that there could be no further violations of socialist legality. Andropov scornfully dismissed noncommunist Western characterizations of the Soviet state security organs as a "secret police," and asserted that the KGB worked in closest harmony with both governmental and societal organizations.

Perhaps the most interesting feature of Andropov's speech was its heavy emphasis upon the ideological functions of the KGB. He asserted that as long as "imperialism" existed, "real danger" would confront the USSR and the forces of peace and progress generally. Andropov said that the security organs were aware that peaceful coexistence was a form of class struggle, in the conduct of which the imperialists were resorting to the most refined methods. He accused the Western, particularly the American, intelligence services of a wide range of dangerous and harmful activities, with particular emphasis on allegations that the "CIA, NTS [Natsionalno-trudovoi soyuz] and other imperialist intelligence agencies" were seeking to blacken the image of the Soviet system and to "weaken the ideological and political unity of the Soviet people." According to Andropov, although there was no longer any social basis in Soviet society for the organization of anti-Soviet activity on the part of any classes or strata of the population, there were still individuals who might, under the stimulus of hostile foreign influence, commit anti-Soviet actions. He noted that a number of foreign agents had engaged in attempts to conduct political and ideological subversion against the USSR, but had been captured by the KGB. None of these persons, he said, had received "any serious support" from the Soviet population. However, he demanded a vigilant effort to guard Soviet frontiers and instill proper political attitudes in the citizenry, so as to assure the highest levels of military, ideological, and political security.

It would be rewarding, even if tedious and costly, systematically to compare official Soviet statements of the Stalin and post-Stalin years regarding the security services. Some significant differences between the statements of the two periods are apparent even from the limited use that has been made of them in the preparation of this study. In the first place, unlike those of the Stalin era, post-Stalin statements strongly emphasize party control over the police. Moreover, emphasis in the post-Stalin era has been upon collective and institutional, rather than personal, control over these agencies. Second, criticism of the excesses committed by the security agencies during the period of Stalin's "cult," and assurances that no return to such arbitrary and unlawful practices would be permitted, differed sharply from the image of infallibility conveyed by propaganda regarding the police during the Stalin era. Such criticisms were toned down in the post-Khrushchev period, however, and by the time of the celebration of the KGB fiftieth anniversary, mention of Stalin or Beria had completely ceased. Silence concerning the past behavior of personnel involved in surveillance and interrogation, and in prison and labor camp operations, left huge blanks in the version of Soviet history that the public was permitted to hear. Third, theoretical and propaganda statements regarding the police agencies are, like statements about other aspects of the post-Stalin system, couched in language of relative sobriety, which differs considerably from the abusive, threatening, and sometimes hysterical tone employed while Stalin was alive, especially during the *Yezhovshchina*.

What, if any, is the political significance of the praise for the KGB's services to the party and state which, especially since Khrushchev's fall, has replaced the retrospective, but often startling, criticism of some of its leaders and rank and file members aired in the communications media and on the rostrum in the early post-Stalin years? Can we infer that the enhanced official image of the security agencies, including not only the KGB but also the MVD, reflects increased influence, as well as status, for those agencies? A cautiously positive answer on both points seems justified. The pertinent evidence indicates that the resources made available by the party to the security agencies have increased and that it has been granted more freedom to do its job of tracking down and punishing dissenters and "trouble-makers." However, this enhanced position and, perhaps, increased influence, must be viewed in the perspective of sharp contrast to the Yezhov or Beria eras. Moreover, it seems likely that to some degree the new image represents an effort to undo the damage done, in the reformist phase of Khrushchev's administration, to the morale of cadres whose willing and effective cooperation is essential to the survival of an autocratic or oligarchic polity of the Soviet type. In this perspective, it appears that the security services, like other major segments of the bureaucracy, have only been getting their share of the rewards that an unimaginative, conservative leadership considers it both prudent and proper to dispense to colleagues and subordinates who echo official views and faithfully execute orders.

Security Agency Representation

It might be argued, with some cogency, that since the influence of the KGB and its predecessor agencies has depended, not upon representation in even the most important party bodies, but rather upon the closeness of the police to the top leadership and to its tradition of disciplined, covert organization, with instruments of intimidation and violence at its disposal, it is idle to look for evidence of their status in data on their membership in the Politburo, Central Committee, etc. Still, it is striking that the representation of police leadership in Stalin's Central Committees was much greater, both absolutely and in percentages, than it has been in the larger post-Stalin Central Committees. In the Central Committee, elected at the Nineteenth Party Congress in October 1952, 3 of the 125 full members and 7 of the 111 alternate members were high officials of either the MGB or the MVD, then the two major security and police organizations, corresponding in current terminology, to KGB and MVD, respectively.[19] These figures do not represent much change from the situation in 1939 when, according to my calculations, 3 of the 71 full members of the Central Committee elected in March of that year and 5 of its 68 alternate members were high-ranking NKVD officials.[20] During the late Stalin era police representation was greater than it appears from congress reports, since, due to the long intervals between the party congresses which formally elect the Central Committee and other party bodies, some powerful police officials were deprived of membership because their tenure of office fell between sessions. For example, Viktor Abakumov, who replaced Vsevolod Merkulov as Minister of State Security in 1946, and disappeared in 1951—he was tried and executed in 1954—was never listed as a member or an alternate of the Central Committee. Sergei Kruglov, who had served as one of Abakumov's principal subordinates in the counterespionage "SMERSH" organization during World War II, and was head of the MVD from just after Beria's arrest in June 1953 until shortly before the Twentieth Party Congress in February 1956, was never a member or an alternate member of the Central Committee.

Apparently the only police officials elected to the Central Committee at the Twentieth Congress were the rather insignificant N. P. Dudorov, a man whose career had mostly been in the construction industry, and who, after leaving his police post in 1962, became head of the Moscow Administration of Building Materials, and the veteran Chekist Ivan A. Serov, who was head of the KGB from its establishment in 1954

[19] Nicolaevsky, *op.cit.*, presents, on pp. 126-129, a careful analysis of the relevant data.

[20] *XVIII Syezd Vsesoyuznoi Kommunisticheskoi Partii* (Moscow, 1939), p. 688.

until his replacement by the rising Young Communist League chief, N. A. Shelepin, late in 1958.[21] Neither Dudorov nor Serov was re-elected to the Central Committee in 1961. The Twenty-second Party Congress in 1961, and the Twenty-third Congress in 1966, continued the practice of electing to either full or alternate Central Committee membership only the chiefs of the two security and police organizations, namely, the KGB and the MVD or MOOP. Shelepin became a full member of the Central Committee, and also a member of its secretariat, in 1961, and after the ouster of Khrushchev in October 1964, became a member of the highest party body, the Presidium. Earlier incumbents (Dudorov and Serov) were replaced in 1961 by Vladimir Semichastny, Shelepin's successor as head of the KGB; in 1966, Semichastny rose from an alternate member to a full member and N. A. Shchelokov became an alternate. Semichastny was succeeded as KGB chairman by Yuri V. Andropov who since 1957 had headed the Central Committee section for liaison with communist parties of "socialist" countries.[22] At the September 1967 plenum Andropov was elected an alternate member of the Politburo, as the Presidium was then renamed.[23]

A very important aspect of KGB representation in the party decision-making machinery which, on the basis of substantial though incomplete evidence, it seems safe to regard as common to the Stalin and post-Stalin patterns is the membership of KGB executives on party oblast committees. Armstrong, referring, apparently, mainly to the Stalin era, asserts that in the Ukraine oblast MVD chiefs were "apparently always full members" of the bureaus (executive committees) of the oblast party organizations.[24] Information published in issues of seven provincial newspapers in 1966 and 1967 revealed that in the seven local

[21] *XX Syezd*, ii, 501-502.

[22] The foregoing section was derived in part from Jerry F. Hough, "The Soviet Elite: I, Groups and Individuals," *Problems of Communism*, xvi, No. 1 (January-February 1967), 28-35, and from the U.S. Department of State, *Directory of Soviet Officials* (Washington, D.C., 1966), I-A3.

[23] Andropov is the second head of the security police to hold alternate status on the Politburo. Yezhov, for a short period, had such status. Beria was a full member of the Politburo for seven years. It is noteworthy that the celebrated Dzerzhinsky never became even an alternate member of Stalin's Politburo.

[24] John A. Armstrong, *The Soviet Bureaucatic Elite* (New York, 1959), p. 56. Armstrong also noted that oblast MVD chiefs were almost never mentioned in the press. Additional data on KGB membership on obkoms, together with some illuminating evidence on the important propaganda functions of the KGB, are supplied, for the Volgograd oblast, in Philip D. Stewart, *Political Power in the Soviet Union* (Indianapolis, 1968), pp. 77, 93.

administrative units involved, the chairman or deputy chairman of the KGB was at least a member, and in most cases either a full or an alternate member, of the obkom bureau.[25]

A special but interesting example of the representation, in this case in both the party and government, of the Soviet "police community," is that of Aleksandr Panyushkin, who was a member of the Central Committee Auditing Commission. As such, his rank in the party hierarchy was below that of either full or alternate members of the Central Committee. Panyushkin, who had earlier been an alternate member of the Central Committee, and who holds the military rank of major general, has had extensive diplomatic experience, including service as ambassador to China, and was once an officer of the MVD. He has, since October 1961, been head of the Central Committee Section for Travel Abroad, which is also sometimes called the Section for Foreign Cadres.[26]

As far as I have been able to determine, representation of the security police and related agencies in both party and government bodies, below the level of the Central Committee, has undergone a diminution since the death of Stalin roughly comparable to that already described above for the highest party organs.[27] Recent authoritative items in the Soviet press have, however, reported a numerical strengthening of the militia (roughly equivalent to "normal" police forces in countries such as the United States or Great Britain), so that it might be speculated that a parallel strengthening of the more secret branches of the police machine has also occurred.[28] It is, incidentally, interesting that K. Nikitin, in his article in *Partiinaya zhizn*, which was published while he was serving as Deputy Minister of Protection of Public Order, stated that, in 1967, more than 10,000 officers of the

[25] The above data are for the Krasnodar, Rostov, Volgograd, Ulyanovsk, and Yaroslav oblasts, the Altai Krai and the city of Ulyanovsk. Professor Jerry F. Hough kindly furnished the above information.

[26] See *Directory of Soviet Officials*, I-A4; and *Who's Who in the USSR 1965-66* (New York and London, 1966), p. 627.

[27] Hough, *op.cit.*, has traced the process at the level of republic party organizations. My check of biographies in the 1962 and 1966 editions of *Deputaty Verkhovnovo Soveta* and of the lists of delegates in the 1956, 1961, and 1966 stenographic reports of party congresses, led to the conclusion that "security" membership at this level was also diminishing.

[28] See, for example, the article by V. Tikunov, then RSFSR Minister of Protection of Public Order, in *Partiinaya zhizn*, No. 20 (October 1965); see also *Izvestia*, June 12, 1966.

"organs of protection of public order" had been honored by election to the Supreme Soviets of union and autonomous republics, as well as to oblast and other local soviets.

Impact of Security Police on Soviet Life

The political influence of the police agencies, and in particular their impact upon the daily lives and peace of mind of Soviet citizens, were sharply reduced by Stalin's successors. The security police has, on the whole, continued to be held in check, so far as ordinary people—although not dissenting intellectuals—are concerned. However, there is evidence that under certain conditions the security services can still play a role in Soviet high politics. Indeed, they may actually have at times exerted a degree of influence greater than was possible while Stalin was in power and held a firmer grip on all aspects of policy and administration than his successors, especially Khrushchev, were able to achieve. It seems almost certain that the conspiracy which managed the ouster of Khrushchev could not have been carried out as quietly and smoothly as it was without the assistance, or at least the benevolent neutrality, of the KGB leadership. The hypothesis of KGB involvement tends to be confirmed by the fact that the ouster was followed by Semichastny's elevation to full Central Committee membership, and Shelepin's promotion to the Politburo.[29]

In addition to its possible role in ending Khrushchev's political career, the KGB, in 1963 and 1964, engaged in a number of other spectacular, presumably anti-Khrushchev, operations. Those included my arrest on fabricated and totally unsupported charges of espionage, the nearly fatal mustard gas attack on an employee of the embassy of the German Federal Republic in the Zagorsk monastery on September 12, 1964, and several cases of violation of the diplomatic immunity of American and British diplomatic and military personnel, some of whom were manhandled. These operations seem almost certainly to have been acts of political sabotage directed against Khrushchev in

[29] For interesting speculation on the role of Shelepin, the KGB, and anti-Khrushchev party leaders in the downfall of Khrushchev, see "How K Was Overthrown," *The Observer* (London), November 29, 1964. Robert Slusser in his contribution to Peter Juviler and Henry Morton (eds.), *Soviet Policy-Making: Studies of Communism in Transition* (New York, 1967), speculates on the possibility that Shelepin joined Frol Kozlov, Mikhail Suslov, and even the aged Poskrebyshev in persistent opposition to Khrushchev as early as 1959 or 1960.

view of their incompatibility with his efforts to improve diplomatic relations with the United States and West Germany.

Glaring incompatibilities of the kind just mentioned have not been clearly perceptible in the post-Khrushchev period. The police, like other conservative forces in Soviet society, were probably favorably impressed by the relatively repressive, "anti-imperialist" domestic and foreign policies pursued by Khrushchev's successors. However, KGB leading cadres may well feel that Brezhnev, Kosygin, and Podgorny have not always gone as far as they should have in putting the lid on expressions of intellectual dissent or in punishing dissenters. The KGB and its conservative party backers may have been angered and alarmed by the repeated success of dissenting intellectuals in communicating to the interested Western public their version of the struggle between themselves and the KGB regarding the right of citizens freely to express and to disseminate unorthodox opinions.[30]

Reflecting upon the above-mentioned matters, one is tempted to speculate as to whether or not the KGB, by screening and interpreting the information that reaches the highest level of Soviet decision-makers, regulates, at least to a significant degree, the conduct of Soviet foreign

[30] *The Christian Science Monitor*, December 30, 1967, reported interesting speculation by "Kremlinologists" in London on the possibility that the KGB was responsible for publication of a threat to re-try the convicted British subject, Gerald Brooke, on an espionage charge—he had been convicted in 1965 for "anti-Soviet agitation"—as an aspect of its struggle against "permissiveness" in Soviet intellectual life. See also Edward Crankshaw's revealing article entitled, "Now the KGB Tries a Soft Sell Approach" in *The Observer* (London), December 10, 1967, and Patricia Blake's contribution to the *New York Times Magazine*, "This is the Winter of Moscow's Dissent," March 24, 1968. Both of these articles add considerable knowledge regarding the increasing energy and sophistication displayed by the KGB in recent years in combating ideological opponents at home and abroad. While Crankshaw's emphasis is mainly on KGB "disinformation and decomposition" abroad, Miss Blake focuses on the increased authority assumed by the political police to undertake administrative and judicial actions against allegedly anti-Soviet intellectuals.

Evidence of KGB concern over the receptivity of Soviet citizens to "bourgeois" intellectual, cultural, and psychological influences or machinations, as apparently the dissemination of non-Soviet information is perceived, came to my attention while under interrogation in 1963. Thus, I was accused of asking Soviet citizens questions, during trips to Russia, calculated to cause them to make statements harmful to the USSR. In a discussion regarding the availability of *Pravda* on New York newsstands and nonavailability of the *New York Times* to the public in Moscow, the investigator in charge of my case justified this lack of reciprocity on the ground that the Soviet public must be protected from "lies." When I asked one of my interrogators what he would think of survey research by a foreign scholar to study Soviet political attitudes, he replied, "That would be ideological espionage."

relations. In the almost total absence of information pertinent to this question it is perhaps wise to confine ourselves to the view that the KGB probably reinforces tendencies, inherent in such a system as the Soviet one, to perceive events abroad, and perhaps particularly the motives of "bourgeois" governments, through lenses distorted by dogma. A restrictive and distorting influence on the accuracy of Soviet information about foreign affairs may be exerted by the KGB through its heavy representation in the staffs of Soviet diplomatic missions; through its ability to restrict the access of the researchers who staff agencies engaged in preparing materials for the use of high-level decision-makers; and in many other ways, including direct proposals, through its own chain of command, concerning foreign situations and problems. A different line of speculation about the KGB's role in foreign affairs is that some of its intelligent young agents, with wide knowledge of foreign systems and cultures, may actually be a force in the Soviet bureaucracy making for realistic, relatively objective, and prudent foreign policy analysis and recommendations.

The Soviet regime apparently still feels the need for exceptionally powerful, somewhat autonomous security agencies in order to survive and function effectively, at least as effectiveness is conceived by the type of leader in power. To perform their assigned tasks the security agencies, in turn, need highly trained, adequately motivated, reasonably contented, loyal personnel. Organizational and functional requirements tend to make of the KGB, therefore, a group with its own interests and some autonomy. It may be one of the paradoxes of a one-party, ideologically legitimized dictatorship that its effort to prevent the development of political pluralism and legitimate opposition forces it to create a watchdog agency difficult to control and even, potentially, capable of destroying its master. At the very least, the role—or roles— of the security agencies bulk disturbingly large in Soviet life.

Of course, the party has many instruments and techniques which it can utilize in an effort to prevent this special-purpose, "anti-interest-group" interest group from getting out of control. The police agencies, as has already been indicated, have usually been divided into various administrations, or directorates, wholly or partially sealed off from one another, subject to intensive party indoctrination and inspection, and susceptible of being played off against one another by the top leadership. Particularly significant is the fact that the MVD-MOOP, or internal public order agency, has always been available to counterbalance the

116

Cheka-MGB-KGB, or political police.[31] Care is, of course, taken by Soviet leaders, such as Stalin, Khrushchev, and Brezhnev, to place in positions of authority over the various security agencies persons whom, on the basis of previous ties, shared destiny, and demonstrated loyalty, they think they can trust, or at least control. The top command always has at its disposal, as its ultimate balance against the power of the police, the regular military forces, whose officers have, as a rule, bitterly resented police surveillance. Control is also exercised through intensive indoctrination and by judicious use of rewards and punishments.

Finally, the party command usually has special administrative agencies at its disposal for the purpose of exercising surveillance and control over the security police. Stalin relied heavily on a special apparatus headed by General A. N. Poskrebyshev which, among other services performed, apparently directed both the 1936-1938 purge and the preparations for the purge planned for 1953.[32] In the exercise of supervision over the police services, the rough equivalent, since Stalin, for Poskrebyshev's special section has apparently been the Central Committee Section of Administrative Organs. The head of this section, from 1959 until his death in an air crash in Yugoslavia in October 1964, was N. R. Mironov. He had served in the Ministry of State Security from 1951 to 1959 and became, presumably by virtue of the requirements of his party post, a vigorous public proponent of restoration of party control over the security agencies, the procuracy, and the courts. In a speech delivered in December 1961, Mironov referred to Yagoda, Yezhov, Beria, Abakumov, and others as "adventurers and provocateurs" and charged that during the period of "the cult of personality of Stalin" the "organs of the NKVD" had behaved arbitrarily and brutally and had resorted to deception and torture. He also pointed out that under Stalin control by the procuracy over the security agencies had become a formality, and that indeed the procuracy officials lived in terror of the MGB. However, it seems likely that with his own police

[31] Paul Wohl, in *The Christian Science Monitor*, January 28, 1969, speculated on the existence of rivalry for influence between the newly established MVD, headed by Shchelokov, who is perhaps politically closer to Brezhnev than Andropov and the KGB. He also noted that available evidence indicated that the MVD, like its presumed rival, had been assigned certain political-ideological functions. Such a line of speculation seems at least partially supported by the TASS report in Soviet newspapers for February 25, 1969, that Shchelokov, as well as Marshal Chuikov and other notables, had attended a ceremony on February 24 in honor of a prominent Soviet painter.

[32] On Poskrebyshev's role, see Nikolaevsky, *op.cit.*, pp. 105-119.

background Mironov was not unsympathetic to KGB needs and interests.[33] Not until May 1968, did it become apparent, and then only by inference from the Soviet press, that Mironov's post had finally been filled by Nikolai I. Savinkin, a veteran political commissar, with military experience.[34] However, Suslov's role in the KGB fiftieth anniversary ceremonies, and other evidence, indicated that, at the highest policy level, it was he, rather than the chiefs of the Administrative Organs Section, who was exercising supervision over the security machine.[35] Before Suslov, Shelepin had apparently been the top party supervisor and overseer of police, security, and related matters.[36]

Since Stalin, despite increased party control, much greater attention to procedural niceties, and a reduction in harshness and brutality, the security agencies have continued to conduct, under conditions of substantial autonomy, operations of enormous scope and impact. Inconclusive, but impressive evidence indicates that after 1953 police personnel was substantially, perhaps drastically, reduced, but that it was subsequently expanded and at least partly restored to earlier levels.

[33] *XXII Syezd KPSS i voprosy ideologicheskoi raboty* (Moscow, 1962), pp. 232-234.

[34] Nikolai I. Savinkin, on the basis of several references, including listing in Vol. II, p. 551, of the stenographic report of the Twenty-third Congress, seemed likely to have replaced Mironov, and the supposition was officially, if indirectly, confirmed when *Pravda*, for May 5, 1968, referred to him as head of an unnamed Central Committee section. Since as recently as February 14, 1968, in *Pravda*, Savinkin had been identified as Deputy Chairman of the Administrative Organs Section, it seems clear that he was shortly thereafter promoted to be its chairman. The long delay in replacing Mironov may indicate the delicacy of this post, and also possibly differences of opinion at top leadership levels concerning the person to fill it.

[35] Interestingly, Suslov, at the celebration of the fiftieth anniversary of the Bolshevik revolution, had been photographed with Brezhnev, carrying flowers to a new statue of Lenin, and had reportedly made public the Central Committee's greeting to the KGB—a fact indicating that he might be Brezhnev's principal lieutenant in top-level supervision of the security organs.

[36] The ascription of the above role to Shelepin is based on the extensiveness and apparent authority of his discussion of security matters in his speech at the Twenty-first Congress in 1959, and the Twenty-second Congress in 1961, and also on references to him as an authority on such matters in the writings of the distinguished jurist, M. Strogovich. No speech by him is recorded at the Twenty-third Congress when Brezhnev made a brief, laudatory statement on the role of the security organs. In his earlier speeches Shelepin bitingly criticized Stalinist injustice and assured the party that the security agencies had returned in their work to the just and humane practices of Feliks Dzerzhinsky. For Strogovich's references see his book, *Osnovnye voprosy sovetskoi sotsialisticheskoi zakonnosti* (Moscow, 1966), pp. 139, 148. It may well be that replacement of Shelepin as overall supervisor of police matters by the veteran *apparatchik* Mikhail Suslov, a secretariat member since 1947, signaled a general strengthening of "conservative" forces in top elite positions.

118

The main reason for a reduction in forces would appear to have been the dismantling of most of the economic empire, based largely on forced labor, over which Beria and his chief lieutenants presided. A series of amnesties of various categories of convicted persons, including one that was announced shortly before the celebration of the fiftieth anniversary of the Bolshevik revolution, and numerous accounts and reports by foreign visitors to the USSR of conversations with Soviet friends and acquaintances who had returned from prison camps, point to the decline, though not the disappearance, of the slave labor system.[37]

The vicissitudes of post-Stalin changes left the KGB with what Deriabin correctly describes as an impressive amount of autonomy and a high degree of penetration of society. As he points out: "The state security has local directorates in every republic of the Soviet Union. These branches in turn control individual KGB networks down through *oblast, krai* and *rayon* compartments, ending with the local case officer in his small dark kingdom of a town, a factory, or several city blocks." Deriabin goes on to list twelve "main directorates" of the KGB, beginning with those for counterintelligence within the Soviet Union; foreign intelligence; army, navy and air force counterintelligence; border troops, etc., and concluding with a directorate for guarding the security of high party and government officials and, finally, a section for atomic energy. Interestingly enough, in view of Kremlin concern in recent years regarding intellectual and artistic dissent, the fifth directorate listed by Deriabin is one which, he asserts, "amounts to the KGB's special police force in charge of eggheads."[38]

In guarded language, Soviet sources, especially law textbooks and specialized works of legal scholarship, tend to confirm the accuracy of the descriptions of KGB structure and functions presented both by Soviet citizens who have communicated their experiences and interpretations to the non-Soviet world, and by Western scholars who have observed—or experienced—its operations. Through the border guards, who are and have been for most of the period since 1948, "a part of the organs of state security," the KGB exercises "political defense" of the Soviet state boundaries and also cooperates with its counterparts in most

---

[37] Some of the most important evidence is presented in Fainsod, *How Russia Is Ruled*, pp. 448-449.

[38] Deriabin and Gibney, *op.cit.*, pp. 92-97. Jeremy Azrael in his article, "An End to Coercion?" *Problems of Communism*, XI, No. 6 (November-December 1962), presents cogent data on the scope of the surveillance functions and power to intimidate at the disposal of the post-Stalin security agencies.

of the communist-ruled countries of Eastern Europe.[39] Referring to another sensitive sphere, a text on Soviet military law states that "investigators of the organs of state security" in cases of treason, espionage, terroristic acts, "diversion and other especially dangerous state crimes," conduct preliminary investigation in the Soviet army and navy.[40] Many important police functions—in addition to normal work in combating crime—including the enforcement of the internal passport system and the strict rules regarding possession, use, and registration of firearms, typewriters, mimeograph machines, and other reproducing devices are exercised by the militia. The militia, on appropriate occasions and for certain purposes, collaborates closely with and is sometimes supervised by KGB officers.[41]

From time to time, as has already been noted, items published in the Soviet press indicate the existence of something which might be described as a "police community." For example, in April 1965 there was a conference in Moscow devoted to "important problems of the further improvement of the activity of the capital's militia." Among the participants listed at this conference were Semichastny, Tikunov, at that time Minister of Protection of Public Order of the RSFSR, and other high government and party officials.[42] Occasionally the Soviet press provides specific, albeit limited and laconic evidence on the involvement of the police community in the control of Soviet intellectual life. Thus, among those who participated in April 1967 in a "conference of ideo-

---

[39] V. A. Vlasov and S. S. Studenikin, *Sovetskoye administrativnoye pravo* (Moscow, 1959), p. 268; A. E. Lunev, *Obespecheniye zakonnosti v sovetskom gosudarstvennom upravlenii* (Moscow, 1963), p. 116. It is significant that Lunev, *ibid.*, asserts that the KGB, and also the militia, are endowed with "significant powers" in the exercise of "administrative supervision" over other administrative agencies. See also the article by Col. Gen. P. Zyryanov, in honor of "Border Guard Day," in *Pravda*, May 27, 1967. According to him, the border defense forces engaged in "coordinated activities" with those of Poland, Czechoslovakia, Hungary, and Rumania, as a result of which hundreds of "violators of the frontier" had been apprehended. Zyryanov, a deputy chairman of the KGB, was at the time of publication of the above article the commanding officer of the border guards. Some indication of the existence of a "socialist commonwealth police community" was also suggested by the presence, reported in the Soviet press, of "delegations" representing the security forces of the "peoples' democracies," at the KGB fiftieth anniversary celebrations.

[40] A. G. Gorney (ed.), *Osnovy sovetskovo voennovo zakonodatelstva* (Moscow, 1966), pp. 387-388.

[41] A. Lunin, "The Lower Echelons of the Soviet Militia," *Bulletin, Institute for the Study of the USSR*, II, No. 11 (November 1955), 3-7.

[42] *Pravda*, April 10, 1965; according to *Pravda*, August 2, 1964, when Shelepin returned from North Korea he was greeted by Semichastny, A. S. Panyushkin, and P. V. Kovanov, then deputy chairman of the Party-State Control Committee.

logical workers" in connection with preparations for the fiftieth anniversary of the Great October Socialist Revolution, was A. S. Panyushkin.[43] Later in the same year, in connection with the designation of Sergei G. Bannikov as deputy chairman of the USSR Supreme Court, it was reported—but this time in the Western press—that Bannikov, a veteran, top level KGB officer had been engaged, while in the KGB, in supervising, lecturing to, and admonishing Soviet literary and cultural figures.[44] Together with Bannikov, KGB Major General Nikolai Chistyakov was also appointed to the Supreme Court. It has, of course, been the KGB that has arrested, detained, interrogated, investigated, and generally managed the cases against dissident Soviet writers.

Many other aspects of KGB activities and influence, in such spheres as censorship, the safeguarding of state secrets, the conduct of foreign propaganda operations, and use of Soviet diplomatic missions abroad as a cover for KGB intelligence, espionage, and political warfare operations, are relevant and significant. Cyrus Sulzberger has estimated that "sixty per cent of the approximately 6,000 Soviet officials stationed outside the USSR today are actually career officers of either KGB or GRU (military intelligence)."[45] According to Louis Fischer, as late as 1930, Maxim Litvinov, then Soviet Commissar for Foreign Affairs, "stubbornly and sometimes successfully resisted attempts of the Soviet secret GPU to infiltrate the Foreign Commissariat."[46]

And yet I do not wish to convey the impression that the Soviet Union today is as purely a police state as it was under Stalin. To be sure, there has probably been some retrogression since the removal of Khrushchev. Everything we know of the Stalin era makes even the limited freedom of expression enjoyed by Soviet artists, writers, and other intellectuals today seem remarkable.[47] It is worth noting, and is

[43] *Komsomolskaya pravda*, April 6, 1967.
[44] *New York Times*, November 10, 1967. Volume II, p. 401 of the stenographic report of the Twenty-third Congress lists Sergei Grigorevich Bannikov, a delegate, as Deputy Chairman of the KGB. Judging from the name, he is the Bannikov who was appointed to the Supreme Court and who according to Patricia Blake, *op.cit.*, issued stern warnings to Soviet writers not to protest against the Sinyavsky-Daniel trial.
[45] *New York Times*, June 20, 1966.
[46] Louis Fischer, *The Soviets in World Affairs* (Princeton, 1951), Introduction to Vol. I, p. x. In this introduction to a major study first published in 1930, Fischer added that attempts by the Foreign Office to oppose the police were no longer conceivable, "for the infiltration now amounts to domination."
[47] Perhaps the best analysis of the struggle of Soviet intellectuals for increased freedom, and its political implications, is Timothy McClure, "The Politics of Soviet Culture, 1964-1967," *Problems of Communism*, XVI, No. 2 (March-April

perhaps encouraging, that while police membership in the Central Committee has been decreasing, that of bona fide natural scientists has increased, although it is still very small.[48] However, on the negative side of the balance we must consider basic features of Soviet law, especially the laws dealing with "political" crimes—the broadly construed Soviet concept of "economic crime" is also relevant here—and the continued exercise by the KGB of jurisdiction over the investigation of "political crimes" which is one of the bases of its relatively autonomous and highly privileged position within the Soviet political, legal, and administrative structure. The KGB's freedom of action benefits from the hunting license provided by the vague language of pertinent laws, such as RSFSR criminal code Articles 65 and 70, dealing, respectively, with espionage and anti-Soviet propaganda, and Articles 190/1, 190/2, and 190/3, which are even looser and from the point of view of Western law, more objectionable than Article 70.[49] Also of fundamental importance is the right of judicial investigators, in all criminal cases, and not only in "political" matters, to hold suspected, detained, and accused persons *incommunicado*, without access to the services of attorneys, for up to nine months, pending completion of preliminary investigation of their alleged offenses.

A Personal Experience

Since data on the *modus operandi* of the KGB, from sources other than censored and processed Soviet ones, is so extremely scarce, it may be useful if I present a brief interpretive account of the legal aspects of my own experience at the hands of the KGB in 1963.[50] The reader should of course, bear in mind that this is based on memory, since I

1967), 26-43. See also Blake, *op.cit.*, on the mounting intensity, especially in 1967-1968, of the struggle between resistant intellectuals and the party and police authorities.

[48] In a useful unpublished study, prepared for presentation at the October 21-22, 1966 meeting of the Southern Conference on Slavic Studies, Yaroslav Bilinsky observed that while neither in 1961 nor in 1966 was the secret police represented on the Central Committee by a "professional," the number of genuine scientists in the Central Committee, had, in the same period, doubled.

[49] English translations of Article 65, and of Article 70—under which Gerald Brooke and the Soviet writers, Sinyavsky and Daniel were convicted—are available in Harold J. Berman and James W. Spindler, *Soviet Criminal Law and Procedure* (Cambridge, Mass., 1966). The text of Articles 190/1, 190/2, 190/3 is contained in *Vedomosti Verkhovnovo Soveta RSFSR*, 1966, No. 38, item 1038.

[50] See also Frederick C. Barghoorn, *Politics in the USSR*, pp. 330-332.

had no opportunity to make or retain notes. Also, in attempting to appraise the significance of what transpired it is necessary to keep in mind the fact that not only are we dealing here with a single case, but that this case concerned a foreigner. Whether or not this rendered the treatment of the accused less, or more, severe or in any other way distinguished my experience from that which would have befallen a Soviet citizen similarly accused, must remain a matter of speculation. It is my belief that had I been a Soviet citizen I would have been treated more harshly.

It would serve no useful purpose for me to attempt to reproduce the entire experience here. Perhaps the most important single feature of the entire episode was that the case against me was a pure and simple fabrication from beginning to end. I was accused of military espionage, despite the fact that I had neither the training and background nor the contacts or opportunities which might have lent some semblance of verisimilitude to such a charge—leaving out of account, of course, the fact that I never made an attempt to engage in such an activity. This point is stressed at the outset, because it sheds a vivid light on the credibility of KGB charges in accusations that Soviet citizens or foreigners may have committed military or political crimes and confirms the widespread view that in political cases Soviet justice is not squeamish about tailoring facts to suit ideological and political requirements.

I recognize that, in terms of the abnormally suspicious, ideologically colored standards of the KGB, I may have appeared to be a somewhat undesirable individual. I had been employed by the United States Embassy in Moscow for somewhat more than four years, in 1942-1947, during which time I had purchased Soviet publications of various kinds for transmission to United States government agencies and had engaged in political reporting, most of which, however, was of an unclassified nature. In 1949-1951, I had been employed by the United States government, in West Germany, in interviewing Soviet refugees, most of whom were at the time recent defectors. Although this work had been of a political rather than military character, there is no doubt that any organized effort to obtain information from Soviet persons who have fled the USSR arouses bitter hostility in the Kremlin. Perhaps also the critical tone of my publications on various aspects of Soviet propaganda and foreign policy, particularly, one may guess, my attempt to analyze critically Soviet behavior in the field of cultural exchanges, partly on the basis of observations made in the Soviet Union, might have incurred

123

sharp displeasure. It is interesting, in this connection, that all the efforts I made during my imprisonment and interrogation to turn the conversation to the subject of my academic teaching and research were ignored by the interrogators.

Whatever the motives of my kidnapping and imprisonment may have been, the action was most likely taken in reprisal for the arrest by the FBI of a Soviet citizen, one Ivanov, who, like this writer, did not have a diplomatic passport. The value of the experience, for the purposes of this study, consists in the light it shed on the privileged position occupied by the KGB in the Soviet bureaucratic machine and on the methods by which its interrogators and jailers process prisoners. Generally speaking, I cannot complain that I was harshly or brutally treated. In fact, more often than not, I was treated with an amused and slightly cynical courtesy. Also, after a few days of very bad food, I was fed probably better than most ordinary Soviet citizens. However, various aspects of my experience vividly displayed the enormous overwhelming psychological pressure that a secret police machine of the KGB type can bring to bear upon an individual.

Between about 7:30 in the evening of October 31, 1963, and 4:00 P.M., on the afternoon of November 16, when, about two hours after my release from the Inner Prison of the KGB, usually known as Lubyanka (from its location on Lubyanka Lane, near Dzerzhinsky Square) I departed by air for London from Moscow, I passed through three stages—as detainee, suspect, and accused person—each of which was officially initiated by the presentation of a legal document by an officer of the KGB. Throughout the experience, from beginning to end, the continued high status of the KGB within the Soviet political-social structure was indicated in a variety of ways. Thus it was certainly strange that a person could be dragged, shouting and scuffling, from the sidewalk fronting a big hotel, on a busy street, without causing a single passing citizen to display curiosity or to alert a foreign embassy or news service.

During the five or six hours that elapsed between my abduction in front of the Metropole Hotel in central Moscow and my incarceration in a cell in the Lubyanka, I was forced to sit with my hands in tight-fitting handcuffs, was frequently photographed, and was requested to sign a confession that I had committed military espionage. This experience, in which the dominant factor was an exceedingly unfriendly and scornful KGB officer, was one of several that were presumably calculated to convey to the victim a sense of his helplessness. By far the most important factor conducive to imbuing a prisioner with a sense of the overwhelming power of those who have taken control of his destiny is probably isolation. I was held *incommunicado* throughout my entire stay in the Lubyanka. So complete was my isolation that I never saw another prisoner. Perhaps the most trying aspect of the experience was the period of two days during which I was not interrogated. These two days, ironically enough, coincided with the November 6 and November 7 holidays. Strengthening the impression of being completely cut off from the non-Soviet world was the fact that all requests for permission to communicate with the American Embassy were refused on legal grounds. My concern was also heightened when I was told that Soviet law permitted my interrogators to devote nine months to preliminary investigation of the case. I was also told that refusal to answer questions, or the giving of false answers to questions, were offenses punishable by imprisonment in addition to the penalty for the crime of which I was accused. Although for the most part the interrogations were not conducted in a harsh or threatening tone, there were a number of occasions on which I was given to understand that failure to cooperate would lead to extremely unpleasant consequences. Needless to say, the physical surroundings in the prison and the adjoining KGB office building and the general setting and regime tend to reinforce a prisoner's sense that he is engaged in a very unequal contest.

As was to be expected, I was told that I would not have access to defense counsel until the KGB investigators (*sledovateli*) had completed their preliminary investigation. Although perhaps not very important in political cases generally, where the powers of the KGB are so enormous, and particularly in cases involving foreigners, for whom a Soviet attorney could not be expected to conduct a vigorous defense against the accusation that he had seriously harmed the interests of the Soviet state, this feature of the situation of the accused is nevertheless highly significant. It is an integral part of the Soviet pattern of "political justice." The chief investigator assigned to my case was an impressive individual, eloquent and quick-witted, with a sense of humor and with histrionic talent of a high order. When I, after being introduced to the chief investigator on the second day of my imprisonment, declared that the entire accusation rested upon a fabrication, the investigator replied, "The FBI does things like that but we don't." The basis of the strategy of interrogation apparently consisted of an effort by the chief investigator, gaining the prisoner's confidence and by clever questioning, to elicit the desired confession, while leaving routine interrogation to a subordinate who took a much harsher and more unfriendly attitude than did his chief.

Such a division of labor is well calculated to create in the accused a sense of dependence upon the more lenient and indulgent of his two principal interrogators. Several other interrogators entered the case at various times and, at least once, uniformed personnel, perhaps officials of the procuracy, sized me up, but did not speak to me. After about the first ten days of interrogations, during which the investigators conformed to the post-Stalin regulation that no interrogations may be conducted after ten o'clock in the evening, a very aggressive individual entered the case. He brought with him notebooks which apparently contained information regarding my activities while an employee of the State Department in West Germany in 1949-1951. Although some of the information at the disposal of the investigators was partially incorrect or distorted, much of it was accurate and extremely detailed. For example, I was questioned for two or three hours one afternoon about a trip I had made to the Ukraine in the fall of 1946, of which I had naturally forgotten many of the details.

The entire experience greatly deepened my understanding of the process by which individuals can, given enough time, be brought to perform, in a court trial, in the fashion desired by the Soviet authorities. Fortunately for me, I was innocent of the charges, I was held only for a short time, and my release was vigorously, and successfully, demanded by President Kennedy.

Recruitment and Training of Personnel

An important element in the situation of the security forces, which bolsters their character as a coherent group, is the considerable degree of control which their leaders exercise over the recruitment and training of the personnel commanded or supervised by them. As is to be expected, information on these sensitive subjects is defective. However, it is known that the KGB and the militia, like some other branches of the Soviet state administration, operate their own in-service training institutions. Also, representatives of the diplomatic service, the KGB, the military establishment, and other agencies seeking to recruit personnel for sensitive fields are often included in placement commissions which select, for further in-service training, graduates of higher educational institutions.[51] There is reason to believe that the KGB is allowed to recruit its pick of the ablest graduates of Soviet institutions of higher legal training. However, it appears that with the decline of terror and the rise in the level of aspirations of Soviet youth since Stalin, the KGB has found it increasingly difficult to secure desired personnel and has been forced to resort to persuasion, rather than the methods of coercion and dragooning which earlier sufficed. Some observers see evidence of this new pattern in the public relations campaign of recent years, in journalism and in works of fiction, to "sell" the attractions of KGB service by glorifying its role in general, and the patriotic services of individual Soviet intelligence officers, in particular. In any case, as a result of improvement in practices both of recruitment into the security and police services, and of in-service training, the educational and cultural levels of personnel in these services has risen rapidly since the death of Stalin.[52]

While the available evidence indicates that the security and police services enjoy a considerable measure of autonomy in the recruitment and training of their staffs, it is also noteworthy that Soviet sources stress the primacy of the party in the recruitment and supervision of such personnel. Semichastny's article in *Pravda* on May 7, 1965, stated that the Central Committee directed "all of the practical activity of the organs of state security" and called the attention of the Chekists to the necessity of "constantly increasing their political vigilance."[53] It seems reasonable to assume that, within the limits of party guidance and supervision, the security services are permitted and even encouraged to develop a sense of professional and organizational identity. Other factors besides recruit-

[51] *Staffing Procedures and Problems in the Soviet Union*, prepared by U.S. Senate, Subcommittee on National Security Staffing and Operations (Washington, D.C., 1963), p. 17; see also Slusser and Wolin, *op.cit.*, pp. 306-321, and Deriabin, *op.cit.*, pp. 58-69.

[52] Both Tikunov, *op.cit.*, and Nikitin, *op.cit.*, stressed the rapid rise in educational levels of the personnel of the militia. According to Nikitin, the militia operates five higher educational institutions, and dozens of special higher schools, which employ many doctors and candidates of science, and professors. Both authors also emphasized the importance of training in advanced technology for the Soviet police services. Of course, they were describing developments in the militia, rather than in the KGB, but it seems reasonable to suppose that parallel developments, presumably on a more advanced level, are occurring in the KGB.

[53] Tikunov, *op.cit.*, besides stressing the same points, emphasized the importance, for effective functioning and proper indoctrination of the militia, of the introduction of deputy commanders for political-educational work in all units with more than fifty staff members.

127

ment, training, and indoctrination practices appear to foster such identity. Like the regular military services, the security and police agencies have their own recreational and sports organizations, their own uniforms, service routines, buildings, etc. A very important prerogative of the KGB consists in its high degree of control over its internal communications flow, records, files, and archives.[54] The KGB is also in a sense its own press agent. There can be little doubt that the glorification of the KGB during the last four or five years, in Soviet journalism and fiction, was, at least in part, the result of its demands on the party leadership that its good name, which had suffered during the vigorous early stages of de-Stalinization, be restored. It may be assumed that the KGB exercises wide discretion in organizing and conducting propaganda operations against foreign governments.

The experience of the Communist Party of the Soviet Union in building, maintaining, at times partially dismantling, but always rebuilding, a network of political and ideological security agencies seems to suggest that part of the price which is exacted by the struggle to maintain monolithism is the subjection of the citizenry, sometimes up to the very highest levels, to personal insecurity and even terror. The security services have survived as a privileged and powerful subcommunity within the Soviet system because they have performed valuable services to the leadership. Like the party dictatorship itself, the security services are the product of deeply rooted elite attitudes of fear, hostility, and mistrust toward the international and internal socio-political environments, which, in turn, reflect ideological, cultural, and situational factors. Presumably the attitudes which sustain the status of these organs will continue to flourish as long as the conditions which engender such attitudes and foster the healthy existence of an overdeveloped security apparatus persist. To say this is not, of course, to forecast their permanence. Like other aspects of the Soviet system, the functions and style of operation of these agencies have changed since the death of Stalin, in a direction which from the point of view of democratic values is positive, but their continued existence in anything like their present scope, magnitude, and power is from the same point of view deeply disturbing.

The party apparatus and its police allies still dominate Soviet Russia. However, their dominance is not as overwhelming as it once was. They are forced to take into account, and sometimes at least partially to yield

---

[54] See Slusser, *op.cit.*, on KGB control of records.

128

to, the demands of other groups in society, such as scientists and writers, for a measure of autonomy and independence far greater than Stalin would have permitted. Further strengthening of the sense of identity and confidence of the independent public opinion now emerging in the USSR, along with other aspects of the increasing maturation of Soviet society, may gradually subject to public control the once capricious and unpredictable action of the "sword of the revolution." In this connection, it is significant and encouraging to those who regard individual and professional freedom as precious values, that liberal Soviet jurists have, in the post-Stalin era, added their voices to the chorus of demands for a curtailment of arbitrary and extra-legal administrative behavior. There has developed an alliance, or at least a parallelism of professional interests which may yet curb the excesses of police power. However, the unshackling of Soviet society, which has been proceeding for some years, will probably be a long, slow, tortuous process. The police agencies can almost certainly be counted on to resist it and will be supported in this resistance by other forces with a vested interest in the *status quo*.

The security agencies, according to the still-established official doctrine, are the guardians of the interests of society, and in particular of the interests of the party elite. Their capability to continue to play this assigned role will depend on many factors operating within the USSR and in the international environment. It will be reduced by the growth of internal forces of liberalization in Soviet Russia and by whatever links and ties and common perspectives develop between those, in Russia and in the outside world, who seek evolutionary, adaptive change in the direction of rationality and freedom. Needless to say, evolution will be impeded, and the elitist and crisis impulses which sustain the power of the KGB will be fed, by the continuance or the heightening of international tensions.

CHAPTER V ~ BY ROMAN KOLKOWICZ

The Military

Introduction

THE concept of interest groups in a political system presupposes two conditions: (a) distinct sets of interests and values shared by groups or institutional memberships and (b) the existence of "conflict" in the system, i.e., a modicum of tolerance for the public and private articulation of policy-relevant interests and values which are not necessarily those of the ruling elite. In pluralistic systems we have come to accept the idea and reality of interest groups as a vital factor in the political process and social transaction in which the leaders manipulate or accommodate various group demands. In a totalitarian or authoritarian system, however, where a single party claims hegemony of political and social authority, the concept of interest groups needs some clarification, since the single party denies the very existence of such particularistic entities and views the possibility of their emergence as an anathema.

Writers in the Soviet Union, when dealing with political and social processes, rarely talk about interest groups as we know them in the West, i.e., a set of aggregate "constituencies" whose objectives are intrasystemic and not anti-systemic, and whose purpose is to influence policymakers in favor of their particular interests, which are largely derived from their functional, regional, professional, economic, or social group orientations. Communist theoreticians tend to view articulated group interests as a sign of anti-systemic alienation from society and state, as a remnant of the bourgeois past, and such dissent, unless it can be directed and usefully channeled, must be eradicated. Institutional or particularist group loyalties and objectives which significantly depart from those of the party are viewed as being "pathological." The only "interest groups" Soviet theoreticians and leaders recognize are the economically and historically conditioned social classes: the proletariat, the peasantry, and the intelligentsia. They are assumed to have varying interests and values derivative of their class consciousness. Even these class differences, however, are eventually to be eradicated and subsumed within the classless communist society.

We are clearly dealing here with a political doctrine and social values which diverge in a basic way from those of Western pluralistic societies. It is apparent that a set of political and social goals, which stresses uniformity, harmony, and unity as basic desirable objectives, would seem antithetic to the formation and growth of particularist interest groups. Soviet leaders and theoreticians have in the past viewed their society as an amorphous entity which the party could manipulate by means of various deliberate devices in order to keep it malleable and committed to the party's goals, and to prevent it from crystallizing groups and institutions whose spokesmen could challenge the party's hegemony. This view of society was embodied in various declarations by Stalin, notably the familiar one describing "the transmission belts, the 'levers,' the directing force, the sum total of which constitutes the system of the dictatorship of the proletariat."[1]

Western accounts of life and politics in the Soviet Union in the past four or five decades were permeated by the vision of a rule of terror over an undifferentiated populace, and of a small group of men whose Byzantine intrigues and struggles for power absolutely determined the fate of the state, its institutions, and the individual citizens. Such accounts confined all political activity to a single level at the apex of the party hierarchy. In defense of this simplistic presentation of a complex society we must remember how relatively little reliable information on the Soviet Union was available to the West for many years, so that researchers had to make the most of official communications and the statements of party leaders, and try to derive both meaning and facts from the often laborious scrutiny of these sources. This task was the more difficult because of the distorted, idealized view of the Soviet scene—an idyllic picture of a classless, tranquil, and wisely guided society—that was propagated by the party-controlled media. Soviet society was presumed to be permanently "frozen" in an ideologically and politically determined mold and firmly ruled by the party, changes in the top leadership notwithstanding.

In reality, as we came to know, underneath the inhibiting forms of Stalinist dictatorship, the Soviet Union was being transformed into a

---

[1] Paraphrased by and cited in Roman Kolkowicz, *The Soviet Military and Communist Party* (Princeton, 1967), p. 16.

complex industrial society, divided into a number of functional groupings, and included several institutions with strong loyalties and parochial interests, each constantly striving for a greater measure of autonomy. After Stalin's death, there occurred an accelerated process of loosening of political controls over society and the divergent institutional claims, which theretofore had been suppressed, began to be publicly advocated with various degrees of vigor. This trend toward moderation in Soviet political and social life, the growing body of information on the Soviet Union, and the pressures for emancipation among Soviet satellites caused many Western students of communist affairs to abandon a static view of the Soviet Union and to base their research on expectations of social and political change, and on the premise that Soviet society is in a process of transition. This study of the military's role as an interest group belongs to this category.

We begin by positing several basic assumptions about the nature of Soviet political and social life. In the first place, that the political leaders and the basic political values and the ideology are inherently anti-military, i.e., there is a profound distrust of the professional military men who possess the weapons and technology of war, the "experts in violence."[2] Second, that the political norms of the Soviet system reject any particularist interests, be it of institutional, functional, ethnic, or other nature, if such interests are articulated outside the norms of the party. Third, that this rigid insistence on party hegemony and this suppression of the expression of group interests have been undergoing a progressive transformation brought about by several forces of change: modernization of the economy and the management of the state; erosion of ideological imperatives and the emergence of a new form of pragmatism, which considers certain forms of institutional or functional autonomy as necessary for the efficient management of the state; the vast growth of Soviet political and military commitments around the globe which, within the delicate relationship of nuclear deterrence, necessitate substantial inputs into policy processes by experts of various sorts; and a general lessening of the once-pervasive fear of delegating decision-making authority to

[2] Carl Friedrich and Zbigniew Brzezinski have found that totalitarian parties exert constant "efforts to prevent the armed forces from developing a distinct identity of their own" and as a result, the military lives "in an atmosphere of an armed camp surrounded by enemies." They maintain that "the Soviet handling of the army . . . comes closest to the model image of the complete integration of the military into the totalitarian movement." See their *Totalitarian Dictatorship and Autocracy* (Cambridge, Mass., 1956), p. 281.

functional or institutional entities without direct and constant control by the party *apparat*.[3]

The emergence of articulated group interests, then, is a concomitant of a society which is becoming internally complex and which is politically pledged, at home and abroad, to a grand political design which depends on an efficient technological, economical, and managerial substructure. It might be inferred that the "pluralization process" in the Soviet Union is both of the "grass-roots" variety and is partly engineered from above, i.e., the pressures of professional and institutional freedoms and group interests are selectively and carefully tolerated, and at times encouraged, insofar as such developments do not threaten the basic norms of the political system and insofar as they serve to improve the problems of managing a multifaceted society. Such tolerance of interest group articulations may also serve at times the purpose of releasing political pressure from below at a low cost.

Among studies of various Soviet interest groups, that of the military establishment seems to be a promising but at the same time a difficult one. By virtue of its "apartness" from society, its formalized structure of authority and status, a clearly discernible value system, and frequent disagreements and occasional conflicts with the political leadership, the military would seem to be well suited to scrutiny. The military establishment satisfies many of the analytical criteria used by Western sociologists and political scientists in their definitions of an interest group. Its value system is elitist and "inward" oriented and tends to reinforce an institutional awareness and positive self-image. The military's "apartness" from the larger society fosters a sense of exclusiveness and engenders a strong reliance on the military community. The military's modes of dealing with the environment are in some respects similar to those of well-defined interest groups in other societies.

Yet the analyst who attempts to investigate the role and place of the military by using Soviet sources encounters enormous difficulties, the primary one being that of identifying and defining the military's separate institutional identity: its interests, objectives, and values. The reason for this apparent paradox stems from the fact that the Communist Party

[3] In 1959 Khrushchev stressed the desire of the party for "the inclusion of the widest strata of the population in the management of all affairs of the country" and argued that such "an implementation by public organizations of several functions which at the moment belong to the state will broaden the political functions of the socialist state." Speech at the Twenty-first Congress of CPSU, January 27, 1959 (*Pravda*, January 28, 1959).

denies the military such a distinct identity. Through all available media it seeks constantly to reinforce an image of the military as a fully integrated part of a totalitarian system. A large network of political controls within the military organization is designed to keep the latter fully responsive to party guidance, initiative, indoctrination, and other forms of manipulation. This effort, however, has not fully succeeded in suppressing or concealing the many strains and disagreements that exist between the two institutions.

Recent attempts to reappraise the role of the military and other interest groups in the Soviet Union have been aided by a vast increase in the information on the Soviet Union, by a noticeable success in the efforts of the military to obtain institutional autonomy, and by the departure, in Western academic disciplines, from totalitarian monolithic concepts of Soviet political life. In short, it is possible to begin a revaluation and reappraisal of the nature of the Soviet political and social processes by means of applying, with the necessary reservations and adaptations, certain analytical criteria and hypotheses used in the study of Western political systems.

Changing Role of the Military as an Interest Group

What emerges from a study of the Soviet military is a realization that its institutional characteristics are those of all large professional establishments, regardless of their political environment: a high degree of professionalization and demands for professional autonomy; a professional ethos, including a strict code of honor and discipline; and an organizational structure whose levels of authority are easily discernible and stable.

As an interest group the military tends to be highly self-centered, competing with other groups for status, resources, and influence.[4] The military employs a variety of ways of influencing policy and social planning, both of a "direct" and "indirect" kind. Although it possesses substantial potential and inherent political power, it rarely chooses to challenge the party head-on, even when its basic interests are denied. It may nonetheless present its case publicly through speeches and articles, often in a somewhat veiled and esoteric way. It often, however, tends to resort to a form of "passive resistance" acting as a modifier or spoiler of policy by means of institutional inertia, bureaucratic obstruc-

---

[4] See later section of this chapter.

135

tionism, appeals to sympathetic party factions, appeals to "political generals," and denial of its expertise, which leads to erosion of efficiency, discipline, and morale. When viewed from the historical perspective of the past two decades, these methods of dealing with undesirable party policies seem to have been successful for a variety of reasons. These include: the complexity of the military establishment and of warfare in the nuclear age; the rising political and military commitments of the Soviet state which lead to a greater dependence on the military professionals; the realization among military people, under a regime of collective leadership, that a direct challenge to party supremacy tends to unify the party leadership against them, while a selective, patient exploitation of opportune political circumstances serves their ends much better.

Although the military shares some of the characteristics of other interest groups in the Soviet Union, it also differs profoundly from them because of its ambiguous position in the communist state: it is both the mainstay of the regime and a principal potential rival for power. The history of the military's relations with the party has therefore been rather unstable. The party leaders who have had little difficulty in dealing with many other groups and institutions that have challenged or threatened their hegemony are faced with the problem of how to control, and when necessary to coerce, the military without reducing its vigor, efficiency, and morale. Various attempts of the party to keep the military loyal and politically responsive without destroying its effectiveness have had mixed success.[5]

The disparity between the military's vital function in the state on the one hand, and its unclear internal role and political influence on the other, have led to ambiguous Western assessments of its place, status, and influence on Soviet policies. The main reasons for this uncertainty must be sought in the unique political context of the Soviet Union. The attitudes of the various communist ideologues toward professional armies have always been equivocal.[6] Both Marx and Engels originally saw the revolution as a massive uprising of the lower classes led by a communist vanguard. Lenin remained vague about the military's role in a future communist society. However, with the establishment of the Soviet state,

[5] See Kolkowicz, *The Soviet Military*, pp. 340-342, and *passim*.

[6] Roman Kolkowicz, "Heresy Enshrined: Idea and Reality of the Red Army," in Kurt London (ed.), *The Soviet Union, A Half-Century of Communism* (Baltimore, 1968), pp. 223-245.

and the recognition of its growing need for a professional army, the party evolved a *modus operandi* with respect to the military. Stalin, after having ousted Trotsky in 1925, defined the Red Army's organizational structure, its relationship with the party, and its social and political role. The Red Army became an adjunct to the party's ruling elite; the emerging officer corps was denied the full authority necessary to practice properly its profession; the officers' careers were kept in a state of perpetual uncertainty; and, finally, the military community was forcibly exposed to the party's scrutiny through a complex system of control and indoctrination.

Despite the controls and the incessant indoctrination imposed by Stalin, the military establishment did not develop exactly along the lines desired by the party. The officer corps soon began to exhibit some of the characteristics of professional military officers in other political systems. They stressed the need for greater professional autonomy. A typical military ethos developed, marked by elitism and detachment from society and expressed by heroic symbols and a code of honor. The authority of the political commissars was considered destructive and restricted. These tendencies toward institutional autonomy and professional independence were clearly incompatible with the party's objective of a politicized and controlled military organization.

The party's anxieties regarding the military are understandable. As the state makes no formal provisions for the transfer of power, party leaders came to view groups and institutions as potential rivals and challengers. The military, because of its organization, weapons, and philosophy represents the greatest single threat: it controls vast means of physical coercion; it is an integrated mechanism that can, in theory, respond to a few commands and can be rapidly mobilized; and it is a closed group with an elitist, anti-egalitarian value system. Officers share common experiences, schooling, and a language common to their careers. Its members are cliquish with a firm sense of solidarity. And finally, the officers are trained to command, to demand obedience, and to respond to a chain of command.

As long as the terror machine was operational, the military had few opportunities to develop spokesmen who could have articulated its objectives and grievances. After Stalin's death, however, with the party leaders divided by the struggle over his succession, the stabilized control mechanisms were weakened, and the military's views and interests emerged into the open. The brief tenure of Marshal Zhukov as Minister of Defense (1955-1957) strengthened the morale and stature of military professionals. Although his ouster in 1957 brought a temporary setback, the military has continued to gain in professional assertiveness and institutional maturity. This improvement in the military's position has been aided by several developments. The influx of new and complex technology into military science, and the complexity of nuclear warfare and the strategies and doctrines for the conduct of such war have had a liberating effect on the officer corps, endowing experts with greater authority and role, reducing the power of the political control organs. The officer corps is being transformed from a group of relatively expendable commanders with minimal skills into a group of younger, more sophisticated and self-assured technocrats, who are becoming increasingly indispensable, individually and collectively, to the defense and political interests of the party. The Soviet Union's extensive political-military commitments as a superpower would be severely compromised by a major open crisis between the two institutions, so that the party is forced to be more circumspect in its treatment of the military. The party's new pragmatism and higher appreciation of most professional groups—the managers, scientists, and the military among them—has further strengthened the latter's position in the state.[7]

In other words, while conditions for the development of an inner cohesion and institutional self-awareness were inauspicious during the oppressive Stalin era, the years since, having witnessed a progressive ideological disillusionment, a new stress on functional and professional excellence, the disappearance of the terror machine, and acceptance of the principle of collective leadership, have greatly favored the military's role as an articulate interest group.

Interests and Objectives

A vital aspect of an interest group is the fact that it has certain interests and that it seeks to influence decision-makers in order to maximize such interests. The military's basic interests may be divided into two categories: "ideological" and "functional." In addition to such broad, all-military institutional interests, one can discern several subgroup interests which are usually related to certain policy and inter-service problems.

[7] Ibid.

138

The ideological interests of the military refer to the traditional values, self-images, and beliefs of the profession. Their idealized self-image finds expression in numerous public statements by officers, as, for instance, the following by General Makeyev, the influential editor-in-chief of *Krasnaya zvezda* (*Red Star*), the main military organ: "The concept of military honor has existed since time immemorial; it is as old as armies . . . bravery, selfless dedication, and military skill were re-vered. . . . There is a saying: the soldier is at war even in peacetime. But the soldier serves his prescribed time and departs into the reserves. The officer, however, . . . is at war for a lifetime. How many inconveniences, how many trials! But the officer withstands all, overcomes all. He holds high his honor, the honor of the officer and citizen."[8] Makeyev rejects those views which impugn the social utility of the officer, and asserts that his contribution to society is "no less necessary to the father-land than that of a *kolkhoznik*, agronomist, engineer, teacher or doctor." He also rejects the unconcern and antipathy of those in society who pur-sue their normal lives: ". . . while they sleep thousands of officers carry on their difficult duties."

The officers' idealized image of their profession, their duties, and their selfless service to the country (which are found in many other military establishments)[9] is resisted and rejected by the party functionaries. The latter reject the "ideology of militarism" and the "idealistic philosophy" of the military which strive to "show the beauty and wisdom [of military life]."[10] Moreover, such idealized conceptions of the military tend to contribute to elitist tendencies and to a sense of apartness from society and its problems—both unacceptable to the party.

The party's concern with the need constantly to politicize the officer corps is well known. The main objectives of this politicizing and indoc-trination process have been set forth in numerous guidelines to the po-litical control organs in the military:

> The political organs strive to . . . guard daily the uninterrupted in-fluence of the party on all activities and affairs of the Armed Forces. . . . They must always approach problems in such a manner that the interests of communism are given priority. . . . The party demands that all aspects of military life be systematically penetrated. . . . The

---

[8] General Makeyev, *Izvestia*, February 12, 1963.

[9] See M. Janowitz, *The Professional Soldier* (Glencoe, 1960) and numerous other works cited in Kolkowicz, *The Soviet Military*, pp. 24-26, and *passim*.

[10] V. I. Skopin, *Militarizm: istoricheskie ocherki* (Moscow, 1957), p. 35.

political organs must extend their influence into all facets of the activities of the forces . . . they must react to even the smallest deviations from Marxism-Leninism, to any opposition to the policies and directions of the party.[11]

The political control organs are instructed "to explain thoroughly the advantages of Soviet society and state system over the capitalistic system . . . to inculcate in the military . . . an indestructible faith in the ultimate victory of communism." They are also urged to give "serious attention to the recording of discussions" during party meetings when the peculiar ritual of *kritika/samokritika* is performed. The reason for this constant scrutiny is explained: "A well-established informational system enables the political organs always to be on top of things and to react at the right time to deficiencies in the activities of the officer personnel. . . . Party information must correctly define the state of political morale among personnel."[12]

The political control organs play the key role in the effort to politicize the officer corps. Their functions may be summarized as follows: to observe activities in the units and to pass on information to higher levels of the *apparat*; to conduct intensive indoctrination and political education; to regulate the advancement of officers so that only those politically desirable are promoted; to supervise and control military as well as political activities in the units; and to prompt desired action or conduct through intimidation, threats of dismissal, public humiliation, or outright coercion. In addition to these measures the party also seeks to keep the military from institutional "closure" by involving it with social and party groups on the "outside": "Close contacts with party organizations, and collectives of workers in factories, sovkhozy and kolkhozy help soldiers and officers to understand better national interests and to prevent *the emergence of castes* in the military."[13]

THE FUNCTIONAL INTERESTS

The functional interests and objectives of the military are derived from the nature of its primary function to defend the country against aggres-

[11] This citation is from a basic handbook "intended for party-political workers" to assist them "in the organization of party-political work among the personnel of the Soviet army and navy." *Partiino-politicheskaya rabota* (Moscow, 1960), pp. 47-70.

[12] *Ibid.*

[13] Colonel Rtishchev, *V pomoshch ofitseram izuchayushchim Marksistsko-Leninskuyu teoriu* (Moscow, 1959), p. 125 (italics added).

140

sion by the organized and rational use of means of violence. This enjoys top priority whenever international tensions are high, when war threatens, and during actual hostilities. At times of international relaxation or détente, during periods of political and diplomatic passivity, or when other social programs are paramount, the role of the military deteriorates and declines in importance. The need to compete with other social groups and institutions for resources and status motivates the military continually to impress upon the decision-makers the urgency and importance of their role to the welfare and survival of the country. These pleas and demands of the military focus on several clear-cut objectives:

1. Maintenance of a high level of investments in heavy industry, since this sector of the economy is fundamental to the defense industry's needs.
2. Maintenance of high levels of military budgets and expenditures necessary to an efficient and effective military establishment.
3. Maintenance of a certain level of international political tension in order to provide the rationale for large military budgets and allocations.

While these three categories of interests may be described as generic to all military establishments in industrialized societies, the fourth derives from the particular socio-political context of the Soviet Union.

4. A degree of professional autonomy and institutional independence necessary for the military leaders in the formulation of strategic doctrines, in the conduct of military planning at high levels, and in the execution of established military policy.

(1) Maintenance of a high level of investments in heavy industry, since this sector of the economy is fundamental to the defense industry's needs. This is probably the "military interest" with which Western readers are best acquainted and represents a fundamental objective of the military establishment. The policy debates and disagreements on the proper proportion of investment in this sector of industry are as old as the Soviet state.[14] The most recent military claims and the party's counterclaims on the proper proportions of investment were made by First Secretary Brezhnev and by the Chief of the General Staff Marshal Zakharov.

[14] For historical surveys see J. Erickson, *The Soviet High Command 1918-1941* (London, 1962); D. Fedotoff-White, *The Growth of the Red Army* (Princeton, 1944); and Kolkowicz, *The Soviet Military*.

Said Brezhnev: "The national economy must develop harmoniously, it must serve the interests of achieving . . . the constant rise in the people's living standards. The development of heavy industry must be subordinated to the requirements of constant technical reequipment of the whole economy. . . ."[15] The Marshal responded to this several months later in an argument for larger allocations to the heavy and defense industries: ". . . the Soviet people have in the past not for a moment failed to carry out V. I. Lenin's legacy: always to be on the alert, cherishing the defense capabilities of our country and our Red Army as the apple of our eye." He then employed a historical analogy to make his case for "a powerful heavy industry—the foundation of foundations of the whole socialist economy and the firm defense capabilities of our country."[16]

(2) Maintenance of high levels of military budgets and expenditures necessary to an efficient and effective military establishment. As in the case of heavy industry, spokesmen for the military usually seek to impress the political leaders with the urgency of the military's needs for large budgets, and high levels of allocations. A recent example of this tug-of-war between the military's views and those of party spokesmen was a series of statements by military and political spokesmen on the eve of the Twenty-third Party Congress. The military representatives emphasized the "economic base of the defense capabilities" which determines the "essence of a policy and the actual essence of war,"[17] and stressed that "the nature of a war and its success depends more than anything else on the domestic conditions of the country."[18] They emphasized that "in a possible missile-nuclear war, economics will determine its course and outcome first of all and mostly by what it [the economy] is able to give for defense purposes before the war begins, in peacetime."[19] Consequently, "he who does not learn to defeat his enemy in peacetime is doomed to defeat in war."[20]

The party's response to these military pressures was to accommodate such demands while publicly asserting that the consumer interests would

[15] *Pravda*, November 7, 1964.
[16] *Krasnaya zvezda*, February 23, 1965.
[17] Colonel P. Trifonenko, *ibid.*, November 26, 1965.
[18] Colonels Rybnikov and Babakov, *ibid.*, December 7, 1965.
[19] Colonel Trifonenko, *Kommunist vooruzhonnykh sil*, No. 1 (January 1966), pp. 8-16.
[20] Colonel Grudinin, *ibid.*, No. 3 (February 1966), pp. 40-47.

142

receive mounting attention in resource allocations.[21] Consequently, since sizable military research and development programs were continued, and indeed increased, and since the production of offensive and defensive strategic weapons as well as of conventional weapons and technology was also increased, the military could accept and publicly endorse the party's official line on consumer interests.[22]

(3) Maintenance of high levels of international political tension by depicting various persons and situations as dangerous, unpredictable or aggressive, in order to provide a rationale for large defense allocations and a high political status for the military. It may be asserted that military professionals in all political systems tend to depict the international environment as threatening the security of their societies for both objective and "subjective" reasons.[23] In 1954 the military in the Soviet Union had sought to impress the political leadership with the fact that "the easing of international tension should not be overestimated,"[24] whereas the political leader who resisted military demands asserted the opposite.[25] In 1965 military spokesmen saw "the current international situation as characterized by a sharpening of tensions and increased danger of war,"[26] while the political leader, who wanted to curtail military expenditures, had suggested that "of late a certain relaxation of tensions has become apparent in international affairs."[27]

Assertions by the military concerning threats from the international environment are usually related to the party's attempts to reduce its allocations, authority, or status. They therefore serve the military as correct and patriotic means for pressuring those party factions which would put the interests of the consumer or the "stomach" above the basic interests of survival of the nation or the communist system.[28] Another example

[21] *The Dilemma of Superpower: Soviet Policy and Strategy in Transition,* Institute for Defense Analyses, Research Paper, P-383 (October 1967), pp. 30-46.
[22] Marshal Zakharov, in *Tekhnika i vooruzhenie,* No. 4 (April 1966), pp. 1-9.
[23] R. Kolkowicz, *The Red Hawks on the Rationality of Nuclear War,* Rand Corp., RM-4899, Santa Monica, Cal., 1966; *Dilemma of Superpower.*
[24] Marshal Timoshenko, November 1954, cited in Kolkowicz, *The Soviet Military,* p. 385.
[25] For Malenkov's programs, see *Pravda,* August 9, 1953.
[26] *Kommunist,* No. 7 (May 1965), pp. 15-27.
[27] Khrushchev, in 1964, cited in Kolkowicz, *The Soviet Military,* p. 383.
[28] After Khrushchev's ouster, his opponents criticized most of his policies, among them the following: "It would be incorrect to see as the central purpose of Communism mainly the satisfaction of the 'needs of the stomach.' " *Ibid.,* p. 384.

of such military rhetoric can be found in the deliberations prior to the Twenty-third Party Congress when the Five Year Plan was being debated. The military's arguments emphasized that "the policy and actions of the imperialists are intensifying the danger of a new world war" and this "is an undisputable truth,"[29] that nuclear war still serves as a rational instrument of politics, and that any "a priori rejection of the possibility of victory is harmful because it leads to moral disarmament . . . fatalism and passivity."[30]

(4) Retention of authority to manage the internal affairs of the military establishment and to formulate strategic policies. The military has been engaged traditionally in a constant effort to secure greater freedom from the confining embrace and intrusions of the party *apparat*. This basic interest is usually articulated not so much in terms of a particular group or institutional interest, nor as opposition to the party's right to exercise its supreme powers, but rather in terms of the best and most proper use of military expertise. They therefore resist "civilian" intrusion and domination within their own professional areas because, they argue, this tends to undermine the efficiency, readiness, and responsiveness of the military organizations.[31] Although Soviet controls in the forms of politicizing and indoctrinating the officer corps have frequently been discussed in Western studies, less attention has been paid to another aspect, namely, the delineation of the authority of the military to formulate strategic policy. During the Stalinist era the dictator usurped this authority, and the military played a limited role. Only after Khrushchev came to dominate the party did the military assume a minor partnership. After his ouster the military, motivated by real concern that the political leadership might commit the armed forces to situations and policies for which they were inadequately prepared, demanded a larger part in the development of strategic doctrine and in planning activities involving the defense of the country.

The military used as arguments that nuclear war is so complex that, in the words of Marshal Zakharov, military dilettantism in party leaders could be very detrimental, especially if they lacked "even a rudimentary knowledge of military strategy"[32] and that most major Western powers

[29] Colonel I. Sidelnikov, *Krasnaya zvezda*, January 28, 1966.

[30] Colonel Rybkin, "On the Essence of a Nuclear-Missile War," *Kommunist vooruzhonnykh sil*, No. 17 (September 1965), pp. 50-56, and reiterated in various writings in the winter of 1966.

[31] See *Dilemma of Superpower*, pp. 30-46.

[32] *Krasnaya zvezda*, February 4, 1965.

had entrusted their military leadership with the power for full strategic planning while their Soviet counterparts played a minor part in these processes.[33] The party's attitude, as expressed in 1967, was that "attempts to prove that in modern war the political leadership has possibly lost its role has been decisively refuted by logic," that "Marxist-Leninists do not assign the roles of generals absolute importance" since "the influence of even brilliant generals was at best limited to adapting the method of warfare to new weapons," and "because of their destructive properties, modern weapons are such that the political leadership cannot let them escape its control." Finally, the military was told that because of various complex tasks facing modern states, "it is absolutely obvious that the solution of these tasks falls completely within the competence of political leaders."[34]

Subgroups in the Military

Subgroup activities in the military seem to correspond to the degree of political permissiveness in Soviet society. The early post-revolutionary period was a time of great activity by numerous splinter groups and factions whose interests ranged from ideological utopias, to ethnic, nationalistic, parochial, professional, and political stratifications.[35] During the long rule of Stalin, who preferred a submissive, atomized, and uniform military establishment, subgroup activity was reduced to a minimum. Only after his death in 1953, when the military found itself freed from the excesses of the terror machine, did particularistic interests and views emerge into the open once again. While Stalin had preferred a monolithic officer corps (except for *agent provocateur* activities by the security organs), his successors considered an internally divided corps as more desirable and as offering some insurance against the emergence of Bonapartism.

It is difficult to generalize about the subgroups in the military. Some have a more formal and permanent tenure (reflected in inter-service rivalries); others are a by-product of political struggles between factions in the party and the military; some are creatures of technological and professional innovations and progress; still others are of the "sociological" category, representing various interests of generational and

[33] Marshal Sokolovsky, in *Kommunist vooruzhonnykh sil*, No. 7 (April 1966), pp. 59-66.
[34] V. Zemskov, *Krasnaya zvezda*, January 5, 1967.
[35] Kolkowicz, *The Soviet Military*, pp. 36-50.

145

cultural groupings. The subgroups generally advance their particular interests and values through the public media (and presumably through private channels) and usually refrain from directly challenging party supremacy or ideological legitimacy. There is only sketchy evidence to support assumptions about concerted collaboration among various subgroups for tactical purposes of defeating some other subgroups, or for exerting more effective pressure on the political leadership.

The emergent subgroup activities, next to serving their particular ends, also have some broader positive and negative effects on the corporate influence of the military community. On the one hand, it makes the party's controlling tasks easier, since it prevents the officer corps from taking unified action. On the other hand, it introduces a sense of self-assertiveness and denotes a lessened fear of party coercion.

ORGANIZATIONAL SUBGROUPS

The Soviet military establishment is organizationally and functionally divided into several services and arms branches: the Ground Forces, the P.V.O. (Air Defense Forces), Strategic Missile Forces, the Air Forces, the Naval Forces (both surface and subsurface), Forces of the Rear, the Military Academies, and the Central Administrations of the Ministry of Defense, including the General Staff. Although there is some evidence to suggest inter-service conflicts and power struggles, such evidence is inadequate for useful analysis and persuasive conclusions. One can detect, however, pervasive and discernible conflicts of interests, values, and objectives between two broad subgroups: the "radicals" in the Strategic Forces, subsurface Naval Forces, and among the technologically advanced units, and the "conservatives" in the Ground Forces, surface Naval Forces, Tactical Air Forces, and Forces of the Rear.

The central objective of these two broad subgroups is to persuade the political leadership of the soundness and urgency of their advice, and consequently, of the need to base the national planning, allocational, political, and military policies upon their assumptions and proposals. At stake are budgetary allocations, size and role of the various branches of the services, as well as strategic doctrines and policies.

This subgroup activity emerged into the open soon after Stalin's death, and it has continued until the present.[36] The radical subgroup gained

[36] The Western literature on the subject includes T. W. Wolfe, *Soviet Strategy at the Crossroads* (Cambridge, Mass., 1964); A. Horelick and M. Rush, *Strategic*

ascendance during the Khrushchev administration, while the conservative one made impressive gains after his ouster. Their respective arguments may be summarized as follows. The radical credo was that nuclear war would be very different from any previous war; consequently, old military processes and doctrines have become obsolete. Believing that nuclear war has ceased to be politically and militarily meaningful, they placed strong emphasis on deterrence policies and asserted that political wisdom rather than sheer military expertise should be given the decisive role in both pre-war and wartime functions. They also maintained that resources allocated by the party to the defense establishment were adequate, especially since they were receiving a growing share of the total military budget. The radicals, satisfied with Khrushchev's preferential treatment of their needs, were in agreement with his military and political doctrines and policies and actively challenged the conservatives by denigrating them as "old fogeys" who had not learned the lessons of the nuclear age and who had made a fetish of command experience and orthodoxy.[37]

The conservatives accepted the premises of the newer strategic doctrines, but firmly rejected those implications which negatively affected their special interests and the larger security interests of the state. While agreeing with the radicals that a new war would be radically different from any preceding one, because of its speed and destructiveness, they disagreed on the necessary size, role, mission, and effectiveness of the conventional forces. They maintained, therefore, that mass armies were still necessary in a nuclear war; that overreliance on mechanisms and policies for preventing war, such as nuclear deterrence, would be dangerous, since they would not prepare the country adequately for fighting a war; that the needs of the defense establishment must be given priority in national planning, subordinating domestic economic objectives to the defense needs; and that in matters concerning the complexities of modern war, the military experts were, in the final analysis, more competent to make judgments than political dilettantes.

As this intra-military conflict of interests continued to intensify in

---

Power and Soviet Foreign Policy (Chicago, 1966); Herbert S. Dinerstein, *War and the Soviet Union* (2nd ed., New York, 1963); and the introduction to *Soviet Military Strategy*, ed. by Marshal Sokolovskii, trans. by Dinerstein *et al.* (Englewood Cliffs, 1963).

[37] A typical "radical" rejoinder to conservative strategic views is found in the virulent broadside of General S. Kozlov, *Kommunist vooruzhonnykh sil*, No. 11 (June 1961), pp. 52-53.

the early 1960's another subgroup—identified here as the "moderates"—emerged and sought to conciliate the other two while selectively promoting the less extreme aspects of the radicals' and conservatives' policies and interests.

All three subgroups used similar methods of communicating their public views, and advancing their interests. While the proponents of the politically safe radical views (because they reflected Khrushchev's interests and biases) pressed their case with sharpness and self-assurance, the advocates of the less acceptable conservative and moderate stance continued a rear-guard action from a position of political disadvantage. Only after the protector of the radicals, Khrushchev, was removed from office, did the moderates and conservatives obtain at least some of their objectives.[38]

POLITICAL SUBGROUPS

The party leader's constant concern about the military is reflected in the elaborate control machinery, geared to prevention as well as coercion, which the party maintains within the military establishment. The main purpose of political control and indoctrination is to instill party loyalty in the military and to prevent anti-party behavior. However, the party leader is also anxious about the personal loyalty of the military; he needs a reliable military elite on whose support he can count in the perennial intra-party power struggles, as well as in cases when the party's policy meets with opposition from some military circles. He seeks, therefore, to assure himself of such support by cultivating a personally loyal military elite, whose careers depend on his own fortunes.

The party leader stands to gain important advantages from this encouragement of a loyal elite. He acquires a body of professionally reliable military experts whom he can trust, who will execute his policies, and who will support him in the event of military opposition to them. The existence of such a loyal group assures the party leader of stability at the highest levels of the military hierarchy, since admission to this elite occurs through cooptation of politically reliable officers. Finally, by cultivating such an elite, the party leader injects an element of divisiveness into the military community which hinders the coalescence of a unified military point of view and the emergence of a single spokesman.

[38] See *Dilemma of Superpower*.

In fact, both Stalin and Khrushchev were substantially aided in their rise to power by the support of personal followers in the military, and both employed these Trojan horses to control the military.[39] The similarity between Stalin's and Khrushchev's uses of such personally loyal subgroups is indeed striking. Though decades apart, the party leaders formed a loyal military following among disaffected officers in the field commands. Acting as the protectors of the field commanders' interests against the encroachments of the central authorities based in Moscow, they gained the commanders' loyalty, and made it possible eventually to combine resources and to link the careers and fortunes of the commanders with the figure of the emerging dictator or single party leader.

Both Stalin and Khrushchev found their military following respectively from among those commanders who participated in the battles around Tsaritsyn (later Stalingrad) during the Civil War, and the battle of Stalingrad (later Volgograd) during World War II. The Tsaritsyn group included such future prominent leaders as Marshals Voroshilov, Budenny, Timoshenko, Tukhachevsky; the Stalingrad group, Marshals Konev, Malinovsky, Moskalenko, Chuikov, Biryuzov, Yeremenko, Zakharov, and Krylov. Both the groups actively aided their benefactors in their rise to power; both were rewarded with the highest military and political places. Yet, in the long run, despite the preferential position of these elites, professional and institutional loyalties and interests tended, with some exceptions, to override personal loyalties to the benefactors and to cause divisions and crises.

THE COMMANDERS AND THE TECHNOCRATS

The introduction of the new technology into the armed forces of various countries has deeply affected their internal processes, institutional values and mores, authority structures, and traditional roles. This development raises several problems: how to retain a military ethos (personal sacrifice, dedication, bravery, and heroism) and commanding authority in the age of computerized war? As M. Janowitz has suggested: "The history of the modern military establishment can be described as a struggle between heroic leaders, who embody traditionalism and glory, and military 'managers.' "[40]

In the Soviet Union, as in many other countries, the military elite has

[39] For a detailed analysis see "The Rise of the Stalingrad Group," in Kolkowicz, *The Soviet Military*, pp. 220-281.

[40] See R. Kolkowicz, "The Impact of Modern Technology on the Soviet Officer Corps," in *Armed Forces and Society*, ed. by Jacques Van Doorn (The Hague, 1968), pp. 148-168.

149

traditionally come from the military academies. The graduates of these institutions, who assume command, enter an officer community dedicated to camaraderie, mutual support, and other traditional military virtues. The ideal Soviet officer combines bravery, manliness, and leadership skills with staff and command abilities. He is more likely to earn the respect of his subordinates by courage and personally inspired authority than by clever staff work or technical expertise. In the past, technical expertise, though acknowledged as desirable in an officer, did not rate very highly among his qualities. After World War II, and especially after Sputnik, when the Soviet armed forces underwent extensive modernization, large numbers of engineers and technicians entered the officer ranks. They are found predominantly in such elite bodies as the Air Defense Forces, the Strategic Missile Forces, and the submarine navy. This influx of well-trained officers into the military community is changing the image of the commanders and is threatening the traditional officers' dominant positions and careers. Thus the rise of the technocrat has introduced new and potentially far-reaching problems. The technocrats among the officers are usually younger, better trained, and more pragmatic than the traditional commanders. They are also less susceptible to pressures and intimidations by the political organs and by the commanders. They have desirable options in civilian life, with good jobs usually waiting for them. Moreover, since their functions are more complex and more vital to the armed forces, they are also less expendable than the commanders.

The initial impact of the influx of technocrats into the officer corps was profound. In the first place, the very size of this technocratic invasion was a factor. The Chief of the General Staff described this by suggesting that while in the past "one could count the engineers in the military on the fingers of one hand, at present 72 percent of officers in the Soviet missile forces are engineers and technicians," and in the Air Defense Forces the "number of engineers and technicians exceeds the number of officers who have graduated from officer schools and higher military academies."[41]

Secondly, the technocrats' self-assurance and contempt for the traditional ways of the commanders introduced widespread friction. Technical officers maintained that "it is not only bravery that counts but also

[41] Marshal Biryuzov, in *Voenny inzhener—aktivny vospitatel* (Moscow, 1962), p. 5.

the mastering of the technology."[42] An exchange between such younger officers was indicative: ". . . I must say that the old champions are played out. There is no use talking to them. There are sputniks, rockets and electronic equipment all around, but they blather on about the importance of internal routine and their frontline experience. Who needs frontline experience now? All this is hopelessly out of date."[43] The commanders resisted these virulent attacks on their prerogatives, values, and careers. The threat to their careers was quite direct. The military cadre organs have in the last decade systematically weeded out the older and unskilled commanders. The extent of this *chistka* alarmed the Defense Minister who rebuked the cadre organs "who are trying to get rid of experienced commanders only because they are 35 years old and . . . therefore have no prospect for advancement. Not even regimental commanders are assured of remaining in their positions. If they do not have an academic education, then the cadre organs do not even want to talk to them."[44] Another prominent military leader warned against technocratic predominance since "a disproportionate stress on theoretical training may lead to the separation of officers from life" and may "transform officers into 'scholastics' who do not understand life at all but are merely capable of citing the book."[45]

The initial impact of a changing technology was such as to debilitate the officer corps. Large numbers of traditional commanders were replaced by technical officers, and traditional military values came to count for less than technical expertise. Gradually, however, the shock effect of these reforms on the military has been subsiding and countertrends are discernible.

YOUNGER VERSUS OLDER GENERATIONS

Although the conflicts between the commanders and technocrats contain a strong generational element, there is another aspect of this latter problem which needs separate treatment. It seems that the younger elements in the military reject many of the basic values of the officer community, frequently expressing their views in anti-military and pacifistic terms. While the older elements among the officers, mainly those

[42] General V. Petukhov, *Krasnaya zvezda*, March 23, 1964.
[43] *Ibid.*, March 4, 1964.
[44] Marshal Malinovsky, in *K novomu podyomu partiino-politicheskoi raboty v Sovetskoi Armii i Flote*, ed. by Major General Z. S. Osipov (Moscow, 1960), p. 12.
[45] Marshal P. Rotmistrov, *Krasnaya zvezda*, January 30, 1963.

who have seen service in World War II, retain a nostalgic and romantic attitude toward service, duty, and the "beauty" of the military profession, the younger officers and soldiers frequently spurn such views, at times arguing that "there can be no beauty [of profession] where . . . people are training to kill others"; "while the officer profession is necessary at present, it is uninteresting and unromantic"; and "any civilian profession is better than the military."[46]

Another instance of this anti-militaristic trend among the young is reflected in a withering remark to a young man contemplating a military career: "Don't be a fool, Igor; only failures put on a gray overcoat voluntarily, and you are a bright boy."[47] Or in the vehement rejection of a military profession by another one: "Where can there be beauty? In the daily routine where everything is figured out to the last minute? Or in the days which all seem alike? To see in them the beauty of life means to be a limited person."[48]

The pacifistic and anti-military trends among the young have caused profound concern in the military and in the party. *Komsomolskaya pravda*, the daily newspaper for the youth, printed several anti-military articles and was subsequently rebuked severely for describing a typical Soviet officer as "a veritable horror, an aberration, a spiritual Quasimodo" and for presenting "this monstrosity, without concern to the public."[49] Defense Minister Malinovsky showed his alarm by blaming Soviet writers and artists for "mistaken tendencies in representing the last war" and for introducing "motifs of pacifism" and an "abstract rejection of war into Soviet arts, literature and the movies."[50] General Yepishev, head of the political control system in the military, sharply criticized writers and artists for the same reasons and urged them to "teach youth to be brave and courageous, steadfast and firm."[51]

MUSCOVITES AND STALINGRADERS

The political uses of history, or more properly, historical writings, play an important role in military as well as in party life. Two key battles of World War II, the battles of Moscow and Stalingrad, have become a source of bitter disputes between several powerful factions or subgroups in the military.[52] These running feuds seek in part to set the

---

[46] *Ibid.*, January 13, 1963.   [47] *Ibid.*, August 26, 1962.
[48] *Ibid.*, December 26, 1962.   [49] *Ibid.*, January 29, 1961.
[50] *Ibid.*, February 9, 1964.   [51] *Kommunist*, No. 5 (March 1964), p. 73.
[52] For extensive discussion, see "The Dialogue on Historical Roles" in Kolkowicz, *The Soviet Military*, pp. 174-219.

historical record straight and to make claims for larger shares in the military glory of the participants. Their main purpose, however, is to serve as a vehicle for making demands and criticisms concerning current problems of policy, influence, and status. Historical dialogues are properly suited for such policy debates, as the party demands that open disagreements on vital issues be transmitted through esoteric, indirect, and politically "neutral" media. In order to maintain the fiction of a harmonious society and avoid posing direct challenges, the participants in the historical discussions abide by this etiquette.

In these debates, the battles of Moscow and Stalingrad have taken on a symbolic meaning greater than their actual significance. Those who claim that the battle of Moscow was the major, decisive operation in the initial stages of the war tended to be followers of Marshal Zhukov. Those who claim that the decisive battle of World War II was Stalingrad were adherents of Khrushchev and the Stalingrad group. These two battles have been a bone of contention between the Zhukovites and the Khrushchevites in the military and have been exploited by each for political purposes. For the Zhukovites (those generals and marshals who resented the growing influence of the Stalingrad group members who were loyal to the party leadership in general, and to Khrushchev in particular) these continued arguments served several purposes: to denigrate Khrushchev's claims to military genius and management capabilities; to criticize his strategic policies; to reject and resist civilian intrusion into the properly military domains of the officer corps; and finally, to undermine the prestige, influence, and authority of members of the Stalingrad group in the military establishment. After the ouster of Khrushchev, the Zhukovites obtained major concessions from the new political leadership and as a result the historical feud abated.

Dealing with the Environment: Case Studies

In this section we shall briefly describe three case studies in order to discern how the military deals with challenges and threats from its environment. In describing these cases we shall emphasize some of the basic interests of the military establishment which have come into conflict with the party and the government: the military role in developing strategic and foreign policy; the military's share in the government's budgetary and resource allocation policies; and the role of the party's control organs within the officer corps. Each of the case studies centers on a crisis situation in the Soviet Union: two of the cases involve a change of leadership in the party and government; the third deals with a critical situation brought about by a sweeping change in strategic and economic policies which deeply affected the military establishment. In examining these developments we shall be guided by the following queries: what were the issues involved and how did they affect the military's interests? What resources and tactics did the military employ to influence the party's and government's decision? How was the conflict of interests resolved?

THE MALENKOV PROGRAMS

After Stalin's death several would-be successors to his position entered a tense and unstable coalition. The spokesmen of several powerful institutions—the security organs, the party *apparat*, the governmental and managerial bureaucracies and the military—maneuvered for place in the struggle for power. The fall of Beria removed the security organs from the running. Of the remaining three only the party *apparat* and the governmental bureaucracies, with Khrushchev and Malenkov as their respective spokesmen, continued an intense competition for control of full power over the state.[53] The military, long conditioned by Stalin to remain apolitical and neutral in the inner affairs of the party, were quiescent. Moreover, neither Khrushchev nor Malenkov could be regarded as a strong friend of the military's basic interests. However, this indecisiveness soon gave way to commitment as the military began to realize that Malenkov's political and economic programs were threatening their basic interests. Those programs were premised on a desire for a détente with the West and on a rejection of the political utility of nuclear war. In 1953 Malenkov asserted that "the international situation at present is characterized first and foremost by the great success achieved by the Soviet Union . . . in easing international tensions"; he suggested that a thermonuclear war would result in a "new world slaughter . . . and would mean the destruction of world civilization." He also stressed that "our main task [is to] ensure the further improvement in the material well-being of . . . all Soviet people."[54] In fact his budgetary proposals clearly reflected his détentist and consumer-oriented policy leanings. Whereas Stalin's last announced defense budget (1952) had amounted to 113.8 billion rubles, Malenkov's budget fell to 100.2

[53] For a useful analysis see R. Conquest, *Power and Policy in the U.S.S.R.* (London, 1961), pp. 195-263.
[54] *Pravda*, August 9, 1953.

154

billion rubles. Moreover, he decided to use state reserve funds (generally reserved for war emergencies) in order to accelerate consumer programs.[55]

There is little doubt that the Malenkov programs posed a profound challenge to the military's interests and aspirations. Having endured Stalin's highhanded and frequently misguided policies and instructions for the defense establishment, they hoped for a larger role in setting their house in order and for larger allocations to some badly neglected sectors of the armed forces. The most reasonable strategy for the military to follow, in the face of these dire consequences, was to align with Khrushchev, and thereby force Malenkov out of office. This was indeed the course on which the military embarked during 1954 and 1955. Having clearly stated its position in the authoritative organ of the General Staff, "heavy industry is the foundation of foundations of our socialist economy,"[56] the military mounted a public and private campaign aimed at the ouster of Malenkov. The crisis came to a head in the winter of 1954-1955 when secret debates were taking place in the Central Committee on the subject of the 1955 state budget. Numerous prominent military figures exerted pressure on the proceedings by means of speeches and occasional interviews and articles which uniformly stressed the dangerous international environment and the need for heightened vigilance and economic sacrifices in order to increase Soviet defense capabilities.[57]

Under the collective pressure from the Khrushchevite and other factions in the party and from the military, Malenkov caved in and formally resigned in February 1955. The price of the military's support to Khrushchev was impressive. The day after Malenkov's "resignation" Marshal Zhukov, the arch-opponent of Malenkov's programs, received the post of Minister of Defense. Marshal Bulganin, a "political general," became Prime Minister. Eleven generals were promoted to the prestigious rank of Marshal of the Soviet Union. Numerous delayed promotions were rapidly bestowed on various loyal generals. Stalinist strategic doctrines, which were bitterly resented by the majority of the military, were publicly debated and criticized and eventually rejected. Political controls in the officer corps were reduced to insignificance, and the authority of the political functionaries was confined to morale-build-

[55] See Kolkowicz, *The Soviet Military*, pp. 112-113.
[56] Colonel I. N. Nenakhov, in *Voennaya mysl*, No. 10 (October 1953), p. 8.
[57] For various statements by Marshals Bulganin, Konev, Zhukov, Sokolovsky, and others, see Kolkowicz, *The Soviet Military*, p. 110.

155

ing and educational activities. These major gains, in the next few years, caused mounting concern in the party *apparat*. Khrushchev finally recognized the dangers of an overbearing and politically active officers corps and sought to reverse the process, as we shall see in the next two sections.

THE REFORMS OF 1958-1959

Between 1954 and 1957 the military was twice placed in the position of coming to the aid of the First Secretary of the party, Khrushchev. In 1954-1955 the result was the ouster of the Prime Minister Malenkov, and in 1957 the effect was the political demise of Khrushchev's enemies among the so-called "anti-party group." Having reached a position of unchallenged authority in 1957, Khrushchev realized that his allies in the military had assumed an unprecedented political role and that their appetites and claims were beginning to show a dangerous intensity. He therefore set about curbing the military, seeking to reduce it to a subordinate and malleable instrument of the party *apparat*.

The October 1957 plenum of the Central Committee has been presented by Soviet leaders and publicists as proof and symbol of the party's ability to crush any Bonapartist trends in the military. In the words of a prominent party writer, the plenum indicated "the logic of the basic party moral: anyone who attempts to oppose the party, to take over its functions, loses its trust no matter what the achievements of such an individual."[58] The impact of that meeting cannot be overestimated. Indeed, the plenum achieved more than merely the removal of Marshal Zhukov from office. It became a point of departure for a program of far-reaching reforms designed to integrate the military with other social institutions, to reestablish party dominance at all levels, and thus to prevent the emergence of another Zhukov.[59]

The charges against Zhukov and his "line" were initially made by Presidium member Suslov, the party's chief ideologue, at the meeting of the Central Committee. He stressed the fact that "we were dealing in this case not with isolated mistakes but with a system of mistakes . . . that was leading to a dangerous isolation of the armed forces from

[58] Yuri Petrov, *KPSS—rukovoditel i vospitatel Krasnoi Armii (1918-1920 gg.)* (Moscow, 1961), p. 464.

[59] For details, see Kolkowicz, *The Soviet Military*, pp. 220-281. The statutes which were to implement the broad directives of the October plenum included: *The Statute on Military Councils*, April 1958; *Statute on the MPA*, April 1958; *Statute on the Political Organs in the Soviet Army and Navy*, October 1958.

the party" and, more important, "was tending to keep the Central Committee out of the decision-making on crucial matters affecting the affairs of the army and navy."[60] This indictment against Zhukov was explained further, at the Twenty-second Congress, by the Head of the Main Political Administration (MPA) in the armed forces, Marshal Golikov, who described in some detail the "Bonapartist" policy followed by the ex-Minister of Defense and depicted the 1955-1957 period as one of "growing drift toward unlimited authority in the army and the country."[61]

After a "cooling-off" period following the October plenum, the Central Committee began the implementary work on the reforms. Their specific objectives were as follows:

(1) To break down the barriers between the ranks; to engage actively the professionally less-committed and malleable *Komsomol* in various party-related tasks in the military; to inhibit elitist tendencies in the officer corps by reducing their disciplinary powers.

(2) To limit severely the commanders' full authority within their commands by lodging much of that authority in the party organizations within the units. This change offered the commanders a carrot-and-stick alternative. Commanders who were party members automatically became heads of the party organizations within their units and directed their activities. Those who were not in the party, or who refrained from taking an active role in party affairs, lost much of their command authority, and "came to learn very well from their experience, that [they were] simply unable to carry out their assigned duties."[62] This innovation forced even the commander who was an active party member to derive his authority less from his military rank than from his position as head of the party organization in his command.

(3) To strengthen the party's channels of access to the inner structures of the military establishment; to improve its controls and authority by enhancing the role and influence of the MPA.

[60] XXII *Syezd Kommunisticheskoi Partii Sovetskovo Soyuza, stenog. otchyot* (Moscow, 1962), III, 67.

[61] *Ibid.*

[62] This admission of the effects of the *Changes in the instructions to the Party Organizations in the Soviet Army and Navy* (Paragraph 2), April 1958, was made during a tense period in party-military relations in the summer of 1962. The author was a general of the Guards, Kh. Ambaryan, in an article pointedly titled "Full Commanding Authority—The Most Important Principle in Developing the Armed Forces," *Voenny vestnik*, No. 8 (August 1962), pp. 12-15.

(4) To integrate the military units more closely with the civilian party organizations and with "cultural" and civic organizations, seeking thereby to prevent a "closure" of the military.

(5) To assert firmly the party's authority to define military theory, doctrine, and strategy by assigning most of these functions to the Central Committee and the Presidium.

The general impact of the statutes and regulations on the officer corps was profound. Military commanders became very dependent on the political functionaries in their own units, and *yedinonachaliye* (one-man leadership), the central objective of the officer corps, became a meaningless fiction. The political organs actively pressed for an intensification of *kritika/samokritika* which was "no longer limited to the sphere of party work but was also applied to the military sphere," and commanders "began to reorganize their activities, to listen to the voices of those under their command, to consult with them, and to show concern for them."[63]

The first stirrings of the military's resistance to the reforms and the accompanying coercion appeared late in the spring of 1958. During the summer the military press began to reflect the widening rift between commanders and the political organs. Reports of a serious deterioration of discipline and morale in the military and of rude and arrogant treatment of commanders by their political assistants led *Krasnaya zvezda* to conclude that "all these facts indicate that the problem of strengthening commanders' full authority . . . demands urgent attention."[64]

It gradually became apparent that the military's method of dealing with the threats to their prerogatives, careers, professional interests, and values was to encourage an erosion of discipline, efficiency, and morale which seriously threatened the viability of the forces, and which would render the military incapable of dealing with the influx of modern weapons and equipment into the armed forces or with the contingency of a nuclear war.[65] The military especially resented one of the reform measures, namely, a massive attempt by the political organs to replace commanders with political functionaries at every opportunity and under any pretext.[66] The unfortunate effects of these arbitrary sub-

[63] Marshal Grechko, in *K novomu podyomu*, p. 35.

[64] *Krasnaya zvezda*, August 9, 1958.

[65] For a fuller analysis see Kolkowicz, *The Soviet Military*, pp. 135-150.

[66] For statistics on such replacements (amounting at times to 43 percent of commanding personnel) and on the resistance by officer personnel, see the report

stitutions, especially in combination with the general decline of morale and discipline, motivatived Defense Minister Malinovsky to warn the political organs that the proper way of introducing the reforms was "not by replacing . . . commanders, just because you have presumably more experience." He also told them that "If you interfere with the commander's work, if you go over his head, the result will be destructive and will end in disorder, and where there is disorder, there is conflict, struggle and catastrophe."[67] He demanded that the commanders be given greater authority to carry out their duties and that the political organs curtail their excessive activities.

Encouraged and presumably supported by most ranking military personalities, middle-level commanders unleashed their own anti-reform campaign in print. The main theme of their counterattack was as follows: modern warfare will be a dynamic and complex process and will require complex technical equipment and weapons; both large and small units will presumably be separated from the main forces and headquarters, so that commanding officers will have to conduct their own operation independently. Given these changed conditions commanders must possess broad authority; they must be self-reliant and permitted to take risks on their own. To allow him enough time to practice his craft and improve his training, the officer must be freed from the burden of constant party requirements. He must be spared the harassment of political organs, who challenge his authority in front of his subordinates, and who arbitrarily interfere with his plans and programs which they supplant with their own *ad hoc* and irrelevant solutions.

The military's strong resistance to the reforms was substantially aided by the fact that the party and the government were at the time attempting to modernize and reequip the armed forces. Moreover, the excesses of the political organs in the military severely disturbed even the loyal pro-Khrushchev members of the High Command whose concerns with the long-range effects of such a coercive campaign undoubtedly were related to memories of the Stalinist excesses in the 1930's, which led to a near collapse of the Red Army. In any case, by the end of 1958, and especially early 1959, it became clear that a compromise solution was going to be attempted. The compromise formula seems to have

---

of the Head of the Cadres Department in the MPA, L. Vakhrushev, in *Kommunist vooruzhonnykh sil*, No. 23 (December 1962), p. 27.

[67] *Krasnaya zvezda*, November 1, 1958.

been based on a mutual agreement to curtail the most extreme demands of both the military and the party. Under the advice and tacit pressure from his military associates from the Stalingrad group, Khrushchev weakened his thrust into the private domains of the military establishment and limited the political organs' freedom to manipulate the officer corps. The military, in its turn, agreed to a removal of the Zhukovites remaining in their midst. A collectivist approach and method were agreed upon: the wide authority of the political organs was to be transferred, to a substantial extent, to collective bodies within the military. Political sections and departments at various levels of the military hierarchy were to be transformed into party committees, which presumably were less objectionable to the military. At the same time, practical control over these collective bodies was retained by higher level functionaries from the MPA. The frictions and tensions between the military and the party abated during 1959 and major attention was focused on the adaptation of the new military technology that was by then pervading the armed forces. The party, however, did not give up its efforts to eviscerate the officer corps and to deprive it of its prerogatives and authority. As it turned out, Khrushchev had merely delayed this effort until a more propitious occasion and had already begun laying the groundwork for the next stage of reforms, which were to emerge the following year.

THE STRATEGIC REFORMS OF 1960-1962

On January 14, 1960, at the Fourth Session of the Supreme Soviet of the USSR, Khrushchev announced a series of measures of profound importance to Soviet foreign and domestic policies, and of specific importance to the defense establishment. The central thrust of Khrushchev's statement, which in many ways recalled Malenkov's programs of 1953-1954, was that "the general trend is toward reduction of tension in international relations," and "under present conditions war is no longer completely inevitable." Having asserted that "reduction of the numerical strength of the army will not prevent us from maintaining the country's defense capabilities at the necessary levels," he announced a proposed reduction of the military by 1.2 million men (from 3,623,-000 to 2,423,000), including a cut of 250,000 officers. Khrushchev argued that the greater role of the strategic missile forces and the generally changed dynamics of warfare would minimize the role of conventional forces as the defense of the country "is determined not by the

THE MILITARY

number of our soldiers under arms . . . but by the total firepower and the means of delivery available." He further stated that the savings from such reductions of armed forces would amount "to about 16 to 17 billion rubles per year" and that this represented "a large additional amount for the fulfillment and overfulfillment of our economic plans."[68]

The new defense policies of Khrushchev had a shock effect on the military establishment. They not only threatened careers, vested interests, "institutional empires," but also caused serious concerns among strategists in the High Command and among Khrushchev's most trusted associates in the military, who viewed this "all-or-nothing" massive-retaliation type of strategic doctrine as dangerous to Soviet political and military interests. Some of the immediate effects of Khrushchev's new policy were destructive of the military's morale, efficiency, and traditional institutional interests.

The manpower cuts had a most severe impact upon officers in the conventional forces. The release of a quarter of a million officers caused deep resentment because it cast out into an unfriendly social environment a large number of professional men who had become used to a relatively good standard of living, high social status, and a sense of professional and economic security.[69] As civilians most of these people faced a bleak future in which it would be difficult to earn a livelihood and support their families in an environment that had little need for their craft. Demobilization meant wholesale demotion from a privileged social group to the lowest levels of workers and *kolkhozniks*. The plight of the demobilized officers caused serious concerns in the higher levels of the military hierarchy and was reflected in the Defense Minister's statement that "the demobilization of more than 250,000 officers will be accompanied by various difficulties." He urged these officers "not to be discouraged because of the necessity to change profession or because one has to leave the armed forces without having served the necessary period to be eligible for a pension."[70] He gave little comfort, however, in citing statistics which indicated that only 35 percent of officers released from service in recent years had found

[68] *Pravda*, January 15, 1960.

[69] An extensive research analysis of problems connected with the early retirement of officers in communist armed forces found that "the officer's transfer into the reserves and the return to the social group from which he entered the military was viewed by many of those interviewed as a social degradation." *Studia Sociologiczno-Polityczne* (in Polish), No. 14 (1963), p. 31.

[70] *Krasnaya zvezda*, January 20, 1960.

work comparable to their previous military positions, whereas the rest had had to take jobs as ordinary workers.

The second blow to the military's interests was Khrushchev's massive degradation of the most powerful and "traditional" sector of the Soviet armed forces—the conventional forces. Most of the 1.2 million reduction was to come from the Ground Forces, surface navy, Tactical Air Forces, and various support services. These were the oldest, most entrenched, tradition-bound branches of the military. Khrushchev's decision to reduce this vast institutional empire not only destroyed careers and vested interests, but also threatened the morale and the *esprit de corps* of these sectors. Moreover, such a wholesale reduction of conventional forces, paralleled by an increase in size, role, and influence of the newer branches of the military (the Strategic Missile Forces, the subsurface navy, and the Air Defense Forces), caused widespread concern as to the mobility and responsiveness of the Soviet defense establishment.

Although Khrushchev presumably anticipated only limited resistance from the military, he did not leave events to mere chance. After his formal and public statements on the new policy the party *apparat* moved into action through a multipronged effort to overwhelm any potential resistance from the officer corps. Political controls and general interference in the military were greatly intensified. The reduction of a quarter of a million officers provided an opportunity for a "cold purge" of undesirable elements. The party-controlled media launched a vast campaign of intimidation, hammering away on the single theme that the party was the ultimate authority in the military and that the commanders' authority, from the lowest ranks to the highest, was at the pleasure and mercy of the party organs. In May 1960 Khrushchev appointed 450 new generals, many of them younger men presumably more loyal to him than the hundreds of generals being released from the military. Finally he convened, for the first time since the critical postpurge days of 1938, a vast All Army Conference of Party Secretaries, who were given firm directives on how to implement the reforms and on how to deal with potential resistance.

Despite these massive countermeasures, or more properly, "prophylactic" actions, the military began a campaign to withstand the radical policies of Khrushchev and to halt and reverse some of the implementation already underway. Most military people recognized Khrushchev's policies toward the armed forces as a major threat to many of their traditional prerogatives, interests, and values. With each new regulation, statute, or policy statement, it became clearer that the party leaders envisaged ultimately a severely truncated military organization, shot through with an effective network of political controls and divided between the strategic forces, to be given preferential treatment, and the conventional forces, to perform a greatly reduced role. This vision included an officer corps divested of meaningful professional authority, in which commanders were essentially *primi inter pares* in their own commands, dependent on collective bodies and subject to harassment from the *Komsomol* at the bottom, the MPA and the political departments at the top, and civilian *apparatchiki* on the outside.[71]

At first, there was little that the broad sectors of the officer corps could do to resist the assault. Khrushchev still had the support of the top layer of the military establishment, consisting mostly of trusted associates from the Stalingrad group, and thus felt free to coerce the middle and lower echelons, whose officers had few spokesmen at the highest party levels. Nor did they have any protectors within the military establishment against the pressures from the MPA and the political organs. Moreover, deliberate inequality in the assignment of priorities and roles to the various branches of the military created an internal dissension that prevented a single "military" viewpoint from crystallizing. By 1961, however, Khrushchev's military policies began to affect strongly the upper layers of the officer corps as well as the middle and lower ones. This development provided a common bond of disaffection throughout the military and placed them in a better position to begin counteraction.

[71] The extent of dissatisfaction among highest military leaders, is reflected in numerous public statements. See, for example, Marshal Krylov's attack on Khrushchev's reform plans. Stating that "Lenin taught us that military affairs, more than anything else demand strictest unity of action . . . the subordination of the wills of thousands to that of one man—the single commander," Krylov warned against the excessive use of *kritika/samokritika* by political functionaries, stating that "it is necessary to use this sharp instrument very skillfully . . . not just for the sake of criticism." He further maintained that *"yedinonachaliye* presupposes full independence of the commander . . . who is able to use his full authority boldly, decisively, without looking back over his shoulder" so that the commanders do not have to "waste a lot of time while making decisions or when giving orders because they are obligated to consult ahead of time literally all their assistants and helpers, and to listen to their opinions and suggestions." *Krasnaya zvezda*, September 27, 1961.

In December 1960, the political organs began to report alarming signs of a growing inertia, deterioration of discipline, and general obstructionism in the military.[72] A month earlier, in November, Khrushchev's strategic doctrine was implicitly criticized by General Krasilnikov.[73] He was joined by other ranking members of the military hierarchy, including the Minister of Defense, Marshal Malinovsky, who, from the forum of the Twenty-second Party Congress, clearly disassociated himself from Khrushchev's monistic views on war and the obsolescence of large, conventional forces: "We also believe that under modern conditions any future war would be waged . . . by mass armies of many millions."[74] It became apparent that substantial numbers among the Soviet High Command were deeply concerned with Khrushchev's strategic doctrine and that they were going to resist it. They presented the following arguments: mass armies, far from becoming obsolete in modern war, were still a vital factor indispensable to victory; investments in heavy industry must be maintained at high levels; monistic theories in the development of concepts of war were dangerous; it was absolutely necessary to have large, modern armies and weapons systems *prior* to the outbreak of war.[75]

In the spring of 1962 Khrushchev ordered the MPA to undertake a sweeping reassessment of the military's resistance and opposition. In March 1962 the MPA reported that it had uncovered "serious deficiencies" in the central apparatus of the Ministry of Defense.[76] These included the throttling of *kritika/samokritika* practices, serious breaches of discipline, and obstruction of the control function of the MPA and party functionaries. In April, the Central Committee, by then deeply concerned with the extent of the military's intransigence, ordered the MPA to call a meeting of the chief political personnel to deal with the problem. The session found the officer corps guilty of grave offenses:

[72] Marshal Golikov, Head of MPA, in *Kommunist vooruzhonnykh sil*, No. 5 (December 1960), pp. 16-25; also Colonels Tarasov and Illin, *ibid.*, pp. 26-32.
[73] "O kharaktere sovremennoi voiny," *Krasnaya zvezda*, November 18, 1960.
[74] *Pravda*, October 25, 1961.
[75] General of the Army V. Kurasov, "Voprosy sovetskoi nauki v proizvedeniakh V. I. Lenina," *Voenno-istorichesky zhurnal*, No. 3 (1961). Similar views were expressed in the important Soviet volume, *Military Strategy*, ed. by Marshal Sokolovskii in 1962. For analysis, see Thomas W. Wolfe, "A First Reaction to the New Soviet Book 'Military Strategy,'" Rand Corp., RM-3495, Santa Monica, Cal., 1963.
[76] *Kommunist vooruzhonnykh sil*, No. 5 (March 1962), pp. 55-57.

officers were said to be "full of deviousness" and insidious loyalty to one another; they were found guilty of covering up for one another; instructors from the MPA were cited as having tried to shield their comrades by preventing party organs from seeing their files.[77]

The degree of military resistance finally persuaded Khrushchev to fire the head of the MPA (Marshal Golikov, a professional officer of good party standing) and replace him in May 1962 with General A. A. Yepishev, a close associate of Khrushchev, with a long career in the security police organs. Yepishev was clearly selected as the man to break the military's resistance once and for all.

In August, Yepishev made public the first findings of his thorough survey of the military establishment.[78] He singled out three targets in his extremely critical report, the apparatus of the Ministry of Defense, the Ground Forces, and the military academies, which were a traditional breeding ground of military professionalism and élan. His report was a wholesale indictment of these three important parts of the military establishment. The personnel of the General Staff and the ministry administrative apparatus were said to ignore directives of the Central Committee. The Ground Forces, the main object of Khrushchev's socio-political and strategic reforms, were found to be a major source of disobedience, bureaucratic obstructionism, and general decline of military efficiency.

This encroachment by the MPA into the private preserves of the military hierarchy aggravated the situation. The officer corps reacted sharply to this challenge. In the subsequent months both the officer corps and the political control organs began to attack each other in the press with growing boldness and intensity.[79] Finally the Central Committee convened a meeting, attended by high level military and Central Committee members, in order to stem the evident alienation between the two institutions. From subsequent sparse public reports it would appear that the impasse was not overcome. The Defense Minister, Malinovsky, published a scathing statement in which he warned the political organs that "we do not need criticism for its own sake, but only that which is principled and helps us strengthen our armed

[77] See a report by the Head of the Party-Organizational Department of the MPA, General A. Bukov, *ibid.*, No. 10 (May 1962), pp. 22-28.

[78] "O rabote partkoma i partiinykh organizatsii shtaba i upravlenii sukhoput-nykh voisk," *ibid.*, No. 15 (August 1962), pp. 38-41.

[79] Kolkowicz, *The Soviet Military*, pp. 266-269.

forces."[80] Yepishev retorted by accusing the internal apparatus of the Defense Ministry of "having remained for years outside of any controls."[81] He also pointedly said that "we think it is very important to explain to the military cadres the essence of *yedinonachaliye* in the Soviet armed forces. . . . It is absolutely necessary that all officers, generals, and admirals clearly understand that the indispensable condition for their retention of commanding authority . . . is the cooperation given to commanders by party and *Komsomol* organizations, their ability to direct their activities. . . ." He further warned the military that the party had some "well-established means for dealing with all negative phenomena, including perversions of commanding authority."[82]

The deteriorating relationship between broad sectors of the officer corps and the political organs was suddenly overshadowed by the Cuban missile crisis of 1962. In its aftermath the party sought to blame the military for the Cuban fiasco, while firmly rejecting implied military criticism of Khrushchev's management of this ill-fated affair. Khrushchev continued to bully his military opposition, firing the chief of the General Staff, Zakharov, and replacing him with a loyal marshal, Biryuzov, haranguing the military for their wasteful expenditures, and seeking to transform national planning policies from a defense-oriented economy toward a consumer-oriented one.[83] As he embarked on a détente policy with the West and a "goulash-communism" policy at home, he alienated many entrenched bureaucrats in the government, and thus it became only a matter of time before Khrushchev, like Malenkov before him, would fall victim to a party-military cabal. In October 1964, Khrushchev was ousted from his various positions in the party and government, and in the months after his removal the military became the most virulent critic of the deposed leader.[84] One might speculate, on the basis of the Malenkov, anti-party group, and Khrushchev affairs, that any political leader who persistently and profoundly threatens some of the military's basic interests invites his own political demise.

[80] *Krasnaya zvezda*, October 25, 1962.
[81] *Ibid.*, December 8, 1962.
[82] *Kommunist vooruzhonnykh sil*, No. 19 (October 1962), p. 9.
[83] See Kolkowicz, *The Soviet Military*, pp. 291-300.
[84] A fuller analysis is to be found in R. Kolkowicz, "Die Position der Sowjetarmee vor und nach dem Sturz Chruschtschows," *Osteuropa*, No. 10 (1966), pp. 671-684.

Conclusions

The burden of this inquiry was to discern whether the Soviet military can be described as an "interest group," and if so, what kind of influence it exerts on society, the government, and the party. The conclusion is that the military may indeed be described as an interest group. It has a distinct identity, self-reinforcing values, a set of mutually shared interests and objectives, and a certain *modus operandi* in dealing with its environment. At the same time, the military is in many ways a unique group or institution. Unlike many other groups, it seeks and usually achieves distance and separateness from the larger society and its problems. It is essentially a guildlike organization, seeking closure from the outside, living by certain orthodox rules and mores, and constantly guarding its privileges and prerogatives. Consequently, as long as its basic needs and interests are satisfied, the military finds it easy to live with any kind of political leadership. It has shown itself to be very loyal to the party and its leadership, rarely questioning their wisdom or their right to exercise full authority over society. Only when the party challenged the military's basic interests and objectives did the latter resist or oppose the party's initiatives.

As we have seen, the military is a complex amalgam of numerous and varied interests, objectives, and parochial attitudes and is not therefore a monolithic and homogeneous institution. Whenever threatened by a challenge to its basic professional and institutional prerogatives and values, it tends to close ranks and to offer a fairly unified response to such a challenge. On the other hand, when such basic interests are not involved, the military community has shown itself to be a veritable battleground of ideas, objectives, and proposals which reflect the relatively recent blossoming of subgroup activities.

A vital question usually raised in connection with a political interest group is the problem of its access to the decision-makers and its ability to rally support on its own behalf. While the military is represented in the Central Committee and in various lesser political bodies in the state, it is very difficult to speak with assurance about the actual ways and means used by the military to secure access to the political decision-makers. One might speculate that this occurs by invitation or cooptation, rather than by pressure from below. As we have observed, the military achieved its highest levels of political influence during periods

ROMAN KOLKOWICZ

of profound internal crisis in the party, when one of the warring factions
sought military support in order to defeat another faction. Once the
party healed its internal strife the military found itself without too much
influence and open to retaliation from the party. Yet its numerical representation in the Central Committee reached greatest strength during
periods of distinct political inferiority.[85]

What influence may the military have on the evolving Soviet society?
Potentially the military might serve as a major vehicle for change, since
it has a monopoly of the means of violence which, under certain circumstances, could upset the internal political balance. Moreover some
of the military's institutional interests might have a modernizing and
liberalizing effect. The military, it may be speculated, opposes police-
state controls and presses for a greater autonomy of managerial, professional, scientific, and functional groups and a wider dispersal of state
authority. Some of the younger and more highly skilled elements in the
officer corps stress a new form of functional and social pragmatism
which rejects ideological intrusion and determinism.[86]

The military, however, seems unlikely to undertake a progressive
role. It is essentially an institution of conservative members who prefer
the *status quo* and firm governmental rule of an orderly society. A community of guildlike professionals, the officers, it may be assumed, view
radical social, cultural, economic, and ideological positions—sometimes
defended by other groups—as undesirable and alien to their own moral
code. In this respect their views are similar to those of the more conservative party functionaries. The military also embodies an acute sense
of nationalism, fostering patriotic attitudes in its members and seeking
to engender such values in the populace. Moreover, in seeking to further
its basic institutional interests, the military interferes with and opposes
various modernizing and liberalizing trends in the country. The officer

[85] *Party Congress*

	Total CC Membership	Total Military Membership	Percentage of Total
Sixteenth (1930)	137	5	3.5
Seventeenth (1934)	139	8	6.0
Eighteenth (1939)	139	15	10.7
Nineteenth (1952)	236	26	11.0
Twentieth (1956)	255	20	7.8
Twenty-second (1961)	330	31	9.5
Twenty-third (1966)	360	32	8.9

(From Kolkowicz, *The Soviet Military*, p. 331.)

[86] Kolkowicz, "The Impact of Modern Technology," pp. 148-168.

168

corps generally prefers a social planning policy which subordinates consumer interests to defense needs, urging large allocations to heavy industry.

Unlike the intelligentsia, youthful dissenters, some managers, ethnic groups, and others with particular interests in various kinds of change, the military does not normally seek change, nor does it evoke any camaraderie or trust from other groupings. If anything, it is looked upon as a consumer of badly needed resources, as a blind instrument of the various regimes, as a residue of orthodoxy and of blind adherence to party dictates. The military is also seen as the institution which has most to gain from a deteriorating international environment, and possibly as the one which seeks to prevent the relaxation of international tensions. Consequently, the military has a limited national "constituency," except perhaps in certain quarters in the party and in those managerial circles concerned with defense-oriented industries. Only as a protector of the country from external threats does the military gain support and respect from society. But such heroic and historical roles are rather quickly forgotten in the long inter-war periods when society's interests turn toward economic, social, cultural, and private pursuits. In sum, the military differs profoundly from those interest groups in Soviet society whose particularistic interests are also the larger objectives of people who seek long-postponed changes in the social, political, and philosophical realities of an authoritarian system.

CHAPTER VI ~ BY JOHN P. HARDT AND
THEODORE FRANKEL

The Industrial Managers

THE SOVIET industrial managerial group is large, currently numbering over 100,000. For several reasons this group of industrial enterprise managers continues to be more homogeneous in training, performance, and behavior than the more extensive group of Soviet managers and planners as a whole. But whereas there has been considerable continuity in the characteristics and group identification of those industrial managers who came onto the scene during the Stalin era, in recent years a Soviet version of the entrepreneur with a more sophisticated knowledge of management science has become increasingly important. The simple and overriding gross output criterion has been progressively replaced by multiple criteria, including sales and profit.

During the course of Stalinist rule a professional management group was built up whose degree of autonomy was related to its political reliability. The Stalinist model of economic planning and management shaped a class of production-engineer managers well suited to the narrowly defined goals of forced industrialization.[1] The establishment of the professional Stalinist manager has not, however, met the requirements of management in the post-Stalin economic system. The new manager required is more of a demand-oriented businessman and less of a supply-oriented production engineer. The emerging comprehensive, optimal approach to planning is responsive to the needs of improved economic

[1] There are a number of studies available on the Soviet manager which focus primarily on the Stalinist period. Our approach deals with this period as a base for relating the managerial group to changing Soviet society and thus differs from that of the many useful studies available. See Joseph Berliner, *Factory and Manager in the USSR* (Cambridge, Mass., 1957); David Granick, *Management of the Industrial Firm in the USSR* (New York, 1955); Jeremy R. Azrael, *Managerial Power and Soviet Politics* (Cambridge, Mass., 1966); Barry M. Richman, *Soviet Management: With Significant American Comparisons* (Englewood Cliffs, 1965); Barry M. Richman, *Management Development and Education in the Soviet Union* (East Lansing, 1967).

171

efficiency that also generate pressures for a new system of economic management. However, it is likely that the implementation of an optimal planning system for the economy as a whole will have to precede changes in management, if only because the professional economists and statisticians appear to be available to staff the transition, while a comparable supply of appropriately trained professional managers for managerial reform does not appear available. The complex and time-consuming task of creating a new class of businessmen-managers to replace the entrenched production-engineer managers is proceeding very slowly. The increasing divergence which results between the characteristics of the existing managerial and the required managerial group may be a central source of conflict within the Soviet management group as a whole. A proper response to the new requirements of the economy may necessitate both a very large educational effort in management science and the replacement of the majority of the current managerial cadres.

Other issues are emerging between the managers and other large groups such as the top party leadership, the party apparatus, the military, the security forces, etc. Unsatisfactory economic performance accounts for the persistence and general acceptance of a need for planning and management reform. All groups would share in the advantages of improved economic performance if the management group were modernized or appropriately professionalized. At the same time, professionalization of managerial or other groups resulting in possibly improved efficiency needs to be weighed against a diminution in direct party control and a reduction in the influence of governmental organs including the security and police groups, whose *raison d'être* is to carry out party control. Moreover, the changes apparently required in the managerial group seem to be so extensive as to put in question the ability of many senior managers, who are also members of the party elite, to survive as active members of the group. Whereas the parochial production-oriented professionalism of the Stalinist period generated little group conflict with other institutions, the new professionalism cuts across institutional lines—a fact which impedes its acceptance. Similarly, those features of the economic reform that aim at reducing party control do not produce guaranteed results in improved economic performance, especially in the short-run.

Despite what may be interpreted as significant changes or the beginning of significant changes in the Soviet managerial group since Stalin, a case can still be made from available empirical evidence that only a modification of the Stalinist approach to planning and management has occurred. Thus, modest changes to date could be viewed as reversible and indirect in their impact on the managerial group in terms of its enduring character and relationship to other elite groups. In our view, however, although minor reversals may occur, the trend of change in the managerial group is not likely to be turned back—not as long as the pressures for improved economic performance continue, and particularly if these pressures heighten.

In spite of many changes in personnel and in the characteristics of the managerial group as a whole, the core of managerial cadres in industry appears to represent a group with common interests and identification. Although not having direct channels of access to the top leadership, as a group they have usually had elite representation. Moreover, in the post-Stalin period the core group has begun to represent a broader, larger group of managers and planners.

Conflict within the managerial group may well build up to a point where much more rapid and sudden alteration in management is likely if the pace of Soviet social change is not accelerated. Moreover, among the institutional groups influencing Soviet policy, the managers and the economists, as interest groups, may represent forces of institutional change, as contrasted with groups such as the military and the police which stand for the *status quo*. Hence in the broader context of conflict and change, the managerial group may in future prove to be a significant factor in Soviet political development. Accordingly, our approach in the pages that follow is to appraise conflict within the Soviet management group as a whole and between the managers and other institutional groups in the Soviet elite. In this, reference will first be made to the Stalinist manager and then to the changing role of the industrial manager since 1953.

The Stalinist Model of Economic Planning and Management

Management in the USSR is not conducted *in vacuo*, but in the context of the economic planning process. It is primarily through the plan that priorities for resource allocation are set and criteria for performance are established. The manager receives his guidance concerning the top leadership's economic decisions through the plan. To this extent then the economic planning process developed during the period of Joseph

173

Stalin's power had a pattern and an internal rationale. It is conventionally referred to as the Stalinist model.

To plan in the Stalinist context meant, in effect, to mobilize and concentrate all the resources in the society for the purpose of *maximizing* one primary set of economic goals. This was not in any conventional sense comprehensive planning of the production and distribution processes throughout the economy but rather a form of selective, controlled mobilization of certain key products that may be described in the following fashion:

> In implementing the Stalinist economic model Soviet planners have acted "as if" the maximization of output of only *one* sector of the economy—heavy industry—were important. They have acted "as if" the interest of the other sectors could be safely ignored or held constant (*ceteris paribus*) while heavy industrial output was expanded as rapidly as possible. And finally, they have acted "as if" production of the other sectors was of value only insofar as it provided additional increments of materials, labor, and capital for the expansion of the heavy industrial sector. These "as ifs" gave the Soviet planner a set of simple imperatives in planning resource allocation:
>
> *First,* allocate to the military establishment the resources (labor, materials, capital) needed to fulfill strategic requirements. Also, lay aside the minimum amounts of resources needed for consumption and the preservation and necessary growth of the infrastructure.
>
> *Second,* maximize the flow of resources into the heavy industrial sector. Then specify how resources are to be combined to maximize output. (The Soviet planner assumed that fixed, functional relationships held between units of steel, energy, and machine equivalents. A simple application of these production functions helped him determine the crude end-product mix, as well as proportions between factors and production. These production functions changed little over time.)
>
> *Third,* distribute residuals of unrequired or unsuitable resources among other sectors such as agriculture and light industry.[2]

[2] John P. Hardt and Carl Modig, "The Industrialization of Soviet Russia in the First Half Century," in Kurt L. London (ed.), *The Soviet Union: A Half-Century of Communism* (Baltimore, 1968), pp. 295-326.

The application of this plan involved primarily the systematic expansion of the priority industrial sectors through a detailed control and allocation mechanism. Administratively centralized day-to-day management was possible as it only had to be applied within the selected priority sectors. Moreover, during the early stage of industrial development of the Soviet Union in the twenties and thirties, the primary goal was the establishment of a coal, steel, and simple machine-building base, and for that purpose the political leadership could employ a simple physical output criterion of performance for administering management.[3] The characteristics and attitudes of the managerial group during the Stalinist period, discussed below, were consistent with these planning and management criteria.

The operational center of the industrial group directing the Soviet economic planning and management system under Stalin was the director of the industrial enterprise or *predpriyatiye*. Although loosely representative of a much more extensive group of managers and planners, the industrial group itself was large in number; under Stalin, tens of thousands, and in recent years, over 100,000.[4] This central management group grew increasingly homogeneous in training, performance, and behavior in the Stalinist period. Detailed plans were formulated and published in many other areas, but these were described by Soviet and Western economists alike as "buffer sectors" or areas in which planning was less consistent in formulation, implementation, and control.[5] Success was well rewarded in the industrial enterprise (and more particularly so in heavy industry), while failure was severely punished. The use of criminal law to control and enforce the management system reached its extremity with the development of the forced labor camp system in the late thirties.

Specifically, the terms "industrial enterprise directors" or "industrial managers" used in this chapter correspond to the Soviet term "directors, leaders, and managers of enterprises," as used in the 1959 Census, which apparently covers the managers of all Soviet enterprises in heavy and light industry. It does not cover the 120,000 managers of enterprises in

[3] John P. Hardt, "Soviet Economic Development and Policy Alternatives," in Vladimir G. Treml (ed.), *The Development of the Soviet Economy: Plan and Performance* (New York, 1968), pp. 1-23.

[4] See n. 6, below.

[5] See John P. Hardt, Dimitri M. Gallik, and Vladimir G. Treml, "Institutional Stagnation and Changing Soviet Strategy," in Joint Economic Committee, Congress of the United States, *New Directions of the Soviet Economy* (Washington, D.C., 1966), pp. 19-62.

construction, transportation, and forestry nor the more than 1,200,000 managers in trade, public dining, supply, housing, communal economy, day-to-day services, health, culture, and education.[6] It will be assumed, however, that the group of industrial enterprise directors serves as a reference group (and acts in some ways as a spokesman) for the total group of managers. The 1959 Census lists 128,712 directors, leaders, and managers of enterprises in industry; within this group there is a leading subgroup comprising the directors of the some 43,000 enterprises operating on economic accountability (*khozraschyot*), with the core group constituted by the 11,000 directors of those enterprises which produce 75 percent of Soviet industrial production.[7] Practically all enterprise directors in heavy industry are party members.[8]

While it seems safe to conjecture that the group of industrial enterprise directors is subdivided along branch and regional lines and is further split on such matters as investment and labor resources allocation, there is insufficient evidence to pursue the matter in this essay. For the same reason, the generational conflict, which can be expected to reach a high point within the next decade, will not be treated here.

The Stalinist Manager

During the quarter-century of Stalin's rule, the characteristics that distinguished the group of industrial enterprise managers from other interest groups underwent decisive change. The change resulted from the necessity of harnessing this group, in particular, to the overriding Soviet commitment to speedy industrialization on the Stalinist model. The outstanding features of this adaptation were an explosive growth in numbers; homogenization in terms of political affiliation, education, experience, and, to a lesser extent, social background; and the fostering of an engineering approach to economic management.

To gauge the depth of these changes, it might be desirable to consider briefly the characteristics of the industrial managers for the period 1920-1928, the years of War Communism and the New Economic Policy (NEP). In view of the dearth of hard information on the subject,

[6] Tsentralnoye Statisticheskoye Upravleniye, *Itogi vsesoyuznoi perepisi naselenia 1959 goda, SSSR, Svodny tom* (Moscow, 1962), p. 148 (henceforth *Itogi 1959*).

[7] See *Ekonomicheskaya gazeta*, No. 9 (February 1967), p. 17. Cf. Ya. Kvasha, "Kontsentratsia proizvodstva i melkaya promyshlennost," *Voprosy ekonomiki*, No. 5 (May 1967), pp. 26-31.

[8] V. Zaluzhny, "Ideinost khozyaistvennovo rukovoditelya," *Kommunist*, No. 7 (May 1968), pp. 85-95.

considerable caution must be exercised in making numerical estimates; with this caveat it is estimated that there were about 20,000 industrial managers in 1926.[9] Of these, 5,000 were old Bolsheviks,[10] i.e., Red Directors who had had some experience in industry before the revolution, with the rest consisting of "bourgeois" and Menshevik specialists. This high dependency of the new regime on noncommunists led very speedily to an arrangement under which the nominal manager (the *khozyaistvennik*) was a party member with little technical know-how who was "assisted" by the technical director, frequently a politically unreliable engineer. In terms of social origins, a rather high percentage both of Bolsheviks and non-Bolsheviks was recruited from white-collar families; the social background of a sample group of directors in 1922 showed that one-third were former managers and owners of factories, one-fifth were former office workers, while only one-third were former factory workers. The educational background of the same group was as follows: 13 percent of enterprise directors had higher education, 24 percent had a secondary education, and 63 percent had an elementary education only.[11]

The Stalinist period saw a very rapid change in all these characteristics. The size of the managerial group grew about sixfold, from about 20,000 in 1926 to about 131,000 in 1957,[12] and 128,712 in 1959.[13] The greatest increase took place in the period of rapid industrialization during the first two Five Year Plans from 1928 to 1938-1939; at the

[9] Calculated on the basis that the number of enterprise directors in all categories grew approximately six times from 1926 to 1956. See Alf Edeen, "The Civil Service and its Composition and Status," in Cyril Black (ed.), *The Transformation of Russia* (Cambridge, Mass., 1960). The figure may be a bit high in view of the fact that Tsentralnoye Upravleniye Narodno-Khozyaistvennovo Ucheta SSSR, *Narodnoye khozyaistvo SSSR* (Moscow, 1932), p. 429, gives a 1926 figure of 4,094 Group A enterprises and 4,422 Group B enterprises. However, since these enterprises include only those counted in the census, they probably underestimate the true 1926 figure. If the Soviet figure is more accurate than the estimate given here, the increase in the number of managers would be even steeper than assumed.

[10] Azrael, *op.cit.*, p. 65.

[11] S. N. Prokopovicz, *Russlands Volkswirtschaft unter den Sowjets* (Zurich-New York, 1944), p. 205.

[12] Nicholas De Witt, *Education and Professional Employment in the USSR* (Washington, D.C., 1961), p. 498. It should be noted that De Witt's figure includes directors, chief engineers, and other leading specialists and their deputies. However, the 1959 census figure (see n. 13, below) gives 128,712 directors, leaders, and managers *exclusive* of chief engineers and other leading specialists. It is therefore believed that De Witt's 1957 figure is comparable to the 1959 census figure.

[13] *Itogi 1959*, p. 148.

latter date, the number of enterprise directors stood at about 95,000.[14] The growth from 1939 to 1956 occurred at a considerably lower rate.

The composition of the group was subject to similarly abrupt changes. Beginning with the so-called "Wreckers' Trial of 1928," increasing numbers of Mensheviks and "bourgeois" specialists were purged over the next years; their places were taken by graduates from engineering colleges, the enrollment of which grew precipitously from 16,500 in 1928 to 114,500 in 1932.[15]

These new cadres were not merely better educated than the men whose places they took; they were also politically far more reliable. Although in 1923 only 47 percent of the directors of 264 of the largest enterprises were communists, 93 percent of all enterprise directors were party members in 1929.[16] (Not all of them were, of course, college graduates. A good many were Bolshevik workers promoted from the bench to the administrative staffs, and others were Mensheviks who "had seen the light" and joined the Bolsheviks; but the proportion of the new graduates grew from year to year.) It is not surprising, then, that the regime found it feasible by 1929 to proclaim the replacement of the old troika of enterprise director, party official, and trade-union functionary with the "one-man" leadership of the enterprise manager.

The next major change came with the purge of 1938-1939 among whose special targets were the independent-minded Red Directors who apparently were slow to accept Stalin's sovereignty over the economy.[17] Lazar Kaganovich characterized the thrust of the purge of industry in the following terms: "In 1937 and 1938 the leading personnel of heavy industry were thoroughly renewed . . . in some branches it was found necessary to remove several layers." However, he continued, ". . . we now have cadres who will perform . . . any tasks assigned to them by Comrade Stalin."[18]

[14] *Ibid.* Calculated on the basis of the assumption that the number of enterprise directors in all categories grew by 30 percent from 1939 to 1959. A recent source puts the growth of the larger, but related, group of "leaders of enterprises and of their structural subdivisions" between 1939 and 1959 at 26 percent. See V. S. Semenov, *Klassy, sotsialnye sloi i gruppy v SSSR* (Moscow, 1968), p. 147.
[15] Gregory Bienstock, Solomon M. Schwartz, and Aaron Yugow, *Management in Russian Industry and Agriculture* (Ithaca, 1948), p. 104. See also TsSU, *Kulturnoye stroitelstvo SSSR* (Moscow, 1959), p. 203.
[16] V. Zaluzhny, *op.cit.*, and Prokopovicz, *op.cit.*, p. 204.
[17] Merle Fainsod, *How Russia Is Ruled* (2nd ed., Cambridge, Mass., 1963), p. 506.
[18] *Eighteenth Congress: The Land of Socialism Today and Tomorrow: Reports and Speeches* (Moscow, 1939), p. 392, cited in Azrael, *op.cit.*, p. 100.

By 1941, there was in office a new generation of communist-raised managers, cleansed of "bourgeois" and Menshevik specialists and of the Red Directors, politically reliable and technically trained. The tenure of enterprise directors rose from something like an average duration of three years in the 1930's to as much as ten years by 1953. All in all, the change accommodated the requirement for managers willing to obey without reservations the commands channeled from above.

While size, educational level, and political affiliation of the managerial group changed in direct response to the demands of the Stalinist model of industrialization, the changes in social background followed a more complex pattern. The regime's initial impulse was to replace the great majority of managers having white-collar background with men of more acceptable proletarian background. (Technically social background in Soviet statistics is presented in two major categories: "social position" which refers to the principal type of work previously engaged in, and "social origin" which categorizes the parents' mode of earning a living. Both categories are divided into the subcategories: workers, peasants, and white-collar workers.)

As a result of the purge of the "bourgeois" and Menshevik specialists in 1928 and the promotion of workers from the bench, the background of enterprise directors had by 1936 radically changed in favor of former workers. In terms of "social position," former workers then accounted for two-thirds of all enterprise directors.[19] In terms of social origins, in 1936 roughly one-quarter of enterprise directors was of peasant origin, and the proportion of those of proletarian origin was twice that of directors with white-collar origins (i.e., 50 percent).[20] It seems reasonable to conclude that enterprise directors with proletarian (and peasant) antecedents and with experience at the workbench were clearly being favored.

This trend apparently slowed down considerably after 1938, when it was recognized that the policy was yielding poor results. From this time on, while efforts did not cease to advance proletarians to managerial positions, people with white-collar background were again permitted to take a disproportionate share of managerial positions. Bienstock, Schwartz, and Yugow mention that in the second half of the thirties, promotion of workers directly from the bench into administration almost stopped. The influx of workers and workers' children into collegiate institutions fell off markedly after 1933; thus, while in 1933

[19] Granick, *op.cit.*, pp. 46-47.   [20] *Ibid.*

manual workers and their children accounted for 64.6 percent of students training at higher institutions for industry and transportation, their share in 1938 had dropped to 43.5 percent.[21] By 1938, when the party resumed large-scale recruitment, local organizations made a major effort to enlist the technical intelligentsia, old and new, into their ranks.[22]

While no hard figures exist for 1941-1955, it seems reasonable to accept Granick's conclusion that during this period Soviet industrial managers were upgraded both in "social origin" and "social position." The men occupying directors' positions in this period had been department superintendents in the thirties, at which time 80 percent of their number were graduate engineers and 45 percent had fathers in white-collar occupations.

It is interesting to conjecture as to the reason for this policy reversal and its impact on the managers' group. Granick speculates that the home training of white-collar families makes them more achievement-oriented; if so, the policy reversal of 1938 constitutes a tacit recognition of this phenomenon by the Soviet regime. In equally speculative terms, the implications of the continued predominance of former "bourgeois" elements in the managerial group can be construed—at least in the thirties and forties when the myth of the proletarian was still strong—as meaning that a great many managers were uncertain of, and uneasy about, their status in society and were for that reason particularly eager to conform to Stalin's *diktat*.

In contrast to this speculation must be put the curious fact that the proportion of those with "worker" background was higher for enterprise managers than for either their superior or subordinate groups in management. In terms of "social position," the heads of the ministerial main administrations were—in the late 1930's—two-thirds former white-collar personnel and one-third workers (i.e., the exact opposite of the directors), while 92 percent of the chief engineers were classified as white-collar. Similarly for "social origin": heads of main administrations and chief engineers with white-collar parents were up to three times as numerous as those with worker parents, while for the enterprise directors the relationship was two to one.[23] This relationship apparently persisted for a considerable period of time.

[21] Bienstock *et al.*, *op.cit.*, p. 122.
[22] *Partiinoye stroitelstvo*, December 1, 1938.
[23] *Pravda*, September 7, 1929, cited in Granick, *op.cit.*, p. 47.

The implications of both the relatively low social standing of the enterprise directors in comparison to their supervisors and their subordinates and the lesser degree of social homogeneity are not entirely clear. It may be speculated that the result was a lessened degree of cohesiveness, possibly undermining the group's solidarity.

The overall trend of the educational qualifications of the directors' group showed a sharp drop after 1929 from the already low levels of the 1920's, followed by a rapid rise in the thirties and forties. By 1929, the purge of Menshevik and "bourgeois" specialists had resulted in a situation where 93 percent of all directors were Communist Party members. Of these, a sample showed that only 2.6 percent had a higher education as compared with 13 percent of the 1920 sample mentioned above.[24] However, by 1933, directors of enterprises, their deputies, and subordinates showed 21.5 percent with higher education and 13 percent with secondary education;[25] and by 1939, 27.7 percent of the directors of industrial enterprises had a higher education.[26]

It should be noted, however, that the directors' education was persistently inferior to that of their immediate superiors and subordinates. Thus, in 1933 the percentage of persons with higher education was considerably greater among the directors of superior industrial associations and trusts, as well as among the subordinate department heads, than among enterprise directors. Similarly, during the period 1934-1936, 60-65 percent of the heads of the ministries' main administrations had engineering degrees and up to 90 percent of the enterprises' chief engineers were graduate engineers, as compared to 24-36 percent in the directors' ranks. Among the department superintendents, the proportion with engineering degrees grew from 55 percent to 80 percent, and such men were almost never graduates of the lesser industrial academies.[27] It must also be stressed that throughout the entire period the education of the managers was oriented almost exclusively toward engineering, with very little attention given toward management, trade, or the humanities.

The available data permit only a general comparison on the matter of tenure between the periods before and after the purge of 1938. Not surprisingly, before 1938 the tenure of enterprise directors on the

[24] Report of the Central Committee to the Sixteenth Congress of the CPSU (Moscow, 1931), pp. 187-188.
[25] *Socialist Construction in the Soviet Union, Statistical Handbook* (Moscow, 1935), pp. 513-519.
[26] Zaluzhny, *loc.cit.*   [27] Granick, *op.cit.*, p. 43.

job was short. Despite a 1929 Central Committee directive to keep directors of firms at the same post for longer periods of time, studies in 1934 and 1936 showed that only 3-8 percent of directors had held the same job for over 5 years, 16-20 percent for 3 to 5 years, and another 40-55 percent for 1 to 3 years. Twenty-five to 35 percent had held their jobs for less than 1 year.[28]

These changes exaggerate somewhat the degree of personnel turbulence in the industry as a whole, for 1934 figures show that 25 percent of all directors had worked in their branch for over 10 years, and another 40 percent had worked there from 5 to 10 years. Even so, the turnover of directors was much higher than for either heads of main administrations, 60 percent of whom had been in the branch for over 10 years, or for chief engineers, 48 percent of whom had been in the same branch for the same period of time. All in all, the poorer-educated and lower-class directors seemed to have been in a more exposed situation than other managerial groups.[29]

The outlook for managerial tenure apparently changed drastically after 1938. Azrael has come to the conclusion that ". . . a conservative interpretation of the scattered evidence available suggests that no less and probably considerably more than half of the men who headed Soviet enterprises in 1953 had held the directorship of similar posts for over a decade."[30]

Overall, the characteristics of the managerial group under Stalin's rule changed radically. In the first decade, the number of managers grew rapidly, their political allegiance changed decisively, their background became more heterogeneous with the influx of proletarians, the educational level was significantly raised, and they experienced an exceptional degree of personnel turbulence. The 1938 purges constituted a distinct turning point. Subsequent to that date, the growth in numbers decelerated, the group became more homogeneous in background and education, their political loyalty was undivided, their educational level rose and became ever more narrowly technical, and personnel turbulence declined significantly. Stalin had succeeded in creating a group of managers that suited the requirements of his approach to industrialization.

[28] TsUNKhU, *Sostav rukovodyashchikh rabotnikov i spetsialistov* (Moscow, 1936), pp. 15-17.

[29] Granick, *op.cit.*, p. 47.   [30] Azrael, *op.cit.*, p. 107.

Group Attitudes

Despite the discontinuities in characteristics outlined above, members of the managerial group retained a common set of attitudes. The causes for this continuity may briefly be posited as follows. One, the strict limits imposed by the Stalinist industrial system (public ownership of property, the plan, party supervision, severe labor laws) produced a common set of environmental problems for the managers and directed their reactions into similar patterns. Two, the managers' social position as *nouveaux arrivés* and as creatures of the state, as deviants from the ruling ideal of the proletarian, and as socially and academically inferior to both the higher echelons and subordinates shaped their attitudes along similar lines. Three, the position of the industrial managers, who were simultaneously the key producers of the system and the lowest functionaries of the hierarchical bureaucracy set up common pressures and produced common attempts to relieve them.

Before proceeding to consider the attitudes of the managers, it is perhaps desirable to utter a caveat as to the difficulty of obtaining data on the attitudes of Soviet groups over a period of three decades—particularly those such as the industrial managers who include tens of thousands of people. With this proviso, it may be stated that a number of managerial attitudes were articulated with considerable consistency throughout Stalin's regime.

OPERATIONAL AUTONOMY

One of the most salient attitudes was the demand for greater operational autonomy from ministerial and party interference. As early as 1923, the Old Bolshevik, Leonid Krasin, made himself the spokesman for the managers (and especially the Red Directors) when he criticized "agitators and journalists" high in party councils for "interfering with the recovery of production."[31]

Though vigorously attacked at the Twelfth Party Congress in 1923, this sentiment could not be wholly stilled. Thus, at the beginning of the Five Year Plan (and one year after the Wreckers' Trial) one of the most eminent of the Red Directors, S. P. Birman, asserted that the interests of production required a reduction in industrial control and demanded that no specialists or engineers be removed from their posts

[31] Cf. Adam B. Ulam, *The Bolsheviks* (New York, 1968), p. 577.

without managerial sanction and that the secret police stop equating misjudgment with sabotage.[32] In 1929, Stalin bowed to the demand for managerial autonomy, at least formally, by calling for one-man leadership by the enterprise director. In 1933, enterprise directors were still struggling vigorously for autonomy, as can be deduced from the Commissar of Heavy Industry Ordzhonikidze's puzzlement at the incessant demands by enterprise managers for one-man command.[33] In 1935, S. P. Birman still enjoyed a widespread reputation for independence and had to be trapped into jacking up his plan targets.[34] In 1940, two years after the dread purges, four Leningrad enterprise managers felt free to publish a letter in *Pravda* complaining about the constraints put on them,[35] and in 1950 a Leningrad factory director still complained about interference—apparently with impunity.[36]

In sum, due to the party's claim to leadership over all aspects of Soviet life, restrictions on the industrial managers were constant throughout the Stalin period, and so apparently was their attitude that such restrictions were unjustified and dysfunctional.

PROFESSIONALISM

Closely linked to the demand for operational autonomy was the demand for professionalism. There were two aspects to this demand: one was the managers' insistence that their performance be judged in terms not of political but of professional criteria; the second concerned the nature of these criteria.

The demand for professionalism was raised as early as December 1917 by the Congress of Officials of Factory, Plant, and Trade Industrial Enterprises, which proclaimed its members' willingness to render diligent and responsible service provided the regime respected the fundamental canons of economic rationality.[37] Indeed, S. V. Utechin has suggested that professionalism was the outlook of the "majority of . . . bourgeois specialists" entering the service of the Bolshevik state.[38] Bolshevik managers had much the same attitude. Leonid Krasin stated

[32] *XVI Konferentsia RKP (b), avril 1929 goda, stenog. otchyot* (Moscow, 1962), pp. 459-461, cited in Azrael, *op.cit.*, p. 92.
[33] G. K. Ordzhonikidze, *Stati i rechi* (2 vols., Moscow, 1956), II, 447, cited in Azrael, *op.cit.*, p. 93.
[34] *Za industrializatsiyu*, February 2, 1935, cited in Granick, *op.cit.*, p. 123.
[35] *Pravda*, September 10, 1940.
[36] *Leningradskaya pravda*, May 12, 1950.
[37] Azrael, *op.cit.*, p. 35.
[38] S. V. Utechin, *Russian Political Thought* (New York, 1964), p. 184.

in 1923 that the party's aim should be a "minimum of control." He protested against excessive party interference in the selection and disposition of industrial personnel and the displacement of skilled managerial personnel by "some commonplace replacements from the party's manpower fund." In so doing, he did little more than echo the cry that managers in the field were reported to have addressed to provincial party committees: "Comrades, you are not competent in economic questions."[39] Krasin was supported at very high levels by Y. A. Preobrazhensky, V. P. Nogin, and P. A. Bogdanov, the chairman of the VSNKh (Supreme Council of the National Economy) Presidium. The latter wanted no less than a truly professional personnel policy administered by the managerial elite itself.[40]

The Twelfth Party Congress, in April 1923, was apparently a turning point in party-manager relations; at this time, the right of the party generalists to supervise and guide all aspects of industrial management was decisively asserted. As a result, and with the growing influx of the graduates of engineering schools into managerial positions, the criterion of professionalism shifted away from economic rationality and toward demands for greater technical proficiency in engineering, both in terms of education and experience. Unfortunately, proficiency conceived in terms of such exclusively quantitative norms blinded managers to the element of economic choice in production; and what was worse, once this kind of managerial orientation had been fixed, it perpetuated itself through its influence on the curriculum of Soviet engineering schools and the cooptation of those who were considered promising managers.

PERSONAL ENRICHMENT AND STATUS

A major attitude shared by plant managers in Lenin's and Stalin's days—and indeed assiduously fostered by Stalin—was the striving for the maximization of personal income via the bonus system. This goal was not one that appeared in discussions in the Soviet literature, but it has been firmly established by the investigations of Joseph Berliner.[41]

The assumption that the drive for personal enrichment and status was central for the managerial group has enormously important implications. One, it provides a focal point for managerial aspirations and serves

[39] Azrael, *op.cit.*, pp. 73-74.
[40] *XII Syezd RKP (b), stenog. otchyot* (Moscow, 1923), p. 334, cited in Azrael, *op.cit.*, p. 75.
[41] Berliner, *op.cit.*, pp. 12-56.

as the lowest common denominator for the objectives of apparently all members of the group. Two, the regime's open acceptance of this attitude as justifiable in the case of the managers and their ideological condemnation of such egoism in all other segments of the population set the managers apart and thus served to consolidate feelings of group solidarity. Three, the centrality of income maximization in the attitudinal scheme of the managers should predispose this group toward the values of efficiency and rationality and against the claims of ideology.

Interviews in depth with Soviet managers also uncovered a number of other objectives, such as dedication to the progress of industrialization in the USSR, love of the fatherland, and service to the nation and their fellow men. However, these were objectives which did not differentiate the managers from other Soviet citizens, and therefore they will not be discussed here.

Interest Articulation and Channels of Access

Given that the managers of the Stalin period shared a number of attitudes, did they merely constitute a congeries of individuals or small groups evincing similar reactions to the same basic situation, or were they welded by these shared attitudes into an interest group with at least some of the attributes of comparable groups in Western countries? The answer to this question hinges largely upon whether the managers succeeded in articulating their interests and in bringing them to bear upon the top Soviet decision-makers. Some observers have tended to answer in the negative.[42] However, if one argues—as Azrael does—that the Soviet managerial group did emerge after Stalin's death as a cohesive body, it seems reasonable to expect fairly structured interest group activities during the Stalin era. In fact, a close look reveals that there were opportunities both for interest articulation and for the realization of demands.

For example, throughout the Stalin period professional conferences took place in which group attitudes could not help but be expressed. In the brief period from January to March 1936, there were four conferences of 700 engineers and foremen from various ferrous metallurgical firms. In the period from February to May 1936, there were

[42] Gabriel A. Almond and G. Bingham Powell, Jr., *Comparative Politics: A Developmental Approach* (Boston and Toronto, 1966), p. 79.

over twenty branch conferences of machine-building firms which were working sessions rather than indoctrination meetings.[43] Such meetings were not exceptional and served to articulate the interests of the managers involved. While these confrontations might also have helped to promote the kind of hierarchical, departmental, and factional divisions considered by Azrael, such factionalization could also be a first step toward interest aggregation. The schools and institutions which the regime had established for the Red Directors and which proved to be veritable hotbeds of dissidence were another source of interest articulation, at least during the first Five Year Plan.[44] Finally, enterprise directors throughout the Stalin period confronted their superiors in the industrial ministries in the protracted bargaining that constituted the planning process. While the bargaining was cast in terms of specific input and output figures, it must have solidified a cognizance of shared and opposed interests on both sides.[45]

In short, the managers did have the opportunity to develop an awareness of shared attitudes and to articulate common interests throughout the Stalin period. Paradoxically, the very turnover of personnel within the various branches probably contributed to increased personal contacts among managers and to a greater articulation of interests.

The managers' opportunities for bringing their demands to the attention of the ruling elite groups appear to have been surprisingly good. Stalin's monopoly of ultimate decision-making must not be permitted to hide the fact that at the operational level enterprise directors had access to and influence over leadership groups in both the state administration and the party apparatus. In the industrial ministries, Gosplan, various state committees, and functional ministries managers were engaged in close contact and bargaining with officials. These negotiations, even in Stalin's heyday, were two-way streets. They permitted the directors to "lobby" on behalf of their own interests and to acquaint their opposite numbers at the second and third echelons of state power with managerial sentiments.

Another important channel of access took the form of personal con-

[43] A. Tochinsky and V. Rikman, in *Planovoye khozyaistvo*, No. 6 (1936), p. 44, cited in Granick, *op.cit.*, p. 100.
[44] Cf. Lazar Pistrak, *The Grand Tactician* (New York, 1961), pp. 61-68.
[45] Cf. Herbert Levine, "Recent Developments in Soviet Planning," in Joint Economic Committee, Congress of the United States, *Dimensions of Soviet Economic Power* (Washington, D.C., 1962), p. 47.

187

nections between powerful enterprise directors and ministers, based upon common interests in efficient enterprise performance, personal ties, and sometimes bribery.

Finally, there existed what Almond and Powell have called elite representation on behalf of interest groups. This took the form of "the presence of a group member in the rule-making structure, or of sympathetic representation by an elite figure" permitting "direct and continued articulation of interests by an involved member of the decision-making structure."[46] There can be little doubt that at least until the purge of 1938, men such as Ordzhonikidze, with impeccable credentials, did act in this way. After the purge no such independent elite members remained in the state apparatus, but various top party leaders continued to be identified with different aspects of the economy and within the limits of Stalinist absolutism presumably endeavored to advance the interests of their "constituency."

The relationship of the party apparatus to industry was delineated in general terms at the Twelfth Party Congress in 1923, when the ascendancy of the party apparatus over the enterprise directors was established. The exact relationship was, however, subject to frequent change, at least on the policy level. In 1929 Stalin decreed the one-man principle of leadership, i.e., the predominance of the manager in the factory. By 1933 official complaints were heard about the laxity of party supervision over industry. In 1937 Stalin indicated that the party organization had gone to unacceptable extremes in economic supervision. In 1939 the emphasis was reversed again and the party organizations in the enterprises were given formal rights of supervision. After the war Stalin ordered curtailment of party participation in enterprise management, but the principle of party predominance was never revoked.

The party's chief representatives in dealing with the enterprise directors were the oblast committee (obkom) first secretaries and the republic first secretaries in republics without oblasts. The hold of these functionaries over the enterprises was implemented by three main instrumentalities, over and above their general position as the center's provincial "prefects," to use Hough's term: (1) the *nomenklatura* control over managerial positions in the enterprises, (2) the supervision exercised over the enterprise via subordinate party bodies at the raion, city, and enterprise level,[47] and (3) the day-to-day economic services

[46] Almond and Powell, *op.cit.*, p. 83.
[47] Cf. I. M. Kriulenko, "O podbore, rasstanovke i organizatsii ucheby kadrov

rendered by the obkom (or raikom and gorkom) industrial departments in the fields of expediting and procurement. In this latter sphere, they were truly indispensable, as can be seen from Grossman's description: ". . . the lower and intermediate party levels owe their functions and powers in the economy precisely to the failure of other institutions. So far, those levels of the apparat have to do a job because of inadequate incentives, improper signals, improper coordination within the economy, conflicting goals and standards, shortages of all sorts, and other functional defects."[48]

These relationships established a direct link between the managers and the second echelon of the party hierarchy (the oblast secretaries in the RSFSR, for example, were directly subordinate to the central party apparatus in Moscow). As long as the channels between this second level and the first party level were open, enterprise directors had meaningful and significant, if indirect, access to the highest positions of power. There are several complicating factors, however. One is that, in the process of transmission to the top, the presentation of managerial interests may have been distorted. Two, the channels between the second and first echelon of party power were not always wide open, e.g., during Stalin's purges of the party. Three, the lateral relationship between enterprise directors and party apparatus was complicated by vertical enterprise ties to their ministries. Finally, it must be remembered that the main flow of information and pressure was from the top to the bottom, from the party to the enterprise director. Despite these reservations, there can be little doubt that the link between the party apparatus and the enterprise directors—whatever its other advantages or disadvantages—ordinarily provided the directors with reasonably quick and efficient access to the sources of real power in the Soviet system.

Post-Stalin Changes

Circumstances after the death of Stalin and particularly after the abortive sixth Five Year Plan of the mid-fifties made necessary a new

---

v period mezhdu XXI i XXII syezdami KPSS," in *Istoria kommunisticheskoi partii Sovetskovo Soyuza* (Moscow, 1967), VI, 53; A. Kandrenikov, "Novye uslovia—novye trebovania k kadram," *Kommunist*, No. 5 (March 1967); and L. Morozov, "Vospitanie rukovodyashchikh kadrov v promyshlennosti—iz praktiki raboty Volgogradskovo obkoma partii," *Ekonomicheskaya gazeta*, No. 40 (October 1968), p. 4.

[48] Gregory Grossman, "Economic Reforms: A Balance Sheet," *Problems of Communism*, XV, No. 6 (November-December 1966), p. 55.

and more complex system of planning and management. Comprehensive economic planning became mandatory as the requirements of light industry, consumers, and the infrastructure of the Soviet economy, especially transportation and housing, became relevant elements of economic demand. At the same time, the traditional military requirements for resources became dramatically more expensive as nuclear missilery provided a new and costly set of military demands on top of the continuing conventional armaments needs. Moreover, the preferred industrial sector could be, and indeed needed to be, converted from a simple coal/steel type economy to one more consistent with the industrial technology of other countries using more sophisticated energy and metal sources. These increasingly complex supply requirements in the traditional heavy industrial-military sectors of the Soviet economy had also to be reconciled with the burgeoning requirements of consumer-goods and housing materials production. Incentives were required to provide a basis for improved labor and management productivity. The population appeared to be less willing to accept stable or declining living conditions, whether in the city or the countryside.[49]

These problems of expanding demand and diminishing supply were reflected in a reduction of the overall indices of Soviet economic growth, either calculated in terms of the annual rate of increase in the gross national product (GNP) or simply in terms of annual increments in industrial output segments of GNP. The rate of increase in the early sixties was substantially less than the average during the fifties (4.5 percent per annum as compared with about 7 percent).[50] This retardation could be explained partially by poor harvests, bad weather, and other factors not directly relevant to the system of planning and management. However, the slowdown in industrial growth which persisted through most of the sixties cannot be explained by factors external to Soviet economic planning and management. The hard choices were between changes in the resource allocation pattern (e.g., reducing the military budget) or improved efficiency in economic administration. The *ad hoc* solutions imposed at the top by Nikita Khrushchev in his agricultural "campaigns," including the new lands policy, fertilizer expansion, the abolition of the machine tractor station, etc., were followed

---

[49] Hardt and Modig, *op.cit.*, p. 6.

[50] See Stanley H. Cohn, "Soviet Growth Retardation: Trends in Resource Availability and Efficiency," in Joint Economic Committee, Congress of the United States, *New Directions of the Soviet Economy* (Washington, D.C., 1966), pp. 99-132.

by a more comprehensive approach to pricing and enterprise management under the leadership of Brezhnev and Kosygin, which promised a change from maximal to optimal planning. These changes may be viewed at best as modest, and the unsatisfactory performance of the economy continues to provide a source of pressure for further movement away from the Stalinist system of planning and management toward a different approach.[51]

These changing aspects of demand and supply have directly challenged the central features of the previous economic model, as may be noted by contrasting the following remarks on the post-Stalin situation with the Stalinist model described above on p. 174.

First, military allocation levels can be only provisionally set aside, both in the aggregate and in the trade-off between alternative military uses (e.g., missiles *vs.* conventional divisions). The fluctuating military budgets of Khrushchev and his successors bear witness to the fact that defense is now a variable rather than a preferred "given."

Likewise, consumption is no longer a nonpreferred "given." Production to provide for improved living conditions is a variable—if only as a stimulant to productivity.

Second, the simplifying assumptions of fixed product relationships are increasingly untenable as the structure of heavy industry becomes more complex, servicing technologically advanced space programs, traditional military and investment projects, and new requirements in the economic infrastructure.

Third, no longer can Soviet planners treat light industry, transportation, and agriculture as though they were primarily suppliers of "surplus" labor, raw materials, and capital for heavy industry—and consumers of whatever residuals are left after heavy industrial output is maximized.[52]

The old system of economic planning and management has been eroded and in some ways changed basically. A new system, however, has not yet emerged. The possibility of the development of comprehensive optimal planning and management based on a marketlike system seems to be accepted by many Soviet economists, and by some Western economic specialists, including the authors of this paper. It is both theoretically possible and rational in the context of the Soviet system. How-

[51] See Hardt *et al.*, *op.cit.*, p. 7.   [52] Hardt and Modig, *op.cit.*, p. 6.

ever, these factors do not alone guarantee its existence. The system to date is still much closer to maximal Stalin-type planning and day-to-day centralized management.

Against this background one might expect to observe a change in the behavior and interests of the managerial group. This expectation would be all the stronger in view of the changes in the institutional environment of the Soviet managers, such as Khrushchev's 1957 decentralization which abolished the industrial ministries, the 1962 split of the party (at the oblast level and below) into industrial and agricultural organizations, as well as the economic reforms effected by his successors. Before addressing ourselves to this question, it might be useful first to consider the basic characteristics of the managerial group as a whole in terms of size, composition and education.

The size of the enterprise directors' group during and since the Khrushchev period has stabilized or even declined. Thus, the 1957 figure for enterprise directors may be estimated as 131,000,[53] while the 1959 Census gave a figure of 128,712.[54] Although hard data are not available, some surmises can be made concerning the composition and social background of today's managers. The first is that with the disappearance of the older groups (Red Directors, Menshevik, and "bourgeois" specialists) the present group is rather homogeneous. Both those members recruited in the 1940's and the emergent new generation were born under Soviet rule and are the products of Soviet training and indoctrination. The second is that of today's top group of managers approximately half come from white-collar families[55] so that their backgrounds are rather similar. Presumably, white-collar origin and social background are no longer the outsider's mark as they were in the 1920's and 1930's, and consequently enterprise directors feel less uncertain about their social status. Their sense of security is probably also boosted by the greater homogeneity of the group's composition.

There is little question that the educational qualifications of enter-

[53] De Witt, *op.cit.*, p. 498.

[54] The diminution of the group of enterprise directors is, of course, closely connected with the long-term trend toward the merger of small plants which apparently overbalances the effect of the addition of new plants. Cf. TsSU, *Narodnoye khozyaistvo v 1956 godu* (Moscow, 1957), p. 48, which explicitly refers to a drastic merger of small plants in 1955. Incidentally, this volume's reference to 206,000 large and small enterprises in 1955 (*ibid.*) clearly includes a number of marginal plants whose directors are not comparable to the group discussed here.

[55] Granick, *The Red Executive* (Garden City, N. J., 1960), p. 40.

prise directors, as a group, were improved during and after the Stalin period. In 1967, 68 percent of industrial directors had a higher education,[56] with the percentage significantly higher in heavy industry and perceptibly lower in light industry, particularly in the provinces.[57] There can be little doubt that of the enterprise directors with higher education, the majority had specialized in engineering rather than in economic or business management. De Witt's figures show that the number of professional engineers and other specialists working in industrial enterprises grew from 153,000 in 1941 to 442,000 in 1959; by contrast, the economists are shown working in state ministries and state agencies other than enterprises.[58]

In view of the preponderance of engineers among enterprise directors it is worth noting that only 7-8 percent of the curriculum time at higher engineering institutions is devoted to political and socio-economic subjects,[59] and of this time probably a high percentage goes to the study of Marxism-Leninism. Even the courses in engineering economics (which are designed to train planners rather than engineers) offered by the Moscow Institute of Engineering Economics devote 40 percent of curriculum time to "hard" science and engineering subjects, 17 percent to political courses, and 36 percent to business administration (production, management, accounting, business law, finance). In the light of the foregoing it seems safe to conclude that the arts of management still occupy second place to the science of engineering in the education and orientation of enterprise directors.

The current economic reform has changed this picture in only one major respect: the party has been running hundreds of seminars and courses for directors, deputy directors, and other leading personnel designed to orient managers away from the old goals of quantity production toward profits and sales.[60] It is too early to say to what extent

[56] Zaluzhny, *loc.cit.* See also A. Muzhitsky in *Izvestia*, June 22, 1968.
[57] Morozov, *loc.cit.*   [58] De Witt, *op.cit.*, pp. 794-798.
[59] *Ibid.*, p. 283.
[60] To give one example of many: In February 1967, the Lvov Gorkom, in conjunction with the Lvov Division of the Economic Institute of the Ukrainian Academy of Science, the Philosophical Institute of the Ukrainian Institute, and the Lvov Polytechnical Institute sponsored a scientific conference on "Social Problems of the Economic Reform." The First Secretary of the Lvov Gorkom, in his address, stressed that a manager accustomed to operate only under instructions from above or on the basis of his experience and intuition cannot manage properly. He called for better training and more initiative for management cadres. A. Zaitsev, "Sotsialny problemy ekonomicheskoy reformy," *Ekonomika Radianskoi Ukrainy*, No. 5 (May 1967), pp. 51-54.

courses embodying the goals of the new economic reform (managerial initiative, attention to consumer demands, cost efficiency) have been incorporated into the curricula of Soviet schools. Should such courses be added, it would take a number of years before they could significantly affect the attitudes of incumbent directors.

The tenure of enterprise directors has been relatively long and steady since Stalin's last decade. It was disturbed briefly in 1959 when Khrushchev embarked upon a "renewal of cadres" at the middle and lower levels of the industrial establishment, on the grounds that these cadres were not able to cope with the new requirements imposed upon Soviet industry. By the end of 1962, he seemed ready to apply his policy of replacement to the enterprise director, only to turn, at the last minute, against the party cadres proper in his bifurcation of the party in November 1962. However, lately there have been scattered indications of fairly severe managerial shake-ups in the provinces. Thus, in one raion of Volgogradskaya oblast, 43.5 percent of directors and chief engineers were changed in the last two years; and in another raion, during the same time, 32 managers of industrial enterprises were changed, 10 of them for unsatisfactory work.[61]

In conclusion, the post-Stalin period continued the stabilizing trend of the last decade of Stalin's rule, despite the rather drastic institutional rearrangements by Khrushchev and their reversal by his successors. The size of the managerial group, its composition and background, its education and tenure have remained stable or altered only slightly. More important, the image which the directorial group has of its functions and the nature of its interests has remained largely unchanged, despite the slow emergence of a fresh generation of directors and the very considerable pressure toward change exerted by the party. It is too early to say whether the party is willing and able to effect a more rapid transformation in managerial attitudes by a rejuvenation of managerial ranks.

Group Attitudes

OPERATIONAL AUTONOMY

While there is little direct evidence of managerial self-assertiveness in the post-Stalin years, there are many indications of a continued desire to achieve operational autonomy—particularly in the reactions of Khru-

[61] Morozov, *loc.cit.*

shchev and his successors to the managers. Specifically, in the 1957 reorganization, which formally subordinated industry to the obkom first secretaries, Khrushchev was very careful to concentrate his fire on the central ministries and to reassure the enterprise directors. Thus, in the Central Committee decree of February 14, 1957, repeated reference was made to the need for raising the role of local organs in the economy.[62] Khrushchev's speech in the Supreme Soviet on May 7, 1957,[63] again emphasized the desirability of enlarging the rights of the local economic, administrative, and party organizations. These assurances to the local economic organs, including the enterprises, followed sweeping decrees in 1955 and 1956 giving enterprise directors additional rights in initiating production plans and in recruiting personnel. It is no surprise then that the enterprise directors, believing that Khrushchev was bolstering their autonomy, reacted favorably to the 1957 reorganization, at least at the outset.[64]

Subsequently, beginning as early as 1958, the creeping recentralization of industry cut back whatever gain in authority may have been achieved by the directors in 1957. For one thing, the various divisions of Gosplan, bypassing the *sovnarkhozy*, kept a tight control over the enterprises;[65] for another, the many new State Committees assumed in substance many of the supervisory functions of the disestablished ministries;[66] and finally, the *sovnarkhoz* system itself was progressively centralized, with the establishment of regional *sovnarkhozy* and ultimately a national *sovnarkhoz*. The 1962 bifurcation of the party further undermined the grant of authority to the enterprise directors and alienated this group from Khrushchev.

Khrushchev's successors, too, played up to the directors' desire for autonomy. The reform of 1965 reinstituting the economic ministries was explicitly intended to enlarge the operational autonomy of the enterprise directors, both by keeping down the ministries' control (through reduction of the number of performance indices set by the ministries) and by changing the style of guidance from direct administrative interference to indirect guidance via financial incentives and penalties. The initial reaction of the enterprise directors to the proposed buildup of their autonomy was, surprisingly enough, negative. There is

[62] *Izvestia*, February 14, 1957.   [63] *Pravda*, May 8, 1957.
[64] Wolfgang Leonhard, *The Kremlin Since Stalin* (New York, 1962), p. 241.
[65] Alex Nove, *The Soviet Economy: An Introduction* (New York, 1966), pp. 79-80.
[66] *Ibid.*, p. 75.

ample evidence that the directors, as a group, were timid in asserting the additional rights granted to them and that they permitted the ministries to encroach steadily upon enterprise autonomy.[67]

On the face of it, this reaction would seem to contradict the thesis of the desire of directors for autonomy, but a closer look reveals that what the incumbent directors objected to was not autonomy per se, but the conditions under which that autonomy was being offered. This involved the speedy replacement by more modern entrepreneurs of the engineering managers who were bound to the production process and were oblivious to cost and marketing considerations. What made the situation serious for the incumbents was that it was the party which set this high price for entrepreneurial independence. Thus, V. Akhundov, First Secretary of the Central Committee, CP of Azerbaidzhan, has written that the old type of manager, the thoughtless performer and pusher, will disappear. The new type of manager will be a man capable of thinking and acting according to scientific data, a resourceful man with a mercantile spirit.[68] F. Tabeyev, First Secretary of the Tatarskaya ASSR, noted for his willingness to encourage economic experimentation, called for party encouragement of a new style of managerial leadership.[69] Similarly, Professor L. Leontyev stipulated that the success of the economic reform was contingent upon major changes in managerial psychology: "The personnel of enterprises must be freed from the habit of waiting for or requiring instructions from above on the questions which now come within their competence."[70] V. Firsov, director of the V. I. Lenin Machine-building Plant, excoriated the old timid "psychology" which had not changed.[71]

If the initial reaction of enterprise directors to the reform was hesitant because it did not offer them autonomy on their own terms, recent responses seem more positive and more assertive. In February 1966, when most of his fellow directors were still defensive about the economic reform, G. Kulagin, director of the Sverdlov Production Asso-

[67] Joint Economic Committee, Congress of the United States, *Soviet Economic Performance: 1966-67* (Washington, D. C., 1968), pp. 131-132; Theodore Frankel, "Soviet Economic Reform: A Tentative Appraisal," *Problems of Communism*, XVI, No. 3 (May-June 1967), 32, 34-35.
[68] V. Akhundov, "Sovetsky khozyaistvennik," *Kommunist*, No. 17 (November 1965), pp. 22-31.
[69] F. Tabeyev, "Partiinaya organizatsia," *ibid.*, No. 1 (January 1967), pp. 37-46.
[70] *Pravda*, April 29, 1966.
[71] V. Firsov, "Novizna," *Literaturnaya gazeta*, February 1, 1966, p. 2.

ciation for Construction of Machine Tools in Leningrad, demanded that while "orders issued by higher administrative organs should be binding upon the enterprises, the specific methods, ways and means of implementation be left to the enterprises themselves."[72] By August 1967 he was loudly demanding that the investment funds allocated to enterprises be increased ten times.[73] K. Rudnev, Minister for Instrument Building, Means of Automation and Control Systems, has written half-jokingly about one of his directors who refused for months to work according to the reform and had to be "coaxed" by the ministry.[74] Many directors now complain publicly about being deprived by their ministries of funds for the assimilation of new technology.[75] One director has asserted his independence to the point of denying workers of the staffing section of the oblast finance department access to his records and refusing to divulge information on the structure of the enterprise administration.[76] A recent article by Ye. Liberman mentioned the attitude of enterprise directors who defend the economic interests of their enterprises against encroachment from the ministry.[77] Finally, in a recent study of 2,000 "middle-level" managers at machine-building factories in Moscow and Kharkov, "almost all expressed their dissatisfaction about the insufficient degree of independence given to them in their work."[78]

More important, enterprise directors have been successful in asserting their autonomy vis-à-vis the primary party organizations in their factories. A recent article in the party journal, *Partiinaya zhizn*, stated unequivocally that "in accordance with the principle of one-man leadership the right to appoint, shift or dismiss a worker belongs exclusively to the economic manager, whether he is a member of the party or not. . . . If the party organization [differs with the manager] on an issue, it may raise the question with higher party and economic bodies."[79] In the same vein, a local procurator's office in the Ukraine countermanded the

[72] G. Kulagin, "Obedineniye predpriatii i ministerstvo," *Kommunist*, No. 3 (February 1966), pp. 82-91.
[73] *Pravda*, August 9, 1967.   [74] *Ibid.*, July 5, 1967.
[75] A. Novgorod, cited in "Reforma i tekhnika," *Ekonomicheskaya gazeta*, No. 33 (August 1967), p. 11.
[76] V. Selyunin, "Yeshchyo raz o lishnikh zvenyakh," *ibid.*, No. 14 (April 1968), pp. 14-15.
[77] Ye. Liberman and Z. Zhitnitsky, "Ekonomicheskiye i administrativnye metody khozyaistvennovo rukovodstva," *Planovoye khozyaistvo*, No. 1 (January 1968), 19-28.
[78] G. Kozlov, "Shkola upravlenia," *Novy mir* (August 1968), pp. 201-218.
[79] A. Plokhotnikov, "Kak reshat vopros o kadrakh?" *Partiinaya zhizn*, No. 9 (May 1968), p. 32.

veto rights ceded to several factory Komsomol organizations on personnel questions.[80]

At present, then, managers' aspirations for autonomy seem to be more openly avowed and more stubbornly defended than at the beginning of the economic reform of 1965. The reason for this turnabout in attitude may lie in their growing appreciation of what can be gained from even the present limited autonomy.

It should be noted that at least one student of Soviet affairs has detected a somewhat longer-range trend (1952-1965) for Soviet elite groups, and particularly the economic elite, to assert themselves. Professor Lodge finds that the economic elite has increasingly articulated a conviction that it should participate in decision-making and has pressed this claim, with ever greater assertiveness, in the technical press.[81]

PROFESSIONALISM

To judge from directorial contributions to public discussions of the economic reform, directors have strong feelings as to the importance of expertise, pride in professionalism, and a warm desire to make professional judgment rather than political needs decisive in industrial operations. It is less certain that this professionalism is of a kind designed to fit the reform's requirements for "business administration" and "industrial management," for it is predominantly of the engineering type. Barry Richman has shown that in 1960, of all professionals employed in industrial enterprises, 76.5 percent had graduated from engineering programs and only 9.8 percent from economics programs.[82] In this connection it is worthy of note that in the technical institutes for engineers, the economic disciplines occupy only 5 percent of all class time.[83] Richman also estimates that at least 90 percent of all enterprise top executives are engineers by vocation and training, although many have not received a higher education.

It is this continuing engineering orientation which is one of the reasons why the incumbent industrial managers—largely the products of the Stalinist period—oppose the current economic reform with its

[80] V. Proskura, "Protest prokurora," *Komsomolskaya pravda*, May 22, 1968.

[81] Milton Lodge, "Soviet Elite Participatory Attitudes in the Post-Stalin Period," *American Political Science Review*, LXII (1968), 827-839.

[82] Richman, *op.cit.*, p. 67.

[83] N. I. Mokhov, "O podgotovke ekonomistov i povyshenii ekonomicheskoi kvalifikatsii khozyaistvennykh kadrov," *Planovoye khozyaistvo*, No. 7 (July 1968), pp. 67-80.

abandonment of "hard criteria," such as volume of production, and its switch to "soft" nonengineering criteria, such as profits and sales. There can be little question that the necessary shift in managerial attitude is being accomplished at a slow rate despite the party's crash program to orient hundreds of thousands of leading industrial cadres toward greater independence, profit-mindedness, etc.

Nor does it seem likely that a new generation of managers can be educated quickly. For one thing, the magnitude of the task is staggering. Soviet sociologists have estimated that 60 percent of all administrative personnel in industry—including directors, deputy directors, chief engineers, heads of service departments, and shop foremen—are in their fifties and sixties. It is estimated that in the next five to ten years, when thirty- and forty-year-olds will move into responsible positions, approximately 4 million people will have to be trained for administration. This will amount to 40 percent of all such positions in industry. The number of managerial specialists (presumably above the shop level) to be brought into industry is estimated at 1½ million.[84]

Moreover, there are still no institutes wholly devoted to problems of industrial management, despite the frequent discussions of American schools of business and recurring proposals to establish Soviet counterparts.[85] To be sure, the State Committee for Labor and Wages Questions has founded an "All-Union Scientific-Methodological Center for the Organization of Labor and Production Management,"[86] and numerous engineering and economics institutes have introduced courses designed to acquaint the students with problems of management.[87] These innovations, however, cannot be expected to change the basic engineering orientation of the students, as can be seen from the following citation from a recent article on managerial training:

Enterprise managers in industry and construction are now being trained in faculties for organizers of industrial production associated with the Moscow, Leningrad, Kharkov, and Sverdlovsk engineering economics institutes. Specialists with higher education, *as a rule engineering education*, who have worked for a number of years in enter-

[84] Kozlov, *loc.cit.*

[85] See *Voprosy ekonomiki*, No. 3 (March 1968), p. 25; Kozlov, *loc.cit.*; V. Ozira, "Kak uchat v shkole biznesa," *Literaturnaya gazeta* (October 9, 1968), p. 11; and N. Veselov, P. Zhukov, and Ye. Makarov, "Ekonomicheskoye vospitaniye i obrazovaniye," *Kommunist*, No. 8 (May 1968), pp. 62-72.

[86] V. Lisitsyn and G. Popov, "O kadrakh upravlenia," *Planovoye khozyaistvo*, No. 5 (May 1968), p. 3.

[87] Mokhov, *loc.cit.*

prises as supervisors of shops, divisions and other services, are being trained in these faculties for work as enterprise directors.[88]

In the same vein, two authors demanding the establishment of a Higher Academy of Management, for "command personnel" of the economy, still insist that management students should initially be trained for production-specialization, to be followed by a postgraduate course in management.[89]

PERSONAL ENRICHMENT AND STATUS

While some qualified Western observers have come to doubt that the "bonus drive" is a distinctive trait of the Soviet managerial class, the top political leadership since Stalin has always acted as if the pursuit of the ruble and the desire for status are *the* keys to managerial motivation. Khrushchev continued Stalin's policy of paying managers in heavy industry high salaries (as much as ten times the average wage of unskilled workers), bonuses amounting to 30-50 percent of basic salaries, plus benefits such as the use of company cars and preferential housing.[90] It has been assumed in the West that such emoluments were given on the premise that they would induce enterprise directors to fulfill and overfulfill what was then the regime's primary target: maximum quantitative output.[91]

It seems to the writers of this essay that Brezhnev and Kosygin rely for the success of the current economic reform primarily on the manipulation of the managers' presumed propensity for bonus maximization. The current reorientation of production from the maximization of physical output to considerations of enterprise efficiency and consumer demand has been accomplished by linking the size of the managers' bonuses to enterprise sales and profits (the latter are now the only source of managerial bonuses). Indeed, the structure of the incentives system under the reform is such that a highly qualified observer has concluded that its purpose is to induce the manager to maximize the incentive fund (or funds).[92] And the plethora of instructions that come from the Soviet press concerning the incentive funds testifies to their importance in the present scheme of things.

[88] *Ibid.*
[89] V. Lisitsyn and G. Popov, *Pravda*, January 19, 1968.
[90] Richman, *op.cit.*, pp. 124-125.
[91] A. Bergson, *The Economics of Soviet Planning* (New Haven, 1964), p. 75.
[92] Gertrude E. Schroeder, "Soviet Economic Reforms: A Study in Contradictions," *Soviet Studies*, xx, No. 1 (July 1968), 1-21.

Interest Articulation and Channels of Access

The extent of interest articulation can safely be assumed to have increased since Stalin. While personal confrontation between individual managers and their superiors in economic councils and ministries probably continued much as before, large-scale inter-personal meetings of managerial personnel vastly increased in frequency over the post-Stalin period. The transition to the current economic reform, in particular, witnessed a veritable explosion of conferences and professional forums, bringing together hundreds and thousands of directors with representatives of state executive organs, soviets, and the professions. In one recent series of meetings, close to 9,000 personnel of this description met in 10 zonal conferences in the RSFSR.[93] Similarly the All-Union Conference on Perfecting, Planning, and Improving Economic Work in the National Economy (May 14-17, 1968) brought together 5,000 planners, administrators, and economic managers. There can hardly be any doubt that such meetings offer ample opportunities for directors to exchange opinions and to form a concensus or divide into factions, as the case may be. There has been increased opportunity for the ventilation of managers' views in the columns of technical journals, such as *Ekonomicheskaya gazeta*; and while many of these views pertain to the technicalities of the reform, they presumably contribute to the establishment of a group opinion and to the rise of group spokesmen.[94]

Significant also is the recent report on a "Club for Professional Meetings" in Leningrad, bringing together the city's top directors for informal get-togethers and discussions on topics ranging from the impact of the price reform on production and matters of personnel morale to enterprise relations with state organs. A recent series of formal talks dealt with the topic: "The Modern Director: What He Is and What He Ought To Be."[95] It is noteworthy that no party sponsorship was mentioned in connection with these meetings.

Stalin's death may be said to have drastically improved the managers' access to the seats of power, because the liquidation of his one-man

[93] K. Gerasimov, "Slagaemye effektivnosti," *Ekonomicheskaya gazeta*, No. 45 (November 1967), pp. 10-11.

[94] A good example is A. Rudkovsky, director of the S. M. Kirov turbine plant in Kharkov, who has repeatedly been a coauthor of articles with Ye. Liberman, e.g., Liberman and Rudkovsky, *Pravda*, April 20, 1966.

[95] S. Strushentsov and G. Emdin, "Dorogoye vremya direktora," *Ekonomicheskaya gazeta*, No. 31 (August 1967), pp. 9-10.

command immediately upgraded the power of the state officials to whom enterprise directors had routine approach. Conversely, Khrushchev's reorganization of 1957, which well-nigh destroyed the central state apparatus in industry, abolished the central contacts established by enterprise directors in Moscow. With the reestablishment in 1965 of the central ministries, the directors' access to the highest state executives (or at least to their deputies in the ministries' main administrations) was reestablished. While the ministers do not share—as many Western observers seem to assume—a complete community of interests with the directors, the similarity of interests is sufficiently large to ensure easy entrée of the directors to the ministers. It can, therefore, be assumed that the Council of Ministers, of which these ministers are members, is quickly cognizant of directors' demands and grievances.

The general relationship of "mutual involvement" between party functionaries, particularly at the local level, and enterprise directors has not changed in its essentials from the Stalin period—despite the very extensive structural changes in party and industry organization effected by Khrushchev and revoked by his successors. The 1957 reorganization of Soviet industry should have led, on the face of it, to a much closer access of enterprise directors to the party, particularly to the oblast apparatus which patently was intended to take over much of the policy and guidance function formerly exercised by the central ministries. However, the 1958 reduction of the party apparatus (possibly in excess of 25 percent) and the concomitant recentralization of the industrial administrative apparatus had the paradoxical effect of overburdening the apparatus and making party functionaries less accessible than before.

Likewise, the results of the 1962 bifurcation of the party were not what might have been expected. Here again the system on paper favored an almost total control of industry by the oblast apparatus—with a resultant increase in accessibility of party functionaries to enterprise officials. As matters worked out, the split of the party organs at the oblast level and below into industrial and agricultural bodies and the continuing recentralization of industry destroyed the parallelism between party and industry structures (i.e., there were close to 90 oblast industrial party committees and fewer than 50 economic councils) and seriously hampered the access of enterprise directors to their party contacts. It also seriously eroded the apparatus's ability to fulfill its economic function of assisting enterprise directors in procurement and coordination problems, due to the disruption of the party's horizontal links to the state apparatus.[96]

Against this background, the current regime's liquidation of Khrushchev's reorganization of the party (1964) and industry (1965) restored, *inter alia*, the access of enterprise directors to both party and state. It is all the more important to stress this point since it was at first believed by Western and certain Soviet observers that the economic reform was undercutting the party's ties to industry. Similarly, there was considerable anxiety in the lower ranks of the party that the economic reform, with its emphasis on material incentives, would do away with the need for the kind of propaganda and agitation which had been their *raison d'être*. However, it has become apparent that the hold of the party, at least at the oblast level and below, has been strengthened rather than weakened by the economic reform. Once again, the united party apparatus—particularly at raion and city level[97]—functions as expediter and trouble shooter along horizontal lines of communication (which are being neglected by the vertically structured state apparatus). Furthermore, continued stress on propaganda and agitation, and the organization of "socialist competitions" has reassured the local cadres that they are still necessary. More important, the party as a whole has been invested with the responsibility for the success of the reform, specifically for the retraining of the management cadres. All these developments entail strong and close relationships between party and enterprise managers and a degree of access which is far closer than in Khrushchev's time and more meaningful than in Stalin's.

The post-Khrushchev period has seen an increase in the strength of the managerial group, as far as numbers, level of education, social homogeneity, and security of tenure are concerned, as well as in the attainment of some of their most cherished objectives: increased income and status, and greater autonomy. At the same time, their freedom to articulate their interests (within limits) and the opportunity to bring them to bear on the powers that be at all levels of the party and government structure have also improved. But even as it improved its capability and in many ways showed willingness to play the role of an interest group, the managerial group has not experienced changes in

[96] Cf. Jerry F. Hough, "A Harebrained Scheme in Retrospect," *Problems of Communism*, XIV, No. 4 (July-August 1965), 26-32.
[97] Tabeyev, *loc.cit.*

self-image or in the concept of its interests to match the changes that have occurred in the economy and those that must occur sometime in the future.

Prospects for the Managerial Group

It is paradoxical that at a time when many of the long-term aims of Soviet managers are being met their future seems to be especially uncertain. The requirement for a more professional type of manager has spread from heavy industry to light industry and indeed throughout the economy. Managers have been granted a degree of autonomy, at least from direct party intervention, that would seem more than satisfying, considering their past experience. Moreover, their living conditions have improved. If the Fiat auto deal of 1966 was designed to provide the material basis for more incentives to managerial performance, then we may assume that both the real income and the range of expenditure choice are improving.[98] Yet the managerial group may be less satisfied with its rising income than with stable income and the assured status of the past. The general rise in real income—the average increase in personal disposable money income has been 7.5 percent from 1964 to 1967—probably exceeded price changes and narrowed the differential advantage of managers over others in the labor force.[99] Similarly, in spite of the passenger car example, the widening of the managers' choice of remuneration has apparently been slow. Continued slow improvements in housing and other aspects of communal living may lead expectations to run ahead of opportunities. David Granick likened the Stalinist "Red Executive" to a skilled American black in a northern city who had an increasing income but suffered sharp restrictions on choice of expenditure outlets, e.g., for housing.[100] We might speculatively posit another parallel between the two groups in the fact that the quantitative measures of income and expenditures may run sharply counter to the psychic satisfaction of the recipient. Of course, satisfaction and performance are not necessarily directly related. Dissatisfaction may indeed spur performance, although this does not appear to be the case.

More disturbing to the Soviet managers is the prospect that their

[98] Joint Economic Committee, Congress of the United States, *Soviet Economic Performance, 1966-67* (Washington, D.C., 1968), p. 105.
[99] *Ibid.*, p. 91.
[100] Granick, *The Red Executive*, p. 123.

professionalism may become obsolete just when they may be allowed to employ it with less external intervention. A leading article in a prominent Soviet economic journal illustrates this:

At present the economic managers (*rukovoditeli*) who grew up in the days when administrative methods were supreme, do not meet the new requirements of the economic reform and the technological revolution. . . . To be a "manager" under present-day conditions means having a special profession, means having a post that can no longer be held by an engineer or an academic economist. The personal capabilities of a man are the conditions for practicing this profession, and these capabilities can only be brought to perfection by hard practice, combined with a constant broadening of one's knowledge of the theory of management.[101]

This situation poses difficult problems for the managerial group. The leading managers may endanger their own careers by pressing for change in the managerial group. Moreover, if they attempt to conform to policy directives to encourage the development of a new managerial style, they must realize that there is no quick and efficient way to change from a Stalinist production engineer into a management "businessman." The old Stalinist problems of relieving bottlenecks in the production process were relatively straightforward technical and administrative ones. The new manager has to deal with problems that require improved data and modern systems of analysis. He may have to be familiar with linear programming and the use of digital computers.

Furthermore, managers' success indicators are derived not from supply considerations, as in the past, but from demand. Sales, quality, and profits—the demand-derived criteria—are more than a set of new administrative indicators; they call for a change of psychology which must accompany the transition from a seller's to a buyer's market. And the buyer may now be increasingly the individual citizen in the market place, rather than another enterprise director or his expediter (*tolkach*). Thus, demand-related criteria may be replacing supply in Soviet enterprise management as constraints and measures of performance.[102] This was illustrated in a keynote speech by N. K. Baibakov, the Chairman

[101] Lisitsyn and Popov, *loc.cit.*

[102] B. N. Mikhalevsky and U. P. Solvyev, "Opyt opredelenia srednesrochnoi perspektivnoi potrebnosti v osnovnykh produktakh (raschet po 1975 godu na primere chernoi metallurgii)," *Ekonomika i matematicheskiye metody*, No. 3 (1968), pp. 315-334.

of Gosplan (State Planning Commission) in May 1968: ". . . We consider that in future the order book should be the starting point for the long-term plan of the factory. Long-term direct links create the conditions for the gradual reduction and consolidation of the assortment of products laid down in the state plan, and for the development of wholesale trade in the means of production."[103] Clearly the market mechanism has not yet taken over,[104] but it is evident that the administratively centralized method of detailed day-to-day management in the key sectors of Stalinist planning is being challenged, perhaps irreversibly. Cleavages within the managerial group have thus developed along educational, generational, and functional lines. If the leadership chooses to move ahead in replacing the old production-engineer type of manager with another generation of managers schooled in a Soviet version of management science, then the fissures will probably deepen within the managerial group.[105]

The Soviet leadership also has its dilemmas. The old manager cannot be easily replaced by one trained in management science. The Soviet educational system does not appear to be geared either qualitatively or quantitatively to supply thousands of "businessmen" managers. The decision of the Stalinist leadership to replace managers and economists with politically reliable production engineers provided some options.[106] These less well-trained engineers "learned en route" to relieve production bottlenecks in the important industrial sectors. The economic costs incurred in the form of inevitable delays and shoddy output could be absorbed by the lower priority, consumer-oriented

[103] N. K. Baibakov, "Zadachi sovershenstvovania planirovania i uluchshenia ekonomicheskoi raboty v narodnom khozyaistve," *Ekonomicheskaya gazeta*, No. 21 (May 1968), pp. 3-10.

[104] See especially Schroeder, *op.cit.*, and "The 1966-67 Soviet Industrial Price Reform: A Study in Complications," *Soviet Studies*, xx, No. 4 (April 1969), 462-477.

[105] Deputy Chairman of the Council of Ministers USSR, Chairman of the State Committee for Science and Technology, V. A. Kirillin, in *N.T.O. SSSR* (Nauchno-Technicheskoye Obshchestvo), No. 12 (1968), p. 4. "On instructions from the Council of Ministers USSR, Gosplan USSR and the State Committee for Science and Technology are preparing at the present time proposals to improve the training of specialists in the field of management of the national economy. In these proposals there is in particular a provision for the creation of a special training institution in an Academy for the Management of the National Economy."

[106] G. Grossman, "Scarce Capital and Soviet Doctrine," *Quarterly Journal of Economics*, LXVII, No. 3 (August 1953), 311-343.

activities. At present there may be no buffer areas left, and the cost of mistakes in management and planning is increasingly visible in the form of poor products and unclaimed inventories in the capital goods as well as consumer sectors. Adoption of criteria based on profits, sales, and other monetary considerations would surely be more accurate and useful in the context of comprehensive financial planning than as disconnected parts of the *ad hoc*, selective approach of the current reforms. This leads us to look for changes toward comprehensive optimal, financial planning to *precede* significant changes in management.

In turn, the problem of reforming economic planning may lie less in the development of the appropriate professionalism than in allocation changes. The military-heavy industry establishment may oppose the adoption of a new planning system, promising long-run improvements in efficiency, if it threatens them with budget reductions. This broader constraint may be the kind of factor which slows the introduction of comprehensive planning and thereby impedes progress toward improved management. Therefore, given the interrelationship between managerial planning and broader Soviet policy, it is important for us to put the manager-planning changes in a broader societal context.

The emerging pluralism within the Soviet elite has produced conflict between contending groups, most evident in decisions on resource allocation. Some liberal professional economists tend to favor investment in industry and agriculture over further increases in military outlays, so that they may have common cause with the new managerial group. Economic professionalism has not only resource implications, for the professional attitude is itself a common bond among professionals in different spheres. For instance, it is interesting to note the number of articles on economic reform that find their way into the pages of such liberal literary journals as *Novy mir* and other wide-ranging specialized publications. Professionalism in the arts may be less portentous in practical life than the application of professional economic standards in comprehensive planning, but it reflects a common interest in the delegation of party decision-making power. A common *laissez-faire* attitude of professionals throughout the Soviet elite may press effectively for changes in the relationship of the party to the various key institutional groups. As a result not only the monopoly of power in the hands of the top party leaders but their intimate involvement in decisions and policy implementation may be at stake. Thus, through economic reform the changing role of the manager may be linked to more general challenges to the overextended control system of the Soviet government.

Conflict concerning professionalism, however, cuts across institutional lines and ranges some professionals and party generalists on one side against a similar grouping on the other side. The managerial elite is probably involved in interaction with other elites ranging from support of significant change in Soviet society to defense of the *status quo*. Nonetheless, the longer-run interest of the managers would appear to be in an increase in professionalism within a context of more limited party control. The development of a new kind of Soviet manager may be interwoven with a similar development of other new groups, such as planners and the military, throughout the whole fabric of the Soviet elite and may be tied to fundamental changes in the top leadership. When and if a new managerial group finally emerges it may be a part of a very different Soviet society.

CHAPTER VII ~ BY RICHARD W. JUDY

The Economists

THE BROADEST possible definition of Soviet economists would embrace all individuals educated or occupied as economists. So defined, the members of the group would share few attributes beyond those of the definition itself. A definition and analysis based purely on occupational or educational considerations would present little of interest. This study concentrates instead on the elite group of professional Soviet economists who occupy leading academic, planning, and administrative positions and who articulate viewpoints on major questions of economic theory, policy, and research methodology. An early finding was that this set of elite Soviet economists is heterogenous with respect to the positions that they adopt on these questions. Given this fragmentation, a search was made for attributes which might characterize significant opinion groups. The attributes of age, degree of mathematical proficiency, and institution of main occupational affiliation were found to be most useful in characterizing these groups and in predicting an economist's position on controversial issues.

In this essay I have attempted to do several things. First, I have presented certain characteristics or attributes of Soviet economists which correlate well with their opinions on issues of theory, policy, and methodology. Secondly, the essay reviews leadership-economist relations during the Stalin era and since 1953. Thirdly, I have examined two sample issues on which opinion group activity is evident among economists. The particular issues examined concern the "Liberman" debate and the basis of price formation in the Soviet economy. These are but two of many significant issues that might have been studied had limitations of scope and space not precluded it. Finally, there is a concluding assessment of the significance of opinion group activity for the formation of Soviet economic policy.

Groups Among Economists

INSTITUTIONAL AFFILIATION

The majority of articulate and influential Soviet economists are associated with various institutes of the Academy of Sciences, with central governmental agencies and, to a lesser extent, with the leading universities. The following sections indicate the most important of these institutions and the most prominent economists associated with them.

The Academy of Sciences. Economic research is done in a number of institutes of the USSR Academy of Sciences and its filials. Most of the republican academies also have institutes of economic research.

The interest of the academy's top leadership in economic theory, policy, and methodology has varied greatly over the years. Greatest intensity was displayed in the period 1955-1964 when the party and academy leaderships conducted an energetic campaign to redirect Soviet economics. It will be shown below that the academy's presidents, A. N. Nesmeyanov and M. V. Keldysh, have been valuable sources of support for the advocates of radical change in Soviet economics.

Enormous influence was long exercised by the highly orthodox economist, K. V. Ostrovityanov. A former director of the Institute of Economics, and chief editor of *Voprosy ekonomiki* (1949-1953), Ostrovityanov became vice-president of the academy in 1953. From these and other posts he has exercised a very conservative and orthodox influence on Soviet economics.[1] Another economist, A. M. Rumyantsev, has recently taken a leading role in the affairs of the academy. He is vice-president of the academy and a proponent of more fundamental reform in economics.[2] Originally from Kharkov, Rumyantsev has long known

[1] K. V. Ostrovityanov was born in 1892 and joined the Communist Party in 1914. He graduated from the Moscow Commercial Institute and taught in Moscow during the 1920's. After the purges of the economists in 1929-1930, Ostrovityanov's star rose rapidly. He was prominent in the Communist Academy by 1930; by 1936, he was a corresponding member of the Academy of Sciences and head of the Political Economy Section of the Institute of Economics. He led the organization of the Economics Faculty at Moscow University in 1941 and chaired the Kafedra of Political Economy. In 1952 he became a candidate member of the Central Committee of the CPSU and was listed in that capacity in the records of the Nineteenth and Twentieth Party Congresses. His power and influence waned steadily from about 1956. He died in 1969.

[2] A. M. Rumyantsev was born in 1905 and graduated in 1926 from the Kharkov Economics Institute. After military service and work in the Ukrainian Commissariats of Agriculture and Justice, he taught economics from 1930 to 1943. Between 1943 and 1949 he did party work in the Kharkov obkom. From 1950 to 1952 he was director of the Institute of Economics and head of the

of his fellow Kharkov economist, E. G. Liberman. As chief editor of *Kommunist*, Rumyantsev provided Liberman his first national forum.[3] From his powerful party and academic positions, he has provided valuable support to the reformist forces.

The Economics Section was established in 1962 and charged with coordinating economic research in all institutes and filials of the Academy of Sciences, USSR, in the republican academies, and in higher educational institutions.[4] During the late 1950's and the 1960's, a number of bitter conflicts raged among the academy's economists. One major function of the Economics Section has been to moderate these conflicts and to impose the academy's discipline on the contending factions. The academic secretaryship of the section is obviously a position of considerable power. The post was held first by A. A. Arzumanyan (1962-1965)[5] and then by A. M. Rumyantsev (1965-1967). N. P. Fedorenko succeeded Rumyantsev but his tenure was brief. The fourth and present incumbent is T. S. Khachaturov, a rather cautious reformer.[6]

Before the creation of the Economics Section in 1962, the coordination function was exercised by the Section of Economic, Philosophic and Legal Sciences. From 1953 to 1962, the academic secretary of this

---

Social Science Section of the Ukrainian Academy of Sciences. In 1952 he went to Moscow to become head of the Science and Higher Education Section of the Central Committee. He was chief editor of the journal *Kommunist* between 1955 and 1958, and from 1958 to 1964 chief editor of *Problemy mira i sotsializma*. In 1964-1965 he was chief editor of *Pravda*. Between 1965 and 1967 he was academic secretary of the Economics Section of the academy. In 1960 he became a corresponding member of the academy; in 1966 he was promoted to full academician. In 1967, he became vice-president of the academy.

[3] See *Kommunist*, No. 10 (July 1956), pp. 75-92.

[4] *Vestnik Akademii Nauk SSSR*, No. 8 (1962), pp. 9, 110.

[5] A. A. Arzumanyan (1905-1965) was for many years head of the Institute of World Economics and International Relations. He was a party member from 1921 until his death, and also a deputy to the Supreme Soviet. He became a full academician in 1962. As a member of the Presidium of the Academy of Sciences and academic secretary of the Economics Section, he was in a position to advance the cause of mathematical economics. His portrait stands with that of V. S. Nemchinov in the office of N. P. Fedorenko, Director of the Central Mathematical Economics Institute. This, together with a glowing obituary in *Ekonomika i matematicheskiye metody*, No. 4 (1965), bears witness to the gratitude that Soviet mathematical economists feel to Arzumanyan.

[6] T. S. Khachaturov was born in 1906. His early research was concerned with the economics of transportation. After World War II he became interested in the problem of capital investment criteria. His main positive contribution to Soviet economic thought was his support in the 1950's for the "coefficient of relative effectiveness," a surrogate for the rate of interest. He became a full academician in 1966.

section was V. S. Nemchinov, a radical reformer.[7] Between 1949 and 1953, the post was held by the orthodox K. V. Ostrovityanov.

At present, there are five full academicians among the economists: N. P. Fedorenko,[8] T. S. Khachaturov, K. V. Ostrovityanov, A. M. Rumyantsev, and S. G. Strumilin.[9] Fedorenko is aligned with the mathematical, relatively liberal reformers. Khachaturov, once regarded as a reformer, has been outdistanced by the swift developments of the last decade and must be located somewhere in the middle of the radical-orthodox spectrum. Ostrovityanov and the venerable Strumilin are, of course, extremely orthodox. Rumyantsev is moderately reformist but hardly to be counted among the radicals.

The Institute of Economics. The oldest and best known economics research group in the Academy of Sciences is the Institute of Economics.

---

[7] V. S. Nemchinov was born in 1894. His early work was in agricultural economics and statistics. From 1926 to 1934 he was chief of the agricultural statistics section of the Central Statistical Administration. His studies of peasant grain production and marketing laid the statistical basis for Stalin's famous speech "Na khlebnom fronte" ("On the Grain Front") of May 28, 1928. (See I. Stalin, *Voprosy Leninizma* [11th ed., Moscow, 1953], p. 193.) From 1928 to 1948 he headed the Kafedra of Statistics at the Timiryazev Agricultural Academy. From 1940 to 1948 he was director of that academy. In 1946 he became a full academician. For his public defiance in 1948 of Lysenko's genetic theories, Nemchinov was removed from his responsibilities at the Timiryazev Academy. In 1949 he became head of the Council for the Study of Productive Resources under Gosplan. In the 1950's, Nemchinov became convinced of the great potential of mathematical economics. He gathered about fifteen young economists, mathematicians, and engineers to form in 1958 the Laboratory of Mathematical Economic Methods. The rest of his life was devoted to a passionate struggle, against bitter opposition, to advance the acceptance of mathematical methods. His efforts culminated in 1963 with the establishment of the Central Mathematical Economics Institute. He died in 1964. For his contribution to mathematical economics he was posthumously awarded the Lenin Prize in 1965; he shared the honor with L. V. Kantorovich and V. V. Novozhilov.

[8] N. P. Fedorenko was born in 1917. Most of his research before 1963 focused on economic problems of the chemical industry. He became a corresponding member of the academy in 1962 and a full academician in 1964. He is director of the Central Mathematical Economics Institute.

[9] S. G. Strumilin was born in 1877. An early revolutionary, he participated in the Stockholm and London congresses of the Russian Social Democratic Party. He was appointed by Lenin to the initial State Planning Committee and worked in Gosplan and the Central Statistical Administration for many years. He has been an academician since 1931. Much of his energy in recent decades has been devoted to an attempt to make the Marxian theory of value relevant to price formation and other problems of a socialist economy. His ideological and revolutionary zeal has not waned with the passage of time. He has been an ally of the very orthodox economists, although he is considerably more capable than they are. Strumilin accommodated himself to Stalin's dicta in the field of economics.

Founded in 1930 and merged into the Academy of Sciences in 1936, the Institute of Economics has been a bastion of conservative political economists. From this key organization and through the editorial board of the monthly journal, *Voprosy ekonomiki*, the orthodox economists have wielded immense influence over the Soviet economics profession. The present director is the conservative L. M. Gatovsky.[10]

The Central Mathematical Economics Institute (TsEMI). In 1963, after a long struggle to establish mathematical economics in the USSR, the Central Mathematical Economics Institute was established. The TsEMI was initially staffed by economists from the previously existing Laboratory of Mathematical Economics of the academy, the Mathematical Economics section of the academy's Main Computer Center, a mathematical group from the Institute of Economics, and several other groups. V. S. Nemchinov was the driving force behind the creation of TsEMI but, due to his failing health, he selected N. P. Fedorenko to become director of the institute.

TsEMI is in the vanguard of innovative economics in the Soviet Union. Its offices in Moscow and Leningrad house research groups which are exploring the most novel approaches to Soviet economic problems. The organ of TsEMI is *Ekonomika i matematicheskiye metody*, a bi-monthly journal of high scientific caliber. In addition to many young economists, mathematicians, and engineers, TsEMI is also host to several veterans whose contributions to analytical economics began in that remarkable period of the 1920's before Stalin crushed the economists. Such sages include A. L. Lurye, V. V. Novozhilov, and A. L. Vainshtein.[11]

[10] L. M. Gatovsky was born in 1903. He has written on a number of topics in the conventional vein of Soviet political economics. He collaborated with Ostrovityanov and other ideologists from the Institute of Economics to write the famous *Textbook of Political Economy* published, finally, in 1954. He has displayed considerable agility in accommodating himself to changes in the political winds and is not a principled dogmatist as is Ostrovityanov. Since 1960, he has been a corresponding member of the academy.

[11] V. V. Novozhilov was born in 1892 and graduated in 1915 from Kiev University. For many years he taught and did research at the Leningrad Engineering-Economics Institute. He is now director of the Leningrad branch of TsEMI. He has made important contributions to mathematical economics in the USSR. Even more significant was his discovery and advocacy of the concept of opportunity cost for which he was severely attacked during the Stalinist period. As indicated, in 1965, he, with V. S. Nemchinov and L. V. Kantorovich, received the Lenin Prize for his contributions to mathematical economics.

A. L. Vainshtein was born in 1892. He was educated first as a mathematician and worked in aerodynamics. After studying economics, he began his work in

RICHARD W. JUDY

The Siberian Section of the Academy of Sciences. Two interesting groups are located at the Siberian Section of the Academy of Sciences in Novosibirsk. The first of these is the Branch of Mathematical Economic Methods of the Institute of Mathematics headed by L. V. Kantorovich, a pioneer in the use of mathematical methods in economics and a passionate reformer of Soviet economics.[12] Among his close associates is V. M. Makarov, a young economist turned mathematician. Kantorovich's group publishes the occasional journal, *Optimalnoye planirovaniye.*

The second Novosibirsk group is the Institute of Economics and Organization of Industrial Production headed by A. G. Aganbegyan.[13] Over 500 persons are employed by the institute. Much of its attention is directed to economic and sociological problems of Siberia. Mathematical methods and other unorthodox techniques are typical of Aganbegyan and his institute. Close working relations are maintained with Kantorovich's group.

---

analytical economics in 1924 with his article "Matematicheskoye ischisleniye srednevo rasstoyania polei ot usadby pri razlichnoi konfiguratsii ploshchadi zemlepolzovania i rasnom mestopolozhenii usadby" in the book *Optimalnye razmery selskokhozyaistvennykh predpriaty* (Moscow, 1922). He worked in Kondratyev's Institute of Economic Fluctuations in the 1920's. Stalin disbanded the institute and Kondratyev was shot. Vainshtein was imprisoned from about 1940 until about 1955. After his release he became associated with V. S. Nemchinov and the Laboratory of Mathematical Economics. He has made several important contributions to mathematical economics. Recently, he has devoted considerable energy to rehabilitating the reputations of Soviet mathematical economists of the 1920's, e.g., S. A. Feldman (*Ekonomika i matematicheskiye metody*, No. 4 [1968], p. 669).

Few biographical details of A. L. Lurye are available. He was born in the nineteenth century and has recently contributed significantly to mathematical economics.

[12] L. V. Kantorovich was born in 1912. He made important contributions to mathematics in the mid-1930's. In 1939, he published the first application of linear programming. This highly original work lay dormant until the late 1950's when its true importance was recognized in the USSR and abroad. Kantorovich is a radical reformer and has helped to bring powerful groups of Soviet mathematicians and physical scientists to the side of radical innovation in Soviet economic theory, policy, and methodology. He is utterly contemptuous, even in public speech, of the dogmatic defenders of economic orthodoxy. He became a full academician (of mathematics) in 1964 and in 1965 was a corecipient of the Lenin Prize.

[13] A. G. Aganbegyan was born in 1932. A very energetic and pragmatic economist, he runs a quasi-consulting firm from his base in Novosibirsk. Clients are planning agencies, enterprises, and ministries who pay fees for services rendered by Aganbegyan's analysts. Mathematically inclined and oriented toward reform, Aganbegyan is someone to watch in the future. He became a corresponding member of the academy in 1966. It is rumored that A. I. Mikoyan is his father-in-law.

214

Many ministries and planning agencies also have groups of staff and research economists. There is an extremely large number of these government agencies and institutes, and only the main ones are mentioned below.

Gosplan USSR. The State Planning Committee (Gosplan) is the main economic planning agency in the USSR. Gosplan maintains a large staff of economists and publishes the important monthly journal, *Planovoye khozyaistvo.* The Scientific Economic Research Institute of Gosplan has been under the directorship of A. N. Yefimov since its establishment in 1955 and is an active and innovative center of economic research.[14] It has done much to introduce the techniques of input-output to Soviet planning. Other groups associated with Gosplan are the Council for the Study of Productive Resources and the Institute of Complex Transportation Problems.

The Central Statistical Administration (TsSU). Many economists are employed by the Central Statistical Administration. The key position of this organization in the collection and processing of data enables it to determine what information is made available to other economists. In addition, the staff edits the monthly economic and statistical journal, *Vestnik statistiki* which is published by TsSU.

Other Ministries. Among the most influential of the ministerial institutes is the Scientific Research Institute of the Ministry of Finance. The ministry publishes the monthly journal *Finansy SSSR.* In general, the reputation of the ministry is very conservative on matters of economic policy and methodology.

Other groups of economists work in the ministries of foreign trade, agriculture, domestic trade, and in the state committees for construction affairs, labor and wages, and science and technology.

Higher Educational Institutions. Some thirty specialized engineering-economic, economic, financial, and trade institutes provide higher education for economists. Nearly 200 economics faculties exist in univer-

---

[14] A. N. Yefimov was born in 1908. He taught at the Urals Polytechnic Institute and studied the economics of the machine-building industry. From 1948 to 1955 he headed an economic research unit at the Urals filial of the Academy of Sciences. He became a corresponding member of the academy in 1964. Much of his recent work has focused on the development of mathematical methods (especially input-output analysis) and their introduction into Gosplan's practices. For this work, he and several colleagues were nominated for the Lenin Prize in 1967. He has international ties through Comecon and UNESCO.

sities and other higher educational institutions. The most significant of these institutions are Moscow State University, Leningrad State University, Moscow Institute of the National Economy, Moscow Financial Institute, Moscow Economic Statistics Institute, Leningrad Finance-Economics Institute, Moscow Engineering-Economics Institute, and the Leningrad Engineering-Economics Institute.

AGE GROUPS

There is a strong correlation between the ages of Soviet economists and their positions on questions of economic policy, theory, and methodology. Three age groups are distinguishable:

1. The pre-revolutionary generation consists of economists who were born before 1900. They were young adults in 1917 (Strumilin was forty years old!). Many participated in the remarkably creative developments in economics during the 1920's. These men survived the purges and continued their work through to the 1960's.
2. The Stalinist generation consists of people who were born in this century before 1917. Most numerous are those born in the decade 1900-1909. These men were under thirty years of age when Stalin's purges of analytical economists began in 1930. Many advanced rapidly to responsible positions in the 1930's. Their formative years were those of the purges and of great emphasis on ideological doctrine.
3. The post-revolutionary generation was born in 1917 or after. These men had only indirect contact with the purges of the 1930's. They grew up in a Stalinist environment but most were under thirty when Stalin died in 1953. They were young enough to adapt rapidly to the changing demands placed before Soviet economists after 1955.

The pre-revolutionary generation is sharply split between highly orthodox political economists such as K. V. Ostrovityanov, and analytical economists such as V. V. Novozhilov and A. L. Vainshtein. The former are much concerned with the quasi-ecclesiastical aspects of Marxism-Leninism-Stalinism. The older analytical economists feel a strong continuity between the 1960's and the 1920's when Soviet economics was oriented toward policy and was rigorous in method.

With a few notable exceptions, the Stalinist generation of political

216

economists consists of dreary hacks, who benefited by Stalin's purges, and are often of mediocre ability. They form the backbone of orthodoxy in Soviet economics. They tend to be clustered in the Institute of Economics of the Academy of Sciences, in higher educational institutions, and in some ministries—especially the Ministry of Finance.

The post-revolutionary generation of economists, as a group, is remarkably receptive to change and innovation in economic theory, methodology, and policy, which disconcerts their orthodox elders. K. V. Ostrovityanov recently complained, "Young economists sometimes give undeserved tribute to Böhm-Bawerk and Tugan-Baranovsky; they don't know the history of the struggle of Marxism with subjectivism." He called for an attack on "incorrect theories of domestic production."[15]

GROUPING BY DEGREE OF MATHEMATICAL PROFICIENCY

Mathematical proficiency is the litmus paper for testing Soviet economists. There are rare exceptions to the generalization that mathematically proficient economists are also innovational in theory and policy.[16] Those of the pre-revolutionary generation of economists who are mathematically inclined (e.g., A. L. Vainshtein and A. L. Lurye) are, without known exception, innovational. Extremely few of the Stalinist generation are mathematically competent; the application of mathematics was proscribed during the Stalinist period.[17]

The younger post-revolutionary economists have been strongly drawn toward mathematical economics. A Kafedra of Mathematical Economics (or Economic Cybernetics) has been established at both Leningrad and Moscow universities. N. P. Fedorenko is head of the Kafedra of Mathematical Economics at Moscow University. The kafedra enrolled 250 students in 1966-1967 and the quality of these students is said by some Soviet observers to be much higher than that of other students in the

[15] *Voprosy ekonomiki*, No. 8 (1966), p. 142. E. von Böhm-Bawerk was a prominent member of the Austrian "marginal utility" group of economists who opposed Marxist economics in the late nineteenth century. M. Tugan-Baranovsky was a Russian economist of the late nineteenth and early twentieth centuries who attempted a marriage of Marx's labor theory of value with Austrian marginalism.

[16] But many innovational economists are not mathematically proficient.

[17] A prominent exception is A. Ya. Bayarsky who was born in 1906. He is the author of several works in statistics and mathematical economics and is very orthodox in his concern for doctrinal purity in economic theory. He is head of the Kafedra of Statistics in the Economics Faculty of Moscow State University and director of the Scientific Research Institute for Planning Computer Centers and Systems of Economic Information of the Central Statistical Administration.

faculty. Many of the best of these students do their graduate study in the Central Mathematical Economics Institute.

The affinity of young economists for mathematical methods has made it difficult for the Institute of Economics of the Academy of Sciences to attract qualified graduate students (*aspiranty*) and young research staff. This has alarmed the older economists in the Institute of Economics. M. V. Kolganov, a senior institute staff member, complained:

> Youth is excessively attracted to mathematical methods. . . . And, incidentally, there is a noticeable prejudice against the political economy of Marxism among a number of our young economists. Talk with such a young man and you will find that he knows mathematical methods but doesn't know the elementary basics of Marxist political economy. This induces the most dismal thoughts. One fine day we may face the same situation that the writers did when they were confronted with modernism in the arts.[18]

This section has set forth three principal attributes of Soviet economists which are useful in categorizing Soviet economists: age, degree of mathematical proficiency, and institution of main occupational affiliation. If one knows nothing about an economist beyond these three attributes, it is possible to predict with considerable accuracy the position he will take on major problems of economic policy, theory, and methodology.

Economics and Economists under Stalin

To indicate the manner in which opinion groups characterized by the attributes of age, degree of mathematical proficiency, and institution of main occupational affiliation have come to be associated with positions on major issues of policy, theory, and methodology, we turn to a review of the relationships between economists and the Soviet leadership during the Stalin era and after the old dictator's death.

The Stalinist period was a nightmare for analytical economists. The 1920's saw a great creative outburst during the N.E.P. with the work of V. A. Bazarov, V. G. Groman, and others, but Stalin cut off these promising developments before they reached maturity. V. G. Groman

---

[18] *Ekonomisty i matematiki za kruglym stolom* (Moscow, 1965), pp. 163-164. M. S. Kolganov was born in 1911 and died in 1966. In addition to his senior post at the Institute of Economics, Kolganov held a faculty position at Moscow University.

was removed from Gosplan in 1929; two years later, he was convicted in the "Menshevik Trial." V. A. Bazarov disappeared in late 1930.[19] Many others followed these men into obscurity; few returned. Stalin assailed economists who foresaw the consequences of his lopsided development policies. He suspected economics with its talk of markets, prices, and "equilibrium." He excised from the body of political economy all concern with planning and economic policy. Thus mutilated, political economy was to confine itself to discovering economic "laws" and guarding doctrinal purity. The tools of planning and economic policy were to be wielded only by practical planners and managers. Into the places left vacant by the purged analytical economists slid common drudges ready to mind Stalin's insipid economic "laws." The few remaining economists with analytical potency disguised it or scurried to safety in less vulnerable disciplines.

Early attempts to restore vitality to Soviet political economy were squashed. Sensing that the question of price formation was crucial to the proper treatment of the economic system's ills, some Soviet economists tried to study that question in the late 1930's. But in 1938, Molotov forbade the continuation of a discussion on questions of price formation on the grounds that prices were the concern of policy, not of economists.[20]

Some creative work continued during the worst days of the Stalin era. V. V. Novozhilov developed a belabored but ingenious study of value and price. His reward for these novel and unorthodox ideas was, for many years, abuse. One of Novozhilov's most aggressive critics, P. S. Mstislavsky, attacked him because his logic proceeded from the "super-historical idea of 'maximum effect with minimum expenditures' which was long ago unmasked in Marxist literature."[21] The idea of

---

[19] V. A. Bazarov was a Menshevik economist who worked in Gosplan. His ideas on the use of capital charges were in advance of notions proposed in the USSR as late as 1968. He disappeared late in 1930. V. G. Groman was another Menshevik economist whose significant contribution to the theory and practice of economic planning was his work on the "Control Figures" in Gosplan. He was removed from this responsibility late in 1927, fired from Gosplan in 1929, and sentenced in 1931.

[20] Reported by A. A. Arzumanyan to the Presidium of the Academy of Sciences, USSR. See *Vestnik Akademii Nauk SSSR*, No. 9 (1964), p. 7.

[21] *Voprosy ekonomiki*, Nos. 7 and 10 (1948). For a contemporary Soviet report of these attacks see A. L. Vainshtein, "Vozniknoveniye i razvitiye primenenia lineinovo programmirovania v SSSR," *Ekonomika i matematicheskiye metody*, No. 3 (1966), p. 25. F. S. Mstislavsky is a veteran member of the Institute of Economics.

optimality in the use of resources was so foreign to Soviet political economy that it could be used as a flail by a defender of the doctrine.[22]

A second significant contribution to Soviet analytical economics during the Stalin era was the development of linear programming by the Leningrad mathematician, L. V. Kantorovich. Although it preceded by nearly a decade the independent development of linear programming in the West, Kantorovich's important work was ignored or suppressed in the Soviet Union until the late 1950's.[23]

Finally, some courageous Soviet economists and technicians attempted to suggest improvements in the design of the Soviet economic system even during the darkest hours of the Stalinist night.[24]

The situation for Soviet economic science deteriorated further during the last years of Stalin's reign. The involvement of N. A. Voznesensky with the cultural purges of the late 1940's brought points of economic controversy into the dangerous arena of high Kremlin politics.[25] E. S. Varga, head of the Institute of World Economics, was attacked by Voznesensky in 1947 for his view that the economic collapse of capitalist countries was avoidable. Robert Conquest relates some details of this encounter:

On May 4, 14, and 21, 1947, a meeting of economists and political experts was organized under the presidency of Ostrovityanov (who was to be the economic spokesman of the "left" throughout this

[22] It will be argued later in this paper that it is precisely the acceptance of the goal of optimal resource use that basically distinguishes the Soviet "new economics" from the sterile Stalinist political economy.

[23] The original work of Kantorovich, *Matematicheskiye metody organizatsii i planirovania proizvodstva* (Leningrad, 1939), lay dormant and neglected until references began to be made to it in mathematical economics literature during the late 1950's. Kantorovich's 1959 monograph on the most efficient use of resources, *Ekonomichesky raschet nailuchshevo izpolzovania resursov* (Moscow, 1959) was written in 1941 or 1942 and the author delivered reports on its contents and conclusions to the Leningrad Polytechnic Institute in 1940 and to the Institute of Economics in 1943. See Vainshtein, *op.cit.*, p. 25.

[24] Z. V. Atlas, a veteran Soviet economist now at the Moscow Financial Institute, wrote that he proposed in the late 1940's that enterprise profitability be used as an index of enterprise performance and that it be tied to the use of fixed and circulating capital. (He refers to *Izvestia: otdeleniye ekonomiki i prava, Akademia Nauk SSSR*, No. 5 [1949], p. 387.) Atlas states that this question was again raised in connection with the problem of price formation in the economic discussion of 1951 by L. A. Vaag. The material of this discussion was never published. See Z. V. Atlas, *Khozraschyot, rentabelnost i kredit* (Moscow, 1966), p. 14.

[25] See Robert Conquest, *Power and Policy in the U.S.S.R.* (New York, 1961), pp. 88-111.

220

dispute and has lately figured as a supporter of Khrushchev). The discussion was referred to and Varga was criticized in *Bolshevik* of September, 1947. And in the following months *Pravda* and other papers made a full-scale attack on the moderates.[26]

Varga was censured, his journal *World Economy and World Politics* was suppressed, and his institute was merged into the Institute of Economics under the directorship of Ostrovityanov. The journal *Voprosy ekonomiki* began publication as the official organ of the institute with Ostrovityanov as its editor-in-chief, who, in the first issue, assailed Varga for his ideological sins.[27]

On March 13, 1949, *Pravda* announced that Voznesensky had been removed from his position as head of Gosplan; he was later liquidated. After 1949, Voznesensky was not again mentioned in the Soviet press until after the publication of Stalin's *Economic Problems of Socialism in the USSR*, which appeared in *Pravda* on October 3 and 4, 1952.[28] In this opus, Stalin reiterated his views that economics had no relation to economic policy. He said: "Political economy investigates the laws of development of men's relations of production. Economic policy draws practical conclusions from this, gives them concrete shape, and builds its day-to-day work on them. To foist upon political economy problems of economic policy is to kill it as a science."[29]

This publication of Stalin's had an immediate impact on the Institute of Economics. Sycophantic praise of Stalin's genius was mixed with confessions of error by senior members of the institute. The Scientific Council specified a series of tasks which amounted to calls for more praise and propaganda for Stalin's encyclical.[30] Great stress was placed on the necessity for guarding doctrinal purity.[31]

The heavy ideological artillery opened fire on Voznesensky with an

[26] *Ibid.*, pp. 88-89.

[27] *Voprosy ekonomiki*, No. 1 (March 1948).

[28] Conquest, *op.cit.*, p. 103. See Joseph Stalin, *Economic Problems of Socialism in the USSR* (New York, 1952), p. 72, and I. V. Stalin, *Works*, III (XVI), Robert H. McNeal (ed.) (Stanford, 1967) (in Russian), 188-304.

[29] Stalin, *Economic Problems*, p. 72.

[30] *Voprosy ekonomiki*, No. 12 (1952), pp. 102-116. Several economists admitted that they deserved Stalin's criticism but their contrition was judged inadequate by the editor of *Voprosy ekonomiki* (Ostrovityanov).

[31] *Ibid.*, p. 116. It is significant that there was a total absence of any specified task directing members of the institute to undertake studies designed to promote better or more efficient operation of the economic system. Alone of the institute economists, T. S. Khachaturov emphasized the need to become involved in real economic problems.

article by M. Suslov in *Pravda* on December 24, 1952. After more than three years as a "nonperson," Voznesensky suddenly became the posthumous target of a barrage of charges that his economics was "idealistic," "voluntaristic," "dangerous," and "anti-Marxist." He was alleged to have made a "fetish" of the law of value and to have seen it as a "regulator" of the allocation of resources among branches of the national economy.[32] It seems doubtful that his economics was the major reason for Voznesensky's demise since no effort had been made in 1949 to correct the notions found to be so harmful in 1952. All the more reason, therefore, why many Soviet economists may have interpreted Stalin's *Economic Problems* and Suslov's *Pravda* blast as the opening rounds of a major attack on other economists whose ideas Stalin opposed. Indeed the *Pravda* article accused the journal *Voprosy ekonomiki* of propagandizing Voznesensky's anti-Marxist views and of failing to unmask dangerous economic heresies. The editors of the journal took cover in the lead editorial of the January 1953 issue

---

[32] The charge of "voluntarism" implies that Voznesensky considered the power of planners to be unconstrained by objective circumstances. To have a "fetish" about the law of value presumably means to favor using market forces as a means of allocating resources in the economy; in the words of Soviet jargon, it means ascribing a "regulating role to the law of value."

It is difficult to reconcile these apparently contradictory charges. Two alternative interpretations suggest themselves: (1) Logical consistency among the charges was unimportant because they were being used against individuals and not against economic ideas. (2) A group of economists, including possibly even Voznesensky, had expressed ideas favoring significant redesign of the Soviet economic system which would attempt to reconcile planning and market forces. The fact that the material of the November 1951 discussions on the draft textbook of political economy has never been published suggests that radical ideas may have been advanced at that time. Professor Z. V. Atlas (*op.cit.*, p. 14), tells us that the subject of price formation was raised in those discussions. From Stalin's criticisms of Yaroshenko, we know that the reorientation of socialist political economy toward the design of optimal planning systems was considered by some of the participants at the 1951 conference. Furthermore, Atlas wrote in 1966 that the material of the 1951 discussion was ". . . of importance for the history of economic thought in the USSR and some of the ideas and propositions made there retain their significance and timeliness to the present day." He urged its publication.

By 1966, the economic debate had turned explicitly to questions of "optimal economic planning" and to a search for a rational design of the economic system. Professor Atlas was arguing the case for sweeping decentralization of economic decision-making and the use of market forces in his 1966 book. It was in this context that he mentioned the 1951 debates and noted their relevance for 1966. It is hard to imagine that he would have thought that the 1951 discussions were still pertinent if there were not ideas therein that supported his position. This is all quite speculative, however, and it would be premature to form firm judgments about what actually was said at the 1951 discussions or what motivated Stalin's *Economic Problems* and Suslov's attack in *Pravda*.

behind abject confessions of guilt and passed the attack on to a dozen individual members of the Institute of Economics.[33] Stalin's death on March 5, 1953, arrested the development of the campaign against errant economists before it attained its destined momentum. But it had accelerated sufficiently to frighten badly many of the most prominent Soviet economists.[34]

Soviet economics was in a very sorry state at the time of Stalin's death. Analytical economics had been denied a role in the political economy of socialism and competent economists had been liquidated or driven underground. Political economy had become a vapid ecclesiastical catechism, characterized by sterility and sycophancy. As Academician A. A. Arzumanyan phrased it in 1964:

> Stalin's wrong treatment of the subject of political economy and particularly of the political economy of socialism and his false perception of the role of this science led to an impoverishment of its content and to an emasculation of its revolutionary-practical significance. . . . Stalin regarded political economy as the antipode of economic policy. His mistaken proposition doomed economic research to be an abstract, closed and scholastic study of socialist property ownership. Theoretical economics became significantly isolated from life and from the study of economic problems. Several important facets of our economic life were simply dropped from political economy.[35]

In 1962, Academician L. F. Ilyichev described the effect of Stalinism on Soviet economics in the following words:

> One of the most harmful phenomena of the period of the cult of personality in economic science was the encouragement of economists who could not analyze concrete factual material but who instead could adroitly manipulate citations.

[33] Ostrovityanov admitted that he had erred in praising Voznesensky's "dangerous, anti-Marxist" book, *Voennaya ekonomika SSSR v period Otechestvennoi voiny* (Moscow, 1948), *Voprosy ekonomiki*, No. 1 (1952), pp. 3-15.

[34] The economists singled out for criticism in late 1952 and early 1953 were mainly those who, by the standards of the economic debate of the late 1950's and 1960's, were most docile and orthodox. The liberals and radicals of the later era, such men as Nemchinov, Novozhilov, Fedorenko, Atlas, Vaag, Konius, Lurye, Vainshtein, and Khachaturov emerged unscathed from this fray.

[35] *Vestnik Akademii Nauk SSSR*, No. 9 (1964), pp. 4-5. These remarks were made to a meeting of the Presidium of the Academy of Sciences.

Objectively, the science retreated from questions of production; economists isolated themselves from real life. Their first concern was not with harmonizing economic policy with the demands of economic laws but rather with the "adaptation" of political economy to the major deficiencies that prevailed in practice, i.e., apologizing for those deficiencies.[36]

Academician V. Nemchinov in 1957 spoke of economic statistics in words applicable to all of economics:

Many scholarly statisticians lost their creative individuality and their initiative; they were turned into commentators and interpreters of I. V. Stalin's few utterances on statistical questions. Scientific creativity was displaced by dogmatism and gospel reading; vivifying new scholarly thought was replaced by deadening scholasticism and talmudism. . . . The "citational style" became the dominant if not exclusive method of scholarly exposition and scientific proof. Many "dissertations" and "monographs" consisted nine-tenths of citations that, until mid-1953, were included in quotation marks, and *after that* were without even that external prop.[37]

The totalitarian "model" provides quite an adequate interpretation of the politics of Soviet economics under Stalin. That individual economists cherished ideas at variance with those promulgated officially is also true. But there is no evidence to suggest that these individuals sharing unorthodox ideas combined into opinion groups which worked for the implementation of those ideas. There may have been small groups of like-thinking economists who took each other into mutual confidence.[38] But Stalin had atomized the opposition to his economic notions and had placed docile and obedient sycophants in powerful positions in the Institute of Economics and elsewhere. These faithful executioners of Stalin's will were content to guard doctrinal purity and to produce a generation of economists who could not even recognize, much less analyze, important economic problems.

[36] *Ibid.*, No. 11 (1962), p. 19.

[37] *Uchyonye zapiski po statistike*, Tom III, p. 6 (italics added).

[38] For example, circumstantial evidence points to a grouping around Novozhilov at the Leningrad Polytechnical Institute. Kantorovich may have been a member of this group. Even if such a "grouping" existed, it seems to have been utterly without power to affect policy during Stalin's era.

The Struggle with Inertia, 1955-1961

Little change in Soviet economics was evident for about two years after Stalin's death. The status of the discipline remained low; political economists continued to occupy themselves with irrelevancies. Ideological considerations retained their dominance, and the ideologues continued to control the important editorial and directoral posts. Controversy about relative growth rates between producers' and consumers' goods sectors was injected into the political struggle between Khrushchev and Malenkov. This indicated that economic debate was still fraught with political danger and discouraged the rebirth of analytical economics. Stalin's *Economic Problems of Socialism in the USSR* continued to be quoted with obeisance. Other than ideological rectitude, little was expected of Soviet political economists.

A major change in party expectations of Soviet economists took place in 1955. After the July (1955) plenum, the party and scientific leaderships began seriously to criticize the economists and to place demanding tasks before them. In September 1955, the Presidium of the Academy of Sciences convened a special meeting to consider the shortcomings in economics and to specify new demands on the discipline. The Institute of Economics was criticized for not responding to the demands put before it by the party and government. These had required the institute to develop the political economy of socialism so that it would be of aid to economic policy and planning.[39] In other words, Soviet economics was instructed to become relevant; the Stalinist conception of political economy was to be broken.

At the Twentieth Party Congress in 1956, the party leadership assailed the economists for their neglect of real problems of the economy. N. S. Khrushchev said that economists' work was unsatisfactory because it shed no light on questions of developing industry and agriculture. The economic institutes and their workers, he said, had divorced themselves utterly from the practical work of communist construction.[40]

---

[39] The institute was said not to have produced a single solid work in the field of the economics of socialism. Several members were accused of dogmatism. Economists were urged to concern themselves with problems of the use of the law of value in planning, price formation, labor productivity, material incentives, industrial location, and the economics of agriculture. The institute was ordered by the presidium to correct the shortcomings, to orient itself toward important problems, and to overcome bureaucraticism in its leadership. See *Vestnik Akademii Nauk SSSR*, No. 11 (1955), pp. 108-111.

[40] *XX Syezd Kommunisticheskoi Partii Sovetskovo Soyuza, stenog. otchyot* (Moscow, 1956), I, 113.

A. I. Mikoyan scorned Stalin's *Economic Problems* and criticized economists for their failure to subject it to a Marxist-Leninist critique.[41] A. N. Kosygin complained that the methodology of long-range planning had deteriorated considerably in recent years; the economists, unfortunately, had done practically nothing to improve the situation.[42] Academician A. N. Nesmeyanov, president of the Academy of Sciences, accepted the criticism levied against the economists and assured the congress that the presidium would not ignore this justified criticism but would take steps to correct the deficiencies.[43]

Following the Twentieth Party Congress, the criticism of economists continued in the press and in various scientific meetings.[44] The Presidium of the Academy of Sciences, fulfilling A. N. Nesmeyanov's promise to the congress, subjected the Institute of Economics to withering fire: its staff had not studied important economic problems; the presidium's directives issued in September 1955, had not been carried out; the leadership of the institute was incompetent. The report of the presidium's meeting continued:

> Criticism and self-criticism in the institute is very weak and this lowers the quality of scientific work. Simultaneously, there have been instances of dishonest and malevolent criticism which had led to an unjustified discrediting of scientific work which may have contained individual deficiencies and mistakes but which, in general, have been written from a Marxist position and which constitute items of scientific and practical value.

> Some staff members of the institute do not produce any kind of scientific output or limit themselves to repetition of familiar truths.[45]

The tasks being thrust upon the economists by the party and the academy's presidium were clearly aimed at making Soviet economics relevant to the problems facing policy-makers and planners. The symptoms of economic malfunctioning were apparent everywhere and anecdotal descriptions of those symptoms were commonplace, but because of the analytical poverty of the political economy of socialism,

---

[41] *Ibid.*, pp. 323-324.   [42] *Ibid.*, p. 323.   [43] *Ibid.*, p. 374.

[44] See, for example, the editorial in *Vestnik Akademii Nauk SSSR*, No. 3 (1956), pp. 5 and 6, the criticisms by Nemchinov and Varga at the general meeting of the Section of Economics, Philosophy, and Law reported in *ibid.*, No. 4 (1956), pp. 118-122, and Nesmeyanov's speech reported in *ibid.*, No. 6 (1956), pp. 12-15.

[45] *Ibid.*, No. 10 (1956), p. 86.

literally no one could provide a cogent diagnosis. Not surprisingly, the tasks thrust upon the economists were stated imprecisely in the confused jargon of the day. The intent shone clearly through the imprecision and jargon; it was to drag Soviet economics into the twentieth century.[46]

It is important to note here that the revolution in Soviet economics was not launched by the economists. No group of economists applied pressure on the nation's leadership to adopt well-formulated new economic policies. Nor was the pressure of economic ideas sufficiently strong to flow vigorously when the party removed the political plug.[47] The political and scientific leadership was forced to "prime the pump" to induce a flow of economic studies and discussion.[48]

Important pressure for improved economic criteria for rational decision-making did, however, come from scientists, technologists, and engineers. Many hopes vested in automation and other forms of technical progress were frustrated by the absence of adequate measures of "economic effectiveness." Without such measures it was impossible to determine where the application of new technology and capital investment would provide the greatest social benefit. Furthermore, without material incentives coupled to the criteria, economic managers would have no incentive to innovate even when it was economically rational to do so. These frustrations produced demands by scientists for rational economic criteria of effectiveness.[49] The scientists helped convince the

[46] The presidium ordered the Institute of Economics to concentrate on the study of the political economy of socialism and on the "theoretical generalization of the experience of communist construction." The study of all questions was to be "closely related to the development of long range plans for the development of the national economy of the USSR and to the economic competition of the two world systems and to the solution of the basic economic tasks of the USSR, and to the development and strengthening of the socialist system of world economy." *Ibid.*, p. 87.

[47] It is ironic that the leaders of the party and the Academy of Sciences initially selected K. V. Ostrovityanov as the prophet to lead Soviet economics into the promised land of relevancy. In mid-1956, he was given the job of coordinating the study of economics in the various scientific divisions of the academy. *Ibid.*, p. 87.

[48] At a coordinating conference of all institutions doing economic research in the academy held in February 1957, L. V. Gatovsky said: *"From us economists, it is justly demanded* that we quickly convert from simple commentary on existing practices . . . to the formulation of new questions which will assist the improvement of practice. . . ." *Voprosy ekonomiki*, No. 3 (1957), pp. 145-149 (italics added).

[49] On October 15-20, 1956, a conference was held in the Academy of Sciences on "Scientific Problems of the Automation of Production." Participants included

227

party leadership that the fruits of technology would go ungathered without improved economic criteria and incentives.

Criticisms of the lag of Soviet economics behind the demands of life and practice were repeated many times in the years following the Twentieth Party Congress. Economists were censured for their inability to formulate the theoretical basis of price formation, to develop criteria for comparing capital investment alternatives, to devise measures of the economic effectiveness of automation, to provide standards for making decisions about industrial location, to improve the system of planning, to formulate satisfactory indexes for assessing the performance of enterprises, to develop ways of stimulating higher productivity and innovation, to employ properly mathematical methods and computers in their research, and to generalize from empirical data. They were accused of dogmatism, pedantry, talmudism, and incompetence. The drumfire of criticism and demands emanating from the highest party levels was amplified by the top leadership of the Academy of Sciences. Mathematicians, physical scientists, engineers, and individual economists joined the attack.

At the Twenty-first Party Congress in 1959, the economists were assailed by N. S. Khrushchev and I. I. Kuzmin, then head of Gosplan and a First Deputy Chairman of the Council of Ministers. The charges were familiar; economists and economic institutions failed to resolve important practical problems, they were divorced from life, their pub-

---

such bright stars in the Soviet scientific firmament as A. N. Nesmeyanov, A. A. Blagonravov, I. I. Artobolevsky, V. I. Didushin, V. S. Kulebyakin, V. A. Trapeznikov, M. V. Keldysh, A. A. Lyapunov, M. P. Shura-Bura, A. N. Kolmogorov, I. S. Bruk, and S. A. Lebedev. The only economists represented were S. G. Strumilin and G. D. Bakulev, two superannuated fossils.

One of the points stressed by the conferees was that economic science had failed to provide the criteria required to choose rational paths of developing automation in production. With apparent impatience, it was noted that the Institute of Economics had only recently begun to study such important problems. See *Vestnik Akademii Nauk SSSR*, No. 11 (1956), pp. 10-15.

L. A. Vaag told a conference on the law of value in 1957 the following:

I am a technician, a specialist in electric stations, and I assert that we cannot decide basic technical questions without the solution of economic questions. We cannot compare the efficiency of thermal *vs.* hydro-electric stations, we cannot exactly determine how much nonferrous metals we should use in the construction of lines for the transmission of electric energy. Such questions raise serious economic problems.

See L. A. Vaag in Ya. A. Kronrod (ed.), *Zakon stoimosti i evo ispolzovaniye v narodnom khozyaistve SSSR* (Moscow, 1959), p. 425. Vaag later became an economist. He is now with the State Committee of the Council of Ministers for Science and Technology.

lications were merely descriptive, they confined themselves to well-known arguments, etc. To promote practicality among economists, Kuzmin suggested the creation of joint undertakings by Gosplan and the Academy of Sciences. These sentiments were echoed by A. N. Nesmeyanov and K. V. Ostrovityanov.[50]

Leading party figures directed more sharp words at the economists during the July (1960) plenum of the Central Committee. This time, A. N. Nesmeyanov was able to claim that the Academy of Sciences was "overcoming the isolation of its economic institutes from the needs of the national economy." He admitted, however, that much more remained to be done.[51]

In 1961, at the Twenty-second Party Congress, the economists were again urged to repair their deficiencies. One reason for the slow progress in economics, asserted P. N. Demichev, was that some prominent economists spent too much time considering the causes for the lag in economic science without doing anything constructive about it.[52] M. V. Keldysh stated that the party was directing economists to organize their research in such a way as "to provide more scientifically grounded recommendations and thereby to promote more effective decisions regarding practical questions of the development of the economy." He urged economists to use mathematical methods and computer technology.[53]

Criticism of economists by the top party echelon was followed by an unremitting campaign of censure and goading by the scientific elite of the Academy of Sciences. In meetings and speeches too numerous to chronicle, this battle was waged by the academy's presidents, A. N. Nesmeyanov and M. V. Keldysh,[54] other high officials of the academy

[50] *Vneocherednoi XXI Syezd Kommunisticheskoi Partii Sovetskovo Soyuza, stenog. otchyot* (Moscow, 1959), I, 61; II, 205-207, 215, 374-378.
[51] *Plenum Tsentralnovo Komiteta Kommunisticheskoi Partii Sovetskovo Soyuza, 13-16 iyulya 1960 goda, stenog. otchyot* (Moscow, 1960), p. 234.
[52] *XXII Syezd Kommunisticheskoi Partii Sovetskovo Soyuza, stenog. otchet* (Moscow, 1962), I, 263. P. N. Demichev was then first secretary of the Moscow obkom. His attack on economists who bemoaned the lag in economics but did nothing seems to have been a slap at Ostrovityanov and other holdovers from the Stalinist era of political economy.
[53] *Ibid.*, p. 412.
[54] For statements by A. N. Nesmeyanov, see *Vestnik Akademii Nauk SSSR*, No. 2 (1957), pp. 32-33, and *ibid.*, No. 3 (1961), p. 10. M. V. Keldysh has been a particularly strong supporter of analytical economics and a champion of mathematical methods and computers in economics. See *ibid.*, No. 7 (1961), p. 38, for an early statement by Keldysh; many more followed in subsequent years.

such as A. V. Topchyev,[55] and prominent individual scientists and economists.[56] Particularly sarcastic remarks came from the mathematician, L. V. Kantorovich, who said:

> Frequently economists, while admitting certain deficiencies, consider that our economic science is not so bad and they cite the truly remarkable growth rates of our economy as proof. . . . But was the role of economists in these achievements so great? . . . Forty-two years after the socialist state was formed our economic science does not know exactly what the law of value means in a socialist society or how it should be applied, nor does it know what is socialist rent or whether there should be a general calculus of effectiveness of capital investment and, if so, how to do it. We are presented as the most recent discoveries in the field of economics such things as, for example, "the law of value does not operate in socialist society, it only operates upon," or that "the means of production is not simply a commodity but a commodity of a particular type," and so on.[57]

The years from 1955 to 1961 brought more than criticism for Soviet economics; it also brought several important new institutions of economic research. The Scientific Economic Research Institute of Gosplan was created in 1955 with A. N. Yefimov at its head. The objective of this institute was and is to study and improve the methodology of planning. In 1958, the Presidium of the Academy of Sciences announced the creation of the Institute of Economics and Organization of Industrial Production of the Siberian Branch of the academy, headed by A. G. Aganbegyan. An independent Laboratory for Mathematical Economics was

[55] Academician A. V. Topchyev was chief scientific secretary of the academy's presidium. See his very strong statements as reported in *ibid.*, No. 1 (1959), pp. 8-9 (heavy stress on use of mathematical methods and computers and need to make economics relevant) and *ibid.*, No. 4 (1959), pp. 24-25 (strong criticism of economists following the Twenty-first Party Congress); and *ibid.*, No. 8 (1960), pp. 6-7 (following the July [1960] plenum).
[56] It was during this period that Academician V. S. Nemchinov began to emerge as a leader of the "new Soviet economics." See his speeches and remarks as reported in *ibid.*, No. 3 (1957), pp. 50-53 and *ibid.*, No. 5 (1958), pp. 70-73. These reports were given by Nemchinov in his capacity as the academic secretary of the academy's Section on Economics, Philosophy, and Law.
See also the contributions of various scientists at meetings of the Presidium of the Academy of Sciences as reported in *ibid.*, No. 4 (1959), pp. 55-63, and *ibid.*, No. 10 (1959), pp. 95-96.
[57] *Ibid.*, No. 4 (1959), p. 60. Kantorovich credited the academy's Section on Economics, Philosophy, and Law with some accomplishments in the preceding one or two years in propagandizing mathematical methods in economics. V. S. Nemchinov headed the section.

also established in Novosibirsk to be led by L. V. Kantorovich. In Moscow, the presidium established in 1960 a Laboratory for Mathematical Economics under the leadership of V. S. Nemchinov.[58] All of the newly created organizations were intended to develop tools of economic analysis and to apply those tools to problems of planning and management. Their establishment and growth provided organizational bases for groups of analytical economists who were often young and well trained in mathematics. Thus, the orthodox Institute of Economics found itself increasingly in the backwater of new developments.

By the end of 1961, the inertia in Soviet economics was beginning to be overcome. Considerable forward momentum had been built up in a number of new institutes. Important questions were being studied, but much more remained to be done before Soviet economics could make the contribution demanded of it. A. N. Kosygin stated his views in a speech to a group of scientists in 1961:

> Economic science still lags behind the demands of life and practice.
> . . . Academic economists devote little attention to developing planning methodology, to problems of raising the effectiveness of capital investments, to the rational use of capital stocks, and to other questions thrust forward by our economic practice. The majority of economic studies . . . are of a general character and it is possible to draw from them very little of practical use. . . .[59]

Kosygin continued by specifying many problem areas in which economists should be providing recommendations to the party and planning officials. At the end of his remarks, he urged economists and planners to make bold and broad use of modern mathematical methods and computers in research, planning, and management.[60]

This section has attempted to show how Soviet economics began to emerge into the twentieth century during the period following the July (1955) party plenum. During this period we have witnessed a most interesting and significant development of opinion group activity among economists. Subtle interactions among certain groups of economists and other groups among scientists and party leaders produced a kind of coalition politics. It is not possible to document fully the shifting lines of these coalitions or alliances. It would seem, however, that the

[58] See *Voprosy ekonomiki*, No. 5 (1957), pp. 137-139, *Vestnik Akademii Nauk SSSR*, No. 4 (1961), pp. 53-56.
[59] *Ibid.*, No. 7 (1961), p. 97.   [60] *Ibid.*, p. 99.

changing strength of these coalitions lies behind the fluctuations in power within the academic economic establishment and in economic policy during the period since 1955. The following section examines the coalitions as they are observed in two significant policy controversies.

Issues in Soviet Economics, 1956-1968

Prodded by some members of the political and scientific leaderships, Soviet economists began to turn their attention to topics of importance in economic planning and management. The poverty of economic science was such that no demonstratively superior answers were available for the questions which vexed the Soviet leaders. It took time to overhaul obsolete habits of thought and discourse to an extent that would allow an intelligent approach to these problems. The period since 1956 has been one of renaissance for Soviet economic science.

During the early part of this period, economists tended to focus their energy on seemingly unconnected questions which were specified by some of the political and economic leaders. Thus, at the meeting of the Presidium of the Academy of Sciences following the Central Committee plenum of July 1955, the economists were directed to study problems of the use of the law of value in planning, of price formation, of raising labor productivity and lowering costs, of material incentives, of industrial location, of the ways of promoting technical progress, and complex mechanization and automization of production, and of the criteria for choosing from among capital investment alternatives.[61] This list of tasks was supplemented in subsequent years; economists were directed to make use of mathematical methods and computer technology and to concern themselves with ways of improving the planning system.

As the studies and discussion of these individual topics gradually developed, it became apparent that these were not separate and decomposable questions but were linked by ties of mutual dependency in a complex economic system. In the latter part of the period, the examination of many of these questions has tended to fuse into a comprehensive study of the most rational design of the entire Soviet economic system. Only since about 1963 has analysis and debate approached a high level of sophistication.

It should be stressed that the problems of the Soviet economy are so complex that highly sophisticated analysis is necessary. Many of the

[61] *Ibid.*, No. 11 (1955), pp. 108-111.

propositions advanced during the time under review were either vacuous, ill-conceived, or seriously deficient, as were those nostrums which were much publicized by the Western press. In retrospect, the caution displayed by the Soviet leadership in implementing these propositions appears prudent.

It is possible to identify the position taken by certain groups of economists in the discussions of policy, theory, and methodology which have taken place since the Twentieth Party Congress. It is beyond the scope of this paper to treat in depth all of the many issues, but it may be instructive to examine in detail the patterns of alliance insofar as they can be discerned. For this purpose, two issues have been chosen: (1) the issue of criteria by which to evaluate enterprise performance and (2) the issue of the basis of price formation. As will be seen, the available literature offers an extremely rich variety of viewpoints on these two issues by opinion groups actively seeking to influence policy.

CRITERIA FOR EVALUATING ENTERPRISE PERFORMANCE

The problem of finding appropriate "success criteria" is common to all complex organizations. It is the problem of devising goals and incentives for subsystems which will lead decision-makers at lower levels to behave in ways that are consistent with the global objectives of the system. In Western neoclassical economic theory, this reconciliation between system and subsystem goals takes place in an ideal system with perfect competition and postulated maximizing behavior by households and firms. In such an ideal system, prices are determined in such a way that they present full information to decision-makers about the relative scarcities of various goods and services. In their maximizing behavior, households and firms are led by Adam Smith's "invisible hand" to behave in a socially optimal way. Of course, the existence of monopolistic elements, imperfect knowledge, and other breaches of perfect competition deny the real economic system these properties of optimality.

The search for effective criteria by which to evaluate the work of Soviet economic enterprises has been long and discouraging. For many years, the main measure of merit was the degree to which an enterprise fulfilled or overfulfilled its gross output plan.[62] This criterion has serious

[62] The reader is presumed to be familiar with the problem of "success criteria" in the Soviet economy. A good source is A. Nove, "Some Problems of 'Success Indicators' in Soviet Industry," in *Economica*, N. S., xxv, No. 97 (January 1958). See also Janos Kornai, *Overcentralisation in Hungarian Light Industry* (Oxford, 1959).

defects, and there has been a proliferation of auxiliary indices (*poka-zateli*) to remedy these flaws. The question of success criteria is closely related to that of the optimal degree of decentralization. So long as the success criteria at the enterprise level tended to encourage behavior that was inconsistent with the global objectives of the economic leadership, it could be and was argued that decentralization of decision-making would lead the system to perform worse rather than better. On the other hand, extensive centralization tends to undermine local initiative and to waste pertinent information about production possibilities and needs which exist at the enterprise level. This dilemma has motivated the search for more effective criteria for evaluating enterprise performance.

The idea that profitability should serve as the main criterion of successful enterprise performance is commonly associated with Ye. G. Liberman of the Kharkov Economic Engineering Institute. Liberman's proposal gained great notoriety after September 9, 1962, when *Pravda* published an article by him entitled "Plan, Profit, Premia." But there were important antecedents to this *Pravda* article.

There is some evidence that Voznesensky favored a greater use of profitability as an index of enterprise performance.[63] A group of economists—including Z. V. Atlas, I. S. Malyshev, L. A. Vaag, V. A. Sobol, and V. O. Chernyavsky—have long championed greater reliance on profitability and the profit motive.[64] The idea that profitability should guide economic decision-making has long been implicit in the works of V. V. Novozhilov.[65]

Professor Liberman's advocacy of the use of profits can be traced back to before 1956, when he had supervised a study in which a number of Kharkov industrial enterprises experimented with the more liberal use of profitability as a success criterion. On the pages of *Kommunist*, in 1956, Professor Liberman argued that the managers of industrial enterprises should be given the incentive to do the right thing and the

[63] See n. 32, above. See also M. Kaser, "The Debate on the Law of Value in the USSR, 1941-1953, in Retrospect," in P. Lavigne (ed.), *L'URSS, Symposium* (Paris, 1966), III, and Jere L. Felder, *Soviet Economic Controversies* (Cambridge, Mass., 1966), Chap. 3.

[64] Z. V. Atlas is a professor at Moscow State University and the Moscow Financial Institute. I. S. Malyshev (1902-1964) was deputy chief of the Central Statistical Administration. V. A. Sobol (1896-1968) was with the Central Statistical Administration and was chief editor of *Vestnik statistiki*. V. O. Chernyavsky has been chief specialist in the Department on Introducing New Methods of Planning in Gosplan, USSR.

[65] See n. 21, above, and N. Ya. Petrakov, *Nekotorye aspekty diskussii ob ekonomicheskikh metodakh khozyaistvovania* (Moscow, 1966), p. 19.

power actually to do it.[66] In that article he wrote, "It is impossible . . . to solve the important economic task of unleashing the initiative of enterprises . . . by means of a purely administrative broadening of the rights of directors. It is true that no matter how wide these powers may be formulated on paper, they cannot be realized without corresponding economic measures."[67] Several months after Liberman's article appeared, the editors of *Kommunist* published an extremely interesting review of a number of articles published in the journal and letters received during the year 1956.[68] This editorial expressed strong support for Liberman and for the idea of using profitability as a single criterion of enterprise performance.

A major conference was held in 1957 on the "Law of Value and its Use under Socialism," but in the main, this was a fruitless exercise in the traditional hairsplitting of Soviet political economy. Some support was expressed for profitability as a criterion.[69] After the Twenty-first Party Congress, *Kommunist* again featured an article by Liberman in which he reasserted the position outlined in the 1956 article.[70]

The discussion of the role of profitability as a criterion intensified in 1962. Late in 1961, the organ of Gosplan, *Planovoye khozyaistvo*, published an article by the Polish economist W. Brus on the use of material stimuli in Poland, which contained all of the ideas usually associated with Liberman.[71] *Ekonomicheskaya gazeta* in 1962 began a regular column devoted to the perfection of planning and economic organization. *Izvestia* followed suit in August by printing what has become a famous article by O. Antonov on the virtues of competition.[72] On September 9, Liberman's celebrated article appeared in *Pravda*. The public discussion reached a peak in the autumn of 1962. The pages

[66] Ye. Liberman, *Kommunist*, No. 10 (July 1956), pp. 75-92.

[67] *Ibid.*, p. 80.

[68] *Ibid.*, No. 1 (January 1957), pp. 47-62. The author wrote: "The system of material rewards must create conditions under which every worker of an enterprise is personally interested in the uncovering of reserves and in the perfection of technology, techniques, and the organization of production" (p. 48). The articles reviewed were published in *Kommunist*, Nos. 5 (April), 7 (May), 10 (July), and 13 (September) (1956) and an editorial in *ibid.*, No. 8 (May 1956).

[69] See *Zakon stoimosti i evo ispolzovaniye v narodnom khozyaistve SSSR* (1959), pp. 55, 237, 358.

[70] *Kommunist*, No. 1 (January 1959), pp. 88-97. The same issue carried articles by Gatovsky and Nemchinov who took positions consistent with that of Liberman. See B. Kerblay, "Les propositions de Liberman pour un projet de reforme de l'entreprise en U.R.S.S.," *Cahiers du monde russe et soviétique*, No. 3 (1963), pp. 301-311.

[71] *Planovoye khozyaistvo*, No. 12 (December 1961), pp. 74-83.

[72] *Izvestia*, August 28, 1962.

of Soviet newspapers and journals featured numerous articles and letters for and against the use of profitability as a success criterion. Opinion ranged from positions more radical than Liberman's to those expressing opposition on ideological grounds. Many agreed in principle while arguing that the scheme would not work without a prior revision of the price system. No consensus had emerged by November 1962, when the Central Committee met in plenary session.

In his speech to the November (1962) plenum, Khrushchev denied that profitability could play the same role under socialism as it does under capitalism, but he noted that for assessing the work of the individual enterprise, profits were of great significance. He asserted: "Without taking account of profits, it is impossible to tell how the enterprise is working or to evaluate its contribution to social wealth."[73] Khrushchev said that many valuable points had been raised in the public discussion of the role of profits. He instructed the planning organs and the Institute of Economics to study the resulting materials and to come forth with ". . . economic recommendations designed to improve production planning and scientific labor organization."[74]

Khrushchev's instruction was handed to the Scientific Council on Economic Accounting and Material Stimulation under the Economic Section of the Academy of Sciences. The Institute of Economics was given prime leadership responsibility. The council worked throughout 1963 under its chairman, I. M. Gatovsky. In April, it received briefs and research results from a number of institutions.[75] According to Gatovsky, the majority of discussants favored widening the economic powers of the enterprise directors, strengthening material incentives, and raising the role of such economic levers as profits, prices, and premia.[76] The recommendations of the council represented the highest common denominator that could be reached in a large and heterogeneous group. They urged better coordination in planning, gradual replacement of the index of gross output by such indexes as "normal value added," greater

[73] *Plenum Tsentralnovo Komiteta Kommunisticheskoi Partii Sovetskovo Soyuza, 19-23 noyabrya 1962 goda, stenog. otchyot* (Moscow, 1963), pp. 58-59.

[74] *Ibid.*, p. 59.

[75] *Vestnik Akademii Nauk SSSR*, No. 3 (1964), pp. 134-135. The following are reported to have delivered reports and briefs: Institute of Economics of the Academy of Sciences; Scientific Economics Research Institute of Gosplan; Scientific Research Institute of Labor under the State Committee on Labor and Wages; Institute of Management Organization and Norms under the Council of the National Economy; Moscow Engineering-Economics Institute; Financial Institute of the Ministry of Finance; and Moscow State University.

[76] *Ibid.*, p. 135.

powers for enterprise directors, wider use of profits as a source of premia and as a success indicator, better schemes of material incentives, and something akin to a capital charge.[77] In June 1963, these diluted recommendations were passed to the Presidium of the Academy of Sciences. After some modification by Gosplan and the State Committee on Labor and Wages, they went to the government for ratification.[78] A series of experiments based on the proposals was begun by the Council of the National Economy. These experiments used "normal value added" rather than profit as the main success criterion.[79]

After the hard-won consensus of 1963 had borne its modest prize, the discussion of profitability as a criterion reintensified in 1964,[80] and with this came a great extension of the debate. More sophisticated economists no longer considered the issue of success criteria in isolation from the system as a whole. Nemchinov, playing a familiar role, lent his prestige to the debate with an article in *Kommunist*.[81]

The debate of 1962-1965 involved so many participants that it defies analysis by fragmentary citations. Instead, an attempt has been made to inventory the major published contributions and to place each author in one of the three following categories:

1. The author agrees fully with the Liberman position on the use of profits as a success criterion or goes farther to suggest more fundamental decentralization of decision-making.
2. The author basically agrees with the Liberman position but differs in some details.
3. The author is opposed in principle to the Liberman position.

The authors were classified by their positions on the issue and by the organizations of their major affiliation. Table 1 displays a tabulation of the classifications of 93 authors whose contributions appeared on the pages of 6 central journals and newspapers between September 1962 and September 1965. The tabulations should be interpreted with great caution. First, although the sample of authors was not consciously

[77] *Ibid.*, pp. 135-136.　　　　[78] *Ibid.*, p. 136.

[79] *Ekonomicheskaya gazeta*, No. 27 (July 1963), p. 6. The "normal value added" criterion had been used experimentally during 1962 in the Tatar *Sovnarkhoz*. See the article by F. Tabeyev, *Izvestia*, August 24, 1962.

[80] See articles by Sidorov in *Izvestia*, April 9, 1964, and Liberman in *Ekonomicheskaya gazeta* (May 1964).

[81] *Kommunist*, No. 5 (March 1964), pp. 74-87. See also Nemchinov's booklet, *O dalneishem sovershenstvovania planirovania i upravlenia narodnym khozyaistvom* (2nd ed., Moscow, 1965).

TABLE 1.

A Classification of Positions Adopted in the "Liberman"
Debate by 93 Soviet Authors in Central Organs Between
September 1962 and September 1965

| | Position taken by authors on "Liberman" proposals | | | |
Organization of Major Affiliation	Agrees or favors more radical decentralization[a]	Agrees in principle but differs in detail[b]	Opposed in principle[c]	Total number of authors in sample
Institute of Economics, USSR Academy of Sciences	1	3	6	10
Other laboratories and institutes of economics in academies of science	3	0	0	3
Scientific Economics Research Institute and other institutes under Gosplan	2	2	1	5
Moscow State University, Moscow Engineering-Economics Institute, and Moscow Institute of the National Economy	1	0	4	5
Other higher educational institutions	2	1	2	5
All gosplans and the Gosekonomsovet	2	2	7	11
Central Statistical Administration	1	0	0	1
Ministry of Finance and its institutes	0	0	3	3
Other ministries or state committees	0	1	0	1
Ministerial research institutes	2	2	1	5
Sovnarkhozy	4	4	0	8
Enterprise directors, engineers, planners, and accountants	13	1	3	17
Other economists	9	4	3	16
Scientists	1	0	0	1
Party functionaries	1	0	1	2
Total	42	20	31	93

ᵃ Into the category "agrees or favors more radical decentralization" were put: V. S. Nemchinov, I. Birman, B. Belkin, I. Malyshev, Ia. Kantorovich, A. Redin, I. Markin, D. Krasavin, I. Proskurin, A. Zholkevich, E. Ivanov, L. Krukovskaya, E. Manevich, S. Doroguntsov, V. Parfenov, N. Petrov, N. Antonov, S. Kvasov, V. Trapeznikov, L. Leontiyev, R. Belousov, A. Nesterenko, Z. Sotchenko, A. Bursanovsky, K. Belyak, V. Shkatov, A. Veimar, G. Sotnikov, O. Volkov, O. Gromyko, V. Chernyavsky, B. Degtyar, B. Borovitsky, G. Kulagin, F. Sabitov, A. Kleshchinsky, S. Zlobinsky, M. Kuznetsova, I. Solomonov, L. Fedorov, M. Alexeyev, and R. Baigaliyev.

ᵇ Into the category "agrees in principle but differs in detail" were put: F. Veselkov, A. Rodigin, V. Kotkin, E. Slastenko, G. Kozlov, D. Lvov, B. Sukharevsky, E. Kapustin, L. Vaag, S. Zakharov, K. Larionov, K. Frolov, F. Kulygin, A. Yevdokimenko, G. Andronov, I. Rumyantsev, V. Shevelev, V. Rydnik, G. Yevstafyev, and L. Gatovsky.

ᶜ Into the category "opposed in principle" were put: M. Fedorovich, B. Smekhov, A. Zverev, K. Plotnikov, S. Ryumin, E. Ivanov, Sh. Turetsky, N. Kurgultsev, D. Onika, B. Kapitonov, R. Karagedov, A. Bachurin, A. Pervukhin, V. Kelpikov, A. Vorobeva, G. Kosyachenko, L. Alter, N. Spiridonova, N. Maslova, E. Rusanov, V. Dementev, A. Kats, M. Bor, V. Kotov, T. Zhemchuzhnikova, L. Rotstein, A. Matlin, A. Stugarev, A. Gromov, S. Nesterova, and I. Kasitsky.

SOURCES:

Pravda:
  1962   September 6, 13, 14, 19, 20, 21, 26, 29, 30; October 3, 5, 7, 9, 11, 12, 19; November 11
  1963   February 7
  1964   May 17; August 23; September 7; October 4; November 13; December 1, 7
  1965   January 22; February 17; April 7; June 23, 24
Izvestia:
  1962   October 28
  1963   August 13
  1965   August 5
Ekonomicheskaya gazeta:
  1962   October 20; November 3, 10
  1963   January 26
  1964   October 3
  1965   January 20; April 7; June 2
Vosprosy ekonomiki, 1962, No. 10; 1963, Nos. 4, 5, 7, 8, 9
Kommunist, 1962, No. 18
Planovoye khozyaistvo, 1962, No. 12; 1963, No. 6

selected with any bias, it has no claim to scientific randomness. It is not a full inventory or a fully random selection of authors who expressed their views in print; much less is it a random sample of all opinion. Second, the sample size is too small to permit hard and fast generalization. Finally, many authors did not fit easily into the category where they were finally placed; alternative interpretations of their contributions to the debate might place them differently.

Despite its shortcomings, the tabulation provides something better than unadulterated impressionism. Some generalization is warranted about opinion groups as they formed on the "Liberman" issue of the use of profits as a criterion of enterprise performance. The data are consistent with the following groupings:

1. A clustering of conservative opinion (i.e., opposed to the broader use of profit indicators) was to be found in central academic and planning organizations. Only about one-third of *all* sampled authors were opposed, as contrasted with more than half of all authors from the following organizations: the Institute of Economics of the Academy of Sciences; Moscow University economics faculties and institutes; Gosplan of the USSR and of the republics, and the Gosekonomsovet; the Ministry of Finance and its institutes.

2. Clusterings of liberal opinion (i.e., favoring broader use of profit indicators) were to be found at the enterprise and *sovnarkhoz* levels of industrial management. Economists from laboratories and institutes of the various academies of science outside of the Institute of Economics of the USSR Academy of Sciences, were liberally inclined. So were economists whose organizational affiliations were not recorded.

In 1964, a set of new experiments was begun using the volume of output actually sold and profit as the two main success indicators. More experiments were inaugurated in 1965 and at the October 1965 Central Committee plenum, Kosygin announced widespread reforms which went far to embrace the "Liberman" position.[82] These reforms did not end the discussion about the future of the Soviet economic system. Indeed the debate has grown in sophistication and interest since that time, and many questions of theory and practice remain to be worked out before new major reforms are announced.

THE BASIS OF PRICE FORMATION

Price theory is the nemesis of Soviet political economy. Marx's labor theory of value holds that only labor creates "value." Most orthodox economists believe that prices in a socialist economy should be related to value. But to establish prices on the basis of "value" immediately poses two unsolvable problems. The first is that it is difficult to measure labor input satisfactorily. Labor is notoriously heterogeneous; inputs of its various types and qualities must be aggregated according to some

[82] *Pravda*, September 28, 1965.

weighting system if they are to be commensurate. Unfortunately, there exist no objective sets of weights. Furthermore, the amount of labor required to produce a given type of good varies with the technology used and with the quantities of other resources which are combined with that labor in the production process. The second problem stems from the fact that the quantity of labor used in producing a given good bears no necessary relation to the amount of that good which is demanded by users or to its scarcity. Nor does it reflect the usefulness or scarcity of the most advantageous alternative employment of that labor. A price system based on the labor theory of value, therefore, would fail to inform users and suppliers of relative resource scarcities. Information of this type is vital if resources are to be used to the best advantage.

Ideologically, however, the labor theory of value is a vital part of Marxist theory. The entire notion of surplus value, and hence, the Marxist theory of exploitation, is based on the proposition that value is created by labor alone. What is necessary for economic efficiency is anathema for ideology; what is vital for ideology is irrelevant for economic efficiency. Stalin may have perceived this in 1930 when he decreed that the "law of value" did not operate under socialism. Subsequently the practice of Soviet price formation lacked a theoretical foundation. Stalin forbade economists even to discuss the subject. Administrators in Gosplan and other agencies followed rules of thumb in setting prices. Limited information about relative scarcity was contained in the prices and many anomalies arose.

After 1955, Soviet economists began a confused discussion of the "law of value" in socialism. The proper role of market forces versus centralized command and the theory of price formation in the socialist economy were the foci of this discussion.[83] Several groupings of opinion were discernible:

1. The "leave well enough alone" group consists of those who see no basic faults in the existing system of price formation. Prominent members of this group are economists, such as Sh. Ya. Turetsky and L. Maizenberg, who have been closely associated with the official price-setting agencies of Gosplan.

[83] For admirable accounts of the price discussions, see M. Bornstein, "The Soviet Price System," *American Economic Review*, LII, No. 1 (March 1962), 64-103, and M. Bornstein, "The Soviet Price Reform Discussion," *Quarterly Journal of Economics*, LXXVIII, No. 310 (February 1964), 15-48.

2. The "labor theory of value" group is headed by S. G. Strumilin. They urge that prices be set equal to cost of production plus an increment proportional to the cost of labor used in production.

3. The "price of production" group has been headed by L. A. Vaag, V. A. Sobol, Z. V. Atlas, V. Chernyavsky and I. Malyshev. They favor setting prices equal to cost of production plus an increment proportional to the value of fixed and circulating capital used in production.

4. The "optimality" group consists of analytical economists who understand that prices should convey scarcity information and promote optimal use of resources. V. S. Nemchinov, L. V. Kantorovich, and V. V. Novozhilov are prominent members of this group.

The Scientific Council on Problems of Price Formation was established in 1962 by the Economics Section of the Academy of Sciences. Since its creation, the council's chairman has been V. P. Dyachenko, a conservative veteran of the Institute of Economics and a corresponding member of the academy. Dyachenko has misunderstood and opposed the arguments of the "optimality group" and has devoted his main efforts to a reconciliation of the three other points of view. In 1962 and 1963, Dyachenko's council held large conferences on problems of price formation. Table 2 indicates the classification of speakers at these conferences and illustrates several facts. First, the work of the council has been dominated by economists from the Institute of Economics and its conservative allies from the various institutions of higher education. The Moscow Institute of the National Economy was particularly well represented. Second, the mathematically proficient economists were conspicuous by their absence; the Laboratory of Mathematical Economic Methods was represented by only one member at the first conference and by none at the second. V. V. Novozhilov and L. V. Kantorovich spoke at the second conference but their role was very restricted. Third, representatives of various planning agencies and institutes were well represented. Fourth, Dyachenko found many allies in the research institutes of various ministries and state committees, especially of the Ministry of Finance.

Dyachenko slighted the mathematical economists and their ideas at the conferences of his Scientific Council on Problems of Price Forma-

TABLE 2.

ROSTER OF ATTENDANCE AT FIRST AND SECOND CONFERENCES
ON QUESTIONS OF PRICE FORMATION
BY ORGANIZATION OF MAJOR AFFILIATION

Organization of Major Affiliation	First Conference November 1962	Second Conference March 1963
Institute of Economics, USSR Academy of Sciences	19	16
Other laboratories and institutes of economics in academies of sciences	5	6
Higher educational institutions	10	15
All gosplans	8	4
Scientific Economics Research Institute of USSR Gosplan	2	3
Laboratory of Mathematical Economic Methods	1	0
Central Statistical Administration	3	0
Ministerial institutes, state committees' institutes	6	22
Sovnarkhozy including USSR Sovnarkhoz	2	3
TOTAL	56	69

SOURCES: *Obshchestvenno neobkhodimye zatraty truda, sebestoimost i rentabelnost*, V. P. Dyachenko (ed.) (Moscow, 1963); *Uchet potrebitelskikh svoistv produktsii v tsenoobrazovanii*, V. P. Dyachenko (ed.) (Moscow, 1964); *Uchet sootnoshenia sprosa i predlozhenia v tsenoobrazovanii*, V. P. Dyachenko (ed.) (Moscow, 1964); *Uchet prirodnovo i geograficheskovo faktorov v tsenoobrazovanii*, V. P. Dyachenko (ed.) (Moscow, 1964); *Voprosy ekonomiki*, Nos. 3 and 7 (1963).

tion.[84] This group counterattacked later in 1963 by making the theory of price formation a focus of work in the Scientific Council on the Application of Mathematics and Computers in Economic Research and Planning. This council is chaired by N. P. Fedorenko and dominated by economists from the Central Mathematical Economics Institute.[85]

[84] See M. L. Lavigne, "Rapport de D'achenko," *Cahiers du monde russe et soviétique*, VI (January-March 1965), 55-62.
[85] *Vestnik Akademii Nauk SSSR*, No. 1 (1964). At the council's meeting of October 23-25, 1963, V. S. Nemchinov called price formation the "key problem"

In June 1965, the Presidium of the Academy of Sciences met to consider problems of price formation and to try to resolve the bitter differences between the forces of the Institute of Economics (led by Dyachenko) and of the Central Mathematical Economics Institute (led by Fedorenko). The fact that the main report was given by Fedorenko may indicate sympathy for him in the presidium—probably from Keldysh.[86]

The battle continued and on December 14, 1965, the general meeting of the academy sat in judgment while Dyachenko and Fedorenko restated their positions.[87] K. V. Ostrovityanov and Ya. A. Kronrod, in discussion, amplified Dyachenko's attack on Fedorenko, Kantorovich, Novozhilov, and other advocates of "optimality" prices. They argued that such prices contradicted the labor theory of value, embraced marginalism, and were totally anti-Marxist. Furthermore, they said, the theory of optimal economic planning did not exist, and, therefore, no prices could be based on it.

Fedorenko and L. V. Kantorovich hotly rebutted, arguing that the theory of optimal planning not only existed but was being used to solve concrete problems. I. S. Malyshev and L. A. Vaag attacked Dyachenko's report for its errors and for its banality. Academicians S. L. Sobolev and M. A. Styrikovich, both scientists, expressed strong support for Fedorenko and prices of the optimal plan; they both had sharp criticisms of Dyachenko and the weak work of his council. M. V. Keldysh, in his concluding remarks, agreed with Fedorenko in principle but said that the theory of optimal planning was insufficiently elaborated to serve as a basis for price formation.

The optimality price group consists principally of economists from the Central Mathematical Economics Institute, the Siberian Section of the Academy of Sciences, and the Leningrad Engineering-Economics Institute. Table 3 displays the distribution of a sample of authors on the price discussions. Physical scientists in the academy have been important allies of the optimality school. Many young economists have also favored optimality prices.[88] Support for S. G. Strumilin's attempt

---

of the economics of socialism. V. V. Novozhilov argued that the use of marginal relations is consistent with Marxism and, indeed, represents a further development of the labor theory of value under socialism (p. 121).

[86] *Ibid.*, No. 12 (1965), pp. 11-16.

[87] *Ibid.*, No. 2 (1966), pp. 62-94.

[88] In May 1966, a conference of young economists was convened in Moscow. Its sponsors were the Institute of Economics and the Moscow Committee of the

to base prices on labor input, the present system, and for V. P. Dyachenko's compromise comes most strongly from the Institute of Economics, a group of conservative Moscow higher educational institutions, and certain party institutes and schools.[89] Most representatives of Gosplan, the Central Statistical Administration, and the Scientific Economics Research Institute of Gosplan favored the price of production scheme of price formation.

One of the most powerful opponents of the optimality price group has been V. K. Sitnin, chairman of the Committee of Prices of USSR Gosplan. He recently attacked the "idealization in the economic literature of the practice of price formation in the period of the first years of the N.E.P."[90] This should be interpreted as an attack on market prices and "prices of the optimal plan" which have much in common with market-determined prices.

The price reform of July 1967 was carried out on the basis of Dyachenko's recommendations as modified by the Committee of Prices of Gosplan. But the debate continues.

Conclusion

This concluding section is addressed to the question: "What changes have taken place over time in the policy-making role of Soviet economists and their various subgroups?" It ventures some generalizations about the nature and significance of opinion group activity among the economists. It also advances some hypotheses to explain the recent growth in such group activity. Finally, it puts forward some speculations about possible future developments.

THE NATURE AND SIGNIFICANCE OF OPINION GROUP ACTIVITY

Soviet economists seek to influence policy by a variety of means. In professional meetings and journals, representatives of the contending opinion groups elaborate various policy options as rationally as they are able. When discussion moves on to more active exposition, pro-

---

Komsomol. Most speakers were from the Institute of Economics; none were from the Central Mathematical Economics Institute. Despite the disapproval of T. S. Khachaturov, the young economists were outspoken in their support of the optimality approach to price formation. *Voprosy ekonomiki*, No. 8 (1966), pp. 146-147.

[89] The Academy of Social Sciences of the Central Committee and the Higher Party School.

[90] *Voprosy ekonomiki*, No. 8 (1966), p. 142.

TABLE 3.

A CLASSIFICATION OF POSITIONS ADOPTED IN THE PRICE THEORY
DISCUSSIONS BY 82 SOVIET AUTHORS IN CENTRAL ORGANS AND
PUBLISHED BOOKS BETWEEN 1957 AND 1967

Organization of Major Affiliation	Position Taken in Price Discussions				
	Optimality Prices[a]	Price of Production[b]	Dyachenko Compromise[c]	Labor Value[d]	Present System[e]
Institute of Economics, USSR Academy of Sciences	3	1	7	6	2
Central Mathematical Economics Institute	10				
Other laboratories and institutes of economics in academies of science	1		1		
Scientific Economics Research Institute of Gosplan USSR		3	1		1
Moscow State University, Moscow Engineering-Economics Institute, and Moscow Institute of the National Economy			2	2	5
Other higher educational institutions	2				1
All gosplans and the Gosekonomsovet		7	1		2
Central Statistical Administration		3			
Ministries and State Committees	1	2	1		
Siberian Section of Academy of Sciences	4	1			
Scientists	4	1			
Party institutes and schools				2	2
Other economists	1	1			1
TOTAL	26	19	13	10	14

ᵃ Into the category "optimality prices" were put: V. S. Nemchinov, I. A. Tikhonov, M. Adonds, L. V. Kantorovich, V. V. Novozhilov, N. P. Fedorenko, A. L. Lurye, I. Kotov, N. Shukhov, A. Virochenko, I. Puzanova, V. S. Dadyan, V. A. Pervushin, S. Lushin, I. A. Birman, N. Brusilovskaya, V. Zakharov, V. Volkonsky, A. Katsenetinboigen, S. Shatalin, Iu. A. Oleinik, V. F. Pugachev, M. A. Styɪikovich, S. L. Sobolev, M. V. Keldysh, and V. M. Glushkov.

ᵇ Into the category "price of production" were put: I. Malyshev, A. Bachurin, L. Vaag, V. Sobol, Z. Atlas, D. Kondrashev, V. Chernyavsky, S. Zakharov, Z. Chukhanov, A. Stepankov, V. Belkin, N. Petrakov, N. Gorichev, A. Zverev, D. Timoshevsky, M. Eidelman, L. Postyshev, V. Pervushin, and A. Berg.

ᶜ Into the category "Dyachenko compromise" were put: L. Gatovsky, M. Kolganov, A. Boyarsky, V. Dyachenko, V. Lipsits, V. Zhukov, L. Oblomskaya, A. Agafonov, D. Timoshevsky, T. Khachaturov, A. Petrov, K. Ostrovityanov, A. Stepankov and A. Pashkov.

ᵈ Into the category "labor value" were put: Ya. Kronrod, M. Bor, V. S. Alkinyov, N. Spiridonova, M. Volkov, I. Kozodoyev, A. Kursky, V. Batyrev, G. Dikhtyar, and V. Simchera.

ᵉ Into the category "present system" were put: A. Kulikov, Sh. Turetsky, L. Maizenberg, V. Kats, G. Kozlov, V. Sitnin, D. Chernamordik, L. Kantor, B. Gogol, V. Korniyenko, A. Mendelson, V. Lopatkin, P. Mstislavsky, and V. Plishevsky.

SOURCES:
Pravda:
    1962   October 24
    1965   December 18
Izvestia:
    1962   November 29
Voprosy ekonomiki:
    1957   Nos. 2, 3, 5, 7, 9
    1958   No. 1
    1959   No. 2
    1963   Nos. 3, 4, 7
    1966   Nos. 5, 7, 8
    1967   Nos. 1, 2, 3, 4, 5
Vestnik Akademii Nauk SSSR, 1966, No. 2
Kommunist, 1958, No. 16
Vestnik Moskovskovo Universiteta, Seria ekonommi, filosofi i prava, 1958, No. 1
Zakon stoimosti i evo ispolzovanye v narodnom khozyaistve, SSSR, 1959
Obshchestvenno neobkhodimye zatraty truda, sebestoimost i rentabelnost, V. P. Dyachenko (ed.) (Moscow, 1963); *Uchet potrebitelskikh svoistv produktsii v tsenoobrazovanii*, V. P. Dyachenko (ed.) (Moscow, 1964); *Uchet sootnoshenia sprosa i predlozhenia v tsenoobrazovanii*, V. P. Dyachenko (ed.) (Moscow, 1964); *Uchet prirodnovo i geograficheskovo faktorov v tsenoobrazovanii*, V. P. Dyachenko (ed.) (Moscow, 1964)
Tovarno-denezhnye otnoshenia v period perekhoda k kommunizmu, A. V. Bachurin and A. D. Kondrashev (eds.),1963
L. M. Kantor, *Tsenoobrazovaniye v SSSR*, 1964
A. S. Mendelson, *Stoimost i tsena*, 1963
A. G. Zavyalkov, *Planirovanyie tsen*, 1962

ponents of various points of view seek to convince their colleagues, other specialist elites, and public opinion through "debates" carried on through the medium of public meetings and the press. An important road to influence lies in controlling the key institutions of the Academy of Sciences and the universities. This route has been followed by many of the younger mathematical economists as they have sought to increase the power and prestige of the Central Mathematical Economics Institute and its filials. The growing importance of kafedry of economic cybernetics in the leading Soviet universities is another example of this. Finally, there is the attempt directly to persuade influential leaders to follow one or another policy option and to reject others. The nature and extent of this personal element is difficult to assess due to the paucity of evidence. What we do see is much jockeying for position and politicking familiar to anyone who has studied or worked in Western bureaucratic organizations.

To some extent, it is possible to discern the influence of various groups of economists on the formation of Soviet economic policy. The recent decisions concerning performance criteria and price formation policy represent compromises laboriously produced from sharply contending positions expounded by competing groups of economists. The younger mathematical economists say privately that they recognize the necessity of a slow, evolutionary approach to economic reform. Too many older and conservative individuals occupy important positions of power in the party, in government and academic organizations and do not comprehend what the younger men are recommending. Lacking understanding, they feel threatened by the proposals advanced by younger economists. The conservatism of age is strengthened by the incomprehensible mathematical language used by the innovators and by the dubious ideological rectitude of their positions.

The ability of the younger mathematical economists to influence policy is heightened by their incomparably greater capacity to define complex economic situations in a logical manner. This is a thing which the political leadership is unable to do for itself and which the older, conservative economists have never been able to do for them. To be able to formulate the problem is often to be able to influence greatly the solution of that problem. So long as the innovators enjoy a near monopoly of the problem-formulation talents among Soviet economists, they will enjoy a large advantage over their older and more conservative colleagues. The conservative opinion groups are greatly strengthened by the economic illiteracy of the top political leadership. Even though they may desperately seek the answer to a vexing economic problem, this prevents them from grasping the essence of any sophisticated argument. Well-constructed economic reasoning and ideological mumbo-jumbo are equally incomprehensible to untutored ears. The common reaction is to urge all economists to forge consensus opinions on controversial issues. This produces ungainly compromises which are rarely satisfactory to any side.

The impact of younger and more sophisticated economic thought on the Soviet political-economic system is perceptible in undramatic ways. One observes a slow process of "creeping economic rationality." The pricing system announced in 1967 was somewhat better than its predecessor. The introduction of capital charges promotes more rational micro-economic decision-making. Propaganda for economic "optimality" enlightens and encourages those who would seek efficiency. There has been a modest decentralization of policy-making. The change generally is in the right direction but very slow.

REASONS FOR RISE IN OPINION GROUP ACTIVITY

One can conjecture several reasons why the Soviet leadership has permitted and, indeed, encouraged the rise of unorthodox economic thinking and opinion group activity among Soviet economists. In the first place, the Soviet economic system has progressed to the point where intuition no longer suffices as a guide to policy formation. The complexity and functional specialization of the economy have made it impossible for the political leadership to lead adequately without expert advice, and widespread economic illiteracy among these men operates to strengthen this factor. As the political leadership gradually perceived the inadequacy of the economic dogma and advice it was receiving from traditional Soviet economists, a campaign began to cultivate a rational and relevant Soviet economics. This cultivation began in the mid-1950's and continues hesitatingly to the present.

By diminishing or removing the penalties for economic heterodoxy, the party leadership invited opinion group activity. This activity has been slow in developing but, by the mid-1960's, economists generally felt free to participate in economic debates within poorly specified boundaries of ideological legitimacy. Increasingly, too, individuals and

249

groups of economists have dared to press for certain policy decisions which they have regarded as good for the country, and, possibly, as advantageous for themselves.

It is difficult and will become increasingly more difficult to place well defined limits on the freedom of Soviet economists to discuss unorthodox ideas and policies. It is certainly true that many of the younger economists hold classical Soviet political economy in deepest scorn even while they accept the basic tenets of Marxian macro-sociological theory. These young economists believe, and I share their belief, that analytical economics is fully compatible with rational humane socialism. It is not compatible, however, with the unfettered exercise of power by a small minority such as the party apparatus. Perception of this may cause the *apparatchiki* to limit or reverse the trend toward freedom of discussion and advocacy among Soviet economists. Another dogged ally of conservatism is the economic illiteracy of the Soviet political leadership. This, together with ideological paranoia guarantees the strength of more conservative forces for years to come.

SPECULATIONS ABOUT THE FUTURE

Soviet economists are not a homogenous group. The positions of any Soviet economist can be predicted with considerable accuracy if information is available on his age, his organization of primary affiliation, and his degree of mathematical proficiency. Groups defined by these attributes engage in energetic struggle for influence with the top Soviet leadership. The competition among these groups will probably continue to exist but its character will gradually shift. The pre-revolutionary group will soon pass entirely from the scene. The contest will then be between the aging Stalinist generation and a more intelligent, better educated, and expanding group of younger economists.

The leaders of the mathematical economists have felt it necessary to promise very much in return for the support they have received from the nation's political and scientific leadership. It seems doubtful that they will be able to make good on the most ambitious of those promises. In particular, the early feasibility of a system of optimal planning based on mathematical models and electronic computers appears in great doubt. But the concept of optimality is penetrating deeply into the core of Soviet economic thought. If mathematical methods and computers cannot be built to produce optimal plans and optimal prices, it seems likely that pressure will increase to obtain the

results in another way. This will open the door for serious consideration of market socialism—a thing calmly discussed by Eastern European economists but still taboo in the USSR. Young Soviet economists
already entertain such thoughts.

There is an old saying that between two economists there are always
at least three opinions on any question. Under Stalin there was usually
only one opinion voiced no matter how many economists gathered.
Seventeen years after the dictator's death, Soviet economists are beginning to behave normally.

The Writers

THE Authors Guild in the United States is a professional interest group concerned with securing the best contract arrangements with its friendly enemies the publishers and with protecting writers against disadvantageous rulings of the courts or government in all matters relating to literature. One thing organized writers in America will oppose to the bitter end is any infringement on their freedom of expression. As an organized group their influence on the country's cultural development, as well as its political and social policies, is considerable. The Soviet Writers' Union may also in theory be regarded as a professional interest group but one whose functions and freedom of expression are directly or indirectly controlled by the state or, more properly speaking, by the Communist Party.

Russian writers have always had to contend with oppressive government and its often rigid censorship in their efforts to create an artistic literature unfettered by external interference. Perhaps because of the form the struggle took in the past, the influence of writers of belles-lettres proved to be of utmost significance in the history of nineteenth-century Russia. Though none of the great writers then escaped police surveillance and some were persecuted, it has been justly said of them that they were the conscience of the nation, the articulate voices of the silent masses. Tolstoy publicly declared that his hero was Truth; Dostoevsky insisted on the necessity of uninhibited artistic expression; and Chekhov, who declared that it was impossible to deceive in art, announced that his holy of holies as a man and a writer was "absolute freedom." Despite persecution and censorship, a superb literature was created in nineteenth-century Russia, for the government tolerated the work of writers, provided they refrained from attacking the fundamental features of autocracy. Artistic individualism, so necessary to the creation of enduring art, was possible and found memorable expression in fiction and verse. Although this noble tradition has been condemned in the Soviet Union, it is still alive.

Though early Russian Marxists inherited the libertarian convictions of the radical intelligentsia of the 1860's, Lenin, in his 1905 article "Party Organization and Party Literature," argued that party writers must conform to party policies. However, he was thinking more of journalism than belles-lettres, for he asserted: "There is no disputing it that literary work lends itself less than anything else to a mechanical equalizing, to a leveling, to the rule of the majority over the minority. Nor is there any disputing it that in this kind of endeavor it is absolutely necessary to guarantee the largest measure of personal initiative, individual tastes, thought and fantasy, form and content."[1] Years later, however, when communist leaders elevated this article to the position of a kind of *locus classicus* to guide writers, it was precisely Lenin's emphasis on *partiinost* (party spirit) that was insisted upon as the essential ingredient of all Soviet literature.

Approach to Party Control

For a few short years after the 1917 Revolution writers enjoyed the freedom and élan of the only revolutionary period of Soviet literature. Various competing movements sprang up and their highly individualistic artistic programs, published in strident manifestoes, condemned the past and called for fresh beginnings. In prose and drama, writers demanded new forms in which to cast the altered content of life, and particularly in poetry the degree of experimentation reflected a determination to preserve individual values in a world in revolt. Though by 1919 the government had established its own publishing network, *Gosizdat*, many private publishers were allowed to do business right into the period of the New Economic Policy. Complaints by the party press that privately published authors were excessively critical of communist doctrine indicate the relative freedom from or the ineffectiveness of censorship in the early years of the regime. Not a few old Bolshevik leaders, often men of considerable literary culture, defended the author's right to freedom of expression. In 1920 when Lenin forced a resolution through the congress of the *Proletcult*, ending that powerful literary organization's insistence that literature and art should be free of governmental or party coercion, the party Central Committee felt it necessary to accompany a statement of the resolution in *Pravda* with

[1] "Partiinaya organizatsia i partiinaya literatura," *Sochinenia*, 4th ed., x, 26-31.

assurances that artists would be guaranteed "full autonomy" in their work.[2]

On the whole, during the first years of the revolution, the party's position was that of referee in the major literary struggle between left-wing groups of writers, demanding hegemony and party sanctions in developing a new proletarian literature, and right-wing and "fellow-traveler" groups, claiming complete freedom to create as they wished. Well-known party figures publicly expressed opinions on the issues. Bukharin, for example, favored the right wing, arguing that the party should avoid directives on literature since its problems could not be solved by political methods. Trotsky, in 1924, declared: "Marxian methods are not the same as the artistic. The party leads the proletariat but not the historic processes of history. . . . The domain of art is not one in which the party is called upon to command. It can and must protect and help it, but it can only lead it indirectly."[3]

For a short time after Lenin's death in 1924 the literary controversy was reflected to some extent in the political struggle for power within the party. Leaders on the right, stressing the individual and aesthetic elements involved in the creative process, believed that literature should be spared direct party influence, whereas left-wing or proletarian leaders, arguing the educational, propaganda, and utilitarian functions of literature, fought for strict party control. The party's Central Committee resolution of July 1, 1925, encouraged both factions and refused to interfere in literature on behalf of the proletarian groups.

However, as soon as Stalin had consolidated his power, the party made its first move to "take over" literature in another Central Committee resolution (December 1928) which ordered all cultural media to support the first Five Year Plan and directed publishing firms to suggest to authors the subjects on which they should write. Once embarked on this course, the party dropped its previous policy of not favoring any of the rival literary groups and gave open support to the powerful Russian Association of Proletarian Writers (RAPP) as best suited to organize literature to promote the success of the plan. With such backing RAPP tyrannized over other writers' groups and eventually felt independent enough to ignore party directives in an effort to develop a literature devoted to realistic and psychological depiction

[2] "O proletkultakh. Pismo TsK RKP," *Pravda*, December 1, 1920.
[3] Leon Trotsky, *Literature and Revolution*, trans. by Rose Strunsky (Ann Arbor, 1960), p. 218.

of the "living man," "to tear away the masks" of Soviet life so as to reveal its evils as well as its virtues.

The party acted with decision. There is reason to suppose that Stalin played a personal role in drafting the Central Committee resolution of April 23, 1932, which dissolved RAPP and ordered the formation of a single Union of Soviet Writers. At this hint all other literary groupings disbanded. In what was probably the last attempt to oppose in print an official party ruling on literary matters, RAPP leaders published an attack on the 1932 resolution in their journal *On Literary Guard*, in which they took exception to the party's insistence on the publicist function of literature and damned party-inspired critics who imposed their ideas on art without knowing anything about it.[4]

The relative success of the first Five Year Plan helped to assure the party's power and Stalin's absolute leadership of it. The party was ready to assume full control of writers and all literary endeavors and bend them to its own purpose. Though the 1932 resolution was hailed as ending RAPP's regimentation, the party's idea of combining all organized literary groups into one huge national writers' union was a patent device for more effective regimentation. In place of RAPP's incomplete regimentation, all literature in the Soviet Union had thrust upon it the direct controls of the party itself.

The Writers' Union and Literary Groups

Up to this point writers as a group had enjoyed a large measure of freedom of action and expression and were loathe to submit to a command from above to organize. It required more than two years of manipulation and party pressure before an attitude of compliance was achieved sufficient to hold the first All-Union Congress of the Union of Soviet Writers in August 1934. Though several writers and critics spoke with candor of the literary artist's obligation to pursue truth in art wherever he might find it, most of the delegates applauded the keynote address of party leader A. A. Zhdanov, who advocated the aid of "the great and invincible doctrine of Marx-Engels-Lenin-Stalin" in overcoming the difficulties confronting Soviet literature. A means to this end, he declared, must be socialist realism, a portrayal of "real life in its revolutionary development," in which "truthfulness and historical

[4] "Otvet kritikam," *Na literaturnom postu*, No. 12 (April 1932), p. 9.

256

completeness of artistic depiction must be combined with the task of ideological remolding and reeducating the toiling masses in the spirit of socialism."[5]

Thirty-three years later, by the time of its Fourth Congress in May 1967, the Writers' Union had developed into a massive bureaucratic organization with chapters in all the republics. Each is under the direction of its party members who take their orders from the national center of the union in Moscow which in turn is controlled in major policy matters by top party leadership. Though the organizational structure of the Writers' Union has altered somewhat over the years, its ultimate power is still supposed to reside in the All-Union Congress which by statute is directed to meet every three years. However, as indicated, it has convened only four times in 33 years. The congress elects a board to exercise authority between meetings and also a first secretary to head the union. Since the board is large (91 members in 1967), it appoints a secretariat (42 members in 1967) which meets frequently and dominates the affairs of the union. Perhaps it would be more correct to say that a small fraction of powerful leaders within the secretariat makes final decisions on a multitude of matters affecting union policies: editorial posts in its own publishing firm, Soviet Writer, and of its paper, *Literaturnaya gazeta* (*Literary Gazette*), as well as of various literary magazines under union jurisdiction; the publishing fate of controversial books and articles; petitions of individual writers, etc. Although the prestigious Moscow writers' division in the union, especially the party fraction within it, has at times influenced policy issues, the secretariat is really the main administrative transmission belt for implementing decisions of the Central Committee of the party on literary matters.

By 1967 membership had grown to 6,608, more than half of whom (3,615) belonged to the Communist Party. Membership is voluntary and election, based on various qualifications which usually include acceptable published works, is on the recommendation of a nominating committee. There are material advantages in belonging and most established, or nearly established, authors eagerly seek admission. Expulsion can be a serious obstacle to achieving publication of one's works. Young nonmembers are given encouragement at regular national writers' con-

---

[5] *Sovetskaya literatura—samaya ideinaya, samaya peredovaya literatura v mire* (Moscow, 1934), pp. 6-14.

ferences where they receive professional guidance from experienced union authors, and the most promising youths are given scholarships to attend the union's Gorky Institute of Literature.

"Our union is quite rich,"[6] reported an official of the Central Inspection Commission elected at the Fourth Congress to audit the financial affairs of the various enterprises of the organization. During the preceding eight years its income averaged 14,200,000 rubles annually, the sources of which were membership dues, 6 percent of the net returns of publishing firms, and 2.5 percent of the gross receipts of theatrical performances, as well as income from union properties. This annual sum helps to support kindergartens and summer camps for children of union members and clinic and doctors' expenses of the ill; it also provides aid to totally disabled or aged members. The union also operates a network of retreats and sanitoriums for its members in nature spots throughout the country. A Literary Fund exists from which writers may obtain money to spend time at these retreats, or to make trips to distant places to collect material for their writing, or loans or outright gifts to enable a hard-pressed writer to live while completing a piece of work. The annual budget of the Literary Fund alone is now 3,600,000 rubles, and judging from the Inspection Commission's complaints over the years, the fund rather than literary production seems to be the main source of income for not a few writers.

Of the 473 delegates at the Fourth Congress, almost half were fifty years old or younger, which suggests that the union has a larger number of relatively young members than ever before, a significant fact in this contentious time in literary development. The importance the government and party attach to the Writers' Union is reflected by attendance of the Presidium or Politburo at opening sessions of the congresses, and occasionally the head of the Communist Party has delivered a major address. Some indication of the honorable, if not glamorous, character of such a gathering may be gained from the following statistics on delegates to the congress in 1967: 16 had received Lenin Prizes; 107, USSR State Prizes; 61, republic State Prizes; one, a Nobel Prize; 30 were deputies to the USSR Supreme Soviet and 42 to local soviets; 2 had been awarded the order of Hero of the Soviet Union and 7, the order of Hero of Socialist Labor; and a total of 407 delegates had received orders and medals for both literary and military services.

The formation in 1934 of the Writers' Union, whose members have

[6] *Literaturnaya Rossia*, No. 22 (May 26, 1967), p. 18.

subsequently accounted for thousands of books, published in many millions of copies, was originally intended to create a kind of arm of the Communist Party that would organize all literary activity so that it would better serve the educational, cultural, and propaganda aims of the Soviet Union. To this end little has been left undone to convey to conforming members a sense of privileged status in order to bind them, with silken chains as it were, to the communist cause by material aids and by showering them with numerous government honors and widespread national publicity for their literary achievements.

Since the party identifies literature with politics, it may be said that the Writers' Union can have no interests other than political, or party interests. The preponderating majority of the members, like the bulk of those in any country who earn their living from literature, are not genuine artists but more-or-less skilled craftsmen of the word. Without any severe wrenching of conscience they conform in their novels, plays, and poetry with the party's prescriptions, regularly upheld by the union's bureaucratic leadership, in form, content, and ideological treatment. At times they may resent editorial revisions in ideological matters, and the more imaginative craftsmen among them may occasionally yearn for a wider field of thematic selection. Conformity, however, tends to become habitual in the process of making a living, especially when the average earnings of even a moderately successful writer are substantial. In short, these writers have no interests other than party interests, and their function as literary propagandists has been extensive and important.

Allied with this group in the Writers' Union exists another and no doubt much smaller one—communist authors who accept party controls as an article of faith in no sense inhibiting the free functioning of art. How passionate a faith communism can be for its sincere devotees requires no demonstration. For them reason ends where faith begins; the artist believes, and hence does not question, the ends achieved by regimentation. Among such writers freedom and authority, in some strange but believable manner, become identical. As the esteemed author and communist Alexander Fadeyev, who for a time was First Secretary of the Writers' Union, once put it: "Both the party and artistic literature in our country have one and the same purpose. Neither the party nor governmental power in the Soviet land interfere in the individual creation of the artist; they have never dictated and have never attempted to dictate themes and characters, to say nothing of artistic forms."[7] These dedicated communists, along with a majority of the large group of literary craftsmen, represent the conservative trend among union members.

From the very beginning of the Writers' Union there has been a third subgroup, the liberals, few in number but growing in significance over the passage of years. They are the legatees of the lofty artistic accomplishments and libertarian spirit of Russian literature of the past. Including some of the most distinguished names in Soviet literature, they are dedicated to an art which is the free expression of the rational and irrational imagination of man. Although these authors appear at times to rebel against certain aspects of party control, they do not ignore the fact that they function within a political and ideological framework which insists that there is only one truth—the absolute truth of communism. Most of them seem to adhere to this truth, but with how much conviction we can never be quite sure.

Stalinism and Zhdanovism

Any genuine competition of interests among these groupings within the Writers' Union seemed impossible during the early years of Stalin's rule. In the 1930's the union leadership supported the party's propaganda demands connected with its feverish drives for agricultural collectivization and industrial reconstruction, with its intensification of "socialist emulation" or "Stakhanovism," campaigns that furnished themes for a steady stream of novels, plays, and poems. The growing menace of Hitlerism, which stimulated the party to launch a nationalist campaign at the expense of Marxian internationalism, was reflected in a spate of historical novels and plays that stressed great moments in the country's past when Russia had to fight for its life against foreign invaders. The recent history of the revolution and the civil war was also revived in literature but was often subjected to a distorted updating, especially when it involved Stalin's participation in these events. His role had to be exalted as the process of mythologizing Stalin in belles-lettres began.

During this period public criticism of literary deviations, real or imagined, was accepted by the writers with a degree of abject submission that could only be ascribed to fear. If a work had been passed by an editorial board and the government censorship (*glavlit*) and yet ap-

---

[7] *Literaturnaya gazeta*, March 2, 1949.

peared in print with some undiscovered ideological impurity, it was certain to be condemned by reviewers. If by chance the attacks overlooked any such shortcomings, an officially inspired statement from an officer of the Writers' Union was published to set matters right. Such a situation invariably elicited public recantations all around—from the author of the work, the editorial head of the responsible periodical or publishing house, from the incautious reviewer, and sometimes from the editor of the magazine in which the review appeared. Very few authors had the temerity to criticize the severity of controls as did Boris Pasternak at a writers' meeting in Minsk in 1936: "The Stakhanovite promises . . . are capable of only depressing us. . . . Art is unthinkable without risk and self-sacrifice of the soul. . . . Is the task of the Writers' Union to instruct you to be daring? That is the task of each of us."[8]

Dictation by the leadership of the Writers' Union manifested itself in a more sinister way once the terrible Stalinist purges began in the second half of the 1930's. As numerous writers were victimized by the terror, unrelenting pressure was placed on their colleagues to sign public denunciations of them. The union lent its authority and aid in providing lists of names to be used against their own proscribed members. The whole period represented a catastrophe of stunted cultural growth, although a few memorable works of literature were produced. Members of the older generation, who escaped death and survived prison, and who might have had something original to say, were compelled to emasculate their talent and existed as artistic eunuchs, hopelessly parroting each other's version of socialist realism. Younger writers were reduced to imitating their elders in the conviction that their idealized pictures of Soviet life with their stereotyped positive heroes contributed to the glory of agricultural collectivization and the grandeur of industrial reconstruction.

During the war the relaxation of censorship and of overt regimentation, either by the Writers' Union or the party, encouraged a sense of freedom that was reflected in patriotic and often movingly subjective literature. In a writers' conference in May 1945, several spoke out against any resumption of interference in literary matters. Even before the war ended, however, certain incidents suggested that the party had begun to think of whipping writers back into the "happiness" of ideological conformity. At the beginning of 1944, functionaries of the Writ-

[8] Quoted by George Reavey in *The Poetry of Boris Pasternak* (New York, 1959), pp. 91, 92.

ers' Union attacked Mikhail Zoshchenko's serio-comic autobiographical novel, *Before Sunrise*, for vulgar, unpatriotic philistinism, and banned publication of further installments. Later that year the second volume of Konstantin Fedin's fascinating literary memoirs, *Gorky Amongst Us*, was widely condemned in the party press for defending the contemplative author and apolitical art, and for preaching the sacrifice of socialist individualism in an effort to restore artistic individualism in general.

These and other forewarnings of a new party literary line in the making led ultimately to a Central Committee decree of August 14, 1946.[9] In addition to spelling out what would be regarded as anti-Soviet, the decree defined the kinds of books that should be written by post-war authors of belles-lettres. It linked literature with the party's ideological shift in its post-war national and international policy and placed emphasis on themes concerned with Russia's glorious conduct of the war, post-war reconstruction, rehabilitation of returning Red Army men, and the hostile designs of the West, especially the United States. Once again, it was made clear that writers must adhere to the guiding principle of *partiinost* which was understood to mean the organic connection between literature and party political ideology. The wartime relaxation in literature had thus ended and the party acted to restore its dominant role in this as in every other endeavor. The decree's directives were reinforced by a scathing denunciation of recent literary offenses by A. A. Zhdanov, the party's chief cultural spokesman, who had delivered the keynote address at the First Congress twelve years before. His name became attached to this most sterile period of Soviet literature—Zhdanovism.

During the next seven years the administrative bureaucracy of the Writers' Union and its minions, in open alliance with the party, conducted a frontal assault on all writers who deviated from the letter or spirit of the new literary decree. Such distinguished authors as Anna Akhmatova and Zoshchenko, who had been denounced by Zhdanov, were expelled from the union; some literary editors lost their jobs; and a number of authors and critics under attack fell silent. Attempts in fiction to portray truly realistic pictures of life were damned as "slanders" against Soviet reality, heroes were exaggeratedly idealized, and dramatic conflict was cautiously toned down or eliminated. Crit-

[9] *Pravda*, August 21, 1946.

icism of purely literary features was avoided in reviews, which concentrated almost exclusively on ideological content.

In the notorious literary controversies that figured so prominently in the press in this period, for example, the anti-cosmopolitan campaign, the struggle against bourgeois survivals, "typicalness" in literature and the no-conflict theory in drama, one detects a spirit of rebellion, however hesitant, among that small group of liberal-minded writers already mentioned. No doubt the expectations which had been aroused by the relative freedom accorded them as writers during the war were now shattered by the attacks of both the union and the party—attacks which at times seemed to reflect on their loyalty to their country. A few courageously spoke out in meetings of the Board of the Writers' Union or in articles such as that of the playwright, Nikolai Virta, who, in discussing the no-conflict theory in drama, declared: "everything living, true to life, sharp, fresh, and unstereotyped was combed out and smoothed out to the point where it was no longer recognizable. Every bold, unstereotyped word in a play had to be defended at the cost of the dramatist's nerves and the play's quality."[10] Yet almost without exception these few brave souls were beaten down in the official press and sooner or later recanted. Even the First Secretary of the Writers' Union, Fadeyev, when reprimanded by the party for his failure to attribute a major role to the adult communist organization portrayed in his celebrated novel, *The Young Guard*, supinely confessed his fault and—on the demand of Stalin, it is reported—undertook a laborious revision of the book.

By 1952, however, it apparently became clear even to party leaders that a regimented literature designed to educate people in ideological orthodoxy tended to turn them into eager readers of the classics of nineteenth-century Russian literature or translations of world literature. Moreover, the fact that theaters were nearly empty for Soviet plays subscribing to the notion of no dramatic conflicts, or conflicts between only good and better protagonists, whereas dramas of Gogol and Ostrovsky played to full houses, provided stark evidence of the apathy created by official controls. Suddenly a *Pravda* editorial of April 7 of that year castigated those critics who condemned authors for depicting negative aspects of Soviet life. It also attacked works whose heroes were described as entirely absorbed in production problems, and pro-

[10] "Pogovorim otkrovenno," *Sovetskoye iskusstvo*, March 29, 1952.

claimed the need for satirists of the Soviet scene, comparable to Gogol and Shchedrin. A sheaf of similar declarations, inspired by heads of the Writers' Union, soon appeared in print. Nonetheless, it was clear that the warning against overemphasizing negative features of Soviet existence, which the *Pravda* editorial also included, was simply a reiteration of a major emphasis of Zhdanovism.

The Thaw

It may be conjectured that no group in the Soviet Union welcomed Stalin's death in March 1953 with as much relief as the liberal intellectuals and particularly the writers among them. The Board of the Writers' Union, at its plenum in October 1953, called for frank discussions in literary matters, and Fadeyev, exploiting this sentiment, charged the union with violating democratic procedures and obstructing the individuality of authors. Such a rare gesture by a leading union functionary, unthinkable before Stalin's death, prompted a series of articles by liberal-minded authors. They were spearheaded by the remarkable one of Ilya Ehrenburg, in which he declared that the writer's proper domain is man's inner world and spiritual life and not simply descriptions of the external conditions of existence.[11] More startling and pointed was V. Pomerantsev's "On Sincerity in Literature,"[12] one of several similar articles in the magazine *Novy mir* (*New World*), edited by the progressive poet, Alexander Tvardovsky, which exposed the artistic blight in belles-lettres caused by Zhdanovism.

The vigorous debate that ensued in the press and in meetings of authors, sometimes punctuated by protests against bureaucratic practices of officials of the Writers' Union, at first provoked no response from the party, perhaps because of a division of opinion about literary affairs among its leaders at this disturbed time. Conservative members of the union and the party press assumed the offensive after the appearance, in May 1954, of Ehrenburg's novel, *The Thaw*. Its title and its frank excoriation of the harmfulness of trying to regiment art provided a name and a theme for the progressive literary movement after Stalin's death. Inspired articles assailed violators of the principles of Zhdanovism in belles-lettres, and the official party journal *Kommunist*

[11] "O rabote pisatelya," *Znamya*, No. 10 (1953), pp. 160-183.
[12] "Ob iskrennosti v literature," *Novy mir*, No. 12 (1953), pp. 218-245.

sternly warned the Writers' Union that its most important task was "to elucidate thoroughly the harm of those alien tendencies which have recently become particularly prominent in dramaturgy and criticism, and to guide the discussion and solution of literary questions along the correct path, and to foster in the organization the necessary creative atmosphere."[13] The Presidium of the Board of the Writers' Union promptly reprimanded the literary dissenters, exposed various "errors" in *Novy mir* articles, and fired its editor Tvardovsky.

With the death of Stalin, however, had come an end to the paralysis of fear, at least the kind of fear that tormented recalcitrant writers with the nightmare of prison camp or even execution. A few well-known authors boldly voiced the opinion that the Writers' Union, whose literary bureaucracy had become a symbol of crippling artistic controls, ought to be abolished. The rising temper of discontent may have had something to do with talk about the necessity of holding the Second All-Union Writers' Congress. That its realization was several times postponed while officials from the Moscow center traveled to preparatory congresses in various republics to cajole dissident members into line suggests the effort expended to create a desirable atmosphere of harmony for such a meeting.

Yet the leaders' attempts, at the opening of the congress on December 15, 1954, to cultivate an attitude of moderation and agreement were less than successful. Their insistence on the high quality of so much of the literature produced during the period of Stalinism and after was ridiculed in oppositional speeches. Dark hints emerged that personal enmity or envy of members of the union's directorate had played a part in recent failures to publish certain books and also in reprimands, denunciations, and punishments of union members who lacked power or protection. Though slight changes were voted in organizational details and in the statutes, there were no alterations that would make union leaders more accountable to the rank and file or would prevent them from exercising the traditional administrative controls over writers and their works. Although opposition spokesmen did attack some long-established dogmas of literary creation, they did not question the party's final authority in the field. However, the very

---

[13] "Za dalneishy podyom sovetskoi literatury," *Kommunist*, No. 9 (1954), p. 26, quoted in Harold Swayze, *Political Control of Literature in the USSR, 1946-1959* (Cambridge, Mass., 1962), p. 43.

freedom of dissent manifested by some participants indicated that a liberalizing trend had at last begun in the Writers' Union and in Soviet literature.

More than any other event, Khrushchev's startling denunciation of the horrors of Stalinism at the Twentieth Party Congress in 1956 served to polarize the hitherto uncertain and fluctuating division of conservatives and liberals in the Writers' Union, a division which has continued to dominate the literary scene to the present time. His speech filled the liberals with a sense of release, with bright hopes for the future of Soviet literature, and with renewed courage to attempt to realize these hopes even if it meant operating in defiance of the administrative controls of the Writers' Union. If these writers and critics began to emphasize truth and talent in literature in their struggle with the conservatives, it was because of their intense revulsion to years of Stalinist regimentation which had resulted in a travesty of truth and an emasculation of talent. Although they still paid lip service to some measure of party guidance, they openly opposed its direct interference in artistic expression. In some quarters the doctrinaire imposition of *partiinost* and socialist realism in the creation of imaginative belles-lettres was frankly ridiculed. Under this impetus the longing of some authors to probe the real problems of Soviet life, and not its propagandized image, found notable expression in fiction, poetry, and drama between 1956 and 1957, two high points of which were the second volume of the almanac *Literary Moscow* and Vladimir Dudintsev's novel, *Not by Bread Alone*, which aroused wide enthusiasm.

The administration of the Writers' Union seemed incapable of moderating the liberals' onslaught, which was largely influenced by the official exposure of Stalin's crimes, so euphemistically understated as "the cult of personality." The party's initial toleration soon vanished. No doubt the Polish and Hungarian revolts at this time, in which writers, artists, and intellectuals played a significant role, also helped to galvanize the party into action. To some extent the party's concern with the spreading ideological disobedience, accompanied by demands of certain authors for "self-government" in literature, was connected with the opinion of the liberals—as the Secretariat of the Writers' Union reported[14]—that belles-lettres must render as typical to mass readers not only the positive features of Soviet life but also the nega-

[14] *Literaturnaya gazeta*, May 16, 1957.

tive ones. Furthermore, it is likely that the liberal-conservative controversy in literature had also become involved in the party's power struggle.

Khrushchev's Middle Course

So consequential did the party regard the literary dispute that Khrushchev, along with several members of the Central Committee, attended the third plenum of the Board of the Writers' Union in May 1957 and spoke on several occasions. Later in the summer, when Khrushchev's power position had been consolidated, he delivered speeches at three separate conferences of writers, artists, and party officials. These speeches were later published as a single article which amounted to a major statement on literature's obligation to the party and the Soviet Union.[15] The moderateness of his position probably represented an effort to win over the dissenters, but he left no doubt that writers, in portraying the positive and negative aspects of Soviet life, must see to it that the positive ones prevailed.

In the course of the following year, when there seemed no disposition on the part of liberals to surrender, a campaign of intensive propaganda in preparation for an announced Third All-Union Congress of the Union of Soviet Writers was employed to bring about compliance with the party's program in literature. The customary browbeating to compel dissenters to repent their sins and conform went on in numerous meetings of the Writers' Union throughout the country. In a characteristic ritual, speaker after speaker berated the victims and sought to make them appear outcasts from a dedicated brotherhood, guilty of defying the Communist Party and of trafficking with the country's foreign enemies. All this was reported daily in the nation's press. The professional union that should exist primarily to protect its members from external encroachments thus identified itself—or at least its power structure did—with the very perpetrators of the encroachments. At first, liberal writers refused either to comply or defend themselves. With some relevance the charge of a "conspiracy of silence" was brought against them, and a decision was taken to weaken their power in the Moscow section of the union, to which most of the liberals belonged, by establishing an RSFSR division of the Writers' Union.

By the time the Third Congress was held in May 1959, most but

[15] "Za tesnuyu svyaz literatury i iskusstva s zhiznyu naroda," *Literaturnaya gazeta*, August 28, 1957.

267

not all of the recalcitrants had capitulated. The congress, with its false emphasis upon harmony, was generally regarded as the most boring to date. The relatively "soft" position adopted, somewhere between the liberals and conservatives, may have been influenced by the sense of shame felt by the leaders for their support during the preceding year of the ferocious vilification of Boris Pasternak and his expulsion from the union because of his novel *Doctor Zhivago*. This middle way in literature was also stressed by Khrushchev in his surprising and garrulous speech at the session. Perhaps realizing that the party had recently wielded the big stick too hard on literature, he even had words of praise for the much-condemned Dudintsev, who, to be sure, had finally recanted his deviations from *partiinost* in his celebrated novel. In a light, humorous vein Khrushchev urged authors to write as they pleased provided they always remembered that the party expected them to help in the building of communism.

New young authors had begun to do precisely that—to write as they pleased—and, so far as communism was concerned, let the chips fall where they may. Often highly talented, and inspired occasionally by the cause of de-Stalinization, they introduced another troublesome dimension to the Writers' Union. With more daring and less political experience, they made common cause with older and at times wavering liberals, such as Paustovsky, Ehrenburg, Kirsanov, Tvardovsky, Ovechkin, and Aliger. Together they formed an "out group" opposed to the conservative "in group." In actuality the situation was not clear-cut in terms of power and influence, for the shadow of the party continually hovered over both the "ins" and "outs." Ideologically, of course, the position of the Communist Party ultimately favored the conservatives, but during Khrushchev's rule party leaders had learned from experience that controls exercised by conservatives resulted usually in a literature of artistic sterility, in silent opposition by talented writers, and even in legal or illegal efforts to circumvent the controls. The party also evinced some awareness that the creation of truly artistic literature was incompatible with telling authors that they were free to write about anything they wished while at the same time preventing them from doing it. The party was under the further disadvantage that the conservative ranks contained many writers with little or no talent who had a vested interest in the mediocrity assured by restraints. Faced with such a situation, the party's only recourse was to endeavor to preserve a balance in the struggle between liberals and conservatives. When the pendulum swung too far in the direction of liberal critical views and literary accomplishments, as it inevitably seemed to do, a conservative reaction, supported or even initiated by the party, was bound to follow.

This was essentially the situation as the Soviet Union entered the decade of the 1960's. Liberals, indulging in some wishful thinking, regarded de-Stalinization as a rejection of dogmatism, administrative controls, lies, cruel social practices, and illegality; and politically incautious young writers among them (Nagibin, Tendryakov, Kazakov, Antonov, Aksenov, Yevtushenko, Voznesensky, etc.) poured forth fiction, verse, and drama that in considerable measure reflected protest, not against the Soviet system or communism as such, but against the evils of the Stalin era and their survival in contemporary life. The sixties had become peculiarly an age of youth in the Soviet Union. Increased opportunity of travel abroad, enlarged contacts with Western culture, a greater degree of economic prosperity, and the cumulative effects of education which, however strictly managed by the party, could hardly fail to stimulate independent thinking—all these factors added impetus to an old struggle for creative freedom on the part of a new generation of writers, artists, and intellectuals.

That many works by young authors found publication at all was probably due to the mild permissiveness endorsed by Khrushchev at the Third Congress, and also because of his own political interest in de-Stalinization at a time when this policy had its opponents in high party circles as well as in the Writers' Union. On at least two important occasions Khrushchev clearly sided with the liberals. At the request of Tvardovsky, who had been restored to his post as editor of *Novy mir*, he forced the party Presidium to accept the publication in 1962 of Alexander Solzhenitsyn's short novel, *One Day in the Life of Ivan Denisovich*, a brilliant and crushing exposure of Stalinist prison camp existence. He also personally sanctioned the publication in *Pravda* (October 21, 1962) of Yevgeny Yevtushenko's poem "Stalin's Heirs," an attack on those Stalinists still alive and biding their time.[16]

Liberals Versus Conservatives

Khrushchev's passionate demand at the Twenty-second Party Congress in 1961 for a resumption of the de-Stalinization drive spurred on the liberal group in the Writers' Union in their own fight for greater

[16] See Michel Tatu, *Power in the Kremlin. From Khrushchev to Kosygin* (New York, 1968), pp. 246-249.

freedom of expression and gave it a legitimate and organized character. However, it must be emphasized that Khrushchev's support was probably determined more by the need for allies in his political struggle than by any suddenly discovered conviction that literature should be released from party bondage. In this respect it was significant that the prominent liberal Tvardovsky was selected to give a speech on literature at this congress, and in it echoed the contention of young dissenting authors that they should be more bold and take advantage of the relative relaxation of controls. The only way to improve literature, Tvardovsky declared, was to banish the remaining traces of Stalinism from Soviet life.

During 1961-1962, for the first time in the history of the Writers' Union, what could be described as an effective liberal opposition, and apparently one with considerable popular support, existed. It is difficult to determine the kind and extent of their party backing, for though there is indirect evidence that top leaders of both contending groups in the Writers' Union had access to major party figures in their search for powerful influence on one side or the other in the controversy, in the nature of things it is impossible to document this concretely. The liberals did have defenders among older distinguished authors, in the ranks of the best literary critics, and also in high places in the Writers' Union and on the editorial boards of publishing firms and leading magazines. On Poetry Day crowds of young men and women on Mayakovsky Square chanted Yevtushenko's name and roared approval of his recitations. In Moscow's Luzhniky Sports Stadium, thousands of listeners wildly applauded Andrei Voznesensky whose formalist or even surrealist verse, so far removed from official socialist realism, symbolized the literary revolt of youth. For example, his "Beatnik Monologue"[17] reads in part:

> Blasting off from its rocket site,
> Sprinkling the world with atomic dust,
> Time spits on me
> And I spit on time . . .
> We are beatniks, and amidst all their insults
>   We are like wolves and beasts
> Toting clanging scandal with us like convict chains. . . .

[17] *Treugolnaya grusha* (Moscow, 1962).

270

The liberals reached a peak of influence in April 1962 when Yevtu-shenko and Voznesensky were elected to the steering committee of the Moscow section of the Writers' Union, whereas eight well-known con-servatives, including L. S. Sobolev, head of the Russian Republic divi-sion of the Writers' Union, were defeated. Such prominent conserva-tives as V. A. Kochetov, N. M. Gribachev, and A. V. Sofronov wisely refrained from standing for election. The liberals, however, were very much a minority in the Writers' Union and did not have everything their own way. In the union's administrative circles and on the editorial boards of publications were many holdover Stalinist appointees whose literary orthodoxy stood in the way of accepting anything new or ex-perimental. Many writers of the Stalin era with limited talent, who had achieved prominence by wholeheartedly espousing party ideology in their works and who now feared that their own positions and prestige were endangered, deeply resented these innovating youths whom they denounced as boudoir poets dedicated to word juggling and bedroom lyricism, "starry boys," "beatniks," and "Broadway youths" who op-posed the party line that there could be no ideological coexistence with the West in literature.

The two factions sharply opposed each other in various committees of the huge complex of the Writers' Union and in the pages of their supporting publications—the conservatives controlled *Oktyabr* (*Octo-ber*) and *Literatura i zhizn* (*Literature and Life*), which opponents scorned as a "yellow rag," and the liberals, *Novy mir* and *Yunost* (*Youth*). At a meeting of the Board of the Union at the end of 1961, its secretary fulminated against young liberal authors who created in their fiction anti-heroes alienated from Soviet life. Later, conservatives made various charges, without specifically documenting them, that liberals in literature and the arts (painting, sculpture, and music were undergoing the same experiences) had demoralized the opposition; that abstractionist painters and sculptors had arranged their own ex-hibitions and sold their works to foreigners; that bourgeois views of art had become widespread and that their Soviet adherents had stigmatized socialist realists as hopeless conservatives; and that liberals had made use of press, radio, and television to challenge the intelligibility of art and to maintain that the masses were incapable of understanding artistic innovation and that there should be art for the masses and art for the elect few.

271

The Freeze

In terms of the syndrome in party controls already mentioned, steadily mounting liberal successes required that the pendulum should swing the other way—in the direction of the conservatives. Though Khrushchev had tolerated and even somewhat abetted the liberal movement in the interests of his renewed de-Stalinization drive, he eventually realized that an overwhelming liberal victory threatened to result in a questioning of party authority and hence his own. He was forced to fall back on Stalinist conservatives to help him to reassert his authority. The start of the organized campaign of conservative and pro-Stalinist forces against liberal elements in literature and the arts occurred at the well-known incident at an exhibition of painting in Moscow in December 1962. There is reason to suppose that the exhibition, and Khrushchev's presence, were arranged by conservatives who were aware of his contempt for abstract art and the popular support such ridicule invariably achieves. His angry and vulgar remarks on the few such canvases shown were printed in *Pravda* (December 4, 1962).

On December 17, Khrushchev assembled a large gathering of prominent representatives of the arts and literature along with members of the party Presidium. The main speech was made by L. F. Ilyichev, new head of the reorganized Ideological Commission. He dwelt mostly on various liberal protests which had been made, and condemned these for supporting the coexistence of ideologies in the arts, thus catering to bourgeois ideals. Little was said about writers, but he drove home the point that "any deviation from the main line of development of our literature and art are intolerable."[18] Nine days later, however, Ilyichev brought together 140 young artists and authors under the auspices of the Ideological Commission and fiercely attacked leading liberal writers. The artist's credo that he formulated would have delighted the late Stalin: "The talent of a true artist is the property of the people. To the young creative intelligentsia we are compelled to state the following: You no longer belong to yourselves. If your creative abilities have been recognized by the people, they have become the people's property and their wealth. You are at the disposal of the people and must serve them loyally. . . . Those in literature and the arts must check their ideological and aesthetic position against the party program. No other

[18] *Pravda*, December 18, 1962.

'program,' no matter how it is expressed in prose, verse, or memoirs, can be adopted by people working in socialist culture."[19]

Here was party backing for the conservatives, but Khrushchev had not yet spoken and seems to have hesitated. At a party Presidium meeting earlier, in November 1962, which had under consideration the petition of a group of conservative artists who asked why the party's position on art had become obsolete, Khrushchev gave an important speech on literature and painting. Though this was never printed, it was rumored in Moscow that he spoke with admiration of Yevtushenko and Solzhenitsyn and their service to de-Stalinization. About this time he was quoted as having said in substance to a Western ambassador: "I favor greater freedom of expression since the level we have achieved in economy and technology demands this. But some of my colleagues in the Presidium think we must be cautious. Obviously we shall have to wait a while before going ahead any further."[20]

It soon became clear, however, that Khrushchev had come to share the anxieties of conservative leaders in literature and the arts that liberals were using the freedom to expose abuses under Stalin as justification for disclosing those of the present. At a Kremlin meeting (March 7 and 8, 1963) of top party officials and many well-known writers and artists, Khrushchev resumed the old insistence on *partiinost* in literature, asserting in his speech: "We are against peaceful coexistence in the sphere of ideology, and art is an ideology."[21] He also partially reversed his stand on de-Stalinization by offering kind words on the dead dictator's services to the country. In effect he also significantly turned against his protégé, Solzhenitsyn, by complaining that publishing firms and magazines were being flooded with manuscripts about experiences of persons in exile or prison camps, and by warning against such dangerous themes by sensation-lovers who only played into the hands of the bourgeoisie. More pointed was his criticism of Ehrenburg's memoirs, which Khrushchev had also initially approved for publication and which, he now discovered, portrayed everything in the Stalin period in gloomy colors. Ehrenburg had suggested in his work that he knew at the time about innocent writers who were victims of Stalin's purges. The implication was that if he, a private citizen, knew, responsible party leaders, including Khrushchev, must also have known.

[19] *Sovetskaya kultura*, January 10, 1963.
[20] This report is given by Tatu, *op.cit.*, pp. 305-306.
[21] *Pravda*, March 9, 1963.

Then why did they not do something? In his speech Khrushchev attempted to answer Ehrenburg's dark implication: "People ask, did the leading cadres of the party know, let us say, of the arrests of people at that time? Yes, they knew. But did they know that people who were innocent of any crimes were being arrested? No. This they did not know. They believed that Stalin was incapable of repressions against honest people devoted to our cause."[22] Such an implausible response to a tragic question haunting the minds of many Soviet citizens could only compound the rational reasons and emotional forces that had in the first place brought about the protests of the liberals.

Fortified by the official approval of Khrushchev's speech, triumphant conservatives in the Writers' Union resumed zealous persecution of the liberals. The ghastly charade of recantations was played out to the bitter end. Though the young rebels at first refused to repent publicly, despite the ceaseless drumbeat of accusations in meetings and in the press, gradually most of them were worn down and made their "confessions of errors." New elements, however, had entered into the customary routine of this prolonged struggle. Many offending young writers enjoyed wide popularity among readers. A few had won much success on trips abroad and were well known there. They did not fear to defend themselves at union meetings called to reprimand them, and liberal critics openly supported them. Still more striking, the campaign against them was roundly criticized by important communists in Italy, France, Poland, Hungary, and elsewhere. No doubt these factors helped to squelch vindictiveness on the part of the literary bureaucracy of the Writers' Union. Liberal editors retained their posts, and though at first Yevtushenko's expulsion from the union was demanded, the matter was soon quietly dropped. In short, though again defeated, the liberals had achieved a victory of a kind in having found the courage to fight back, a first step toward the indispensable freedom of the creative artist. The struggle between the conservative power of the Writers' Union and its liberal minority had clearly not ended.

Continued Group Struggle

The experiences of 1961-1963 emphasized, if that were necessary, the profound political significance which the party still attached to belles-lettres and the arts. Individual writers and their works were

[22] *Ibid.*

debated in the Presidium and the Central Committee, and in times of crisis the party was prepared to usurp the prerogatives of its controlling agency, the Writers' Union, and demand publicly, through the mouth of its leader, conformity to its wishes in literature. Moreover, the experiences further revealed that conservatives and liberals in the Writers' Union had become powerful competing groups, each on occasion acting as a lobby which sought to secure the backing of the party leadership.

This situation continued, although under altered circumstances, after Khrushchev's fall in October 1964 and his replacement by Brezhnev and Kosygin. The party apparatus had never really been a homogeneous entity, and now, lacking the single authority of a Stalin or Khrushchev, there was the possibility that a fracturing of power at the top might produce both a hard and a soft line in literature. In the uncertainties of the period immediately following Khrushchev's ouster, the party stumbled from a hands-off policy in literature to one at first favoring the liberals. Tvardovsky, in a ringing editorial in the January 1965 issue of *Novy mir*, dismissed all Soviet literature before and after the Twentieth Party Congress which, because of the cult of personality or neo-Stalinism, had falsified Russian life. A few party-inspired editorials on literature, which began to appear in the press in January 1965, suggested divided opinions, one stressing the old shibboleth of *partiinost* and another the search for artistic quality and the need for a balanced analysis of life.[23] More indicative of a soft-line party faction in literature was a long, serious analysis of the situation in *Pravda* (February 21, 1965) by its distinguished editor-in-chief and member of the Central Committee, A. M. Rumyantsev, in which *partiinost* was not even mentioned; artistic creation was described as "the discovery of something new, something hitherto unknown"; tolerance for experimentation was advocated; and the criteria of literary judgment were dissociated from political factors and connected with "the free multilateral development of the personality of each member of society."

This startling presentation, published in such a place, aroused concern among conservatives in the Writers' Union and apparently in the party's hard-line literary faction. The answer to Rumyantsev came promptly— a message from the Central Committee delivered by a member of the Presidium, A. P. Kirilenko, at a Moscow Congress of the RSFSR

---

[23] See *ibid.*, January 9 and 17, 1965.

division of the Writers' Union. In a report on the Congress in *Pravda* (March 4, 1965), its conservative head, L. S. Sobolev, succinctly summed up the essence of the message: "*Partiinost* is the sole criterion of our literary activities." During the next few months a curious kind of literary dispute took place between a "liberal" *Pravda* and a "conservative" *Izvestia.* Though this may have reflected merely personal differences between the two editors-in-chief of the party and government newspapers, it more likely reflected differences on literary problems at that time in the higher party *apparat.* Much of the controversy centered in the literary war between the magazines *Oktyabr* and *Novy mir* and their respective editors, the neo-Stalinist Kochetov and the liberal Tvardovsky.

Liberals appeared to gain most from the party's ambiguous position at this time. The first half of 1965 marked the high tide of excited interest in that "golden age," as Ehrenburg called it, of innovative, revolutionary literature of the 1920's before Stalin came to power. A number of these early proscribed authors were revived in new editions; the process of rehabilitating purged writers, begun after Khrushchev's speech at the Twentieth Party Congress, continued; and their sequestered manuscripts were reviewed for possible publication by government-appointed commissions. Even new editions of the old works of Pasternak began to appear. Contacts with Western cultural organizations flourished, and the interchange of writers, interrupted at the time of Khrushchev's crackdown on the arts, was resumed. Delegations from the Writers' Union fraternized with colleagues in Poland, Czechoslovakia, Hungary, and Rumania, some of whom had a more Western orientation in literature and more advanced ideas of freedom of expression than their Soviet counterparts. Soviet authors also sought and obtained membership in Western literary organizations: the European Community, the European Society of Culture, and P.E.N., and even attended meetings arranged by the Congress for Cultural Freedom. Such contacts could not fail to introduce leading Soviet writers into a literary world of tastes, models, standards, and opposition to artistic controls of which they had little personal knowledge. In these circumstances, it is not surprising that the names of European and American authors, such as Kafka, Salinger, Cheever, Updike, etc., hitherto scarcely known in the Soviet Union, became familiar and their works were translated and much discussed. At this time, in fact, an extensive Soviet controversy developed on the subject of Western modernism versus

276

socialist realism, which accumulated a substantial critical literature involving conservative and liberal viewpoints on such concepts as dehumanization of literature, the alienated man, and Marxian humanism. This resumption of a form of the old Russian tradition of emancipated literary and cultural "Westernization" unquestionably exercised a strong influence in increasing the expectations and defining the artistic goals of liberal writers.

Certainly Western modernism has had an effect on what might be described as a subgroup of the liberals—writers of *samizdat*, that is, unpublished underground literature or literature "for the drawer." Mimeographed magazines of such material, sometimes experimental in form and in content unpublishable in the Soviet Union, are distributed, and forbidden stories and poems circulate in manuscript and are read at private literary gatherings. The practice goes back to the repressive days of the tsars and is an indictment as much of Soviet censorship as of tsarist. Some of the best of the underground literature finds its way abroad and is published there either without or with the author's permission and under his name, as in the case of Pasternak's *Doctor Zhivago*, or under pseudonyms, as with the writings of Abram Tertz (Andrei Sinyavsky) and Nikolai Arzhak (Yuli Daniel). Again, as in nineteenth-century Russia, copies of these contraband works are smuggled into the Soviet Union and appear to be read widely. Few of the many writers and intellectuals I talked with in Russia in 1965 failed to be conversant with the contents of such writings.

Repression and Revolt

Whether the reason was that the growing frequency of these contraband publications damaged the Soviet image at home and abroad, or that the mounting successes of the liberal wing of the Writers' Union again called for the pendulum to swing in the other direction, it is hard to say, but a concerted party attack on liberal writers and artists began to appear in the official press about August 1965. The movement took on sinister implications, for at about the same time the new regime quietly began its own drive to rehabilitate Stalin. The concurrence was understandable. Apparently, as in the case of Khrushchev in 1962-1963, the concern was lest liberal writers, to say nothing of underground writers, would insist on probing more deeply into Stalin's misrule and would also widen their social and even political criticism to include evils of the post-Stalin period.

277

In deciding in September 1965 to arrest and bring to trial Sinyavsky and Daniel, party leaders deliberately set out to silence or reform liberal forces by an act of intimidation that had distinct Stalinist overtones. They were in effect warning liberal writers that a heretic is bound to turn renegade, and that a dissenter can become unpatriotic, even an enemy agent. Though they must have realized the risk of an international propaganda defeat, as in the case of the treatment of Pasternak, they presumably thought the risk slight because Sinyavsky was not then well known and Daniel hardly known at all, and they assumed that public sentiment at home and abroad would be slow to rise in favor of the victims. Sinyavsky and Daniel, in their works published abroad under pseudonyms, were charged with violating the law against "agitation or propaganda conducted for the purpose of undermining and weakening Soviet power." If influential conservative leaders in the Writers' Union welcomed the arrests and trial (February 1966), they were unable to prevail upon any of their more distinguished members to offer testimony against the accused either at the trial or in the official press. Among other reasons for this was presumably the revulsion that swept the intellectual and artistic community because of the government's action.

On the other hand, the trial and the harsh sentences handed down by the court provoked a most extraordinary eruption of protest that ranged from street demonstrations to numerous letters and petitions involving hundreds of signers, many of them people of distinction, and addressed to the court, the Writers' Union, government and party organizations, and the leading newspapers. No doubt the climate of limited social permissiveness that set in after Stalin's death contributed to this unique outburst, as did the long struggle of liberal writers whose demands for freedom of expression and release from the lacquered lying of socialist realism were echoed by the defenders at their trial. But the real motivation behind the protest was the lurking fear that the government's harsh action portended a return to the psychopathological conditions of the Stalin era, with its distorted human relations, laceration of the spirit, and persecution mania. Perhaps, too, the conscience of Soviet writers and intellectuals, which had tormented them for so many sins of omission during the years of Stalin, had survived the furnace of doubt and now refused to be silent.

All these reasons were reflected in the courageous and eloquent open letter of the writer Lidia Chukovskaya who, along with 62 others, also signed one of the most impressive petitions. Her letter, copies of which were sent to the Board of the Writers' Union, *Izvestia*, and various national literary magazines, was addressed to a leading proponent of the conservative faction of the Writers' Union, the celebrated novelist, Mikhail Sholokhov. In his speech as a representative of literature at the Twenty-third Party Congress, he berated the liberal-minded defenders of Sinyavsky and Daniel and implied with satisfaction that in an earlier period of Soviet rule the defendants would have been executed as traitors. "You would have liked it better," Lidia Chukovskaya wrote, "if the court had tried these two citizens unhampered by the legal code, if it had been guided not by the law but by its 'sense of rough justice.' " And she concluded her moving letter by declaring that the trial itself was illegal: "Because a book, a piece of fiction, a story, a novel, in brief a work of literature—whether good or bad, talented or untalented, truthful or untruthful—cannot be tried in any court, criminal, military, or civil, except the court of literature. A writer, like any Soviet citizen, can and should be tried by a criminal court for any misdemeanor he may have committed, but not for his books. Literature does not come under the jurisdiction of the criminal court. Ideas should be fought with ideas, not with camps and prisons."[24]

It was some measure of the party's fear of popular reaction that its controlled press tried to keep the general public carefully insulated from any knowledge of these signed letters and petitions of protest, for though many of them were addressed to the press they were not published in Soviet newspapers. However, they circulated in manuscript copies and, by one means or another, a number of them found their way abroad and were often published there. Nor was the groundswell of indignant reaction to the Sinyavsky-Daniel trial from noncommitted sources in the West or from communist parties from Helsinki to Rome objectively reported in the Soviet press.

In the course of the next two years the Sinyavsky-Daniel affair was directly or indirectly connected with the arrests and subsequent trials of a group of young people—Viktor Khaustov, Vladimir Bukovsky, Vadim Delone, Yevgeny Kushev, Alexei Dobrovolsky, Yury Galanskov, Alexander Ginsburg, and Vera Lashkova. They were variously charged with "subversive" activities, participating in demonstrations, sending abroad a "white book" of the Sinyavsky-Daniel trial, and editing and distributing nonconformist underground literature. Accounts of their

[24] *New York Times*, November 19, 1966.

semi-secret trials, frank statements of several of the accused, and a letter on these matters, addressed to "world public opinion," were sent to the Soviet press and abroad by Pavel Litvinov, grandson of Maxim Litvinov, former Soviet Foreign Minister.[25] Interestingly enough, they often based their defense on improper actions of the secret police, the illegality of the trials, and violations of constitutional provisions of freedom of speech, press, and assembly.

This flouting of the law, as well as ominous implications of Stalinism in the arrests and conduct of the trials, were stressed in another outpouring of letters and petitions signed by hundreds of intellectuals and others.[26] Since many of the signers were liberal literary figures, involved in what seemed clearly to be an informally organized protest, the fearful administration of the Writers' Union countered with published denunciations, and some party members among the signers were dropped from the union. Though the assertion cannot be proved, the union's leadership must have lost standing and respect for its behavior in these clearly punitive literary trials of little-known authors or unknown young novices. Whereas party leaders had initiated them for policy reasons, reactionary union officials defended them although, as heads of an organization supposedly representing the interests of writers, they might have been expected, at the very least, to have pleaded for mitigation of the sentences. The net result was probably to strengthen the cause of the liberal opposition in the Writers' Union. Courage breeds courage in such affairs, and perhaps just because the defendants were young, unknown, idealistic writers seeking to distribute their nonconformist stories and poems and daring in open court to criticize the state's execution of justice, their fates stirred widespread sympathy.

The Fourth Congress and Censorship

Holding a congress of the Writers' Union at a time of extreme literary turmoil seems to have become a regular party device for eliminating discord and achieving some semblance of harmony in the organization. No doubt a desire for a national spirit of cooperation in the face of the forthcoming fiftieth anniversary of the revolution also had something

[25] English texts of these statements may be found in *Survey*, No. 67 (April 1968), pp. 133-137.
[26] For samples of two of the most impressive of these published abroad, see *Washington Evening Star*, February 13, 1968, and *New York Times*, March 8, 1968.

to do with it. More than usual care appears to have been employed in the selection of representatives for the Fourth All-Union Congress of the Writers' Union, held in May 1967, for of the 473 delegates, 403 were communists, a very much larger percentage than that of the total party membership in the union. But the reactionary attitude of the union leadership to the Sinyavsky-Daniel trial was more than an outraged memory in the minds of liberal delegates, a number of whom, including Ehrenburg, were not present. Many invited left-wing and communist writers from abroad, among them Sartre and Aragon, refused to attend. Despite the usual dull reports on the theme of the congress, "The Role of Literature in the Building of Communism," a feeling of tension existed among the delegates who expected a response to a remarkable letter, copies of which had been sent to the Board of the Union and many other members, by Solzhenitsyn who had fallen out of favor with the conservatives ever since Khrushchev's altered attitude toward him in 1963. Union officials, however, had banned any answer on the floor of the congress.

Solzhenitsyn's letter was the frankest and most revelatory statement of the negative and even sinister activities of the Writers' Union as the principal group presumed to represent the interests of the literary profession. Dwelling on the practice of censorship, in which the union leaders had always cooperated with the party in manifold ways, Solzhenitsyn declared in the first part of his letter: "Our writers are not supposed to have the right, they are not endowed with the right, to express their anticipatory judgments about the moral life of man and society, or to explain in their own way the social problems or the historical experience that has been so deeply felt in our country. Works that might have expressed the mature thinking of the people, that might have timely and salutary influence on the realm of the spirit or on the development of a social conscience are prohibited or distorted by censorship on the basis of considerations that are petty, egotistic and, from the national point of view, shortsighted." He then called upon the congress to recommend "the abolition of all censorship, overt or hidden, of all fictional writing and release publishing houses from the obligation of obtaining authorization for the publication of every printed page."

In the next section of his letter Solzhenitsyn considered the duties of the Writers' Union to its members. After pointing out that many Soviet authors during their lifetime had been exposed to abuse and slander in the press and often to violence and personal persecution, he continued: "The Writers' Union not only did not make available its own publications for reply and justification, not only did not come out in defense of these writers, but through its leadership was always first among the persecutors. Names that adorned our poetry of the twentieth century found themselves on lists of those excluded from the union or not even admitted to the union in the first place. The leadership of the union cowardly abandoned to their distress those for whom persecution ended in camps and death. We learned after the Twentieth Congress of the party that there were more than 600 writers whom the union obediently handed over to their fate in prisons and camps." He proposed that the relevant section of the union's statutes "clearly formulate all the guarantees for the defense of union members who are subjected to slander and unjust persecutions so that past illegalities will not be repeated."

Solzhenitsyn in the last part of his letter gave a depressing account of how the secret police searched his apartment, impounded the manuscript of his novel *The First Circle*, as well as manuscripts of plays, stories, and all his literary archives, and without his knowledge made the novel and tendentious excerpts from his files "available to literary officials," meaning by this, no doubt, officers of the Writers' Union. Further, he asserted, an irresponsible campaign of slander against him had been conducted during the preceding three years to the effect that in the war he had betrayed his country, pandered to the Germans, and served time in prison as a common criminal, whereas he had had a distinguished military career and had been sent to a prison camp for criticizing Stalin in a letter. He went on to say that since these slanders, his novel *Cancer Ward*, which had been accepted by *Novy mir*, had been refused publication (because, it was said, of the opposition of Fedin, First Secretary of the Writers' Union). His other efforts to publish had been in vain, and he had been cut off from all fruitful literary contacts. "In view of such a gross infringement on my copyright and 'other' rights," he concludes, "will the Fourth Congress defend me, yes or no? It seems to me that the choice is also not without importance for the literary future of several of the delegates."[27]

Not a word of this amazing one-man assault on the administrative center of the Writers' Union appeared in Soviet press accounts of the congress, but beneath the artificial calm of the proceedings seethed a

[27] Translated in *New York Times*, June 5, 1967.

spirit of revolt led by liberal delegates. It was reported in Moscow that some 200 writers and intellectuals sent letters and telegrams to the union or signed petitions in support of Solzhenitsyn's plea, and that well-known authors, including Paustovsky, Kaverin, Aksenov, and Yevtushenko, openly endorsed his condemnation of censorship. It was also reported that 82 members of the Writers' Union, spearheaded by Tvardovsky and Yevtushenko, warned union leaders that Solzhenitsyn's charges must not be ignored. Voznesensky proposed that a one-volume edition of Solzhenitsyn's published works be issued and that a committee of authors examine his rejected writings to determine those suitable for publication.[28] One delegate, the highly respected poet Pavel Antokolsky, is reported to have gone over the heads of the congress to address a letter to P. N. Demichev, secretary of the Central Committee of the party on ideological matters, in which he said in part: "If a Soviet writer is compelled to turn to his fellow writers with a letter like Solzhenitsyn's, this means that we are all morally responsible to him and to our readers. If he cannot tell readers the truth, then I, too, old writer that I am, have no right to look straight into the readers' eyes."[29]

A more striking letter from a much younger author, G. N. Vladimov, was sent to the president of the congress. After insisting that the only free literature in the Soviet Union was that created by underground writers, and that it "is developing and expanding and to withstand it is as foolish and useless as prohibiting alcohol or tobacco," he turned to Solzhenitsyn, most of whose unpublished manuscripts he had read, and exalted him as "the pride of Russian literature." He demanded to know whether it was not the duty of the Writers' Union to defend this author from all the vicissitudes of his individual situation, and concluded: "Solzhenitsyn's letter has clearly become a document over which it is impossible to pass in silence, a silence unworthy of serious artists. I propose to the congress that it discuss this letter in open session, take a new and unequivocal decision on it, and present this decision to the government of the country."[30]

[28] See Stanley Kunitz, "The Other Society Inside Russia," *New York Times Magazine*, August 20, 1967, p. 24.

[29] "More About Solzhenitsyn," *Radio Liberty Dispatch*, January 29, 1968, p. 17.

[30] *Posev* (April 1968), pp. 16-18, trans. in part in *Aspects of Intellectual Ferment and Dissent in the Soviet Union*, prepared by Sergius Yakobson and Robert V. Allen (Washington, D.C., 1968), pp. 45-46.

As we have seen, however, there was never any hope of an open discussion of the letter at the congress. Moreover, officials of the Writers' Union seemed to learn nothing from this experience, for shortly thereafter they became involved, in the course of exercising their arbitrary controls, in controversy with another distinguished author. Perhaps it was Voznesensky's support of Solzhenitsyn, coupled with the displeasure of union bureaucrats over his allegedly uncritical attitude toward the United States, that led them to cancel his return visit to New York to read his poetry at the Lincoln Center Art Festival in June 1967. The reason given to foreign correspondents in Moscow was that the poet had fallen "ill." A very healthy and indignant Voznesensky promptly wrote a letter to *Pravda* (which was not published but appeared in various newspapers abroad), damning officials of the Writers' Union for their trickery and dishonesty. "It is not a question of me personally," he angrily declared, "but of the fate of Soviet literature, its honor and prestige in the outside world. How much longer will we go on dragging ourselves through the mud? How much longer will the Writers' Union go on using methods like these? Clearly the leadership of the union does not regard writers as human beings. This lying, prevarication and knocking people's heads together is standard practice. This is what they do to many of my comrades. Letters to us often do not reach us, and sometimes replies are sent in our name. What boors, what chameleons they are! We are surrounded by lies, lies, lies, bad manners and lies. I am ashamed to be a member of the same union as these people. That is why I am writing to your newspaper, which is called 'Truth' [*Pravda*]."[31]

These words, for which Voznesensky was reprimanded and threatened with expulsion from the Writers' Union, might one day become the epitaph of that organization. In any event, anxious leaders of the Communist Party could hardly fail to regard the expanded and continuing liberal opposition to the literary trials as a dangerous threat. Accordingly, a resolution of the Central Committee in April 1968 announced an extensive campaign for tighter ideological controls of writers and artists and for greater efforts to combat subversive attempts of the West to undermine the patriotism of the Soviet people. One of the key speeches at this party meeting was delivered by a rabidly conservative official of the Writers' Union, G. M. Markov.

[31] *New York Times*, August 11, 1967.

The resolution's mandate was soon reflected in various attacks by conservative critics in the journals and in the banning of plays by liberals. The Secretariat of the Writers' Union also warned that authors who refused to withdraw their signatures from protests against the literary trials, particularly those that had received publication abroad, faced expulsion from the union and loss of privileges. Though the campaign caused deep pessimism and even fear in literary and intellectual circles during 1968, liberal writers continued to be vocal, if more cautiously so. Despite much pressure to change the views expressed in his letter, Solzhenitsyn also remained adamant. It appears that the union secretariat, after discussing his letter, summoned him before them several times, apparently in the hope of convincing him to make a public disavowal that could be used to good effect, especially in the press abroad. When Fedin, the first secretary of the Writers' Union, pleaded with Tvardovsky to help persuade Solzhenitsyn to alter his position, the liberal-minded poet replied: "I do not recall that anyone has even tried to refute a single one of the points in the letter—why is this? The simple reason is that in the main the arguments are irrefutable, and as for me I would subscribe to them with both hands. . . . To solve this 'question of questions' in the work of the Writers' Union and in literary life in general by 'secret' means is impossible."[32]

Solzhenitsyn's fight against censorship also received support from the outstanding physicist and member of the Soviet Academy of Sciences, Andrei D. Sakharov. Though his remarkable memorandum, *Progress, Coexistence, and Intellectual Freedom* (not published in the Soviet Union) had the larger purpose of projecting necessary changes in Russian and American policies that would enable the two nations to cooperate in order to achieve a peaceful world, he dwelt on the problem of censorship in several passages, one of which reads: "The crippling censorship of Soviet artistic and political literature has again been intensified. Dozens of brilliant writings cannot see the light of day. They include some of the best of Solzhenitsyn's works, executed with great artistic and moral force and containing profound artistic and philosophical generalizations. Is this not a disgrace?"[33]

Meanwhile, because of his refusal to recant, the campaign against Solzhenitsyn continued, the publication of his works was still prevented,

[32] *Ibid.*, December 12, 1968.
[33] Andrei D. Sakharov, *Progress, Coexistence and Intellectual Freedom*, trans. by *New York Times*, with introduction, afterword, and notes by Harrison E. Salisbury (New York, 1968), p. 63.

and his fiftieth birthday was passed over in silence. Though he publicly protested that the publication abroad of two of his novels, *Cancer Ward* and *The First Circle*, was done without his permission, the suspicion existed, and perhaps with some reason, that specially edited manuscripts of these works were offered foreign firms by Soviet agents so that publication of them would justify further attacks on him as "a tool of the West."

During 1968 the intense concern of the party and the conservatives of its faithful arm, the Writers' Union, with the question of censorship and the dangers of uncontrolled expression by authors was unquestionably much exacerbated by the reform program in Czechoslovakia which included, among other things, the abolition of censorship. A frank measure of Soviet determination to preserve censorship at home could be seen in its firm insistence upon its reimposition in Czechoslovakia after the occupation. According to Western press reports, a considerable number of Soviet authors sent a letter of protest to their Czechoslovak colleagues over their country's invasion. Though officials of the Writers' Union tried without success to persuade well-known members of the organization to acclaim the invasion, only the secretariat, made up largely of little-known conservative guardians of ideological purity, signed such a statement of approval in the union's weekly, *Literaturnaya gazeta* (October 23, 1968). What was not indicated, however, was that the list lacked signatures of three of the few distinguished authors on the secretariat—Leonid Leonov, Konstantin Simonov, and Alexander Tvardovsky.

Conclusion

The evidence presented in this chapter seems to make abundantly clear the direction that group politics has taken among Soviet writers.[34]

[34] For other studies in English of the writers as a group, see the following: George Gibian, *Interval of Freedom, Soviet Literature During the Thaw* (Minneapolis, 1960); Priscilla Johnson, *Khrushchev and the Arts, The Politics of Soviet Culture, 1962-1964* (Cambridge, Mass., 1963); Harold Swayze, *Political Control of Literature in the USSR, 1946-1959* (Cambridge, Mass., 1962); Peter Benno, "The Political Aspect," in Max Hayward and Edward L. Crowley (eds.), *Soviet Literature in the Sixties* (New York, 1964); Patricia Blake, "Freedom and Control in Literature," in Alexander Dallin and Alan F. Westin (eds.), *Politics in the Soviet Union, 7 Cases* (New York, 1966), Chap. 5; David Burg, "The 'Cold War' on the Literary Front," *Problems of Communism*, XI, No. 4 (July-August 1962), 1-14, and *ibid.*, XI, No. 5 (September-October 1962), 33-46; Vera Dunham, "Insights from Soviet Literature," *Journal of Conflict Resolution*, VIII, No. 4 (December 1964), pp. 386-410; Max Hayward, "The

Since their organization into a national Writers' Union in 1934 by order of the Communist Party, the union has never ceased to be an instrument of the party, and has not acted as a defender of the interests of its members. Indeed, creative writers have been equated with journalists as instruments for conveying propaganda and ideological instruction acceptable to the party. To the extent that literary artistry enhances the reception of propaganda, the party is concerned with it, but artistic considerations must always be subordinated to ideological correctness. Although the party lines of control in the operation of the Writers' Union are clear, the party prefers to permit the union to run its own professional affairs, and to perform the function of controlling writers, provided it does not wander outside the party orbit. Almost from its origin, however, the Writers' Union became involved in political conflict among rival groups of writers, perhaps inevitably in view of the fact that the party identifies literature with politics. Liberal members, devoted to freedom of expression and the individualism so vital in the creation of artistic literature, opposed conservative elements supported by administrative and ideological controls of the organization's leaders, whose ultimate power came from the party.

This long struggle, resulting in repeated defeats of the liberals, assumed different dimensions and a new sharpness after Stalin's death when a little more latitude was allowed writers to express themselves in literature and in the realm of ideas. No doubt the altered situation was aided also by improving economic conditions, the Soviet Union's new international position of power, and inner-party conflicts during the regimes of Khrushchev, and Brezhnev and Kosygin. It is impossible to estimate how widespread this liberal movement in the Writers' Union has become. The liberals are now associated with many natural allies among intellectuals, artists, academicians, university professors and students, teachers, some members of the armed services, many professional specialists, and even some better educated workers. Lately, the

---

Literary Purge in Retrospect," *Survey*, No. 49 (October 1963), pp. 54-62; Priscilla Johnson, "The Regime and the Intellectuals: A Window on Party Politics," *Problems of Communism*, xii, No. 4, supplement (July-August 1963); J. F. Matlock, Jr., "The 'Governing Organs' of the Union of Soviet Writers," *American Slavic and East European Review*, xv, No. 3 (1956), 382-399; Timothy McClure, "The Politics of Soviet Culture, 1964-1967," *Problems of Communism*, xvi, No. 2 (March-April 1967), 26-43; Ernest J. Simmons, "Introduction: Soviet Literature and Controls," *Through the Glass of Soviet Literature*, Ernest J. Simmons (ed.) (New York, 1953), 4-26.

fear of reversion to Stalinist practices by the party and government has brought other Soviet citizens to the side of the liberals.

Underground authors and their literature have contributed to the liberal writers' cause and at the same time intensified conservative and party opposition. During the last ten years some of the best fiction, which could not be published in the Soviet Union, has been smuggled abroad and appeared there. These items, along with foreign publication of a steady flow of letters and petitions of protesters against the political literary trials, transcripts of the trials, and a variety of documents and memoranda bearing on these matters, have imparted a profounder meaning and content to the struggle of the literary liberals and their allies against censorship, ideological controls, and violation of civil liberties provided in the Soviet constitution. Much of this material published outside the country is funneled back into the Soviet Union by a variety of means, and the anxieties of conservatives and party leaders over this situation are magnified by the international awareness of the stubborn conflict. At no previous time in the history of the Soviet Union has there been such a situation of open rivalry between groups, with the accused in the recent literary trials refusing to confess to the "justice" of charges against them and refusing to deny the existence of political persecution.

In these respects liberals in the Writers' Union may be regarded as an important pressure group whose prolonged struggle has served to give purpose and direction to a whole movement intent upon securing certain changes in party practices or guarantees from the Soviet government. The intellectual dissent of liberal writers to censorship and administrative controls in literature has always had wider implications that involve the morbid fears of Soviet leaders, largely fear of truth before their people, whether it be fear of the whole truth of Stalinism, fear of the truth of the literary trials, or fear of the truth about the invasion of Czechoslovakia. The right of the artist to choose truth is the central issue of the struggle of liberal writers and intellectuals. An incessant propaganda of lies and constant campaigns to direct and control artistic expression seems to many Soviet intellectuals more and more incongruous with the real dynamics of Soviet life today. It seems to them almost anachronistic that one of the most powerful nations in the world, an international leader in scientific achievements in outer space, still fears an author's devotion to artistic truth, his desire to think and write about things as they really are in the Soviet Union. In the intimacy of their homes one discovers, as this author has often done, that their search is for a humanized communism, a political system whose values will have no place for the political lie, the real tragedy of Soviet life. A fully controlled press and literature can only end, they believe, in creating a government of lies. Though the gains of liberal writers and intellectuals in their efforts to change or modify the party's position on freedom of expression have been at best minimal to date, there are some reasons to hope that their continued struggle may help to force the regime eventually in the direction of a liberalized form of communism.

CHAPTER IX ~ BY DONALD D. BARRY AND
HAROLD J. BERMAN

The Jurists*

Soviet Jurists as an Interest Group and as a Profession

IN speaking of Soviet jurists as an interest group, we use the language of a school of political science which interprets political processes in terms of groups exerting influence to secure public action in support of their respective interests.[1] Within this school, widely varying definitions have been put forward; depending on the definition, interest groups may include such diverse types of associations as organized labor, the scientific community, and the local Rotary Club.[2] For no apparent reason, lawyers have hardly been mentioned in the literature on interest groups, although they seem to qualify under virtually all the definitions. We believe that the study of lawyers as an interest group would add new dimensions to interest group theory and at the same time would illuminate the existing theories of sociologists and legal scholars concerning lawyers as a profession.

As is so often the case in matters of social science, including legal scholarship, a comparative approach may clarify ideas that seem obscure when related only to one's own society. In studying the Soviet legal profession, the juxtaposition of the two concepts, "interest group" and "profession," is particularly congenial. Those who are interested in the extent to which Soviet jurists constitute a profession are likely also to want to know in what ways Soviet jurists exert an influence on the political life of the Soviet Union, while those who seek an answer to

* This chapter is a revised version of an article which appeared in the *Harvard Law Review*, LXXXII, No. 1 (November 1968), 1-41. Grateful acknowledgment is made to the Russian Research Center of Harvard University for financial support of a portion of the research upon which this chapter is based.

[1] See, e.g., G. Almond and G. B. Powell, Jr., *Comparative Politics*: *A Developmental Approach* (Boston and Toronto, 1960); E. Latham, *The Group Basis of Politics* (Ithaca, 1952); D. Truman, *The Governmental Process*: *Political Interests and Public Opinion* (New York, 1951).

[2] Latham, *op.cit.*, p. 49.

the latter question will discover it in the answer to the former. As we shall show, it is primarily by acting in their professional capacity that jurists exert political influence in the Soviet Union. We believe that this is probably true of professions in other countries, including the United States, as well.

The Soviet legal profession does not fall into the usual definitions of interest groups as easily as does the American legal profession. Soviet jurists are, to be sure, "a group of individuals who are linked by particular bonds of concern or advantage, and who have some awareness of these bonds . . ."; however, they do not clearly fit within any of the classifications into which the authors of this definition subdivide such groups.[3] If another factor is added—that an interest group "makes certain claims upon other groups in the society for the establishment, maintenance, or enhancement of forms of behavior that are implied by the [group's] shared attitudes . . ."[4]—then, once again, Soviet jurists qualify, but with a difference. In the United States, lawyers make claims through bodies which have the special task of protecting and articulating their group interests—particularly, bar associations. In terms of interest group theory, such "specialized structures" are formed for the "explicit representation of the interests of a particular group" and the "formulation of [its] interests and demands."[5] In the Soviet Union, the Communist Party, which, according to the USSR Constitution, is the "leading core" of all state and social organizations,[6] frowns on the creation of specialized structures for the formulation of special interests. In Soviet theory and practice, all interest groups are subject to party control, and all group interests must be reconciled with the party's interests if they are to be considered legitimate. Thus a theory of interest groups can have value for an understanding of Soviet politics only if it transcends the postulates of a free forum in which various self-interested groups compete for influence.

This is not to say, however, that there is no significant competition for influence among various groups in Soviet society. Western scholarship on the Soviet Union has suffered in the past from the exaggerated conception that all Soviet organizations and associations are merely "transmission belts" of party policy, and that public opinion plays no role in determining party policy. As we shall attempt to show, Soviet jurists (like Soviet writers, managers, army officers, and others) have

[3] Almond and Powell, *op.cit.*, pp. 75-79.   [4] Truman, *op.cit.*, p. 33.
[5] Almond and Powell, *op.cit.*, p. 78.   [6] USSR Constitution, Article 126.

distinctive common concerns and distinctive attitudes, and they press these concerns and attitudes on other groups and on the party leadership itself. Nevertheless, the competition of group interests in the Soviet Union is "socialist competition"; it takes place within a framework not of "the market" but of "the plan," to use an analogy from economics. This analogy may be particularly appropriate, for in Soviet politics as in the Soviet economy we have witnessed in recent years an increasing decentralization of initiative and an increasing recognition that political unity itself requires the protection and reconciliation of diverse goals, just as "the plan" requires recognition of the importance of management independence and enterprise profits; yet neither party hegemony nor the planned economy has been sacrificed. Indeed, both may have been strengthened since the party leadership has recognized that its own authority can best be maintained if various groups are given more leeway to pursue independently the general interests of society.

In distinguishing between particular groups pursuing their own interests and particular groups independently pursuing the general interests of society, we may be helped by adding to the concept of an interest group the concept of a profession—a sociological concept of which traditional interest group theory, perhaps precisely because of its pluralistic postulates, has not made sufficient use. A profession, by definition, is concerned with public service and considers its interests to coincide with those of society as a whole. It is true, of course, that non-professional interest groups may also identify their own interests with those of the whole society, on the theory that "What's good for General Motors is good for the country." However, a group which advances its own interests differs in a subtle but important way from a group which advances an interest of society generally and does so through the device of serving other groups. Thus, in the United States the success of a business or an ethnic organization is generally measured by its contribution to the welfare of its members, whereas the success of the teaching profession, for example, or of the legal profession is generally measured by its success in promoting the ideal of a sound education or a just and efficient legal system and by the group's contribution to the welfare of its students or its clients.

Of course, members of a profession may, and often do, engage in the advocacy of measures which enhance the position of their profession, and hence of its members. Yet when such action becomes a principal purpose of a professional organization, there is often criticism and a general feeling that the profession is not living up to its calling. The main influence of a profession is exerted not through express collective advocacy of one policy or another but through the conduct of its individual members acting in their professional (and hence "group") capacity.

Sociological literature on the professions has accepted this distinction. Roscoe Pound defines a profession as "a group of men pursuing a learned art as a common calling in the spirit of a public service—no less a public service because it may incidentally be a means of livelihood."[7] Talcott Parsons speaks of the professions, including the legal profession, as being "collectivity-oriented" rather than "self-oriented," and he refers to their "disinterestedness" and their role of responsibility to others.[8]

To the collectivity-oriented and disinterested character of a profession must be added other traits,[9] and especially what Parsons calls "specificity of function."[10] The profession's influence stems in part from the fact that it performs specific functions which are necessary to the operation of the social system as a whole and which nonmembers are unable to perform. Thus the profession acquires a degree of independence and of deference both through the particularity of its occupational role and through the generality of the concerns it is willing to serve.

If we attempt to apply these remarks about professions in general to the legal profession in the United States, we should look for an explanation of the enormous influence of American lawyers partly in their peculiar combination of general concerns and particular skills: American lawyers are available to appeal to social values on behalf of the widest variety of groups and individuals; and their appeals are made by means of legal procedures with which they alone are thoroughly familiar. At the same time, however, the character of the influence which the lawyer exerts is conditioned, at least in part, by the body of legal doctrine and legal institutions which are the basis of his art; the law

[7] R. Pound, *The Lawyer from Antiquity to Modern Times* (St. Paul, 1953), p. 5.

[8] T. Parsons, *Essays in Sociological Theory* (rev. ed., Glencoe, 1954), p. 36; Parsons, "A Sociologist Views the Legal Profession," in *Conference on the Profession of Law and Legal Education* (University of Chicago Law School Series, No. 11, 1952), pp. 49, 53, and n. 2.

[9] For a list of further characteristics see W. J. Goode, "Community Within a Community: The Professions," *American Sociological Review*, XXII (1957), 194.

[10] Parsons, *Essays in Sociological Theory*, p. 38.

itself furnishes some of the shared attitudes and forms of behavior which the legal profession presses upon other groups in the society.

In seeking to extend this analysis to Soviet society, we must recognize the many striking differences between American lawyers and Soviet jurists. Indeed, we have hesitated to use the word "lawyer" to refer to the Soviet counterpart just in order to avoid a misleading identification of the two groups. "Lawyer" is a peculiarly American term for the description of all members of the legal profession, including not only advocates in court and legal advisers but also judges, prosecutors, and other officials concerned with the administration of justice, law professors, and even persons who, having been admitted to the bar, are engaged in other pursuits. The analogous term in Russian, as in European languages generally, is "jurist" (in Russian, *yurist*). The term "lawyer" has the connotation initially of a legal practitioner, even though in fact it also applies to others, including law professors, while the term "jurist" has the connotation initially of persons trained in the academic discipline of law study, even though these include practitioners.

The question then arises whether we may properly speak of Soviet jurists as constituting a "profession." There is no Soviet equivalent to our term "profession"; the Russian analogue, *professia*, refers to any occupation for which special training is necessary, and the phrase "common calling," which Pound uses, is completely untranslatable into Russian. Soviet statistics concerning jurists sometimes classify them under the heading of "juridical personnel" (*yuridichesky personal*). However, these linguistic differences, as important as they are, should not obscure certain traits that Soviet "juridical personnel" and the American legal profession have in common. In addition to adhering to the idea of public service, Soviet jurists, like American lawyers, have a monopoly on the exercise of a learned art which is indispensable to a wide variety of groups and individuals and which is related to the general interests and values of the society. The Soviet jurist can and does appeal to "the law" on behalf of many different types of causes (including the cause of law reform), and he is an expert in pursuing these causes through the procedures which the law establishes.

Where the comparison of Soviet juridical personnel with the American legal profession reveals the most striking dissimilarities is not in the nature of the activities and responsibilities of the two groups but in the degree of independent influence which each exercises in its respective society. The importance of American lawyers in politics and in business

295

is too well known to need elaboration. In the Soviet Union (as in many countries of Europe) the study and practice of law is not generally a path to success in politics and in industry. Indeed, relatively few Soviet jurists occupy leading positions in government or economic organizations. Moreover, the fact that Soviet jurists may oppose, perhaps by an overwhelming majority, certain features of the Soviet legal system itself (e.g., the 1961 extension of the death sentence to certain types of crimes against state property) does not necessarily weigh heavily in the minds of the Soviet policy-makers who have the power to change those features. In this connection it is worth noting that in 1958 and 1959 a campaign was conducted in Soviet legal publications advocating the creation of an all-union association of jurists of all kinds; all of the published opinions were favorable to the formation of such an association, and most of them were enthusiastic,[11] yet the campaign failed. Soviet jurists have thus far not even had sufficient power to succeed in establishing their own organization.

The existing limitations upon the independent influence of Soviet jurists and upon their organizational unity may create doubts as to whether they should be called either an interest group or a profession. We have attempted to give full scope to such doubts. Yet we would conclude from the data which we shall present that ultimately the doubts cannot withstand analysis. The fact that Soviet jurists lack a unified organizational base for articulating their interests must be weighed against the fact that they do, as we shall see, bring an identifiable and significant point of view to bear on political decision-making within their sphere of interest. The fact that there is no single spokesman or group of spokesmen who can claim to speak for Soviet jurists as a whole and that they themselves are divided on many matters must be weighed against the fact that there are numerous mechanisms, including institutional affiliations, legal publications, meetings of jurists, and public discussions, through which their collective opinion is made manifest. Moreover, Soviet jurists as a profession share with lawyers of other countries the professional functions of advocacy, counseling, legal drafting, prosecution of crimes, adjudication of disputes, legal education, and scholarly criticism of existing law. In themselves, these functions

[11] L. M. Friedman and Z. L. Zile, "The Soviet Legal Profession: Recent Developments in Law and Practice," *Wisconsin Law Review* (1964), 32, 37-38, and n. 13.

constitute interest group activity by persons acting in their professional capacity.

Our perspective, then, is that of a profession performing an interest-articulating function. This approach requires us to do more than simply indicate the modes and extent of the influence of Soviet jurists over political processes. We must also examine rather closely the roles which the legal profession performs in Soviet society and the processes by which its attitudes and values are formed. Thereafter we shall deal more specifically with the ways in which Soviet jurists make claims upon other groups in Soviet society and the extent to which they are able to make such claims effective.

The Legal Profession in Soviet Society

According to official statistics, there were 101,000 persons with higher or intermediate legal education working as jurists in the Soviet Union in 1965.[12] The Soviet legal profession is much smaller than that in the United States where in 1965 there were about three times as many lawyers for a population roughly five-sixths the size of the Soviet.[13] On the other hand, Great Britain in 1965 had approximately the same proportion of lawyers to population as did the Soviet Union. It must also be remembered that some 40 percent of the Soviet population live in rural communities, where the need for lawyers is not nearly so great as in the cities.

The existence of about 100,000 Soviet jurists takes on greater significance when viewed in the perspective of the entire fifty-year history of the Soviet Union.[14] The first point to be noted in this connection is that the jurists have survived the revolution, despite dire predictions to the contrary—predictions coupled from time to time with sharp hostility not only toward jurists but toward law itself. In the first years

[12] Tsentralnoye Statisticheskoye Upravleniye, *Narodnoye khozyaistvo SSSR v 1965 g.* (Moscow, 1966), p. 574 (hereafter cited as *Nar. khoz.*, followed by the year given in the title). The total of 101,000 is made up of 84,600 with higher legal education and 16,400 with intermediate legal education. In 1959 there were only 83,600 jurists with higher or intermediate legal education. *Nar. khoz. 1961*, p. 576.

[13] American Bar Foundation, *The Legal Profession in the United States* (Chicago, 1965), p. 1.

[14] For a more detailed discussion of the history of Soviet attitudes toward law, see H. J. Berman, *Justice in the USSR: An Interpretation of Soviet Law* (rev. ed., New York, 1963), pp. 24-96.

after 1917, it was the official Leninist view that in a socialist society both law and lawyers would become superfluous and would gradually "die out."[15] In the 1920's this view yielded to the practical exigencies of the New Economic Policy; Lenin, himself a jurist by training, called for a restoration of legal institutions as part of the "strategic retreat" to a mixed capitalist-socialist economy. It was during this period that the pre-revolutionary Russian procuracy[16] was restored, the court system was stabilized, and local associations of advocates were established. Legal education, however, was not encouraged. The first few years after the revolution were a time of civil war and of intense economic privation, and during this time, as well as in the N.E.P. period, it was possible in practice to rely to a certain extent on jurists trained in pre-revolutionary Russian universities. At the same time, government officials were usually recruited from the ranks of men not tainted with the bourgeois past, and therefore frequently were without any formal legal education whatsoever. At the end of the N.E.P. in 1928 there were only 15,000 Soviet jurists with a higher or intermediate legal education.[17]

In the early 1930's legal institutions were threatened once again with extinction. A new "revolution from above," associated with the violent collectivization of agriculture, again produced a philosophy of "legal nihilism," as it was later called. It was predicted that the dying out of law and its replacement by "administration" would be accomplished within a few years. Not surprisingly, this prediction resulted in a sharp decline in the number of persons who undertook law studies and in the prestige of the legal profession as a whole. Law departments in the universities were abolished and legal education was confined to "higher law courses" at law institutes, intermediate "law schools," and special six-month and three-month law courses. Altogether there were fewer than 7,000 students registered each year in all these types of law study in the period from 1932 to 1936.[18]

[15] The Russian term *otmirat* is traditionally translated "wither away," although it means simply "die out."

[16] In tsarist Russia, as in the Soviet Union today, the procuracy was the state agency which investigated, indicted, and prosecuted most crimes; in addition, prior to 1864 it was responsible, as it is now in the Soviet Union, for protesting illegal administrative acts of state officials to their superiors. For a fuller discussion of the Soviet procuracy see below in this chapter.

[17] *Nar. khoz. 1961*, p. 576. In 1913 there were 11,147 practicing lawyers in Russia in addition to government lawyers, officials, and judges. M. Gernet, ed., *Istoria russkoi advokatury* (2 vols., Moscow, 1916), II, 3-4.

[18] See Ya. Berman, "O pravovom obrazovanii," *Sovetskoye gosudarstvo* (1936),

In December 1936, in his speech on the Draft Constitution, Stalin reversed his position. He called for "stability of laws" and hailed the new constitution as the cornerstone of a new "socialist legality." True, legality was not to be extended to "class enemies" and could not protect the victims of political and ideological terror, which reached its height in 1937, the year after the constitution was adopted. But for ordinary social and economic relations, not involving politics or ideology, law and legality were recognized as having a legitimate and an important role to play in a socialist society. Indeed, it was said in 1939 that they would continue to exist even when the Soviet Union had passed from socialism to communism. Thus it became respectable once again to be a jurist. After Stalin's death it became still more respectable, for the post-Stalin leadership sought to extend socialist legality not only to everyday social and economic life but even—within some limits—to politics and ideology as well.

Correspondingly, legal education began to be expanded in the late 1930's and the 1940's. University law departments were restored; by 1957 there were 25 university law departments and 4 law institutes.[19] The number of law students enrolled as daytime, evening, and correspondence students in universities and institutes each year in the early 1950's was about 45,000,[20] and the number of graduates increased from 2,000 in 1947 to 5,700 in 1950 and 8,100 in 1955.[21]

By the late 1950's the number of jurists in the Soviet Union had grown so considerably that N. S. Khrushchev was impelled to say to an American correspondent that there had been an "overproduction . . . of jurists."[22] This opinion was implemented by sharp reductions in admissions to daytime branches of university law departments and law institutes. As a result, in 1963 there were fewer than half as many jurists graduating from such branches as in 1956.[23] Nevertheless, in 1962-1963 there were 46,600 law students—more than in 1955-1956; prevented from entering daytime law departments of the universities and

pp. 115, 119, translated in Z. Zile, *Ideas and Forces in Soviet Legal History* (Madison, 1967), pp. 247, 249.

[19] A. F. Shebanov, *Yuridicheskiye vysshiye uchebnye zavedenia* (Moscow, 1963), p. 103.

[20] Tsentralnoye Statisticheskoye Upravleniye, *Vysshiye obrazovaniye v SSSR* (Moscow, 1961), p. 82.

[21] *Nar. khoz. 1960*, p. 776. [22] *Pravda*, November 19, 1957.

[23] P. P. Gureyev and V. V. Klochkov, "Za dalneishy podyom Sovetskovo pravovedenia i uluchsheniye yuridicheskovo obrazovania," *Sovetskoye gosudarstvo i pravo* (hereafter *SGP*), No. 7 (1964), pp. 3, 11.

law institutes, nearly 70 percent of these students were enrolled in correspondence courses and about 15 percent were enrolled in evening schools.[24]

In the summer of 1964, a new party policy concerning the legal profession was announced in a Central Committee decree which stressed the need for more and better jurists and for the expansion and improvement of legal education.[25] It appears that there was a much greater demand for jurists than the existing supply could satisfy.[26] The fact that the negative attitude expressed by Khrushchev did not prevent the increase in the number of jurists but only slowed it down and the fact that under his successors the party has declared that there is a shortage of jurists are evidence of the importance of the legal profession in Soviet society.

The expansion of legal education has had a dramatic effect upon the qualifications of the Soviet legal profession. In 1936 only 7.6 percent of Soviet judges had a higher legal education, and 51.1 percent had no legal education.[27] Similarly, in that year 54.4 percent of the procurators had no legal education whatever.[28] By contrast, in 1959 over 98 percent of all Soviet legal personnel had either higher or intermediate legal education;[29] in 1967 almost 85 percent of all judges and approximately 90 percent of all procurators had a higher legal education.[30] Today it is practically impossible to enter any branch of the Soviet legal profession without a higher legal education, and it is only older legal personnel who lack such training.

We would estimate that of the 101,000 Soviet jurists approximately 40 to 50 percent are engaged principally in the kind of work that an American usually has in mind when he speaks of "the practice of

[24] Shebanov, *op.cit.*, pp. 177-222.

[25] "Nasushchnye zadachi yuridicheskoi nauki," *Kommunist*, No. 12 (1964), p. 70. The text has not been published so far as we have been able to discover.

[26] In 1963 only 30 percent of the requests for jurists from the procuracy, courts, police, and social insurance agencies were filled. A. S. Pankratov, "Yuridicheskuyu nauku i obrazovaniye—na novye rubezhi," *Vestnik vysshiye shkoly*, No. 11 (1964), pp. 7, 8.

[27] In fact only 5.8 percent had any formal higher education at all. See Ya. Berman, *op.cit.*, translated in Zile, *op.cit.*, p. 247.

[28] *Ibid.*

[29] Tsentralnoye Statisticheskoye Upravleniye, *Itogi vsesoyuznoi perepisi naselenia 1959 goda, SSSR, Svodny tom* (Moscow, 1962), p. 183 (hereafter *Itogi 1959*).

[30] V. Baskov, "Gotovit kadry yuristov na osnove tesnovo soyuza praktiki s naukoi," *Sotsialisticheskaya zakonnost* (hereafter *Sots. zak.*), No. 12 (1965), pp. 4, 7 (procurators); V. Terebilov, "Sud, nauka, kadry," *Izvestia*, August 20, 1967 (judges).

law"—namely, assisting individuals and organizations in the exercise of their legal rights and representing them in civil and criminal litigation. The other 50 to 60 percent consist of (a) various kinds of government officials concerned with the administration of justice (including procurators, judges, *Arbitrazh* personnel, notaries, staffs of juridical commissions, and criminal investigators of the procuracy, police, and KGB);[31] (b) legal staffs of USSR and republican supreme soviets, ministries, local soviets, trade-unions, and other legislative, administrative, and social agencies and organizations; and (c) law teachers and legal scholars engaged in research. We now turn to a discussion of these major branches of the Soviet legal profession, the processes by which their attitudes and values are formed, and their role in Soviet society.

THE ADVOCATE

Jurists whose primary job it is to give legal advice and defend the interests of individual clients in court are called "advocates" (*advokaty*)[32] and are grouped into local "colleges of advocates." In addition to serving as defense counsel in criminal cases, the Soviet advocate gives legal advice and legal representation to individuals in civil matters, which make up about 85 percent of all cases in Soviet courts. Generally, the subject matter involved in civil cases is about the same as that involved in most American civil cases—personal injury litigation, contractual claims, inheritance disputes, family law problems, and the like. There are some differences, however; for example, a substantial proportion of civil cases involve rights to dwelling space in state-owned apartments; on the other hand, there are no cases involving corporation-shareholder relations since no economic organizations in the USSR issue stock. Besides representing private citizens in both civil and criminal cases, advocates sometimes represent state economic enterprises in contract disputes. It is reported that in 1963, in the Russian Republic alone advocates gave legal advice to more than 2,500,000 persons.[33]

[31] It should be noted, however, that some of these officials perform legal services for individuals which in the United States are performed by practicing lawyers. This is particularly true of procurators and notaries.

[32] The following pages, on the composite branches of the legal profession, constitute a somewhat shortened version of the authors' "The Soviet Legal Profession," *Harvard Law Review*, LXXXII (1968), 11-28.

[33] A. Ya. Sukharev, "Nassushchnye zadachi Sovetskoi advokatury," *SGP*, No. 10 (1964), pp. 3, 6, translated in *Soviet Law and Government*, No. 3 (Spring 1965), pp. 40, 43.

The survival of the advocate is perhaps the most striking fact in the history of the Soviet legal profession since 1917. There is nothing in Marxist theory or in the spirit of Bolshevism which explains the utility for a socialist society of preserving the office of the professional legal representative, whose task is to present his client's cause in the best possible light and not to pass judgment on the claims or defenses or on the client himself. Indeed, from a Marxist-Leninist standpoint the lawyer's role appears especially dubious when he is defense counsel in a criminal case: here the client has been charged by a responsible state official with the commission of an offense against society and the lawyer must do everything possible, within the limits set by law, to protect the client and frustrate the state.

In part, no doubt, to curb any tendencies toward excessive zeal on behalf of clients charged with political crimes, Soviet advocates have been placed under rather severe organizational restraints. While the colleges of advocates are defined as "voluntary associations," only their members may engage in legal practice of the kind advocates perform. Each local college of advocates elects a governing board (presidium) to manage its affairs; the presidium then designates the heads of law offices, to which the members are assigned. In addition to control by the presidium, the 1962 republican statutes on the *advokatura*[34] gave general supervisory power over the colleges of advocates to the republican ministries of justice.[35] The Minister of Justice may himself expel a member who has shown "demonstrated unsuitability for the performance of the duties of an advocate . . ." or who is guilty of "misconduct which brings discredit upon the name of advocate."[36]

[34] E.g., Law of July 25, 1962, Statute on the *Advokatura* of the RSFSR, in *Sovetskaya yustitsia* (hereafter *Sov. yust.*), No. 15-16 (1962), p. 31. See generally Berman, "Introduction" to *Soviet Criminal Law and Procedure: The RSFSR Codes 119-27*, ed. and trans. by H. J. Berman and J. W. Spindler (Cambridge, Mass., 1966); Friedman and Zile, *op.cit.*, pp. 32-69. Each union-republic now has its own statute on the bar, replacing the all-union decree of 1939. For the differences among these statutes, see Gutsenko, "Novoye zakonodatel'stvo soyuznykh respublik ob advokature," *SGP*, No. 3 (1962), pp. 56, 64.

[35] In this respect, the republican statutes are analogous to the 1939 all-union decree.

[36] Law of July 25, 1962, Statute on the *Advokatura* of the RSFSR, Article 13(2), in *Sov. yust.*, No. 15-16 (1962), p. 34. With the abolition of the republican ministries of justice, their function of supervising the legal profession has been inherited by the juridical commissions.

In the background of these organizational controls lies the pervasive supervision of the Communist Party. Colleges of advocates, being social organizations,[37] are subject to the leadership of the Communist Party group which forms its "leading core," and this group in turn is subject to the leadership and the discipline of the central party agencies. About 60 percent of Soviet advocates are party members.[38]

Much has been written in Soviet legal literature and in the Soviet press generally about the tension between the advocate's duty to his client and his duty to society. On the whole, the weight of Soviet opinion leans more heavily toward the advocate's duty to society than does the weight of American opinion on this question, yet the terms of the argument are about the same in both countries. Professor M. S. Strogovich, a leading Soviet expert on criminal procedure, has stated that "the advocate may do nothing which is harmful to the accused." Another leading Soviet scholar has written recently that "unfortunately, some judges, procurators, investigators, and scholars" hold the view that the role of the advocate is to assist the court to reach the correct decision, but in fact that is not the purpose of advocacy; on the contrary, under Soviet law "the advocate is obliged to make known only matters which support the accused or mitigate his guilt or responsibility. The activity of the defender, in contrast to the activity of the procurator, is one-sided."[39]

In a deep sense, then, the Soviet advocate—like his American counterpart—is committed to a vocation which, by its very nature, depends on freedom of speech. It is often his task to say things that the state, speaking through its prosecuting agencies, does not wish to hear. In pre-revolutionary Russia, advocates successfully pleaded such unpopular causes as those of Vera Zasulich, a revolutionary student who was charged with the attempted assassination of the governor of St. Petersburg, and Mendel Beilis, who in a wave of official anti-semitism was charged with ritual murder. In post-revolutionary Russia reports of successes of a similar magnitude are not to be found, though we do know of some important political cases in which Soviet lawyers have unsuccessfully used all possible means to prevent the conviction of

[37] *Ibid.*, Article 1.
[38] This figure is based on extrapolation from the figure for the RSFSR. See Kukarsky, "Sovetskoi advokature—45 let," *Sov. yust.*, No. 10 (1967), p. 1.
[39] I. Perlov, "Zachem korit zerkalo?" *Izvestia*, February 14, 1965.

their clients,[40] as well as some political cases of less importance in which they have succeeded.[41]

The tension between the Soviet advocate's duty to his client and his duty to society is also reflected in the system of remuneration of advocates. The advocate's fees, paid by the client, are regulated by schedules issued by the republican ministries of justice or their successors, the juridical commissions. However, the schedules may be modified upward by the presidium of a college of advocates upon petition by the advocate where extra work or special expertise is involved, and since the schedules of fees are not kept up to date, such petitions are often made and usually granted. Nevertheless, fees are generally low, and in practice it is not uncommon for the advocate to receive something extra as an inducement to special effort—a breach of law and of legal ethics which can lead to disbarment. Even apart from such abuses, the fee system is an anomaly in Soviet society and contributes to distrust of advocates. A few years ago a writer in *Izvestia* stated: "[t]he defender is still frequently regarded with prejudice. And sometimes, it must be admitted, he is simply tolerated, in deference to the law. To a substantial degree this all happens because the *advokatura* is organized according to a system of pay and working conditions that clearly contradict our way of life."[42]

Such negative attitudes may account in part for the fact that the number of Soviet advocates has remained relatively low. In 1939 there were approximately 8,000 advocates in a population of 191 million. In 1959 there were 12,828 advocates in a population of 209 million.[43]

[40] For accounts of some conspicuous recent examples, see *On Trial: The Soviet State Versus "Abram Tertz" and "Nikolai Arzhak"* (rev. ed. 1967) (transcript of trials of dissident writers Sinyavsky and Daniel); *New York Times*, January 13, 1968 (account of trial of Ginzburg, Galanskov, Dobrovolsky, and Lashkova); "The Trial of Iosif Brodsky," *The New Leader*, August 31, 1964, p. 6 (translated transcript). It has been reported that Boris Zolotukhin, the lawyer who defended Ginzburg at his trial, was subsequently expelled from the Communist Party. *Newsweek*, August 26, 1968, p. 36. It has also been reported that he has been ousted from the college of advocates and is employed as a jurisconsult of a state enterprise in Moscow. *The Sunday Times* (London), January 12, 1969.

[41] H. J. Berman, *op.cit.*, pp. 58-63 (account of politically motivated conviction of criminal negligence in construction of munitions plant reversed on appeal); B. Konstantinovsky, *Soviet Law in Action: The Recollected Cases of a Soviet Lawyer*, ed. and trans. by H. J. Berman (Cambridge, Mass., 1953), pp. 3-4 (account of politically motivated prosecution of employee for mismanagement dropped after consultation with plant legal adviser).

[42] Barkan, "Pravo na zashchitu ili na zaschitnika," *Izvestia*, April 8, 1964.

[43] *Itogi 1959*, pp. 165-166.

Today the number of advocates is approximately the same despite a substantial population increase.[44]

It would be wrong, however, to conclude that because the Soviet profession of advocate labors under handicaps it is therefore without prestige or influence. The more important fact is that the functions of advocacy in giving legal advice and in representing litigants have proved to be essential to the functioning of the Soviet social order. The mere presence of the *advokatura* is a symbol of the preservation of individual rights against all the pressures of a highly organized society. Moreover, the work of the advocate is integral to the work of the other, more prestigious branches of the legal profession.

As is true of many other types of Soviet institutions, legal institutions created by the Communist Party to serve its own purposes have acquired lives of their own and serve as a control over those who have created them. When the Communist Party leadership seeks to stigmatize as criminals dissident writers, or political demonstrators, or persons engaged in certain nefarious economic activities, it must reckon with the right and duty of their defense counsel to make it as difficult as possible to secure convictions. The party leadership and others must also reckon, in all their activities, with sentiments of procedural and substantive justice which it is the task of the advocates to help maintain. When Soviet advocates campaign—as they often do, both in the press and in the courtroom—for wider appreciation of the importance of their mission "to defend the lawful interests of citizens, enterprises, institutions, organizations, and collective farms . . . ,"[45] they are campaigning not only for their right to exist as a profession but also, and more fundamentally, for the victory of civilizing institutions over the arbitrary practices that inevitably accompany a one-party system.

THE JURISCONSULT

Only in recent years have Soviet legal literature and the Soviet popular press concerned themselves very much with the work of juris-

---

[44] In 1968 the president of the Moscow City College of Advocates stated to one of the authors that there were 7,200 advocates in the RSFSR and 13,000 in the USSR as a whole. The figure for the RSFSR is put at "over 7,000" in Sukharev, *op.cit.*, p. 4, translated in *Soviet Law and Government*, No. 3 (Spring 1965), p. 41.

[45] Law of July 25, 1962, Statute on the *Advokatura* of the RSFSR, Article 2, in *Sov. yust.*, No. 15-16 (1962), p. 31.

305

consults (*yuriskonsulty*).[46] As a result less is known about them than about advocates.

Most jurisconsults are officials of state transport, construction, industrial, or trade enterprises, or, in some cases, collective farms. Their main functions are (a) to advise and represent management in legal matters connected with the enterprise's relationships with superior and subordinate organizations, other enterprises, and individual workers; (b) to give legal advice to labor unions, comrades' courts, and other groups in the enterprise; (c) to "visa," or certify as legal, internal regulations issued by management; and (d) to report to the enterprise's superior agencies any violations of law committed by the enterprise. In his performance of this last function, the jurisconsult may have interests adverse to those of the manager, and it is therefore provided that a jurisconsult cannot be appointed, transferred, or dismissed by the manager without the concurrence of the enterprise's superior agency.[47] Enterprises below a certain size generally are not provided with a jurisconsult; in 1959 there were 20,309 jurisconsults for approximately 200,000 enterprises.[48] Those enterprises which do not have jurisconsults on their staff may use the legal services of members of the colleges of advocates, either on an *ad hoc* basis or on contract with the college of advocates. We estimate that a considerable part of the 20 percent increase in the size of the legal profession from 1959 to 1965 (from 83,600 to 101,000) went into the ranks of the jurisconsults, bringing their number from 20,309 to, we would guess, at least 27,000 and perhaps 37,000 or even more.

The influence of jurisconsults over other groups in Soviet society, like the influence of advocates, is not manifested primarily in concerted public activity or behind-the-scenes pressures, although there may be examples of both. Primarily, the jurisconsult, like the advocate, seeks to influence other groups by carrying out his own tasks. He exerts some influence on managers by showing them the significance of legal principles—for example, those relating to the legal personality of the state

[46] The first Soviet book on the work of jurisconsults, L. Shor, *Organizatsia yuridicheskoi sluzhby na predpriatii i v sovnarkhoze* (2nd ed., Moscow, 1964), initially appeared in 1960.

[47] Decree of March 29, 1963, Model Statute on the Legal (or Contract) Department, Chief (or Senior) Jurisconsult, and Jurisconsult of an Enterprise, Institution or Organization (Council of Ministers, RSFSR), in *Sov. yust.*, No. 10 (1963), p. 29.

[48] *Itogi 1959*, pp. 165-166.

enterprise, the rights of workers under labor legislation, or contractual responsibility—in putting the enterprise's economic activity on a more rational basis. By this means some jurisconsults have come to play a dynamic role in plant management, although it appears that most content themselves with simply indicating what the law requires and what it prohibits. A few leading jurisconsults, moreover, have exercised an influential role through assistance in the preparation of legislation concerning economic matters and through articles appearing in both the legal press and the economic and popular papers. In thus bringing the legal problems of state enterprises to the attention of others, jurisconsults have been able to make cogent arguments for the increased legal independence of individual state economic units and for greater freedom of contract between them.

Indeed, it may have been the influence of jurisconsults that gave a decisive stimulus to major economic reforms in Soviet industrial management after 1962. Amendments to the Statutes on Deliveries of Industrial-Technical Goods and of Consumer Goods, adopted in June 1962 and August 1963 respectively, provided that an enterprise may refuse to enter into contract for the purchase of goods directly allocated to it by planning acts of superior agencies if such goods are not needed by the enterprise.[49] As a result of this new rule, which bears the earmarks of the jurisconsults' influence, enterprises began refusing to purchase both producer and consumer goods in a very large number of instances. At that point, it became obvious that it makes much more sense to let the enterprises make their contracts before the planning acts are issued rather than after; and indeed, this practice has been introduced as one of the significant features of the "new method" of Soviet management adopted in the mid-1960's.

THE JUDGE

The Soviet judiciary—like the judiciary of many European countries —resembles a civil service, for it is composed to a considerable extent of persons who have entered upon a judicial career at or near the beginning of their professional lives and who are promoted from lower

[49] Decree of May 22, 1959, Article 14, Statute on Deliveries of Industrial-Technical Goods, *Sobraniye postanovleny SSSR*, 1959, item 68 (Council of Ministers, USSR); Decree of May 22, 1959, Article 13, Statute on Deliveries of Consumer Goods, *Sobraniye postanovleny SSSR*, 1959, item 68 (Council of Ministers, USSR). Both statutes (as amended to 1965) are published in A. Kabalkin (ed.), *Normativnye materialy po Sovetskomu grazhdanskomu pravu* (Moscow, 1965), pp. 238-254, 262-280.

courts to higher courts on the basis of ability. This is true despite the fact that Soviet judges are elected.[50] The paradox of an elected civil service is resolved by the Soviet system of nominations; the candidacy for each judgeship is limited to a single person, usually chosen on the basis of his professional and political qualifications. However, the tenure of Soviet judges is short—five years—and in fact there is always a considerable turnover at elections of people's judges, for reasons which we do not know.

People's Courts have original jurisdiction over all civil cases and over all but the most serious criminal cases. Appeals may be taken from decisions of the People's Courts to intermediate appellate courts, which are organized at the level of district (krai), region (oblast), city, autonomous region, national area (okrug), and autonomous republic. There are 3,502 People's Courts and 147 intermediate appellate courts.[51] Decisions of the intermediate appellate courts may be reviewed by the supreme courts of the fifteen union republics, and decisions of republican supreme courts may be reviewed by the one all-union court, the Supreme Court of the USSR.[52] In addition, there is a network of military tribunals, with permanent professional military judges sitting in nine military districts, culminating in the Military Division of the USSR Supreme Court.[53] We estimate that in 1965 there were about 9,000 Soviet judges. In 1966 there were 7,594 judges sitting on the People's Courts.[54] We do not know how many judges sit on the 147 regional (and equivalent) courts and the supreme courts of the 15 union republics, but would estimate that they average about 10 judges each.

Several facts indicate that the Soviet judiciary constitutes a unified whole, with common concerns and common attitudes. Decisions of

[50] Only judges of the People's Courts, the lowest level trial courts in the USSR, are elected directly by the people. Judges of higher courts are selected by the governmental soviet at the corresponding level (USSR Constitution, Articles 105-109).

[51] G. Z. Anashkin, "O zadachakh i tendentsiakh razvitia sotsialisticheskovo pravosudia," *Vestnik Moskovskovo Universiteta, Seria XII (Pravo)*, no. 4 (1966), pp. 1, 11.

[52] Law of February 12, 1957, Article 11(b), Statute on the USSR Supreme Court, *Vedomosti Verkhovnovo Soveta SSSR*, 1957, item 85 (Supreme Soviet, USSR).

[53] *Ibid.*, Article 12; law of December 25, 1958, Statute on Military Tribunals, *ibid.*, 1959, item 14 (Supreme Soviet, USSR), as amended, law of February 21, 1968, *ibid.*, 1968, item 64 (Supreme Soviet, USSR).

[54] Anashkin, *op.cit.*, p. 11.

lower courts may be reviewed by higher courts, and the Supreme Court of the USSR and the supreme courts of the individual republics have the power to issue "guiding explanations," restatements, and reinterpretations of particular branches of the law which are sometimes fairly elaborate and which are binding upon lower courts. Moreover, judges of lower courts are subject to disciplinary action by the republican supreme courts in cases of misconduct in office. Finally, as we have already mentioned, judges of lower courts are often appointed to be judges of higher courts.

The USSR Constitution states that "[j]udges are independent and subject only to law."[55] In view of the relatively high degree of secrecy of Soviet governmental operations, however, the question inevitably arises whether there are not pressures on Soviet judges to decide cases according to the will of particular party officials or of the party leadership. There are a few reported instances of direct party pressure on judges in particular cases, but there is reason to think that such pressure was exerted much more frequently than has been admitted. The question gains special importance in view of the reduction of the power of the state security agency. In Stalin's time, persons who had incurred the party's disfavor could be subjected to the administrative procedures of the Special Board of the MVD. However, with the abolition of the Special Board in 1953, it became impossible to sentence a person to penal detention except by judgment of a court.

The party itself has condemned interference by party organizations in the trial or decision of particular cases, and we may well believe that this condemnation is seriously intended, since the party leadership would not wish particular party organizations or officials to use the courts as means of finding scapegoats for their own sins. Moreover, although it is easy to assume that the party leadership instructs the judges in important political cases, such as the trial in 1960 of the American U-2 pilot Francis Powers or the trial in 1966 of the dissident writers Sinyavsky and Daniel, it is also plausible that the judges, being themselves trusted party members and more experienced in judging than their political colleagues, are left to do what they believe to be right under the circumstances. On the other hand, the decision to prosecute Powers and Sinyavsky and Daniel was undoubtedly taken at the highest levels with participation of high party officials.

Whether or not the party interferes in particular cases, there is no

[55] USSR Constitution, Article 112.

doubt that it exerts a very important influence on the course of judicial decisions by its frequent "campaigns" against various forms of illegal activity, during which it often calls for more severe punishments for offenders. Under the influence of such campaigns, courts have convicted men who were later shown to be innocent. The press, which is under direct party control, also has an important influence on judicial decisions, even in particular cases, through its discussion of those cases during—and sometimes even before—trial.

The prestige and influence of the judiciary is, of course, affected by the extent of its political independence, but other matters are also relevant. The scope of the judicial function is narrower in the Soviet Union than in many other countries. Soviet judges are not empowered to refuse to enforce statutes on the ground of their unconstitutionality, though they may refuse to enforce administrative decrees on that ground. Also Soviet courts do not have jurisdiction over major economic disputes, these being left to administrative decision or to *Arbitrazh*. Partly because of the limited scope of adjudication in the Soviet Union, Soviet judges (like Western European judges) do not generally come from the ranks of persons with political experience. As in Western European countries generally, few members of the Soviet public would know the names of any judges even of the highest court —with the notable exception of its chairman, A. F. Gorkin, a prominent party member and not a jurist by training, who was appointed in 1957, apparently in order to raise the court's prestige.

In discussing Soviet advocates, we stressed that they stand for the adversary presentation of claims and defenses, and that implicit in this stand is a commitment to the principles of personal freedom, including freedom of speech. Jurisconsults share this commitment, together with an additional commitment to the autonomy of the enterprise and to freedom of contract. Similarly, we may say that the Soviet judge, by his very vocation, has a commitment to the principle of impartial and independent decision-making. Under Stalin, however, the Soviet judiciary leaned over backwards to interpret Soviet legislation in a Stalinist spirit, and even today it is doubtful that many high court judges would ever wish to set up the requirements of the law in opposition to the demands of party policy. Insofar as the Soviet judiciary seeks to influence other groups in the society, it seems to do so by stressing that both justice and efficiency require the strict observance of the law, and that the goals of Soviet society—as reflected in party policy—must be

310

enclosed within the framework of the law if they are to be made workable.

The procuracy is the cornerstone of the Soviet legal profession. It probably contains abler people than any other branch, and it has higher responsibilities. We would estimate that there were about 18,000 procurators in 1965.[56] The overwhelming majority of them are party members.[57] The Procurator General of the USSR, R. A. Rudenko, is the only jurist who is a member of the Central Committee of the Communist Party of the USSR—an honor which undoubtedly has come to him by virtue of his office, for he is not primarily a politician but a professional jurist who has risen through the ranks of the procuracy.[58]

The procuracy is responsible for the investigation of the more serious crimes and for the preparation of indictments, and it conducts all prosecutions. In addition, it has an even more important function called "general supervision" (*obshchy nadzor*), which is the task of protesting all unlawful acts of state officials, including erroneous decisions of judges, to their superior agencies. Like the procuracy of pre-revolutionary Russia, the Soviet procuracy is the watchdog of the central authority, and it ensures that the laws and regulations of the central authority are observed at the intermediate and lower levels. Although the procuracy's power of general supervision does not include the power to annul, the procuracy's additional right to indict and prosecute is a powerful adjunct of the right to protest.

[56] This figure is derived from the 1959 figure of 22,980 judges and procurators. See *Itogi 1959*, p. 165. If we are correct in believing that approximately 8,000 of these were judges, there were about 15,000 procurators. If the number of procurators increased proportionately to the population, there would have been about 16,500 in 1965. We would guess that the number increased somewhat more than that, in view of the very large increase in the number of jurists during that period. (It should be noted that we speak here of procurators and not of the entire procuracy, which includes also a substantial number of investigators with legal training.)

[57] In 1963, 84.6 percent of the procuracy and "almost all" judges were members or candidate members of the Communist Party. N. Mironov, "Nasushchnye voprosy dalneishevo ukreplenia sotsialisticheskoi zakonnosti," *Kommunist*, No. 1 (1963), p. 49.

[58] Rudenko entered the procuracy at the age of twenty-two. From 1944 to 1953 he was Procurator General of the Ukraine. In 1953 he was appointed Procurator General of the USSR. He became a candidate member of the Central Committee in 1956 and a full member in 1961. A. Lebed, H. Schulz, and S. Taylor (eds.), *Who's Who in the USSR 1965-66* (New York and London, 1966), p. 707.

THE LAW TEACHER AND THE LEGAL SCHOLAR

In 1965 there were 3,272 "scientific workers," as they are called, in the field of law.[59] Many of these were teachers in the 4 law institutes and in the 25 law departments of universities, while many others were members of legal research institutes.[60] In addition to planning the publication of books and articles by their members, research institutes also give graduate law training. Members may serve as part-time law teachers in various educational institutions and other organizations, and they also often act as consultants to governmental agencies of all kinds.

The influence of Soviet law teachers and legal scholars on the development of law is proportionately far in excess of their numbers, impressive as those numbers are. As in Western Europe generally, they usually have more prestige than the law practitioner or the judge or other justice official. This is symbolized by the fact that law teachers and legal scholars are the most highly paid members of the Soviet legal profession. We shall discuss the role of the law teachers and legal scholars in more detail in a later section of this essay.

OTHER JURISTS

While the above groups can be considered the most important subdivisions of the legal profession, there are a large number of persons who carry on legal work in a wide variety of other positions. Thus, jurists serve on the legal staffs of the juridical commissions of the councils of ministers of the USSR and of the fifteen union republics as well as on the legal staffs of USSR and republican supreme soviets, individual ministries, local soviets, trade-unions, *Arbitrazh*, and other governmental and paragovernmental organizations. They also serve as notaries and as investigators in the procuracy, the police, and the KGB.

The Cohesion of the Soviet Legal Profession

Having discussed some of the characteristics of the various parts of the legal profession, we turn to those factors which tend to form these

[59] *Nar. khoz. 1965*, p. 710.

[60] The three "leading scientific research institutes in law" are the Institute of State and Law of the USSR Academy of Sciences, which in 1965 had a staff of approximately 200 in its Moscow headquarters, plus others in branches in Kiev, Tbilisi, and other cities; the Institute of Soviet Legislation, which serves the Juridical Commission of the Council of Ministers of the USSR, and which employed some 90 legal scholars in 1965; and the Institute for the Study of Crime, which is attached to the procuracy and the USSR Supreme Court.

parts into a whole. First, it is apparent that the activities of each part overlap the activities of the others. In a single court proceeding, a judge may hear arguments from jurisconsults, procurators, and advocates, who may cite the writings of a law professor or legal research scholar. Moreover, all the branches of the profession are concerned with the same body of law; a particular code—for example, the civil code—contains matters affecting the work of all jurists in the USSR, and through it they are brought into indirect contact with each other.

Second, there is a certain mobility among the different branches of the profession. An advocate may become a jurisconsult, and vice versa; either may become a procurator; a procurator may become a judge and vice versa; and either may become a law teacher or legal scholar. Some leading jurists in the Soviet Union have been employed in virtually every branch of the legal profession.

Third, almost all Soviet jurists have undergone the same type of educational experience, having received their formal training in schools which operate under uniform study plans approved by the USSR Ministry of Higher and Intermediate Special Education. Only in recent years has a certain degree of specialization been allowed in the last years of law study, when students are permitted to choose one of three programs in order to prepare themselves for work, alternatively, with the courts and procuracy, with soviets and other governmental agencies, or with enterprises and other economic institutions.[61]

The socialization of future jurists (in the sense of creating common professional bonds and a common mentality) in legal education is enhanced by emphasis upon the links between legal education and legal practice. Students are required to attend "practical exercises" in which specific cases and specific legal problems are discussed.[62] In addition they are required to spend a portion of each year, ranging from three weeks in the first year to six months in the final year, in "production practice," involving work outside of school in the offices of investigators, procurators, court officials, advocates, and others.[63]

Fourth, the cohesion of the Soviet legal profession is maintained in

[61] Baskov, *op.cit.*, p. 4.
[62] These exercises are referred to as *prakticheskiye* or *seminarskiye zanyatia.* Shebanov, *op.cit.*, p. 130.
[63] See V. Baskov, "Bez praktiki net uspekhov v uchebe," *Sots. zak.*, No. 9 (1967), p. 47; V. F. Maslov, "Kharkovskii Yuridicheskii Institut v borbe za osushchestvleniye postanovlenia TsK KPSS 'O merakh po dalneishemu razvitiyu yuridicheskoi nauki i uluchsheniyu yuridicheskovo obrazovania v strane," *Pravovedeniye*, No. 3 (1963), p. 8.

313

part through a common body of legal literature. The most important publisher of law books is the State Publishing House "Legal Literature" (*Yuridicheskaya Literatura*), whose 1965 plan called for the publication of 160 titles, in editions totaling about 5 million copies.[64] No book can be published without extensive editorial supervision, and most law books must fall within the plans of organizations in which their authors are employed. In addition, there is a substantial body of periodical legal literature, including four journals sponsored by all-union organizations and others sponsored by republican organizations.[65] Although some of the journals appear to act at times as voices of their sponsoring organizations, and occasionally it is possible to discern differences in points of view among them, the fact that many of the same writers contribute to all the journals attests to their unifying character. Any jurist who wishes to keep informed about the development of Soviet law would certainly attempt to read at least several of the leading journals regularly.

Fifth, various kinds of conferences of jurists both manifest and contribute to a common identification among jurists. Such conferences vary widely in character, and include frequent formal discussions by a university law faculty, or by the members of a legal research institute, on particular legal themes; city-wide meetings of procurators and investigators, at which others may also be present, to consider problems of law enforcement; all-union inter-law-school conferences to discuss, for example, new codes; and all-union symposia on juvenile delinquency or on the role of law in the new economic reforms. Articles in legal periodicals describing such meetings usually emphasize that various legal groups were represented at them. At discussions sponsored by the Institute of State and Law of the USSR Academy of Sciences, where one of the authors spent ten months of study in 1961-1962, one could find as participants judges, procurators, jurisconsults, advocates, *Arbit-*

[64] V. N. Avilin, "Obsuzhdeniye plana vypuska yuridicheskoi literatury," *SGP*, No. 8 (1964), p. 141.

[65] The leading journal for questions of theory is *Sovetskoye gosudarstvo i pravo*, the monthly journal of the Institute of State and Law, under the USSR Academy of Sciences. Inasmuch as political science as an academic discipline does not exist in the Soviet Union, this publication also contains important articles on political and social theory. Another important journal for questions of theory is the bimonthly *Pravovedeniye*, published by the USSR Ministry of Higher and Secondary Specialized Education. Journals oriented more toward the problems of legal practice are *Sovetskaya yustitsia*, bi-weekly publication of the RSFSR Supreme Court and Council of Ministers, and *Sotsialisticheskaya zakonnost*, the organ of the procuracy and the Supreme Court of the USSR.

razh personnel, notaries, representatives of the law publishing house, and others, as well as law professors and legal research scholars.

It would appear that the identification of Soviet jurists with sub-groups within the legal profession does not detract substantially from their identification with the legal profession as a whole. In conversation with representatives of every subgroup one hears the expression, "We jurists. . . ." For procurators, self-identification as jurists—that is, as members of the legal profession as a whole—may be somewhat less important than it is for advocates, jurisconsults, and some other branches. The procuracy has its own élan and its own discipline; it is more tightly knit than other subgroups, and its role is more closely linked with social and political factors outside the law. Yet the procuracy, like all the other branches of the legal profession, derives its character from the concern for law and expertise in law which it shares with all jurists.

The chief factor detracting from the group unity of jurists is the policy of the Communist Party to prevent the formation of any group loyalty that might be strong enough to threaten loyalty to the party itself. We have noted that the attempt of jurists to form a single all-embracing organization has thus far been frustrated—presumably by the party. Within the Central Committee, a Section of Administrative Organs has charge of jurists (including courts and procuracy) as well as of the security agencies; rarely does this bureau speak in public, but behind the scenes it supervises the activities of the entire legal profession, including the work of legal scholars.[66] The many party members in the legal profession are presumably particularly responsive to such supervision and are in a position to make it effective. Yet the unwillingness of the party to allow the psychological and sociological cohesion of the legal profession to be expressly manifested in organizational form, and a fortiori in political form, has not thus far prevented that psychological and sociological cohesion from becoming stronger and stronger. And, as we shall attempt to show below, the collective action of the legal profession has in fact had an influence on Soviet politics.

In speaking of the high degree of cohesion of the legal profession, we do not mean to suggest that jurists generally share the same opinions

[66] This agency acts as watchdog over agencies of state security. It is responsible for party pronouncements on matters affecting the legal profession and in addition maintains a network of local branches which check the work of security agencies, courts, and procuracy in that locality. See L. Schapiro, *The Government and Politics of the Soviet Union* (New York, 1965), p. 68.

on major questions of Soviet policy. There are "liberals" and "conservatives" among jurists just as there are among writers, managers, and other groups. Indeed, according to an old proverb, often repeated by Soviets, "Two jurists, three opinions!" In speaking of the cohesion of the legal profession we have in mind that jurists of all the different subgroups perceive themselves as part of a single group and interact with each other as a single group, and in addition, that they all share certain values which are implicit in their role as jurists.

Access of the Soviet Legal Profession to Policy-Making Processes

Unlike American lawyers, who are well represented in the leadership groups of political and business organizations and in government bodies at all levels, Soviet jurists are almost entirely unrepresented in the formal and informal centers of political power in Soviet society. None of the members of the Politburo of the Communist Party has ever been a jurist—except for Lenin, who can hardly be said to have "represented" the legal profession. As of 1968, in the Central Committee of the party, with its 195 members and 165 candidate members, only Procurator General Rudenko (a full member) was from the legal profession, and in the Central Auditing Commission, with its 79 members, only Supreme Court President Gorkin was from the legal profession. Similarly, none of the current 90 members of the USSR Council of Ministers about whom information is available is known to have had legal training or experience. Rudenko and Gorkin were the only jurists, of the more than 1,500 deputies in the USSR Supreme Soviet,[67] and they were the only jurists appointed in 1966 to the 97-member commission to draft a new Soviet Constitution![68] The virtual absence of jurists in the membership of party, soviet, and governmental agencies other than juridical commissions and judicial agencies occurs also at the republican level. Only in the executive committees of local

[67] Of the members of the USSR Supreme Soviet for the past three terms, 4 of the total of 1,378 deputies elected in 1958, 2 of the 1,442 elected in 1962, and 2 of the 1,517 elected in 1966 are listed as having a "legal occupation." R. A. Clarke, "The Composition of the USSR Supreme Soviet, 1958-1966," *Soviet Studies*, XIX (1967), 55.

[68] See *Izvestia*, December 20, 1966. Not reappointed to the commission were Professor A. I. Denisov, former chairman of the Juridical Commission of the USSR Council of Ministers, and Professor P. S. Romashkin, former director of the Institute of State and Law. N. R. Mironov, late chief of the Bureau of Administrative Agencies, who worked closely with Soviet lawyers, was not replaced on the commission after his death.

soviets are jurists represented in governmental agencies in substantial numbers.

Yet, as we have already indicated, jurists participate actively in the work of the higher legislative and administrative agencies—not as members but as staff advisers, consultants, or members of subordinate divisions appointed to assist those agencies. Thus although the membership of the commissions on legislative proposals of the USSR and republican supreme soviets consists of deputies who are not jurists, their subcommissions, which hold hearings and prepare drafts of particular bills, often take jurists as official members or as consultants. In 1963 it was stated that in the previous few years about 450 legal scholars and legal practitioners had been brought onto the subcommissions as members, and that over 350 others had been invited to consult on specific problems connected with drafting laws, and that they came from all branches of the profession.[69] Similarly, jurists are employed on legal staffs of ministries and are consulted by governmental agencies of all kinds. In all these instances, the legal profession has access to policy-making processes not through direct representation in the policy-making bodies but as a group possessing both specialized knowledge and the specialized skills which are essential to the work of those bodies.

With respect to his specialized knowledge, the jurist is in a position, vis-à-vis Soviet policy-makers, analogous to the position of the economist or engineer or other scientific expert. Just as the economist must be consulted for information and opinions concerning the consequences of an increase in taxes or a change in the price structure, or the engineer for information and opinions concerning the problems involved in diverting a river in order to build a hydro-electric station, so the jurist must be consulted with regard to such matters as available alternative programs for preventing increases in crimes of various kinds, or proposed sanctions and incentives designed to induce enterprise managers to perform contracts, or legal aspects of trade agreements with foreign countries. At the very least, a jurist must be consulted whenever any new law or regulation is contemplated in order to explain the extent to which the proposed change will conflict with existing legislation; and usually he will also be asked what other legal changes will be needed to supplement the proposed change. Any such discussion is

[69] S. G. Novikov, "Uchastiye nauchnoi obshchestvennosti v rabote komissii zakonodatelnykh predlozheny Verkhovnovo Soveta SSSR po podgotovke zakonoproektov," *SGP*, No. 12 (1963), pp. 56, 58.

likely to give the jurist the opportunity to express his opinion concerning the wisdom of the proposed change—an opinion which, of course, may be rejected.

Soviet jurists also possess, however, an expertise which is different in kind from that of the economist or engineer—an expertise concerning the form, as contrasted with the content, of policy. All social systems are based in part on rules for the regulation and regularization of social, economic, and political interaction, and the efficient operation of a system depends to a considerable extent on the internal consistency of these rules as well as on consistency in their application. Especially in a large, complex, and highly organized society such as the Soviet Union, where there are many hundreds of thousands of such rules, it is necessary that there be some persons specially trained to maintain the consistency of the system. Thus the Soviet leaders, like those of other countries, are dependent upon persons with legal training, who "hold a monopoly over the technique which alone is able to produce the advantages of orderly government. . . ."[70] In this sense, the jurists possess an indispensable skill which is pertinent not only to law in the narrower sense but also to the whole administrative apparatus of the state, the whole of the planned economy, and, indeed, the whole of Soviet life insofar as it is subject to official regulation.

Probably the most effective channel of access of Soviet jurists to the processes by which policies are made, at least at the highest level of Soviet politics, is preparation of legislation, and especially of law reforms.[71] After 1936, Soviet jurists were called on to prepare new codes of criminal and civil law and criminal and civil procedure. However, they did not succeed in preparing drafts that were thought suitable for enactment while Stalin was alive, and it was only after Khrushchev came to power in February 1955 that a vital movement for law reform began. From 1955 to 1957 elaborate discussions of proposed legislation took place among jurists at universities, legal research institutes, and elsewhere. Over 400 sessions of subcommissions of the commissions on legislative proposals of the USSR Supreme Soviet were held between 1958 and 1962 to consider the proposals.

Among the most important of the subcommissions were those for the preparation of drafts of Fundamental Principles of Criminal Law,

---

[70] K. Grzybowski, *Soviet Legal Institutions* (Ann Arbor, 1962), p. 178.

[71] For a more detailed analysis of the role of the jurist in formulating legislation, which is briefly summarized here, see Novikov, *op.cit.*, pp. 58, 62.

Fundamental Principles of Criminal Procedure, and Fundamental Principles of Court Organization, all of which were adopted by the USSR Supreme Soviet in December 1958. These subcommissions each consisted of from 25 to 45 persons, a large percentage of whom were legal scholars. Subcommissions for the preparation of drafts of Fundamental Principles of Civil Law and Fundamental Principles of Civil Procedure, which were adopted in December 1961, were of a similar composition. Legal scholars acted as "scientific secretaries" of various subcommissions, and in some cases as chairmen or deputy chairmen.

In addition to working on, or with, subcommissions of the commissions on legislative proposals, jurists participate in the legislative process through the juridical commissions of the USSR and republican councils of ministers. The duties of the juridical commissions include the preparation of new laws (including new codes), and in carrying out this task they often consult specialists outside their own staffs. In addition, the Juridical Commission of the USSR Council of Ministers has its own research arm, the All-Union Scientific Research Institute of Soviet Legislation (VNIISZ), which works directly with the commission on the preparation of new legislation. Because there was "no unified means for consideration of [all] the proposals to improve the law," as a result of which "no small number of valuable ideas and proposals was lost," in 1963 VNIISZ was given the duty "to become, above all, the agency to collect such proposals and in this sense to be a unique institute of public opinion on matters pertaining to the improvement of legislation."[72] The fact that VNIISZ thus stands as a middleman between public opinion and the government must serve to increase its access to those who are responsible for making policy.

The drafts of legislation prepared by VNIISZ and other legal research organizations under its supervision are worked out under the direction of those governmental agencies which are most directly concerned with the particular legislation under consideration. Prior to scrutiny and discussion by the Supreme Soviet's subcommissions, or in

---

[72] According to its director and deputy director, "the government has placed the following major tasks before VNIISZ: study and synthesis of proposals to amend and supplement normative acts now on the books, and participation in the drafting of laws; coordination of the work of research institutions engaged in the improvement of legislation; scientific research into codification and systematization of Soviet legislation; study of and the drawing of conclusions from the legislation of foreign countries." S. N. Bratus and I. S. Samoshchenko, "O nauchno-organizatsionnykh formakh sovershenstvovania Sovetskovo zakonodatelstva," *SGP*, No. 4 (1964), pp. 58-59.

conjunction therewith, such drafts are often submitted to lengthy public discussion in legal literature and in the popular press, as well as in meetings of jurists and among selected groups of specialists. In 1962, one of the authors had the opportunity to attend a two-day discussion of the draft civil codes of the RSFSR and the Ukrainian SSR held by the civil law department of Leningrad University. Some ten people spent about twelve hours commenting on and arguing about the various provisions of the two codes. There were sharp disagreements and some strong criticism of the drafts. The discussion was taken down by a stenographer in order to be sent to Moscow, there to be sifted by others. Such criticism and debate of basic legislation are carried on not only in the universities and legal research institutes, but also in ministries, individual factories, jurists' associations, and elsewhere. A preliminary draft of the Fundamental Principles of Civil Procedure, for example, was sent for comments to literally scores of diverse organizations, and the comments were collated and studied by the subcommission in charge. Tens of thousands of persons, both jurists and others, have been drawn into the detailed discussion of the legislative reforms of the past decade.[73]

The fact that legal scholars thus participate in the legislative process gives them a degree of access to the policy-making process that is often difficult for scholars in other fields to achieve. Furthermore, they are thus given access to resources which are practically unavailable to others. For example, as members of the subcommissions on legislative proposals, jurists have the right to seek and obtain all necessary factual information from governmental agencies.

Apart from formal organizations and procedures for transmitting the views of jurists to governmental agencies, there are numerous informal channels through which individual jurists—sometimes speaking for themselves and sometimes for their organizations—have access to the process of lawmaking. The Soviet press, for example, very frequently contains discussions of legal questions by jurists, and there have even been examples of acrimonious debate between editorial boards of different leading newspapers concerning such questions, with jurists contributing on both sides.[74]

[73] H. J. Berman, "The Struggle of Soviet Jurists Against a Return to Stalinist Terror," *Slavic Review*, XXII (1963), 314-319.

[74] *Ibid.*, p. 316; G. P. Fletcher, "The Presumption of Innocence in the Soviet Union," *UCLA Law Review*, XV (1968), 1203, 1204-1205, and n. 10.

There are obvious limitations on the influence and leverage of the legal profession in the policy-making process, as there are on the influence and leverage of other individual interest groups in the Soviet Union. Although consultation with individual leading jurists may take place behind the scenes, there is no public evidence that they participate in making crucial policy decisions even in areas in which they have the greatest expertise. It would appear, for example, that the extension of the death penalty for various economic crimes in 1961 and 1962 was a decision taken by the political leadership wholly independently of the opinion of the legal profession. Similarly, one may surmise that the Procurator General and possibly other leading legal officials were consulted in advance concerning the feasibility of criminal prosecutions of Sinyavsky and Daniel and of other persons charged with anti-Soviet agitation and propaganda in 1965; yet it appears very likely that the decision to prosecute was made by the political leadership with only minimal influence on the part of jurists. Despite these and other examples, however, it is significant that the jurists must at least be consulted, even in matters highly charged with politics, concerning techniques of legislation and adjudication, and that in matters not so highly charged their advice may be sought on policy and, indeed, they may themselves initiate the policy-making process. Whether or not the jurists are bypassed is a matter not for them but for the political leadership to decide; the fact that they are often not bypassed suggests that the political leadership considers that their nonparticipation would be costly in terms of a falling off in the orderly and effective operation of the system. Thus in spite of severe political limitations on their autonomy, the jurists play an important role, and an institutionalized one, in the many areas of Soviet life where policy requires legal implementation.

Examples of Collective Action

Perhaps the best example of collective action by Soviet jurists is their participation in the law reform movement during the fifteen years since Stalin's death.[75] A signal for law reform was given by Stalin's successors

[75] On law reform in this period see H. J. Berman, "Legality vs. Terror: The Post-Stalin Law Reforms," in G. M. Carter and A. F. Westin (eds.), *Politics in Europe* (New York, 1965), pp. 179-205. This study describes the legal changes which comprised the reform up to 1964 and discusses six major tendencies that characterized the period. These were the tendencies toward "elimination of terror," "liberalization both of procedure and substantive norms," "systematization and rationalization of the legal system as a whole," "decentralization and democratiza-

in their first official announcement after his death, when they promised changes in the system of criminal law and procedure. A second signal, this time not publicized, was given when Khrushchev came to power in February 1955; and by the late summer of 1955, the leading jurists had prepared substantial changes not only in criminal law and procedure but also in civil law, court organization, and many other branches of the legal system.[76] The guidelines of the reform, its direction and limits, were set by the party leaders, but the form and substance of the actual changes were largely the work of the jurists. Leading legal scholars, working closely with officials of the procuracy, the Ministry of Justice, and other agencies, produced drafts of new statutes and new codes, which were then considered by jurists generally, were submitted also for comment by representatives of all interested state agencies, and in some instances were widely discussed by the public in letters to the press and elsewhere. In time, new basic legislation was produced in most of the major fields of law.

Given the general secrecy of Soviet government operations, it is impossible to know to what extent the jurists, as a group, merely gave technical formulations of policy decisions taken by the political leaders, on what occasion they were consulted in advance of the taking of policy decisions by the political leaders, and when they exercised initiative in bringing the need for new policies to the attention of the political leaders. It seems evident that the leadership did not need to consult the jurists in making their basic decision to end the Stalinist terror and to raise the slogan of socialist legality as a bench mark of their regime. On the other hand, once that decision was made, extensive consultation with jurists must have taken place, if only to determine how, in the absence of terror, legal controls over dissent could be made most effective. Also, the jurists must have been given the opportunity to suggest, and not merely to implement, some specific policies; for example, it seems very likely that in the general discussion of the protection of the rights of citizens, it was the jurists, or some jurists, or an individual jurist, who first brought forward the idea, later adopted,

tion in decision-making," "the introduction of popular participation in law-enforcement and the administration of justice," and "a return to harsh criminal and administrative penalties against persons who defied what may be called 'the Soviet way of life.' "

[76] See H. J. Berman, "The Current Movement for Law Reform in the Soviet Union," *American Slavic and East European Review*, xv (1956), 179-189.

that a civil suit should be permitted to compel the press to publish retractions of libels.

One way of assessing the initiative taken by jurists would be to examine the public discussions that have taken place in the past fifteen years concerning proposed legislation and to compare the criticisms and suggestions which jurists made in response to the first published drafts with the corresponding provisions of the laws as finally adopted. This would be a research task of considerable magnitude and is clearly beyond the scope of the present chapter. We may, however, take advantage of some work that has been done along these lines with respect to the reform of civil law.

A period of eighteen months elapsed between the publication of the first draft of the All-Union Fundamental Principles of Civil Law in mid-1960 and the adoption of the final version in December 1961, during which time a widespread discussion of the draft, dominated by jurists, took place in the press and in scholarly journals.[77] The impact of the discussion can be seen in the fact that virtually every article in the draft was changed in some way—often significantly—and some 25 new articles were added. Of particular interest is an analysis of the Fundamental Principles presented early in 1961 by a group of legal scholars in Leningrad.[78] the thirteen authors appear to have comprised the full membership of the Department (Kafedra) of Civil Law of the Leningrad University Law Faculty. They made 50 specific recommendations for changes in the draft, and of these 22 appeared in the final version of the Fundamental Principles (often in exactly, or almost exactly, the same wording as the recommendations), 4 others were partially reflected in the final version, and 24 were not adopted.[79] It should

[77] The draft of the Principles of Civil Law may be found in a number of places, including *SGP*, No. 7 (1960), pp. 3-22. The Principles as finally adopted were first published in *Izvestia*, December 9, 1961. For a discussion by a Soviet writer of the influence of the public discussion on the Principles of Civil Law, see I. I. Kovalev, "Shirokoye uchastiye obshchest vennosti v obsuzhdenii proyektov osnov grazhdanskovo zakonodatelstva i grazhdanskovo sudoproizvodstva," *SGP*, No. 2 (1962), p. 17, and esp. pp. 20-21.

[78] O. S. Ioffe and others, "O proyekte osnov grazhdanskovo zakonodatelstva Soyuza SSR i Soyuznykh Respublik," *SGP*, No. 2 (1961), pp. 93-103.

[79] Under each of the major categories of the draft considered by the authors one or more numbered subjects are discussed. The total of these numbered subjects is only 39, but within several of them more than one specific recommendation is made, and the total number of recommendations, by our calculations, is 50. Some of the recommendations that did not find their way into the Principles may still have had an ultimate impact on policy-making. For example, at least one of the recommendations in Ioffe and others (*op.cit.*, p. 101), that there should be specific

be added that a number of the changes recommended by the group were also proposed by other jurists.

A concrete example of a specific change in legal policy proposed by jurists and ultimately adopted concerns the matter of governmental liability for personal injury and property damage resulting from administrative decisions or regulations ("acts") of state agencies.[80] Prior to the adoption of the Fundamental Principles, governmental liability in tort was limited to situations in which an employee of a state agency acted negligently in the performance of his duties (for example, a truck driver negligently ran a man down, and the state enterprise which employed the driver was held liable); the governmental agency was not liable for negligence of an administrative, as contrasted with operational, character—for example, in requiring the trucks to carry explosives with inadequate safety precautions. In February 1957, at a session of the USSR Supreme Soviet, deputy S. V. Stefanik, a lawyer by training and the chairman of the executive committee of the Lvov Oblast Soviet, argued that the existing law "contradicts the principle of socialist legality" and that to broaden governmental liability would "promote the thorough protection of the rights of workers and the improvement of the work of the governmental apparatus." At first the only substantial support for Stefanik's proposal was from a number of jurists in the Lvov University Law Faculty. The influence of these jurists may have been important in the inclusion of a provision in a 1959 draft of a new Ukrainian Civil Code extending the scope of government liability in tort. At about the same time, however, a draft of a new RSFSR Civil Code was circulated which contained a provision restricting governmental liability in the terms of the pre-existing law. At a meeting in Moscow in December 1959, called to discuss the RSFSR draft, there was widespread support for imposing governmental liability for harm caused by administrative acts. One writer asserted, on the basis of the views expressed at that meeting, that "it would be difficult

---

provisions on the tort liability of juveniles and incompetents, was reflected, in part in the form suggested by these scholars, in the RSFSR Civil Code of 1964. See Articles 450 and 452 of this Code. *Zakony RSFSR i Postanovlenia Verkhovnovo Soveta RSFSR prinyatye na tretei sessii Verkhovnovo Soveta RSFSR, Shestovo sozyva* (10-11 June 1964) (Moscow, 1964), pp. 159-160. An investigation would no doubt reveal other examples of such indirect influence of recommendations.

[80] The following discussion is based on D. D. Barry, "The Specialist in Soviet Policy-Making: The Adoption of a Law," *Soviet Studies*, XVI (1964), 152-165. Complete citations, including those for quotations used here, may be found in this source.

to find another question manifesting such unanimous opinion among scientific and practical workers as the question of the establishment of liability of governmental institutions for injury caused by administrative acts." Nevertheless, the 1960 draft of the All-Union Fundamental Principles of Civil Law side-stepped the issue by stating that it would be left to future all-union and republican legislation. This position was strongly criticized in the ensuing discussion. One writer asserted that "the compilers of the draft . . . should listen to the voice of the wide scientific public and of authoritative practicing jurists and should radically change their approach to the liability of governmental institutions for harm caused by administrative acts."[81] Among the proponents of this change were the thirteen Leningrad University jurists referred to earlier. Eventually, the Fundamental Principles were, in fact, changed to meet this demand; however, the reformers did not get all they wanted—certain limitations were introduced in the final version (Article 89 of the Fundamental Principles).[82]

In terms of the process of policy-formation, the above example shows a conflict between, on the one hand, a substantial majority of the jurists concerned with the question and, on the other, those persons who were vested with the ultimate power of decision. This conflict was resolved by a compromise which, on the whole, was favorable to the jurists. In addition, it shows a slight conflict between the legal scholars specializing in civil law and the "practical workers"—that is, the procuracy and Ministry of Justice, the judges, jurisconsults, and advocates; for although the reform had considerable support from the practical workers, it was also from their ranks that such opposition to it as was openly manifested seemed to come. Such conflicts and compromises, sometimes almost taking on the character of organized campaigns, have been common in the law reform movement which has continued unabated since Stalin's death.[83]

[81] See *ibid.*, esp. pp. 160-161.

[82] For example, governmental liability for damages to organizations (as distinguished from individuals) and for damages caused by officials of the courts, the procuracy, and the organs of inquiry and preliminary investigation will be provided by special laws. Such laws have not yet been adopted.

[83] Cf. P. H. Juviler, "Family Reforms on the Road to Communism," in P. H. Juviler and H. W. Morton (eds.), *Soviet Policy-Making: Studies of Communism in Transition* (New York, 1967), pp. 29-60. The most critical issues in the reform of family law have been the relaxation of the divorce law and the removal of any stigma of illegitimacy and the imposition of financial responsibility on fathers of children born of unwed mothers. Juviler speaks of "an evident sense of legal community among jurists, who have met across the land to exchange views and

A more dramatic example of the influence of jurists on high party policy may be found in their resistance to the antiparasite laws.[84] These laws, introduced in the various republics from 1957 to 1961, were part of Khrushchev's effort to enlist popular participation in punishing "antisocial elements" who were taking advantage of the end of Stalinist terror to acquire wealth illegally or simply to live as vagrants. Possibly the antiparasite laws were also intended—although nothing was said about this openly—as a vehicle for supressing lawful dissent; in fact they were used for that purpose on at least one occasion.[85] From Khrushchev's point of view, they were needed because the very improvement in the standards of legality had made it increasingly difficult to deal with persons who were behaving in undesirable ways. If such persons could not, because of more refined procedural requirements, be convicted of a crime and sent to labor colonies, they should, he indicated, be dealt with "administratively" and exiled to remote places.[86]

The antiparasite laws were first proposed for public discussion in February 1957. However, the discussion was strictly controlled by the party. That a large percentage—perhaps almost all—of the jurists were privately opposed to the draft laws was not apparent on the surface, although some letters by jurists raised questions concerning the vagueness of the concept of an "antisocial, parasitic way of life," and the ambiguity of such phrases as "living on nonlabor income" and "working for the sake of appearances only." Also there was some criticism of the original proposal to permit trials of "parasites" by groups of neighbors and popular assemblies.[87]

---

draft collective opinions on reforms." The jurists themselves, however, seem to have been divided on the policy questions, as was the political leadership and possibly the population as a whole, especially if one takes into account the diverse interests and values of the urban population and the peasantry. Rather intricate compromises were reached in new Fundamental Principles of Law on Marriage and the Family adopted by the Supreme Soviet in June 1968. The Fundamental Principles are translated in *Soviet Statutes and Decisions*, IV, No. 4 (Summer 1968), 106-126.

[84] See, for instance, H. J. Berman, *Justice in the USSR*, pp. 291-298; M. Armstrong, "The Campaign Against Parasites," in Juviler and Morton (eds.), *op.cit.*, pp. 163-182; and J. E. Turner, "Rooting Out the Parasites," in J. B. Christoph (ed.), *Cases in Comparative Politics* (Boston, 1965), pp. 384-408. The reforms in criminal law and in criminal procedure are analyzed in detail by H. J. Berman in his introduction to Berman and J. W. Spindler (eds. and trans.), *Soviet Criminal Law and Procedure*, pp. 1-139.

[85] The Brodsky case; see n. 40, above.

[86] See H. J. Berman and J. W. Spindler, "Soviet Comrades Courts," *Washington Law Review*, XXXVIII (Winter 1963), 854-855.

[87] Many of the important expressions of opposition to the laws by jurists are

In the period from 1957 to 1960, most of the smaller republics of the Soviet Union adopted antiparasite laws based on the original model statute. However, the three largest republics (the RSFSR, the Ukrainian SSR, and the Byelorussian SSR), comprising over half the Soviet population, did not—until 1961; and then they introduced important changes in the laws, substituting trial in the regular courts for trial by public assemblies and groups of neighbors. The delay in adoption of antiparasite laws in the major republics until 1961, and the amendments then introduced, undoubtedly reflected, in part, the opposition of the legal profession to the infringements of legality inherent in this legislation. Indeed, in 1959 the chief draftsman of the All-Union Fundamental Principles of Criminal Procedure stated to one of the authors of this chapter that in his opinion the antiparasite laws contradicted the Fundamental Principles and should be repealed in the republics which had passed them.

What happened next was a rearguard action by the courts against abuses of the antiparasite laws. The Supreme Court of the USSR, in reviewing sentences under the laws, began insisting on procedural guarantees for persons charged: they were entitled to public trial, they were entitled to counsel, they could not be convicted if they had not been given warning and sufficient time to find work, etc., etc. Two decrees of the USSR Supreme Court in September 1961 and March 1963[88] so exposed the evils of the antiparasite laws, and so limited their applicability, that amendments in the statutes became imperative, and in 1965 they were so drastically amended as to render them relatively—though by no means wholly—harmless. The 1965 amendments eliminate the references to living on nonlabor income and working for the sake of appearances only, and they eliminate exile except from Moscow and Leningrad. Not only is warning required, but before a person is charged he must be offered a job. Under the new version of the law it would be difficult if not impossible to repeat the 1964 fiasco which resulted in the exile of the Leningrad poet Iosif Brodsky, who was willing to take a job if the court insisted that his free-lance writing and translating

---

collected in Armstrong, *op.cit.*, on which part of this discussion is based. Turner (*op.cit.*, p. 395), commented that the laws adopted during the first phase "came in for considerable criticism from members of the legal profession." See also A. Campbell, "The Legal Scene," *Survey*, No. 57 (October 1965), pp. 58-59.

[88] Decree of the Plenum of the USSR Supreme Court, September 12, 1961, *Byulleten Verkhovnovo Suda SSSR*, No. 5 (1961), p. 8; Decree of March 18, 1963, *ibid.*, No. 3 (1963), p. 13.

did not constitute "work." Nor is it any longer possible, under the 1965 amendment, to resettle as parasites leaders of certain religious sects on the ground that they are working for appearances' sake only, while living off the contributions of their followers. In fact, almost nothing has been heard of the antiparasite laws since the 1965 amendments. Reports of antiparasite proceedings have been conspicuously absent from the Soviet press, and in August 1966 the President of the RSFSR Supreme Court told one of the authors that the antiparasite cases in the courts in 1966 could be counted on the fingers of one hand.

The fall of Khrushchev in October 1964 may have been an important factor in the severe limitations placed on the antiparasite laws by the 1965 amendments. The behind-the-scenes criticism of the laws by jurists may have also been a factor. But the final decision to confine their scope must have been due in large part to the serious abuses in their operation, revealed by the courts themselves, and especially by the Supreme Court of the USSR. Here the Supreme Court was playing a characteristic role of setting forth basic legal principles which have the purpose— or at least the effect—of moderating the influence of officially inspired campaigns on zealous local judicial officers, many of whom may be under the influence of even more zealous party functionaries.[89]

Thus far we have spoken of the jurists as a more-or-less homogenous group, with only individual differences of opinion, and have not faced the question whether it is divided into opposing subgroups. The only major opposition which is apparent—though there may be others behind the scenes—is between the legal scholars and the "practical workers." Thus one can find occasional reproof of the legal scholars—as in an editorial in *Sotsialisticheskaya zakonnost*, then the organ of the USSR Procuracy, in November 1963—for excessive criticism of existing legislation. The editorial stated: ". . . recently some legal scholars have given an incorrect, one-sided presentation of the role of legal science in relation to the legislative activity of our state. They see this role as consisting of criticizing certain laws, even those which have only recently been adopted. . . . It is well known, for example, that after the adoption in 1958 of the Fundamental Principles of Criminal Procedure, which rejected the proposals of certain scholars, some scientific workers con-

[89] See the discussion of the Supreme Court's performance of this function in D. D. Barry, "The Motor-Car in Soviet Criminal and Civil Law," *The International and Comparative Law Quarterly*, XVI (1967), 56-85, esp. 62-64, 71-72.

tinued the dispute instead of actively assisting in the implementation of the legislative act."[90]

Behind this barbed comment lies the opposition of the procuracy to continuing efforts of some legal scholars to extend the 1958 reforms to include the right to counsel from the time the preliminary investigation is commenced, and not only at the time of its completion, as well as various other efforts to reform criminal procedure. Here is a matter in which the procuracy, which has responsibility for criminal investigation and indictment, has a strong vested interest in unrestricted freedom. The conflict between legal scholars and the procuracy has on a few occasions even attained the dimensions of an open attack in the press, with different newspapers—notably, *Literaturnaya gazeta* and *Izvestia*—taking opposite sides.[91]

An even more dramatic conflict has emerged between the jurists and the press itself, involving press comments on pending cases. Under party guidance, the Soviet press often takes a special interest not only in crime as such but also in particular criminal cases, and even makes scathing denunciations of persons accused of crime or, indeed, still under investigation and not yet indicted. In 1964 the Chairman of the USSR Supreme Court, A. F. Gorkin, a respected party member and former Secretary of the Presidium of the Supreme Soviet of the USSR, was quoted in the press as stating: "The press has a major positive role to play in eliminating the shortcomings of the functioning of the courts. At the same time, we cannot fail to mention that the press sometimes carries articles in which persons are proclaimed guilty prior to the trial of the case in the court, and the question of the punishment to be administered (in the majority of cases the maximum penalty) is decided beforehand. The press can and should criticize shortcomings in the functioning of the courts and offer its opinion as to whether their decisions are right or wrong, but to determine the judgment beforehand and thereby to bring pressure to bear upon the court means not to struggle against errors in the activity of the court but to promote the commission of errors."[92] A year later the issue was

[90] "Za vysokuiu ideinost, printsipialnost i deistvennost pravovoi nauki," *Sots. zak.*, No. 11 (1963), p. 8. The most severe criticism in the editorial was directed at the legal scholar M. Shargorodsky, to whom was attributed the opinion (p. 9) that "science may only be considered science when it says 'no' to practice."

[91] See Fletcher, *op.cit.*, n. 74.

[92] *Izvestia*, December 2, 1964.

debated in considerable detail in a series of articles in *Izvestia*. Two practicing lawyers and a legal scholar advocated curbs on press comment on pending cases, while the Chief of the Investigation Administration of the RSFSR Ministry for the Protection of Public Order (renamed, in 1968, the Ministry of Internal Affairs) argued for the existing practice.[93]

Apart from differences of viewpoint among subgroups of the legal profession based upon their vested interests in different legal activities—such as investigation and prosecution of crimes, defense of accused persons, adjudication, legal scholarship, etc.—it is tempting to look also for differences of viewpoint corresponding to our conceptions of "liberalism" and "conservatism." There are, of course, sharp differences of this kind, but they seem to be differences among individuals rather than among groups. It would be hard to find evidence, for example, that the procuracy is "conservative" and the advocates, or the legal scholars, "liberal." Indeed, it is doubtful that these terms have anything like the same meaning in the Soviet context that they have in the United States. We would guess that Soviet jurists as a group have much more in common—especially their vested interest in legality—than do any of the subgroups into which they are divided; and that the opposition between subgroups is subordinate to their common traditions, their common training, and their common goals.

Conclusion

It should not be supposed that the access of the legal profession to those who are in a position to make policy is confined to situations in which the legal profession is seeking to realize or induce changes in existing law or policy. On the contrary, the main role of the Soviet legal profession is to implement and secure existing policies, and the main source of its influence is the fact that it is needed to help maintain stability and order in the society, and not only to help effectuate change. Under Stalin, and under his chief lieutenant for legal matters, Vyshinsky, Soviet jurists not only shared in the general adulation of the leader, or *vozhd*, but also took it to be their principal task to rationalize and systematize and propagandize the legal order which Stalin created—

---

[93] Yu. Korenevsky and K. Sukhodolets, "Otchevo byvayut oshibki," *Izvestia*, March 15, 1966; I. Galkin, "Sud i obshchestvennye strasti," *ibid.*, April 17, 1966; I. Perlov, "Pravosudiye i obshchestvennoye mneniye," *ibid.*, June 30, 1966. These three articles are translated in *The Soviet Review*, VIII (Spring 1967), 3-12.

based, as it was, on the dualism of law and terror. "Socialist legality" has acquired a new meaning since Stalin's death, but it remains the principal task of the Soviet legal profession to rationalize and systematize and propagandize the legal order which the party leadership proclaims. Jurists may privately disagree with party policy, but they are acutely aware of their duty not to disagree with it publicly. The anti-parasite laws were attacked by some jurists when they were first proposed, but after adoption the public criticism of the laws ceased, though dissatisfaction with the ways in which they were administered continued to be expressed. The extension of the death penalty in 1961 and 1962 to large-scale stealing of state property, large-scale bribery of state officials, counterfeiting, and other crimes did not elicit a single word of criticism in Soviet legal literature, though privately a leading Soviet advocate told one of the authors in 1962 that he was against the death penalty altogether except in time of war. In 1961 when two men were sentenced to death under an edict of the Presidium of the Supreme Soviet passed retroactively for their case, the late Professor S. A. Golunsky, chief draftsman of the Fundamental Principles of Criminal Procedure, told one of the authors, "We jurists didn't like it!"—but nothing to indicate such a response was said or written publicly.[94]

It is easy for Western lawyers, with their tradition of "bourgeois freedom" (as the Soviets call it), to denounce Soviet jurists for their unwillingness publicly to oppose unjust party policies. But it must be remembered that Western lawyers for the most part can engage in public criticism of their governments' policies without adversely affecting the interests of the legal profession as a group. The Soviet legal profession, like Western legal professions, wants to be part of the Establishment. The difference is that the Soviet Establishment does not tolerate public criticism of its basic policies—although today its basic policies themselves are certainly more flexible, and permit a great deal more public expression of criticism within them, than was the case thirty or even fifteen years ago. The Soviet legal profession, like other interest groups, is required above all to be loyal to the party and to the political, economic, and social system which the party represents; if it were not, it would surely lose its access to the policy-making process.

The Soviet legal profession is also loyal to law—and law, including Soviet law, embodies values which transcend any given political, economic, and social system. We have seen that the adversary presentation

94 H. J. Berman, "The Struggle of Soviet Jurist," p. 315.

331

of claims and defenses by Soviet advocates is itself an exercise of freedom of speech; that legal representation of state enterprises by Soviet jurisconsults itself presupposes enterprise autonomy and freedom of contract; that adjudication in the Soviet courts necessarily involves some degree, at least, of freedom of the judiciary from interference by outside organizations, including Communist Party organizations; that the tasks of the Soviet procuracy embody the right of citizens to complain against abuses by state officials and the right to have such complaints investigated and considered; that law teaching and legal scholarship in the Soviet Union (as elsewhere) are predicated on the right and duty of law teachers and legal scholars to criticize existing laws and to propose law reforms; and that the complex interaction of those who share professional responsibility for the operation of the Soviet legal system embodies the values of professional association and professional group identity.

These freedoms, rights, duties, and values are inherent in the practical activities of Soviet jurists, as they are inherent in the practical activities of lawyers of other countries. Not only under communism, but in all societies, there is a tension between legal values and political values, a struggle of law against the state. The political authority is concerned with the maintenance of political power; the legal institutions essential to the maintenance of political power necessarily create motivation and offer opportunities to challenge that power, at least implicitly.

The political authority may seek to avoid such a challenge by operating without law—by force, by informal pressures, by corruption of various kinds. But in the long run these techniques are inefficient. As the Soviet Minister of Justice N. V. Krylenko put it in the early 1920's, "a club is a primitive weapon, a rifle is more efficient, the most efficient is the court." Krylenko's view emphasizes the political role of the judge and of jurists generally and is associated with the theory that all law is a manifestation of the will of the state and cannot conflict with state interests. However, the efficiency of legal controls, which recommends them to state authorities, itself depends on factors that limit the power of the state. One such factor is the necessity of maintaining a respect for law on the part of the people whom it is designed to control: if they do not believe in the rightness of the established legal order they will fall victim to the same mistrust and despair which renders the naked exercise of political power inefficient, at least in the long run. Moreover, as we have stressed, an efficient legal system requires the creation of a professional body to maintain it; and as we have seen, the legal profession inevitably has a vested interest in the legal values—and not merely the political values—which its activities presuppose.

The importance of the legal profession in Soviet political life is therefore not to be measured by its power to determine or to frustrate, at any given moment, particular policies of the Communist Party or the government. Its importance lies rather in the significance of what it stands for as a profession seeking to safeguard and implement, within the framework of party policy, the standards and values of that profession.

CHAPTER X ~ BY FRANKLYN GRIFFITHS

A Tendency Analysis
of Soviet Policy-Making

THE ENDEAVOR to employ interest group conceptions in the analysis of contemporary Soviet politics must provoke a sense of uncertainty in the researcher. Not only do Soviet realities resist any ready transference of notions which are derived largely from American experience, but the available theories of group politics and interest groups have notable deficiencies which have to be dealt with. At the same time, the empirical data to which an interest group approach directs us in looking at Soviet politics raise questions not only about prevailing views of the Soviet political system, but also about current conceptions of the political system as such. It is to be acknowledged that the use of interest group concepts can add to our understanding of Soviet policy-formation in ways that are not readily achieved by employing either the totalitarian or "leadership conflict" models of Soviet politics. And yet it seems apparent that interest group activity cannot be regarded as the central phenomenon in Soviet policy-making. If this is so, what analytical framework should be employed to examine the activities of party *apparatchiki*, economists, jurists, military officers, writers, and other politically relevant individuals who occupy an intermediate position, broadly speaking, between the Soviet leadership and the mass of the led?

It is an innate supposition of the group approach that the process through which policies are formed is essentially subsystem-dominant,[1] in that the working of the system as a whole is to be explained in terms of the interaction of its subsystems such as interest groups, government institutions, and the political leadership. A conservative interpretation of Soviet politics would suggest a very high degree of subsystem-dominance by the party leadership and would accord little or no influence

[1] Cf. Morton A. Kaplan, *System and Process in International Politics* (New York, 1967), pp. 16-17, and Chap. 3.

to interest groups. A more discriminating view of the role of Soviet intermediate actors in a setting of subsystem-dominance can certainly be offered. However, a variety of conceptual and methodological difficulties is encountered in defining Soviet interest group subsystems and determining their influence.

An alternate approach to the data of Soviet intermediate activity might be to begin with the assumption of system-dominance. From this perspective the Soviet policy process would be seen in terms of regularities in the interactions of the whole which represent parametric givens for intermediate participation and to which the latter must be accommodated if it is to have any effect. This approach would have the effect of lowering the salience of subsystem-dominance by the party leadership, but then that is one of the purposes of the analysis of intermediate participation. At the same time, it would divert attention from the consideration of autonomous group action, which is entailed in the assumption of subsystem-dominance and which does not readily "fit" the Soviet data. Ultimately, of course, we are not concerned with "pure" subsystem- or system-dominance, for these are matters of degree. At the present time, however, the question is the preliminary one of elaborating a research strategy most appropriate to the analysis of that Soviet experience which appears to be the equivalent of interest group politics in Western societies.

In this essay it will be suggested that the formation and execution of policy in the Soviet Union may be understood in terms of a system-dominant conflict of tendencies of articulation, through which specific values are allocated for Soviet society.[2] From this standpoint, Soviet policy-making on a given issue is to be regarded as a process in which the interaction among individuals who articulate policy expectations results in the emergence of, and selection from, a series of alternate possible directions of value allocation—tendencies of articulation—for Soviet society. The evidence which might normally be viewed in terms of interest group conflict may instead be treated in terms of conflicting tendencies in the articulations of intermediate participants on given issues. Rather than seek to determine how and with what success one interest group makes claims upon other groups and upon the political leadership, the data of Soviet group relations—organization and or-

[2] The view of the political system as a set of interactions through which values are authoritatively allocated for a society is set forth in David Easton, *A Systems Analysis of Political Life* (New York, 1965).

ganizational resources, expertise, career patterns, ideological orientation, social status, access, and so on—may more profitably be employed to help explain the genesis and outcome of the tendency conflicts through which specific Soviet policies are made. The same holds for the structure of centralized controls under which intermediate actors necessarily operate.

In the sections that follow, attention will first be given to problems of applying David Truman's subsystem-dominant conceptions of group politics to the Soviet setting. I will then consider Arthur Bentley on tendency conflict, and also certain Soviet commentators on the "nonantagonistic contradictions of socialism." Subsequently, an attempt will be made to render the commonplace term "tendency" operational for research as part of a system-dominant conception of the Soviet policy-making process. Finally, consideration will be given to some possible reasons for the development of intermediate participation in Soviet policy-making since Stalin.

Truman's Governmental Process *and Soviet Politics*

Arthur Bentley is commonly regarded as the originator of the group theory of politics, and his remarkable volume, *The Process of Government* (1908), may be taken as its initial statement.[3] Bentley's successors, however, have for the most part failed to appreciate fully his vision of the political process. Those with a theoretical inclination have developed approaches to the study of group politics which differ substantially from his original ideas. Others, who have either been relatively unconcerned with theoretical matters or who have rejected outright the assertions of Bentley and his followers, have produced an imposing body of research into the affairs of individual "interest groups" and "pressure groups." While there are of course many differences among those who have written since Bentley, it is fair to treat David Truman's *The Governmental Process* (1951) as broadly representative of research practice in the study of interest group politics.[4] If a version

[3] Arthur F. Bentley, *The Process of Government* (Evanston, 1949). See also Charles B. Hagan, "The Group in a Political Science," in Roland A. Young (ed.), *Approaches to the Study of Politics* (Evanston, 1958), pp. 38-51, and Robert T. Golembiewski, " 'The Group Basis of Politics': Notes on Analysis and Development," *American Political Science Review*, LIV (1960), 962-971.

[4] David B. Truman, *The Governmental Process: Political Interests and Public Opinion* (New York, 1951). Elements of Bentley's thought are clearly evident in Truman's work. But if his views on the group basis of politics are set aside,

of group theory, even a vestigial one, is to be employed in the analysis of Soviet politics, a choice should be made at the outset between the approaches offered by Bentley and Truman.

For our purposes here, three principal considerations may be identified in the theory that underlies *The Governmental Process*. The first is connected with the definition of what constitutes an "interest group." The second arises with the "potential group," and the third is concerned with the theory of group-based politics. At the risk of being pedantic, let us examine Truman's views on these matters closely and in the light of the Soviet data, in order to lay bare some of the assumptions on which an interest group analysis of Soviet politics may have to be based.

Truman regards an interest group as "any group that, on the basis of one or more shared attitudes, makes certain claims upon other groups in the society for the establishment, maintenance, or enhancement of forms of behavior that are implied by the shared attitudes."[5] It is the shared attitudes—the "frames of reference" with which given situations are interpreted, and also the "views of what is needed or wanted" in these situations—which constitute the "interests" of the group in question.[6] A political interest group is present when the expression of these interests leads to the making of claims through or upon government institutions. *The Governmental Process* is largely concerned with the emergence of such groups, their internal features, their tactics for affecting political outcomes, and the factors responsible for success and failure in achieving their aims. From this vantage point, Truman's political interest group is a reified entity, an aggregate of persons which is endowed with human-like abilities to make claims and pursue strategies.

Elsewhere, however, Truman puts forward a different conception of what constitutes a "group," which is not directly incorporated into the characterization of the political interest group given above. Over and above the sharing of attitudes and the making of claims through or upon

---

Truman's approach is broadly similar to that of Harry Eckstein, *Pressure Group Politics: The Case of the British Medical Association* (London, 1960); V. O. Key, Jr., *Politics, Parties and Pressure Groups* (5th ed., New York, 1964); Joseph LaPalombara, *Interest Groups in Italian Politics* (Princeton, 1964); Jean Meynaud, *Les Groupes de pression en France* (Paris, 1958); H. R. Mahood (ed.), *Pressure Groups in American Politics* (New York, 1967), and others. For a related statement of the group theory of politics, see Earl Latham, "The Group Basis of Politics," *American Political Science Review*, xlvi (1952), 376-397.

[5] Truman, *op.cit.*, p. 33.   [6] *Ibid.*, pp. 33-34.

government institutions, the existence of a political interest group is said to require a minimum frequency of interaction among its members.[7] It is this interaction which produces the uniformities of attitude and of claim-making behavior among the individuals involved. Moreover, it is this interaction which is the "group" so far as politics is concerned.[8] Thus, at various points Truman states that an interest group is to be seen as "a standardized pattern of interactions rather than as a collection of human units."[9] From this perspective, the object of inquiry is not an aggregate but a *pattern of interaction.*

Truman does not state what he means by interaction, but it may be seen as a process in which the activity of one or more individuals is stimulated by, or follows upon, and is therefore in some way dependent upon, the activity of others.[10] The dependence among interacting individuals may be unilateral or mutual, in that the conditioning of activity can flow very largely in one direction from one actor to others, or there can be reciprocal conditioning. Where mutual dependence is absent or cannot be demonstrated adequately, it has been suggested that terms such as "informal group," "grouping," or "collectivity" should be employed instead of "group."[11] Truman himself uses the term "categoric group" to refer to a case where interaction is not present (e.g., "blondes"). Accordingly, for the persistent pattern of interaction which Truman calls a political interest group to exist, a degree of mutual dependence should be manifested with a minimum frequency. From this standpoint, the American Medical Association is to be seen not as an aggregate of doctors which makes claims on the basis of certain common interests, but rather as a pattern of interaction which exists among these doctors and which leads to the formation of certain specific attitudes and the communication of corresponding political demands. This pattern of interaction may be termed an "analytic group."

It may be suggested that there is a "level of analysis" problem in Truman's conception of the interest group and, ultimately, of group

[7] *Ibid.*, pp. 23-24.   [8] *Ibid.*, pp. 21, 23-25, 29, 33, 46.

[9] For example, see *ibid.*, p. 508. Truman adds, "The view of the group as an aggregation of individuals abstracts from the observable fact that in any society, and especially a complex one, no single group affiliation accounts for all of the attitudes or interests of any individual except a fanatic or a compulsive neurotic."

[10] George C. Homans, *The Human Group* (New York, 1950), pp. 36-37.

[11] Robert K. Merton, *Social Theory and Social Structure* (New York, 1965), pp. 283-285, and Odd Ramsoy, *Social Groups as System and Subsystem* (New York, 1963), pp. 16-17.

politics as well. Despite his assertions that the interest group is to be understood as a pattern of interaction, *The Governmental Process* is dominated by the assumption that an interest group is more readily treated as a reified or personified aggregate. Thus, he is primarily concerned with such questions as how "it" combats the claims of other "groups," how "it" achieves access to decision-makers and civil servants, what strategems "it" employs to influence public opinion, and so on. This class of question is pertinent at a level of analysis where the discussion is focused on the behavior of aggregates which are credited with a human intelligence and capacity for action. It is not the kind of question that might be posed at the level of a transactional analysis, where the investigator would be concerned with *patterns of interaction and the relations between them.* Nor, of course, is it the kind of question that would follow from a decision to combine the two forms of analysis and inquire how one pattern of interaction "makes claims" on other patterns of interaction by "securing access" to the institutions of government (themselves presumably still other patterns of interaction). The problem here is not merely semantic, but conceptual. Presumably aware of the great difficulties of a transactional interpretation of the political process, and of combining transactional with aggregate analysis, Truman evidently chose to work at a more conventional and familiar level of inquiry. The notion of the group as interaction recedes into the background, and the analysis is made effectively in terms of the shared attitudes, internal cohesion, strategic position, strategy, and influence of reified entities.

In considering the relevance of Truman's interest group conceptions for the study of Soviet politics, we are offered a choice between what might be called the reified group and the analytic group. Leaving the latter aside for the moment, we may note that Gordon Skilling has in effect proposed the use of Truman's reified group, and that the contributors to this volume have to varying degrees been inclined to adopt a similar approach. Zbigniew Brzezinski and Samuel P. Huntington have also employed reified group concepts in their *Political Power: USA/USSR*, as have Sidney I. Ploss, Philip D. Stewart, and Joel Schwartz and William Keech.[12] Despite the substantial advances that

---

[12] Zbigniew Brzezinski and Samuel P. Huntington, *Political Power:USA/USSR* (New York, 1964); Sidney I. Ploss, "Interest Groups," in Allen Kassof (ed.), *Prospects for Soviet Society* (New York, 1968), pp. 76-103; Philip D. Stewart, *Political Power in the Soviet Union* (Indianapolis and New York, 1968); and

have been recorded in this literature, it may be suggested that we do not yet have a clear picture of the aggregates that constitute interest groups in the Soviet setting. In the abstract, a wide range of variables is eligible for inclusion in the construct of a reified interest group.[13] However, an attempt to elaborate a typology of Soviet interest group aggregates would require a prior conclusion that the reified interest group is an appropriate tool for the analysis of Soviet political life.

It may be suggested that the informality of political conflict and political collaboration in the USSR does not greatly favor a view of interest groups as coherent units which possess a human capacity to pursue ends. On first impression, it might seem that goal-seeking aggregates of men taken by profession or formal organization constitute the primary effective groups in Soviet policy-making. While this is what research into Western group politics would suggest, there is as yet little evidence to show that the organized group pursuing a coherent common interest is a frequent participant in the Soviet policy process. Although such activity could occur over certain issues, such as "professional autonomy," central controls would still seem far too substantial to permit autonomous action by whole organizations. Instead, it would appear to be the rule that formal organizations and professions are internally fragmented and do not have an aggregate approach to most issues.

No doubt the remarkable picture of opposing alignments which Richard Judy has drawn for the economists in this volume could be duplicated for other occupational groups: though Donald Barry and Harold Berman regard the jurists essentially as a unified whole, they do observe that differences also exist among jurists in regard to specific policy issues; Roman Kolkowicz discerns a multiplicity of subgroups among the Soviet military; Ernest Simmons observes similar divisions within the Writers' Union; John Hardt and Theodore Frankel envisage a fundamental division among the industrial managers; and even in the state security apparatus the possibility of differences of orientation toward policy is suggested by Frederick Barghoorn.

Joel J. Schwartz and William R. Keech, "Group Influence and the Policy Process in the Soviet Union," *American Political Science Review*, LXII (1968), 840-851.

[13] See, for example, Paul F. Lazarsfeld and Morris Rosenberg (eds.), *The Language of Social Research* (New York, 1967), pp. 290-301, or Richard J. Hall, J. Eugene Haas, and Norman J. Johnson, "An Examination of the Blau-Scott and Etzioni Typologies," *Administrative Science Quarterly*, Vol. 12 (1967), pp. 118-139.

The implication of this and other evidence[14] is that informal subgroups, which Skilling refers to as "opinion groups," are of greater relevance for policy formation than formal aggregates taken as wholes. However, on the basis of the available data, it is open to question whether such informal groups can readily be treated as aggregates that press common claims, rather than as sets of *individuals* who share common attitudes but who may or may not purposely be acting in concert. Concerted action is bound to occur, but its character is largely hidden, making it difficult to determine whether we are dealing with an aggregate, a loose coalition of like-minded actors, or the parallel unilateral articulations of virtually atomized individuals.

If we look for patterns of articulation on specific issues, as opposed to the conflicting articulations that arise from specific formal groups, we find signs of shared outlooks and claims which cut across formal groups. The presence of such cross-group linkages at the regional level is admirably discussed by Jerry Hough in his chapter on the party *apparatchiki*. At the central level, similar informal constellations may well exist, as sets of writers, painters, cinematographers, scientists, party officials, and others vie over the artistic policy of the regime, or as other informal coalitions emerge over "democratization" and in the

[14] Among others see, Patricia Blake, "Freedom and Control in Literature," in Alexander Dallin and Alan F. Westin (eds.), *Politics in the Soviet Union: 7 Cases* (New York, 1966), pp. 165-206; Victor Frank, "The Soviet Literary Climate," *Survey*, No. 56 (July 1965) pp. 46-53; Timothy McClure, "The Politics of Soviet Culture, 1964-1967," *Problems of Communism*, xvi, No. 2 (March-April 1967), pp. 26-43; V. Holubnychy, "Soviet Debate on Economic Theories: An Introduction," in H. G. Shaffer (ed.), *The Soviet Economy* (New York, 1963), pp. 343-359; Marshall I. Goldman, "Economic Growth and Institutional Change in the Soviet Union," in Peter H. Juviler and Henry W. Morton (eds.), *Soviet Policy-Making: Studies of Communism in Transition* (New York, 1967), pp. 61-81; Michel Tatu, "Soviet Reforms: The Debate Goes On," *Problems of Communism*, xv, No. 1 (January-February 1966), 28-34; Gerald Segal, "Automation, Cybernetics, and Party Control," *Problems of Communism*, xv, No. 2 (March-April 1966), 1-12; Raymond H. Garthoff, "Khrushchev and the Military," in Dallin and Westin (eds.), *op.cit.*, pp. 243-274; Thomas W. Wolfe, *Soviet Strategy at the Crossroads* (Cambridge, Mass., 1964); George Fischer, *Science and Politics* (Ithaca, 1964); Paul Hollander, "The Dilemmas of Soviet Sociology," *Problems of Communism*, xiv, No. 6 (November-December 1965), 34-46; A.J.C. Campbell, "The Legal Scene: Proceduralists and Paternalists," *Survey*, No. 57 (October 1965), pp. 56-66; John N. Hazard, "Social Control Through Law," in Dallin and Westin (eds.), *op.cit.*, pp. 207-242; Grey Hodnett, "What's in a Nation?" *Problems of Communism*, xvii, No. 4 (November-December 1967), 2-15; Loren Graham, "The Reorganization of the Academy of Sciences," in Juviler and Morton (eds.), *op.cit.*, pp. 133-162; John A. Armstrong, *The Soviet Bureaucratic Elite* (New York, 1959), pp. 89ff., and "Party Bifurcation and Elite Interests," *Soviet Studies*, xvii (1966), No. 4, 417-430.

making of decisions concerning agriculture, housing, educational policy, and so on.[15] Thomas W. Wolfe, to offer another example, has recently suggested that the alignment on the issue of military participation in policy-making cuts through the party and military, creating a situation in which "the party has been able to summon advocates for its view from within the military establishment and the latter in turn has found allies on the political side of the house."[16] Accordingly, the researcher may frequently be dealing not merely with opposing subgroups within individual organizations, but with opposing and even more informal combinations of individuals with varied occupational and institutional affiliations.

As we penetrate further into the policy-making process, the aggregate of individuals that constitutes the reified group becomes increasingly difficult to conceive of in practice. The formal organization loses a good deal of its significance, and there seems to be little reason to attribute to such diffuse "aggregates" as are observed, a will and purposes of their own in making claims, seeking access, and engaging

---

[15] The line-up on the central budget process is also a case in point and has been discussed in passing in numerous studies. See for example, Carl A. Linden, *Khrushchev and the Soviet Leadership, 1957-1964* (Baltimore, 1966) or Robert Conquest, *Power and Policy in the U.S.S.R.* (New York, 1961). On agricultural and educational policy, see Sidney I. Ploss, *Conflict and Decision-Making in Soviet Russia: A Case Study of Agricultural Policy, 1953-1963* (Princeton, 1965); and George Z. F. Bereday and J. Pennar, *The Politics of Soviet Education* (New York, 1960), in addition to Schwartz and Keech, *op.cit.* Vernon V. Aspaturian has suggested the presence of opposing group alignments in the formation of foreign policy. "Internal Politics and Foreign Policy," in R. Barry Farrell (ed.), *Approaches to Comparative and International Politics* (Evanston, 1966), pp. 212-287. See also Robert Slusser, "Khrushchev, China, and the Hydra-Headed Opposition," in Juviler and Morton (eds.), *op.cit.*, pp. 183-269. On the disarmament issue, a number of conflicting tendencies of articulation are observable as persisting over a fifty-year period. Franklyn Griffiths, "Inner Tensions in the Soviet Approach to 'Disarmament,'" *International Journal*, XXII (1967), 593-617. No doubt, analogous research on issues such as de-Stalinization, "vigilance" campaigns, nationality policy, material versus moral incentives, and so on, would reveal similar patterns of conflicting articulation, reaching with variations from the highest level to local politics. Many of these policy divisions could be described in "progressive versus conservative" terms if provision for intervening positions is allowed. Moreover, it is possible to conceive of individuals and groupings having complementary positions on a variety of issues at once, since many of these seem to be interdependent. For example, what happens in regard to East-West tension affects the outcome of policy on budget, economic decentralization, literary controls, law enforcement, de-Stalinization, and so on. Cf. Zbigniew K. Brzezinski, "The Soviet Political System: Transformation or Degeneration?" *Problems of Communism*, XV, No. 1 (1966), 1-15, and Alexander Dallin and others, *The Soviet Union, Arms Control, and Disarmament* (New York, 1964), pp. 73-81.

[16] Thomas W. Wolfe, "Are the Generals Taking Over?" *Problems of Communism*, XVIII, No. 4-5 (1969), pp. 106-110.

in other activities of a reified group. An alternative might be to concentrate attention on "opinion groups" within the formal organization or profession, as Skilling in effect proposes. But apart from the questionable aggregate nature of such a group, this would remove from the field of vision other and possibly important forms of intermediate participation in the making of policy.

In addition, there is the problem of acquiring knowledge about the influence or effectiveness of a reified group, however its membership is defined. While elements of the military almost certainly sought to block Khrushchev's proposed reductions of conventional forces in 1960-1961 and 1963-1964, for example, it cannot definitely be shown that they had a part in the reversal which both announcements suffered. Schwartz and Keech, in their study of group participation in the educational reform of 1958, perforce confine themselves to the observation that "insofar as groups influenced the outcome of this issue it was through the communication of their expert judgements to people at the top of the hierarchy who *were* in a position to influence outcomes."[17] In this volume, Barry and Berman have pointed to an exceptional and convincing case in which the very language of the decision was identical to the prior recommendations of an aggregate of Leningrad jurists. But it always remains possible that the activity of a given "group" may have little or no bearing at all on the resolution of an issue.[18] Decision-makers may operate arbitrarily, or in an information vacuum which is self-imposed or the result of preoccupation with other business. Alternatively, they may comply with articulations originating from a certain aggregate, but for reasons that have little to do with the arguments from below. A good deal may eventually be learned about the general capacity of interest group aggregates to influence political outcomes through the tendering of expert advice and the mobilization and denial of support. But at present it seems unlikely that the impact of a given interest group on a specific outcome can be ascertained accurately, owing both to the inherent methodological difficulty of relating an aggregate to the process of which its activities are part, and to the informality of the Soviet political process.

Finally, a number of objections can be made to reification as such.

[17] *Op.cit.*, p. 847. Similarly, Philip Stewart is concerned with the "potential influence" of interest groups. *Op.cit.*

[18] Cf. Theodore J. Lowi, "American Business, Public Policy, Case Studies and Political Theory," *World Politics*, XVI (1964), 681.

In the first place it inhibits the observer from perceiving a system of behavior by having the latter appear to be a thing in itself, which possesses purposes and a will of its own and acts independently of the interaction among its constituent parts. Secondly, it inhibits the consideration of a system of behavior as it influences and is influenced by the "external" situation in which it is embedded. The behavior of a group that is directed toward the external setting surely cannot be considered without immediate reference to the influence on members of communications arising from nonmembers and the physical environment. Third, by directing us more to structure than to process,[19] reification also favors the pursuit of "linear causal" or action-reaction explanations of "group" behavior, and minimizes the interpenetration and mutual dependence of groups as systems of action. As Bauer, Pool, and Dexter state in their study of American policy-formation on the issue of foreign trade, "The appropriate general model is not one of linear causality, but a transactional one which views all the actors in to some extent a situation of mutual influence and interdependence."[20] Finally, a reified group consisting of an aggregate of individuals cannot itself influence the behavior of an individual or another group. Rather it is the communicated activities, themselves the consequence of prior communication, which affect the expectations of others.[21] This suggests that the primary object of study should be articulations rather than groups.

The foregoing observations on the use of reified group conceptions are not meant to suggest that it is preferable to employ the analytic group in the study of Soviet group politics. Looking at formal organizations, their subgroups, or at informal coalitions for information on interaction patterns that might represent Truman's analytic groups, we are at once faced with the problem of empirical evidence that characterizes Soviet studies. The investigator is compelled to rely almost entirely upon the printed word, supplemented on occasion by field trips.

[19] The methodological conservatism of interest group analysis is indicated by David Easton, who contends that it is a manifestation of the "strong tendency in political research to move directly to the particular structures, whether formal or informal, through which political interactions manifest themselves." *A Framework for Political Analysis* (Englewood Cliffs, 1965), p. 49.

[20] Raymond A. Bauer, Ithiel de Sola Pool, and Lewis A. Dexter, *American Business and Public Policy* (New York, 1963), p. 456.

[21] It should, however, be acknowledged that this essay, while seeking to avoid reification of the group, tends to reify the individual; for purposes of preliminary analysis he is regarded as an entity or actor in the political process, rather than an open system of action embedded in an environment.

A surprisingly rich variety of outlooks and claims can be demonstrated on this basis, and from these some initial sense of patterned activity can be drawn. But apart from the case where spokesmen refer to and support one another or one another's positions, we are very largely denied the possibility of demonstrating the presence of the interaction on which the existence of an analytic group depends. In practice there may very well be sufficient mutual dependence in the behavior of "liberal" writers, or among "liberal" writers and others seeking greater artistic freedom, to warrant in both cases designation as analytic groups. The same is true of "family groups," certain Crimean Tatars and their supporters, or the "action group" of Soviet Baptists that came into being in 1961.[22] Yet since most of the interaction is not visible to the foreign observer, it is virtually impossible to demonstrate that it in fact occurs. Thus, the use of analytic group concepts would have to take largely for granted that which is most vital to the enterprise: the existence of the "group" under investigation.

But if we cannot clearly demonstrate the presence of interaction in the Soviet setting, can we hope to make scientific statements about Soviet policy-making in the first place? Can we speak seriously of "articulation," for example, if the expression of a demand or interest has political significance only if the communication is received,[23] and if we are unable to determine the connection between this communication and the subsequent behavior of the recipient? Perhaps the Soviet case merely presents in sharper form the fact that the interpretation of interaction in any political setting is to some extent an exercise in impressionism. Under these circumstances, it is preferable to acknowledge that the exercise is impressionistic to a degree and to avoid setting up criteria of scientific investigation that are impossible to observe in practice.

We might therefore consider relaxing the requirement for a rigorous demonstration of interaction and proceed to speak of such groups as "liberal writers," "the KGB," or the "party-military group for party primacy in military policy-making," as analytic interest groups. Yet it remains difficult to see what would be gained by the use of this concept. The paucity of data would continue to prevent clear specifica-

[22] For the latter groups see respectively, *New York Times*, May 3, 1969, and Michael Bourdeaux and Peter Reddaway, "Soviet Baptists Today," *Survey*, No. 66 (January 1968), p. 52.

[23] Heinz Eulau, "Rationality in Unanimous Decision-Making," in Carl J. Friedrich (ed.), *Rational Decision* (New York, 1963), p. 38.

tion of analytic groups and analytic group activity. And if one pursued a transactional analysis of the interdependence and interpenetration of groups as patterns of interaction, further questions would be raised about the distinctiveness of the "group," which would ultimately appear to dissolve into process. In this case, too, our observations are confined to patterns of parallel unilateral articulations made by individuals who apparently share similar views of a situation and of policy requirements. Although we shall later broach the task of presenting a transactional theory at the system level, it seems unlikely that such an approach at the subsystem level, stressing analytic groups, would give any greater clarity than would be obtained with the use of reified group concepts. We are thus led to seek an alternate mode of analysis that would attempt to avoid the methodological shortcomings of the group approach altogether.

Turning briefly to Truman's potential group, or interest that is not expressed by a particular organized interest group, we see that it is characterized as "a 'becoming' stage" of group activity based on "widely held attitudes that are not expressed in interaction," but which may become the basis of interaction.[24] It consists of "potential activities" or "tendencies of activity" such as surround the "democratic mold" or rules of the game in the United States: given a violation of such pervasive norms, the individuals who represent the potential group may be moved to interact, with the result that a political interest group comes or threatens to come into being.[25] Truman observes that the membership of the potential group normally cuts across groups having a narrower interest and may exert substantial influence on the expectations and conduct of more salient actors in the political process.

As a tool of analysis, the potential group is primarily intended to direct attention to the role of relatively unorganized "interests" in the making of policy, and to the process of group formation in evolving political situations. Applied to the Soviet data, it might well be possible to discern potential groups of Stalinists, World War II veterans, Ukrainian nationalists, advocates of increased material incentives to stimulate production, and others whose expectations are taken into account in the formation of Soviet policies. The Czechoslovak experience of 1968 needs only to be mentioned to suggest the variety of "potential groups" that can exist in a "socialist" society and may become actual under appropriate circumstances.

[24] Truman, *op.cit.*, pp. 34-47.   [25] *Ibid.*, pp. 36-37, 129-139, 511-512.

A number of difficulties arise, however, in a detailed application of the potential group concept as put forward by Truman. The ambiguity in his concept of the interest group is also reflected in his approach to the potential group. On the one hand, the potential of the potential group is to become an organized group or aggregate which proceeds to influence policy in a more obvious and direct fashion. On the other, the potential of the potential group is to intensify claim-making interaction so that the dispersed members are united into an analytic group. Unless transactional analysis is consistently employed, it is difficult to see what advantages the potential group concept has over the more familiar notion of the "reference group." Indeed, if the latter is regarded as a set of individuals "who share distinctive norms which are used by a given actor in the determination of his own behavior,"[26] not only the potential group but also the actual interest group would have to be viewed in a different light. The problem of analyzing the mutual dependence between the reference group and the individual political actors concerned would, however, still have to be faced.

If, on the other hand, a transactional analysis were to be employed at the subsystem level, the researcher would be faced with the problem of delineating the process whereby a tendency in the activity of a set of persons (a potential group) is followed by interaction and the formation of an analytic group. Even if this could be accomplished with the available evidence of group relations, the interesting questions in such a process would be, not the formation of analytic groups as such, but the intensification of a particular pattern of articulation by members of the potential and actual groups to the point where it influences or displaces other articulation patterns in official policy on a given issue. On the whole then, it is unlikely that the use of Truman's potential group concept would be advantageous in the analysis of Soviet politics.

Finally, there is the question of the group theory of politics, as advanced by Truman and as it might apply to politics in the Soviet Union. From the foregoing it should be apparent that Truman assigns to interest groups a central role in the determination of political behavior by virtue of the influence they exercise both over their own members and over others in society. As he puts it:

[26] Robert A. Feldmesser, "Social Classes and Political Structure," in Cyril E. Black (ed.), *The Transformation of Russian Society* (Cambridge, Mass., 1960), p. 236.

We have argued, in fact, that the behaviors that constitute the process of government cannot be adequately understood apart from the groups, especially the organized and potential interest groups, which are operative at any point in time. Whether we look at an individual citizen, at the executive secretary of a trade association, at a political party functionary, at a legislator, administrator, governor, or judge, we cannot describe his participation in the governmental institution, let alone account for it, except in terms of the interests with which he identifies himself and the groups with which he affiliates and with which he is confronted. These groups may or may not be interest groups, and all the interests he holds may not be represented at a given point in time by organized units. Organized interest groups, however, from their very nature bulk large in the political process.[27]

While not claiming that group relations are the sole datum of American politics, group affiliation and interaction represent the key to a scientific understanding of politics, in Truman's view. The result, very briefly stated, is a subsystem-dominant or pluralistic democracy in which power is dispersed among contending groups and in which those charged with the making and implementation of decisions are responsive to varying forms of group influence.

Group interpretations of politics as put forward by Truman, Bentley, and others have been subjected to telling criticism along three lines. First, the view of policy as the product of relations between interest group aggregates and government officials overlooks a range of situational factors which affect the actions and effectiveness of these groups. Second, analytic interest group theory is not a theory in the proper sense, but merely a way of talking about politics which does not help to explain anything. Thirdly, it is preferable to confine research to case studies of individual interest groups, taken as aggregates and preferably seen from a comparative perspective.[28] Viewed together, these criticisms, which seem for the most part well taken, suggest that the

[27] Truman, op.cit., p. 502.

[28] See, among others, Merle Fainsod, "Some Reflections on the Nature of the Regulatory Process," in Carl J. Friedrich and Edward S. Mason (eds.), Public Policy (Cambridge, Mass., 1940), pp. 297-323; Harry Eckstein, "Group Theory and the Comparative Study of Pressure Groups," in Harry Eckstein and David E. Apter (eds.), Comparative Politics: A Reader (New York, 1963), pp. 389-397; Joseph LaPalombara, "The Utility and Limitations of Interest Group Theory in Non-American Field Situations," ibid., pp. 421-430; Roy C. Macridis, "Interest Groups in Comparative Analysis," Journal of Politics, xxiii (1961), 25-45; Samuel J. Eldersveld, "American Interest Groups: A Survey of Research and Some

theory of group-based politics is of use principally in bringing to light the role of intermediate actors in the making of policy. There is much to be admired in *The Governmental Process*, but at the theoretical level it is unable alone to suggest a workable framework for the study of policy-making in "pluralist" societies.

So far as the role of group politics in the Soviet setting is concerned, the contributions to this volume indicate that in the post-Stalin USSR a capacity for self-expression is displayed by intermediate political actors. Judy's study points out that elements of the political leadership actively encouraged members of the economics profession to come forward with policy-relevant research and proposals. Within certain fluctuating limits, writers, jurists, managers, party *apparatchiki*, military officers, state security officials, and members of other organizations have also been able to express themselves on matters of current policy. Yet it could hardly be inferred from this and other similar data that the basis of Soviet policy-formation is the conflict and collaboration of interest groups, however they might be defined. In the relatively highly centralized and authoritarian Soviet setting, a variety of environmental factors serves to reduce the importance of group relations even more than is the case with American politics. These include the structure of official institutions and controls; the capacity of political leaders and bureaucrats to shape the immediate situation in which "interest groups" operate; the influence of social structure and the existing power configuration on the nature and possibilities of group action; the impact of ideology and "political culture" in general on group behavior; the role of skill and nonrational elements in individual behavior; and the purely technical limitations on policy arising from bureaucratic procedure, existing legislation, established policies, and the available technology. In the light of these considerations, a theory of Soviet

---

Implications for Theory and Method," in Henry W. Ehrmann (ed.), *Interest Groups on Four Continents* (Pittsburgh, 1958), pp. 177-196; David G. Smith, "Pragmatism and the Group Theory of Politics," *American Political Science Review*, LVIII (1964), 600-610; Mancur Olson, Jr., *The Logic of Collective Action* (Cambridge, Mass., 1965); Stanislaw Ehrlich, Les 'groupes de pression' et la structure politique de la capitalisme," *Revue française de science politique*, XIII (1963), 25-43; Peter Bachrach, *The Theory of Democratic Elitism* (Boston, 1967), esp. Chap. 4; and Lowi, *op.cit.* For examples of Soviet commentary on interest and pressure groups (*zainteresovannye gruppy, gruppy davlenia*) see V. E. Guliyev, "Teoria 'pluralisticheskoi demokratii,'" in *Sovremennye burzhuaznye uchenia o kapitalisticheskom gosudarstve* (Moscow, 1967), pp. 59-88, and S. V. Bobotov, "Vlianie grupp davlenia na apparat vlasti burzhuaznovo gosudarstva," *Sovetskoye gosudarstvo i pravo*, No. 8 (1959), pp. 114-120.

politics which attributed primary importance to interest group activity would seem to this author to be inappropriate. Both on their own merits and in terms of their applicability to the Soviet experience, subsystem-dominant theories of group politics are of limited use in helping us to understand the overall process of policy-making in the contemporary Soviet Union.

Louis Hartz has warned that the attempt to apply the American group approach to European politics, where class and ideological forces are vital, may involve "defining the 'group' in all sorts of odd ways."[29] This seems to be an understatement of the problem where the USSR is concerned. Lacking the possibility either of an overarching group theory of politics or of applying analytic group concepts, we are left with the modest claim that interest group aggregates are an important but neglected element of the Soviet political process. And yet there are substantial difficulties in characterizing even the aggregate group and its role in the formation of policy. Accordingly, there is cause to consider setting interest group terminology aside and searching instead for an alternative method of analyzing intermediate participation. This takes us back to Arthur Bentley and his conceptions of the process of government.

Bentley on Tendency Conflict

Bentley made use of the mechanistic terminology of "groups" and "pressures," but the aim of *The Process of Government* was to reduce empirical political inquiry to the description of process.[30] Hostile to the reification typical of the legal-institutional mode of political analysis, and to prevailing notions of causality associated with the force of ideas and feelings, Bentley perceived the raw material of politics in the activities of interdependent men.

> It is first, last, and always activity, action, "something doing," the shunting by some men of other men's conduct along changed lines, the gathering of forces to overcome resistance to such alterations, or the dispersal of one grouping of forces by another grouping.[31]

[29] Louis Hartz, *The Liberal Tradition in America* (New York, 1955), p. 250.
[30] A debt should be acknowledged here to the work of Norman Jacobson, which influenced the formation of this paper. See Jacobson, "Causality and Time in Political Process: A Speculation," *American Political Science Review*, LVIII (1964), 15-22.
[31] Bentley, *op.cit.*, p. 176.

We have one great moving process to study, and of this great moving process it is impossible to state any part except as valued in terms of the other parts.[32]

Acting men could not be differentiated as concrete entities standing apart from the environment in which they performed, and from which ideas, feelings and behavior were derived. But Bentley did make a partial separation of groups or "differentiated bits of activity" on the part of "speaking-writing-indorsing people," and asserted that when the groups were adequately stated, everything was stated.[33] The group he regarded not as a thing in itself, but as "a certain portion of the men of society, taken, however, not as a physical mass cut off from other masses of men, but as a mass activity, which does not preclude the men who participate in it from likewise participating in many other group activities."[34] Government accordingly became the "actually performed legislating-administering-adjudicating activities of the nation and . . . the streams and currents of activity that gather among the people and rush into these spheres."[35] The subject of study was thus to be "the whole working process, regularities and tendencies and all."[36]

In discussing the differentiated bit of activity, Bentley added that there was no group without its interest. If an attempt were made to take the group without its interest, the result would be nothing at all: "The group is activity and activity is known only through its particular type, its value in terms of other activities, its tendency where it is not in the stage which gives manifest results."[37] Interest, for Bentley, was a "valued activity" of a mass of men who were following a definite course. It was to be defined by observation, and would seem to consist of the content or meaning of activity. On this basis, Bentley identified a host of "interest groups"—organization groups, discussion groups, opinion groups, belief groups, totem groups, and others. All of these, including government institutions (which he characterized as "relatively definite regions in the configuration of social activity")[38] were in a constant state of flux and open to interpretation in terms of subgroup and underlying group activity. This, briefly put, is the conception of the political process with which Truman seems to have begun, but with which he did not persist.

[32] *Ibid.*, p. 178.　　[33] *Ibid.*, pp. 182, 208.　　[34] *Ibid.*, p. 211.
[35] *Ibid.*, p. 180.　　[36] *Ibid.*, p. 168.　　[37] *Ibid.*, p. 213.
[38] *Ibid.*, p. 183.

In addition to these more-or-less manifest forms of group action, Bentley distinguished "certain forms which are not palpable or evident to the same extent," and which could be regarded as "tendencies of activity" in which social processes worked through individuals.[39] He cited the example of the directors' meeting of a business corporation, at which two policies affecting the industrial life of the country were competing for adoption. Here he saw the situation as one of "corporation activity streaming right through the directors toward realization on one line or another."[40]

> The two plans, the two tendencies of the two factions of the directors, reflecting two contacts with the surrounding world, two opportunities, fuse and break away and fuse again until the corporation activities move definitely forth on a positive, clear, visible line. But it is not the plans as abstractly stated, as idea, that thus conflict or coalesce. It is the active groups of men for whom the plans are but symbols or labels.
> The whole situation can be stated in such terms.[41]

Looking from the corporation to the broader social picture, Bentley regarded the notion of such tendencies as a start toward the study of "structural lines of activity of the whole society."[42] We would seem here to be presented with the notion of conflicting tendencies of activity with regard to the authoritative allocation of values for a society.

This account of Bentley's views suggests that the elements of at least two modes of analysis can be discerned in his work. According to the former, which may be regarded as subsystem-dominant, politics is a process of an enormous number of differentiated bits of activity going on with reference to all the issues of the social system at once; the pattern of activities in the performance of a single policy consists of only a somewhat smaller universe of interaction; the activity of the whole polity can only be stated in terms of a microscopic analysis of relations among the totality of its parts.[43] In the latter approach,

---

[39] *Ibid.*, pp. 184-186, 188.   [40] *Ibid.*, p. 190.   [41] *Ibid.*, p. 191.
[42] *Ibid.*

[43] Thus Bentley regards the nation as "made up of groups of men, each group cutting across many others, each individual man a component part of many groups. . . . the whole social life in all its phases can be stated in such groups of active men, indeed must be stated in that way if a useful analysis is to be had. Sometimes the groups, although not territorially distinct, gain a marked separation, so that two opposing parties may face each other with well closed ranks. Then again all is seemingly confusion, and the crossed lines of different groups seem too tangled to be followed." *Ibid.*, p. 204.

which is characterized by system-dominance, policy is seen as the product of conflicting tendencies of the activity *of the whole* with regard to specific issues: instead of a multitude of bits of activity, there is the interaction of a limited number of tendencies of the whole polity; the performance of the whole may be considered in terms of conflicting macro-political tendencies in the handling of individual policy problems.

In this original and highly indeterminate conception of political life, knowledge could at best be impressionistic. And yet it was Bentley's view that impressions of process could convey more about the real essence of politics than the artificial construction of a palpable reality which could be "explained" by the practitioners of a political science alienated from political life.[44] As was observed by Vincent Van Gogh, who like Bentley sought to break out of the narrative form and to capture activity itself in a spontaneous and moving interpretation of life, it was necessary to "exaggerate the essential, and, of set purpose, to leave the obvious vague."[45] Since Bentley, however, transactional analysis has failed to take the place of more conventional interpretations of policy-formation. The study of group politics has been characterized by the use of a reified conception of the group and a linear view of causation with which the analyst seeks to explain phenomena from which he is remains alienated. This state of affairs is to be attributed in part to the inherent difficulty of conceiving and applying transactional theories of policy-formation. It is also based on a reluctance to accept a mode of inquiry which would seem to have little explanatory potential and, therefore, little practical utility.[46] But ultimately it arises from an unwillingness to live with the "fantastic unstructuring of the situation"[47] which would follow from an acceptance of Bentleyan theory.

Of Bentley's two approaches to the political process mentioned above, the system-dominant or "tendency" analysis would seem to be more suited to the data afforded the investigator of Soviet politics. As we have seen in connection with Truman's analytic group, there is inadequate evidence to employ conceptions of patterned interaction at

---

[44] Jacobson, *op.cit.*   [45] *Ibid.*, p. 16.

[46] See also the commentary on the conservative bias of Bentleyan theory in Myron Q. Hale, "The Cosmology of Arthur F. Bentley," *American Political Science Review*, LIV (1960), 955-961.

[47] The phrase is Joseph LaPalombara's, in Eckstein and Apter (eds.), *op.cit.*, p. 422.

354

the subsystem level. In any case, the prospect of examining all component subsystems and subsystem interactions in order to state the working of the whole is too forbidding. Unfortunately, however, while Bentley goes into analytic group discourse at length, there are only occasional remarks about tendencies which stream through the whole. In particular, the nature of a "tendency of activity" is not elaborated upon, nor are we given any indication of how one tendency prevails over another in the policy process. The latter question, and explanation generally, did not greatly interest Bentley. But insofar as the acquisition of a capacity for political control is an objective of political research, some form of causation must be retained. If we are to follow Bentley in an effort to escape the consideration of reified entities and their role in policy-making episodes, it is nevertheless desirable to be able to correlate situational variables with political transactions and thereby obtain some ability to explain and predict outcomes.

If the arguments advanced here prove valid, the problem in investigating what appears to be interest group activity in the Soviet Union turns out after all not to be one of transposing a method derived from the experience of the United States and of other Western societies. Instead, we are better advised to start virtually from the beginning and follow Bentley's lead in developing a method of tendency analysis applicable to the study of intermediate participation in the Soviet context.

In so doing, we should be aware that there is a related Soviet interpretation of Soviet political life. This is the set of views according to which Soviet social development is understood in terms of nonantagonistic contradictions manifested in the conflict of tendencies. As Ts. A. Stepanyan puts it, "We see with our own eyes that the nonantagonistic contradictions of socialist society increasingly take the form not of social opposites, but of substantive differences which express the struggle and clash of different sides and tendencies in all areas and spheres of social development."[48] Or, to quote P. N. Fedoseyev: "Nonantagonistic contradictions in socialist society are thus highly variegated and dissimilar in character and in the sharpness with which they appear. They are manifested in the sphere of economics,

[48] Ts. A. Stepanyan, "Raskrytiye i preodoleniye protivorechy—obshchaya zakonomernost stanovlenia i razvitia kommunisticheskoi formatsii," in F. V. Konstantinov (ed.), *Dialektika sovremennovo obshchestvennovo razvitia* (Moscow, 1966), p. 126.

in the area of social relations, and in ideological life. In each of these areas the range of contradictions and of the forms of their manifestation is extremely wide."[49] The question of nonantagonistic contradictions in socialist formations remains subject to the restrictions of political debate in the USSR. Nevertheless, some observations may be made to clarify further the possible implications of a tendency analysis of Soviet policy-making.

The term "nonantagonistic contradiction" evidently came into use during the period of the Lenin succession. Lenin is said to have initially raised the question in practical form in his comments on Bukharin's *Economics of the Transition Period*, when he noted that antagonism and contradiction were not identical conceptions, and that the former was to disappear while the latter would remain under socialism.[50] Subsequently the concept was elaborated in dealing with the contradictions between proletariat and peasantry: antagonistic contradictions were those involving vital questions, as between the proletariat and the "kulaks"; nonantagonistic contradictions were those involving current problems where a community of interest was present on vital issues, as within the worker-peasant "*bond*."[51] By 1940, however, the notion seems to have been dropped from the Marxist-Leninist analytical repertoire, and the emphasis was placed increasingly on the "moral-political unity of socialist society." Following Stalin's death, the term regained currency, although Stepanyan informs us that only with great difficulty did he have a discussion article on the subject published in *Voprosy filosofii* in 1955.[52] Since then a debate has developed on the presence, nature, and role of nonantagonistic contradictions in Soviet life, with some dialecticians seeking to expand the usage of the term in opposition to others who prefer to restrict its use and to stress the "moral-political unity" theme.

A good deal of the literature on nonantagonistic contradictions in the USSR is concerned with the struggle between the "new" and the "old." G. E. Glezerman argues that "only through the struggle between these opposed forces and tendencies, through the predominance of the new over the old, is the movement of socialist society to communism

---

[49] P. N. Fedoseyev, *ibid.*, p. 92.

[50] See S. R. Dudel, "O vnutrennikh antagonisticheskikh i neantagonisticheskikh protivorechiakh," *Voprosy filosofii*, No. 2 (1953), p. 57.

[51] See M. M. Rozental, "Materialisticheskaya dialektika kak tvorcheski razvivayushchaya nauka," *ibid.*, No. 4 (1953), pp. 30-31.

[52] Stepanyan, in Konstantinov (ed.), *op.cit.*, p. 122.

possible."[53] A similar general assessment is made by V. P. Chertkov, who goes so far as to say that in socialist society "advanced and reactionary ideas are the reflection of advanced and reactionary tendencies which exist in life itself, the reflection of the struggle of opposites which is the source of development."[54] Chertkov argues that there is no "conservative" force in Soviet society, and that the bearers of the old are to be regarded as "separate elements from all classes and social strata" but never as a "compact social group."[55] As for the role of the political leadership, it presumably reflects the base and is not simply a bearer of the "new," particularly where the question of political participation is concerned. Fedoseyev urges that, "the art of leadership lies neither in ignoring contradictions nor in negating the possibility of uniting opposites, but in the ability to take timely note of contradictions, to find forms and methods of combining and overcoming opposing sides and tendencies if they are not antagonistic in character. . . ."[56] The extent to which the Soviet leadership permits or suppresses ("takes note" or "ignores") the expression of nonantagonistic contradictions is the question of whether policy on "within-system" issues is to be the product of interaction in the corporation boardroom, to paraphrase Alfred Meyer[57] and Bentley, or of more widespread but controlled participation in the tendency conflict through which values are allocated for Soviet society.

So far as empirical references to tendency conflict in Soviet politics are concerned, the Soviet literature proves virtually barren. It has little or nothing to tell us either about what constitutes a tendency or how tendency conflict proceeds. The effort to construct a tendency analysis must accordingly begin without the benefit of any direct assistance from either Bentley or Soviet commentators. Though the remarks that follow are necessarily somewhat rudimentary, with further research and generalization it may be possible to offer a coherent tendency analysis of Soviet policy-making and of the role of intermediate participants therein.

[53] G. E. Glezerman, "Moralno-politicheskoye yedinstvo sotsialisticheskovo obshchestva i stiraniye granei mezhdu klassami," *Kommunist*, No. 15 (1956), p. 40.

[54] V. P. Chertkov, *Neantagonisticheskiye protivorechia pri sotsializme* (Moscow, 1958), pp. 214-215.

[55] *Ibid.*, pp. 57-59.

[56] Fedoseyev, in Konstantinov (ed.), *op.cit.*, p. 96.

[57] Alfred G. Meyer, in *The Soviet Political System* (New York, 1965), p. 113, likens the party leadership to the board of directors of an industrial corporation.

Tendencies of Intermediate Articulation

To begin with, the concepts of "system-dominance" and the "intermediate actor" should be examined more closely. The notion of system-dominance implies that despite the appearance of autonomy on the part of actors within the system, their activities are to be regarded as subordinate to the interaction of the whole. The assumptions of subsystem-dominance imply that policies are made through the behavior of subsystem actors, and that the latter are essentially free to influence the outcomes of the whole. System-dominance, however, suggests that subsystem actors must continually conform to the situations with which they are faced, and differentiations in subsystem activity must conform to differentiations in the activity of the system as a whole. The question then becomes one of identifying significant uniform differentiations in the activity of the whole. It is proposed that these differentiations be seen as conflicting tendencies in the total mass of communications through which values are allocated, or policies are made and implemented, for Soviet society. Thus, the articulations of political participants will ultimately be influential only to the extent that they form part of existing tendencies or lead to the setting up of possible alternate directions of value allocation for the whole. At the subsystem level the presence of a tendency would be indicated by a pattern of articulation associated with a loose coalition of actors operating at different levels of the political structure, whose articulations tend in the same direction but who are unlikely to be fully aware of the common thrust and consequences of their activity. Additional characteristics of tendencies and tendency conflict as manifestations of system-dominance will be considered below.

With regard to the term "intermediate actor," it may be noted that William Kornhauser has referred to "intermediate groups" in considering the collectivities that lie between the political elite and the non-elite,[58] and David Truman has stressed the importance of the "intervening structure of elites" for American political life.[59] Although it is still a matter of dispute, Soviet analysts also refer to the "intermediate strata" in capitalist formations, but deny that the intelligentsia, for

[58] William Kornhauser, *The Politics of Mass Society* (Glencoe, 1959).
[59] David B. Truman, "The American System in Crisis," *Political Science Quarterly*, LXXIV (1959), 481-497.

instance, forms an intermediate stratum in the USSR.[60] Karl Deutsch distinguishes between the elite, the passive or underlying population, and the "politically relevant strata."[61] But where the latter includes the entire mass of the politically mobilized population, the term "intermediate actor" will be employed here in a somewhat narrower sense to mean the politically active members of both formal organizations and informal groups who are not members of the political elite for a specific issue of all-union politics.

A more precise definition does not appear possible, especially in view of the fact that the Soviet political elite, like any other,[62] is not fixed in composition, but varies in membership from issue to issue. For some issues Marshal Grechko is clearly a member; for others where his concern or influence is relatively marginal, his capacity to affect outcomes may be equivalent to that of the intermediate actor; and for still others he may have no effect whatsoever. Conversely, it is possible that in dealing with some problems, a lower-echelon secretariat official, a military officer, a jurist, or an economist may be so closely involved in the making of an authoritative allocation as to become virtually indistinguishable from the relevant members of the political elite.[63] Normally, however, we may expect their participation to be less direct and more concerned with the formation and mobilization of support for alternatives in the phases that precede and follow the taking of official decisions. In speaking of intermediate actors in all-union politics, then, reference will be made to party and state officials and professional personnel who do not occupy leading positions in the Central Committee secretariat or the Council of Ministers, and who are neither passive members of formal organizations nor relatively unaffiliated members of the population at large.

Proceeding from the fact that in research on Soviet data sets of

[60] On "intermediate strata" in the West, see V. A. Cheprakov, *Gosudarstvenno-monopolisticheskii kapitalizm* (Moscow, 1964), pp. 334-343. As regards the absence of intermediate strata in the USSR, see, for example, *Stroitelstvo kommunizma i razvitiye obshchestvennykh otnosheny* (Moscow, 1966), p. 161.

[61] Karl W. Deutsch, *The Nerves of Government* (New York, 1963), p. 40.

[62] Cf. Aaron Wildavsky, "The Analysis of Issue-Contexts in the Study of Decision-Making," *Journal of Politics*, xxiv (1962), 730.

[63] For example, it has been reported that following upon severe competition among various Soviet cities and regions to secure the location of the Fiat auto works, the Chairman of the Council of Ministers requested and then acted directly on a recommendation for location from the staff of the Central Mathematical Economics Institute of the Academy of Sciences.

conflicting articulations are observed on problems of current policy, some remarks should be made about articulation in the Soviet context. A political articulation may be regarded as an act of communication in which an expectation about the authoritative allocation of a value or set of values is conveyed by one political participant to another. For articulation to occur, the expectation transmitted must also be received in some form. Without reception there is, as indicated earlier, no political communication, and no political significance save for the individual or individuals seeking unsuccessfully to influence the expectations of others about policy. It must be acknowledged at once that after recoiling from the notion of an analytic interest group partly on the grounds that the requisite interaction is difficult to demonstrate in the Soviet setting, interaction has been reintroduced in the concept of articulation. But while articulation in Soviet conditions can for the most part only be assumed to take place, the study of articulation and articulation patterns from a macro-political perspective raises more modest expectations of proof of interaction than does the attempt to consider it in relatively small groups of men which are to be related to other groups and ultimately to outputs. Moreover, as has already been asked, what is the alternative to a minimal assumption of interaction in Soviet politics? Let us therefore assume in principle the presence of interaction and of articulation and see what can be learned from such data as are available to us.

If we examine the articulations which are made at all levels—political elite, intermediate, and popular—differentiated patterns of activity are observed with respect to specific public policies. Although the number of individuals transmitting a common expectation of public policy will vary from issue to issue, we may regard a mass of common articulations which persists over time as a tendency of articulation. In the articulations that concern a given issue, a variety of tendencies is likely to be displayed. In some cases these may remain confined to specific articulations by subordinate actors within the system, whether individuals, groups, or weak coalitions. Given the condition of system-dominance in Soviet society, however, it is to be assumed that certain dominant tendencies of articulation will emerge from the total system of interaction and form effective alternate directions of policy. On the basis of the available evidence, then, the investigator will have to make a judgment as to which patterns of articulation represent effective variants of policy on the issue in question. The Soviet policy-making

360

process is thus to be regarded as one in which interaction among participants at different levels of the political structure generates a conflict of dominant tendencies of articulation, through which alternate lines of policy are identified, authoritatively decided, and implemented with regard to specific values. To state this in another way, policy on a given issue is likely to be internally contradictory and may be understood as the interaction among conflicting tendencies of articulation prior to, during, and after the taking of official decisions; similarly, fluctuations in value allocation or in the policy "line" may be seen as shifts in the relative influence of conflicting tendencies.

To offer some illustrations, in examining the Soviet approach to nationality policy, Grey Hodnett observes what are in effect conflicting patterns of articulation as expressed by important political figures, semi-official commentators, and specialized analysts at the all-union level.[64] These tendencies of articulation are directed alternatively toward the flourishing, *rapprochement*, or fusion of the Soviet nations. To this picture, similar tendencies of articulation could be added from observation of statements by individuals at various levels within the union republics, down to the men in the street, whose views may to some extent be sampled by the traveler. It can be hypothesized that these three conflicting tendencies, and perhaps others not yet identified, are outward manifestations of the dominant alternatives of the political system with regard to the nationality question, and that the policy of the regime on this issue consists of an interaction of tendencies in which a shifting consensus is produced as now one and then another tendency prevails.[65] Or to take another instance, recent policy on disarmament and limited arms agreements with capitalist countries is characterized by the conflict of three principal tendencies reaching from the top political leadership through the expert analysts to the articulations of the general populace.[66] Again, the activity of the regime would seem to reflect a

[64] Hodnett, *op.cit.*,

[65] Nationality policy is one area in which it is officially acknowledged that conflicting tendencies are at work. For example see Khrushchev's report to the Twenty-second Party Congress, *Pravda*, November 1, 1961, and also A. M. Yegiazaryan, *Ob osnovnykh tendentsiakh razvitia sotsialisticheskikh natsii SSSR* (Erevan, 1965), and P. M. Rogachev and M. A. Sverdilin, "O preobladayushchei tendentsii razvitia sovetskoi obshchnosti," *Voprosy filosofii*, No. 2 (1969), pp. 26-31, for differing views of tendency conflict over the nationality issue.

[66] Griffiths, *op.cit.*, pp. 603-617. Similarly, Marshall Shulman treats the contrasting "syndromes" in Soviet foreign policy in 1949-1953 as tendencies. "What the analyst seeks to do but not overdo," he states, "is to identify the dominant tendency at any one time and the shifts in policy emphasis which make for a

361

moving consensus, as the relative influence of specific tendencies rises and falls in response to changing domestic and external circumstances. To offer yet another example, in a consideration of the issue of legal reform, Harold Berman has pointed to six tendencies in partial conflict.[67] Similar patterns of conflicting articulation could no doubt be observed, if other issues of the Soviet polity were systematically studied. In each case the value-allocating activity of the political system would seem to consist of a process of selection from a number of future directions or expectations of policy which are more-or-less clearly expressed in conflicting tendencies of articulation.

The question may be posed as to why uniformities of individual behavior expressed as tendencies of articulation should arise. Why is there not simply a chaos of individual articulations, or, on the other hand, 22 as opposed to only a few opposed tendencies? The answer would seem to lie partly in the structure of the environment in which the individual is embedded, and in reference to which he assesses the consequences of a given allocation. Aaron Wildavsky, in discussing issue-contexts or situations in which issues arise and provoke structured responses, observes that some situations "exert a severe dichotomizing effect in which opinion is polarized into two opposing groups," while in others not all the participants choose sides, and in still others the participants are fragmented into numerous groups taking a variety of positions.[68] Erving Goffman, however, suggests that interaction usually takes the form of two-team play, or is resolvable into this form.[69] But neither author is able to cast much light on the formation of opposing sides and tendencies. Similarly, James Rosenau, in discussing "issue-areas," acknowledges that it has yet to be shown how "value clusters in a given area evoke distinctive motives, actions, and interactions on the part of the affected actors."[70] The question of why sets of conflicting tendencies arise in the allocation of values could be discussed in terms of how expectations are aggregated and "issues" are generated. More

---

recurrent pattern in Soviet behavior." *Stalin's Foreign Policy Reappraised* (Cambridge, Mass., 1963), p. 6.

[67] Harold J. Berman, "Legality vs. Terror: The Post-Stalin Law Reforms," in Gwendolyn M. Carter and Alan F. Westin (eds.), *Politics in Europe* (New York, 1965), esp. pp. 184-203.

[68] Wildavsky, *op.cit.*, p. 720.

[69] Erving Goffman, *The Presentation of Self in Everyday Life* (Garden City, 1959), pp. 91-92. Also cited in Ramsoy, *op.cit.*, p. 71.

[70] James N. Rosenau, "Pre-Theories and Theories of Foreign Policy," in R. Barry Farrell (ed.), *op.cit.*, p. 85.

closely, consideration could be given to the perceived self-interest of the participants, the impact of social class, professional, and other reference groups on behavior, the role of political-cultural and institutional factors, and also the requirements of role performance. In this it would have to be determined how such environmental regularities serve to order the relations of men so that their interactions serve as channels for the flow of alternate tendencies of the system as a whole.

The extent of participation in the articulation of a given tendency will, of course, vary from issue to issue. In the resolution of policy problems connected with agriculture, food prices, housing, education, or trade-union benefits, for instance, the activities and anticipated reactions of lower participants may be involved in tendency articulation. On other issues, such as military strategy or science policy, the tendencies through which values are allocated may reflect the activity of actors at the intermediate and political elite levels principally. In other areas, such as policy on economic reform or social mobilization and control in the immediate post-Stalin era, innovating elements of the leadership may have read the conflicting articulations from lower levels in the absence of significant participation by individuals at the intermediate level, in view of the relative absence of empirical economists and sociologists at that time. Similarly, articulations by intermediate actors and elements of the general population may find only weak response from the top level, as seems to be the case with tendencies favoring expanded artistic freedom or substantially greater investment in housing construction. Finally, in still other areas, such as the management of foreign policy crises or the appointment and removal of important officials, the articulation of conflicting tendencies of policy will largely be confined to members of the political elite. In each case, then, the extent of articulation of a given tendency will have to be determined separately on the basis of the evidence.

Turning from the articulation of tendencies, we must now consider the information communicated by them. This information may be reduced to an expectation about the authoritative allocation of a value. Three elements may be identified in the content of a political expectation.[71] The first is a value or goal—military security, flourishing of the

---

[71] See Robert A. Levine, *The Arms Debate* (Cambridge, Mass., 1963). Levine's discussion of schools of thought in the American debate on arms policy is conducted in terms of the values, analyses, and recommendations of each school. This approach is broadly similar to David Easton's interpretation of the elements

Soviet nations, *partiinost* in the arts—which may in turn be instrumental for the achievement of other ends.[72] The second is an analysis of the situation in which the individual or organization is to pursue the given value, as for example the interpretations of the latest aggressive acts of "imperialism" which accompany public discussion of military security by representatives of the armed forces, or the particular consideration of the laws of development of nations made by those who favor a multinational Soviet state. Finally, a political expectation is characterized by a recommendation or demand stating how the given value should be allocated in the given situation—for instance, strengthen Soviet defense, further develop the statehood and culture of the people of the USSR, intensify the presentation of socialist realist themes in art—in the implementation as well as formulation of decisions.

The forms in which an expectation is articulated may, of course, be varied in practice—ranging from eloquent silence or physical gestures to a full presentation of value, analysis, and recommendation. In view of the fact that an articulation involves the reception as well as the transmission of signals, the content of the expectation as received may also be quite distinct from that which was subjectively intended, insofar as we are concerned with intentional communication. Given the problems of data, however, research must be confined largely to expectations as transmitted. We cannot, however, read articulations literally as statements of subjective expectation, owing to the esoteric language of politics in the USSR and to the obvious fact that people will often say one thing in order to achieve another. A tendency of articulation is, therefore, to be conceived of in terms of the apparent essential expectations of political actors, and not simply in terms of the overt meaning of individual articulations that is not subjected to contextual analysis by the investigator.

At the same time, it is necessary to bear in mind that there may be a logical interconnection among expectations that ostensibly concern entirely separate issues. It is also true to say that articulations may have unintended consequences that extend beyond the allocation of the

---

of a "reformative political theory." David Easton, *The Political System* (New York, 1953), pp. 83ff.

[72] The problem of distinguishing between ultimate and instrumental values is discussed in Vernon Van Dyke, "Values and Interests," *American Political Science Review*, LVI (1962), 567-576. The investigator must himself cut into the ends-means regression that may arise, identifying ultimate and instrumental values in accordance with analytical requirements.

explicit value in question. It would be a narrow view of Soviet policy-making on agricultural questions, for example, if it were based on research into articulations that referred to agricultural affairs alone. Depending on the situation, the resolution of agricultural issues may be related to politics on issues such as level of support for heavy industry and defense, party organization, economic reform, arms limitation agreements, and others. There may be a mutual dependence of the politics of different issues, whether or not this is perceived or acted upon by Soviet political actors, and whether or not individual participants are consistently "progressive" or "conservative" in their expectations from issue to issue. The point to be made here is that the allocation of a specific value may well be affected not only by tendency conflict in the articulation of expectations explicitly concerned with a given issue, but also by seemingly unrelated masses of articulation on other issues. Accordingly it may be useful to distinguish between "pure" and "syncretic" tendencies of articulation. The former may be regarded as consisting of masses of articulations in which expectations explicitly concerned with the allocation of a given value are conveyed from one participant to another. The syncretic tendency, on the other hand, may entail massive political processes in which a pure tendency is surrounded by streams of apparently unrelated communication which ultimately reinforce explicit expectations.

It may further be hypothesized that the political actors articulating a given tendency will differ in the extent to which they express one or another element of an expectation. Ultimate values—diffuse expectations such as well-being, justice, equality, security—may be articulated most effectively by the mass of citizens in interaction with intermediate actors and the political elite. Analyses of specific situations in terms of ways to achieve instrumental and ultimate values may be carried out principally by nongovernmental and governmental personnel occupying intermediate positions in the political structure.[73] Increasingly, however, intermediate actors appear to be able to make recommendations over and above situational analyses, particularly where expert performance is involved. Finally, instrumental values and effective recommendations

---

[73] It may be noted that in a formal discussion setting, debate among intermediate participants is on occasion concerned not with alternate public policies, but with competing definitions of the situation in which policy is being carried out. Hodnett has pointed to this peculiar feature, *loc.cit.* It is also a characteristic of the 1929-1930 debate at Moscow State University among international lawyers. See *O burzhuaznykh vlianiakh v sovetskoi mezhdunarodno-pravovoi literature* (Moscow, 1930).

to realize both instrumental and ultimate values in given situations are articulated mainly by members of the political elite, especially in the process of taking decisions. Insofar as we are concerned with the role played by intermediate actors in tendency conflict, it would seem to lie chiefly in defining the situation in which values are to be allocated, and in making recommendations which deal only with particular situations.

In political analysis, and especially in the study of Soviet politics, there is a preference for the consideration of power and its exercise by those in authority. It is appreciated but not greatly taken into account that the political decision-maker is generally constrained by the situation in which he finds himself. Not only may he be required to secure the compliance of peers and lesser participants, but he is often called upon to resolve technical problems that try the best of minds. He has, in effect, to deal with both "nonlogical" and "logical" dimensions of the policy situation, which are defined for him primarily by the communicated expectations of other actors. Leaving aside the expectations of other decision-makers and of the mass of the population, we may regard his behavior as being subject to special forms of influence as a result of the articulations of intermediate actors.

Here a distinction may be made between the persuasive and technical aspects of Soviet intermediate articulation, although in practice they may be closely interdependent. Thus, by virtue of the perceived importance of its function and morale, the skill of its leaders, and other factors, the communications issuing from an aggregate such as the military establishment, the KGB, the literary community, or the industrial managers may possess a degree of persuasiveness quite independent of their logical content. In addition, a varying capacity for technical analysis of policy issues (which may not be shared by the decision-maker, who is in any case operating under the pressure of business), gives the intermediate actor further opportunities to shape the situation in which the decision-maker must act. This is particularly true of governmental groupings whose members not only possess technical expertise but also perform important administrative functions.

There may be an implication in the foregoing remarks that the articulation of a tendency represents a "bubbling up" toward the decision-makers of progressively more operational expectations, in a manner analogous to the articulation and aggregation of interests suggested by functional analysis.[74] However, it should be pointed out that the com-

[74] See Gabriel A. Almond, "A Functional Approach to Comparative Politics,"

munication among those articulating a given tendency is better regarded as a two-way transaction. The fate of the 1957 decision to dismantle the central ministerial apparatus and establish a series of regional economic councils is perhaps a case in point. Those at the pinnacle who favored a return to some form of central ministerial pattern no doubt drew support from intermediate and local articulations which assessed the existing situation unfavorably and offered arguments for recentralization. A. M. Rumyantsev notes that several years before the 1965 reorganization, discussions began among scientific and practical workers, "sharp debates" arose in the press, and a stream of letters flowed into newspaper offices.[75] These various articulations doubtless bubbled up to the leadership level as well; ultimately they were collated, analyzed, and incorporated into the proposals submitted at the September plenum and presumably to the leadership before that. On the other hand, the making of these local and intermediate articulations required the signaling of a favorable disposition from the upper levels, if lower participants were to express themselves and be heard. The varied recentralizing measures taken after 1957 presumably reflected such a responsiveness at the top; ultimately, Rumyantsev tells us, the discussion of the economic administration was officially sponsored by party organizations. The implication is that individuals and groups engaged in the articulation of a given tendency are likely to be in a state of mutual dependence as expectations of policy are coordinated.[76]

We are thus presented with pure and syncretic tendencies of articulation which vary both in the range of participation and in the manner in which expectations are expressed at different levels of the political structure. As for the way in which one tendency prevails over another in the process of value allocation, it would seem to be dependent upon changes in the expectations of participants. When looked at closely, the content of a given tendency may be seen to consist of values, analyses, and recommendations having more, or less, in common with those expressed in the opposed tendencies. Under the pressure of events,

---

in Gabriel A. Almond and James S. Coleman (eds.), *The Politics of the Developing Areas* (Princeton, 1960), pp. 3-64, and Gabriel A. Almond and G. Bingham Powell, *Comparative Politics: A Developmental Approach* (Boston and Toronto, 1966).

[75] A. M. Rumyantsev, "Predvidimoye zavtra," *Yunost*, No. 1 (1966), pp. 65-70.

[76] See A. Belyakov and I. Shvets on the need for upward flow of information in party organs, "Partiinaya informatsia," *Partiinaya zhizn*, No. 8 (1967), pp. 27-34.

FRANKLYN GRIFFITHS

actors may reorient their activity from one tendency to another, as analyses, recommendations, and possibly value preferences alter.

The process through which these reorientations take place may be akin to bargaining. As Hough demonstrates, explicit bargaining or coordination of expectations takes place between participants at the regional level. Here the exchange of articulations presumably modifies perceptions and recommendations, if not value preferences.[77] Conceivably this coordination may occasionally include logrolling or pragmatic bargaining across different issue-contexts, as demands in one setting are modified in return for altered articulation in another, thereby preserving the appearance of unanimity which party controls and the Soviet political culture urge upon participants. In addition, informal coordination of the type of "tacit bargaining"[78] may also occur. In this case, the expectations of actors who publicly articulate opposing tendencies on a given issue may be coordinated by a mode of communication in which signals are read and taken into account in the determination of behavior by individuals who are either unwilling or unable to bargain openly. This process may occur with particular frequency in the Soviet setting, where the structure of party controls and ideological considerations militate against strenuous public bargaining. In such ways streams of communicated expectations could be aggregated and disaggregated under the stimulation of events.[79]

In analyzing the complex process of Soviet policy-making, the extent to which individuals and the reference groups they represent are free to influence outcomes within the framework of institutionalized controls has to be weighed against the continual necessity to conform to the requirements of policy-making situations. If the overall consequence of these individual adjustments is the establishment of uniformities or tendencies in the total pattern of articulation on a given issue, a key

[77] For a further indication as to how these modifications might be expected to occur, see the discussion of "reciprocal field control" in Robert A. Dahl and Charles E. Lindblom, *Politics, Economics, Welfare* (New York, 1953).

[78] See Thomas C. Schelling, *The Strategy of Conflict* (Cambridge, Mass., 1960) for the conception of tacit bargaining, which to date has been restricted in its application to problems of inter-state bargaining.

[79] To make another reference to this kind of phenomenon, but from a wholly different context, Henry Cabot Lodge, Jr., has observed that in United Nations bargaining, "Just when the free nations begin to drift apart, which they have a natural tendency to do, being free, a Soviet speaker will say something that is so monstrous and so senseless that you can see the free world getting together right in front of your own eyes." Cited in Robert E. Riggs, *Politics in the United Nations* (Urbana, 1958), p. 41.

operation for research is to characterize the setting which gives rise to these structured responses.

In seeking to explain the emergence and outcome of tendency conflict, we might first be concerned with the collection of data on the variables that account for the propensity of diverse actors to articulate a similar approach to a given policy. These would include organizational affiliation, occupation, role, age, career, ideological orientation, self-interest, and responsiveness to authority. Attention could then be given to the institutional and political-cultural dimensions of the setting as they affect orientations to political action. What, it might be asked, is the institutional framework within which actors are bound to operate? What limitations are imposed by the character of their access to "influentials"? What bearing does ideology and its enforcement have on the nature of articulations concerning a given issue? Next, participants might be related to political resources. A central factor here would be the capacity and willingness of the leadership to mobilize bias and otherwise prevent the emergence of some issues,[80] and to articulate the expectations of different sectors of the party and society on other questions. Additional resources, available to intermediate actors, include professional expertise and operational control of organizations, including media of communication. By examining such factors, which might equally be used to characterize the formation and attributes of Soviet interest groups, it may be possible to offer explanations for the propensity to make a common articulation and for the distribution of potential influence among political actors with regard to specific issues.

Having considered possible sources of observed regularities of articulation by actors from different levels of the political structure, the problem would be to explain the outcome of a given policy-making episode. This would entail an examination of both subsystem-dominant and system-dominant variables as they affected the course of tendency conflict. At the subsystem level, we would be primarily concerned with the skill and effectiveness with which actors consciously utilize political resources to influence the expectations of "fellow travelers," the potentially interested, and those who are opposed. Interaction at the leadership level is obviously an overriding consideration here. Though we possess little direct information on the struggle over power and policy as it affects the leadership's handling of specific issues, it may be suggested that in-

[80] Cf. Peter Bachrach and Morton S. Baratz on "nondecision-making," in their "Two Faces of Power," *American Political Science Review*, LVI (1962), 951.

termediate articulations offer an indication of the policy content of conflict at the top level, and that they are in some cases stimulated by
leaders' efforts to elicit intermediate and mass articulations in the form
of favorable argument and diffuse political support.[81] At the same time,
within the framework of permissible discourse, intermediate actors will,
in accordance with their capabilities, use expert argument, organizational resources, and appeals to wider publics in order to influence one
another's expectations and those of the leadership as well. In most
cases, shifts in articulation from one policy alternative to another will
be predominantly the result of events at the leadership level, to which
lesser actors adjust with varying degrees of precision. In others, particularly where a divided leadership and complex issues are involved, differentiated intermediate articulations will be of special importance in defining the context in which leadership decisions are taken and then
implemented. With such considerations in mind, it may be possible to
offer explanations for shifts of support from one tendency or alternate
line of policy to another as the result of the formation of a "winning
coalition."

Intentional political behavior, however, accounts for only part of the
total volume of communications through which selections are made from
alternate possible directions of value allocation. Actors, even at the
leadership level, are likely to be engaged in, and fully apprehend, only
a limited phase of the total process through which an issue is resolved.
Nor are they likely to be fully aware of the consequences of their actions for actors operating at other levels of the political structure or in
other policy-making situations.[82] Each actor in each policy-making

[81] Cf. Hodnett, *op.cit.*, and Merle Fainsod, *How Russia Is Ruled* (rev. ed., Cambridge, Mass., 1964), pp. 387, 418, 591.

[82] It is also likely that actors will be playing in a number of different policy
games simultaneously, with the result that moves in one game may have reper-
cussions on behavior in other games, which would be decided quite differently if
they were played in isolation. At the leadership level, for example, we need only
refer to the variety of games in which Khrushchev was involved late in 1962—
party reorganization, recentralization of the economy, development of the
chemical industry, arms control negotiations with the United States, the conflict with China, imposition of new controls on writers and artists, enunciation
of the Liberman reforms—to perceive the possibility of tendency shifts being
affected by multiple-game participation. A similar condition presumably holds
for lesser actors who, even if they are not engaged in the resolution of distinctly
varied policy issues, may be playing in bureaucratic and other games as well as
expressing opinions on specific public policies. Interest group theory treats this
problem in terms of "overlapping group memberships." From the standpoint of
a tendency analysis, it is to be assumed that there are uniformities in the consequences of multiple-game activity: a "pure" tendency on a given issue is ac-

situation will be faced with conflicting patterns of articulation which are not of his own making and to which he must to some degree conform, as well as seek to alter. These disparate but related situations may be assimilated into the total political situation over which no single actor or set of actors has total control; similarly, discrete occurrences of pure and syncretic tendency conflict can be assimilated into dominant tendencies of the whole system to which individual articulations must be accommodated. Shifts in the relative influence of such macro-political tendencies may be explained by reference to events in the material, social, and technological environments in which the political system is embedded. For example, in seeking to account for variation in the relative influence of antagonistic and conciliatory tendencies in Soviet conduct toward the United States between the building of the Berlin wall in 1961 and the signing of the test ban treaty in 1963, attention would be given to changes in the international environment, the state of military technology and the strategic military balance, the industrial economy, agriculture, and other factors which favored the dominance of more conciliatory tendencies in official policy.

A tendency analysis of Soviet policy-making would thus proceed in four stages. The investigator would initially determine the presence of uniformities in the articulations of participants in a given episode and characterize the differences between policy at the outset and conclusion. He would then consider such underlying variables that might help to explain the observed propensities of given actors to articulate common or converging expectations of policy, and also their potential influence. The third stage would concern subsystem interaction and its effects on the relative influence of alternate lines of policy. Finally, situational variables would be adduced to explain the course of tendency conflict in the system considered as a whole.

So far as intermediate articulations as such are concerned, it should be apparent that to consider them in isolation would be to wrench specific sets of interactions from the far more extensive processes of which they are part. And yet the empirical data available to us are richest for intermediate articulations. Moreover, by examining intermediate tendencies of articulation on given issues, and bearing in mind their relation to political activities at the social base and leadership levels, we may

---

companied by a mass of seemingly unrelated but supporting articulations of which actors are largely unaware and which serve to determine their behavior.

hope to learn something not only about the process of policy-making, but also about the adaptive and integrative capabilities of the Soviet system. Insight into adaptation may be expected to follow from the fact that intermediate actors play an important role in interpreting developments in the environment, and thus in defining the situation in which policies are made. In the case of integration, intermediate actors are of particular significance in mediating the relationship between state and society. In examining the policy-making activities of intermediate participants in the Soviet Union, therefore, we stand to gain from an orientation that emphasizes issues rather than groups, the process of tendency conflict on these issues rather than the conflict of structures invested with purposes and power of their own.

Concluding Remarks

Where tendency conflict on issues accepted as legitimate in the Stalin era seems to have been largely confined to members of the political elite, in the post-Stalin USSR, it may be suggested, tendency conflict has come to reach more deeply into the political structure. A vertical decentralization of policy-making can be discerned, in which increasing numbers of intermediate participants are engaged in the governmental process. Policy continues to be made in a highly organized context, but informal participation by members of the intermediate structure is serving increasingly to shape the situation in which the political elite acts. Where for centuries a "dual Russia" prevailed in which state and society were alienated, intermediate elements have now emerged in substantial numbers.[83] The fact that the growing intermediate participation is characterized by basic acceptance of the political order, if not all details of its constitution, suggests a trend in the development of the Soviet system to bridge the age-old gap between state and society. At the same time, there are indications of an opposing trend, exemplified in the unwillingness of some participants to permit the analysis, much less the free play, of "nonantagonistic contradictions" in Soviet society.

[83] Robert C. Tucker, *The Soviet Political Mind* (New York, 1963), pp. 69-90, and Henry L. Roberts, "The Passing of Power: Reflections on the Fall of Khrushchev," *Columbia University Forum*, VIII (1965), 15-19. Professor Roberts points out that the intermediate articulation of Russian society had begun in the nineteenth century, only to be set back during the first decades of the Soviet regime. He suggests that the development of the intermediate structure has been resumed in the post-war era. On this point and others that follow below, see also Schwartz and Keech, *op.cit.*

It can be argued that two principal tendencies exist on the question of political participation in the Soviet Union, and that we are not presented only with a widening of the gap between the society and the political system.[84] Furthermore, it may be suggested that the division that exists is not between an elite that has become "a brake on social progress," on the one hand, and increasingly restive "key groups" on the other. Instead, the line of battle would seem to cut across the elite-intermediate boundary and to involve opposing constellations of elite and intermediate participants. We cannot of course foresee the future of this development, but an appreciation of events to come may be gained by considering some of the factors which so far have worked in favor of the trend to intermediate participation.

In the first place, the social, economic, and technological changes that have attended the modernization of the USSR have led to social and functional differentiation and have thus produced potential intermediate participants in large numbers. Simultaneously, the increased social and technological complexity of policy-making may be regarded as having led to an overloading of centralized policy-making facilities.[85] A devolution of participation was required particularly where technical issues were involved: Stalin himself said that science could not develop without "struggle of opinions," and this theme was taken up in earnest after his death.[86] In addition, mobilization of the society to fulfill the increasingly exacting tasks of the regime has necessitated a greater effort to encourage "creative initiative" rather than merely the enforced compliance and coerced enthusiasm which seems to have characterized the Stalin era. But for creative initiative to be unleashed, it was necessary in turn to consider allowing greater personal satisfaction not only of material wants, but also of the needs of human dignity, whether achieved through the passive experience of greater freedom or through outright political participation. At all points, the response to such requirements was doubtless countered by arguments and tendencies of behavior that emphasized the need to maintain the "moral-political unity" of a mobilized society. In this regard, the argument continues to be advanced that socialist society is not characterized by spontaneity but is based

[84] Zbigniew Brzezinski, "Reflections on the Soviet System," *Problems of Communism*, XVII, No. 3 (May-June 1968), 44-48.

[85] Cf. Karl W. Deutsch, "Cracks in the Monolith: Possibilities and Patterns of Disintegration in Totalitarian Systems," in Carl J. Friedrich (ed.), *Totalitarianism* (Cambridge, Mass., 1954).

[86] Stalin's statement is to be found in his "Marksizm i voprosy yazykoznania," *Pravda*, June 20, 1950.

rather on planned social development. Here we see an echo of the fear, so often expressed in the West, that unrestrained activity by intermediate and nonelite participants may lead to "anarchy."

Secondly, internal division in the party leadership would appear to have been an essential pre-condition for the growth of intermediate participation. Although the sources of cleavage in the post-Stalin leadership are manifold, it is intrinsic to the policy-making situation in advanced societies that problems are never fully resolved and debate never fully closed on issues. Closure, of course, occurs, but the leaders for reasons of their own may remain differentially predisposed to a consideration of the continuing articulations from lower levels, with the result that issues are sooner or later reopened. In other cases, such as nationality policy, there is evidently a chronic lack of consensus at the leadership level. The effect is in this case to permit continuing articulation by intermediate participants within the limits of an ambivalent party line.

A further consideration in the rise of intermediate participation is undoubtedly the withdrawal of terror as a ready instrument of leadership control. The expectation has become widespread that it is possible within reason to dissent and live. Dissent was possible in the Stalin years,[87] but with the relaxation of terror a statistically greater incidence of intermediate articulation arises as individuals make modest efforts to shape their environment without fear of imminent reprisal. In particular, articulations issuing from professional groupings have been advanced in the pursuit of what Arnold Wolfers in another context has called "milieu goals": various writers, mathematical economists, jurists, sociologists, military officers, and others have sought in a variety of ways to create a setting in which they could more adequately perform their profession.[88] Nevertheless, the arbitrary resort to coercion remains, as dissident intellectuals and spokesmen of minority nationalities have learned in recent years. Though it would be unwise to generalize about all the issues of the Soviet polity from such cases, it is evident that

[87] Thus, having survived the "Varga affair" of 1946-1949, Eugene Varga chose again to challenge orthodoxy in the autumn of 1951 at a conference called to discuss a planned party text. Virtually everyone seems to have disagreed with his view that inter-imperialist wars were no longer inevitable, and the argument was passed for decision to the "chief arbiter of the conference," Stalin, who also opposed Varga. E. Varga, *Ocherki po problemam politekonomii kapitalizma* (Moscow, 1965), p. 78.

[88] Arnold Wolfers, *Discord and Collaboration* (Baltimore, 1962), p. 73.

there are countervailing trends in the matter of terror, whose short-term consequences are difficult to predict.

The decline in the use of terror is linked in turn to another enabling condition for intermediate participation: the relative improvement in the international situation of the Soviet Union. Stalin justified terror in large part on the grounds that the USSR existed in a "capitalist encirclement" and was subject to the threat of subversion and "imperialist aggression." By 1969, capitalist encirclement had ceased to preoccupy the Soviet leadership. Despite the incessant propaganda concerning "imperialism," the nuclear deterrent is no doubt regarded by some as assuring the basic security of the state, as Khrushchev once intimated.[89] The expectation of war has somewhat declined, and with it the "rally 'round the flag" mentality of earlier years. It thus becomes possible to consider a degree of regional and vertical decentralization of the economic and political systems, and to permit increased dependence upon lower participants. On the other hand, members of the military and police establishments continue to harp on the "imperialist threat," to campaign on behalf of patriotism, and to counteract the penetration of "bourgeois ideas." In so doing, they endeavor to maintain a mobilized, unified society that is inimical to extensive intermediate participation. They may be aided in this by the conflict with China. Thus, the Soviet system would seem to be a penetrated one with regard to political participation, as the conflict of tendencies is to some extent influenced by communications received from beyond the national frontiers.[90]

Additional variables could be considered, but the underlying point may already be clear. To speak of a widening gap between state and society is to regard Soviet political structure essentially in terms of elite and nonelite. When intermediate participation is introduced, the picture becomes somewhat more complex and, it is suggested, true to

[89] Arnold L. Horelick and Myron Rush, *Strategic Power and Soviet Foreign Policy* (Chicago, 1966), p. 106.

[90] Soviet authors assert that the development of democracy in the USSR is partially dependent upon the international situation. See Fedoseyev in F. V. Konstantinov (ed.), *op.cit.*, p. 53; F. M. Burlatsky, *Gosudarstvo i kommunizm* (Moscow, 1963), and in D. A. Kerimov (ed.), *Demokratia i kommunizm* (Moscow, 1962), p. 211; Yu. M. Kozlov, in *Sovershenstvovaniye demokraticheskikh printsipov v sovetskom gosudarstvennom upravlenii* (Moscow, 1966), p. 19; or A. Visnyakov, "K voprosu o dialektike razvitia sotsialisticheskovo obshchestva," *Kommunist*, No. 10 (1953), p. 30. In some cases these statements may be justifications for the failure to proceed with democratization, and in others they may be arguments in favor of a tension-reducing policy toward the West.

life. Instead of an elite vs. nonelite dichotomy, or indeed an elite-inter-mediate participant cleavage, the effective alignment is between oppos-ing coalitions of elite and intermediate actors. To this a further precision may be added, in that the more conservatively minded intermediate actors may be less "intermediate" than their relatively progressive colleagues: the Ostrovityanovs and Kochetovs would not appear to have detached themselves from their leadership patrons to the same degree as the Nemchinovs and Tvardovskys whose expectations have favored the "new" as opposed to the "old." Will the varied proponents of the "new," the *forces vives* of Soviet society, succeed in furthering not only their own expectations of policy, but, as a consequence, integration and adaptation of society and polity?

If we were to consider only recent leadership actions and the capacity of the leadership to entertain major institutional reforms, the answer would surely be negative. But insofar as the problems of integration and adaptation are ones of expanded participation, a good deal could be accomplished in the Soviet Union without significant institutional reform. Through intensified use of public and professional discussions, conferences, opinion polls, mass participation in the affairs of public associations and the state apparatus, informal participation could be extended in ways that would continue to circumvent the organs of rep-resentation and leave intact the position of the party as the leading force. Whether progress will be made in taking even such modest steps as these will depend not only on the predispositions of the leadership, but also on developments external to, as well as within, the USSR. Although the countervailing forces should not be underestimated, an examination of intermediate participation and the secular trend toward its expansion since 1953 suggests that the Soviet system possesses a significant potential for political adaptation.

To conclude, this essay represents an attempt to fashion a tool for the analysis of processes which are inherently diffuse and about which we have only little information. Even if it is accepted that the scope of participation is as large as presented here, some may conclude that Soviet policy-making remains essentially inexplicable or is not a fit subject for process analysis. Others may find it preferable to treat inter-mediate activity in terms of interest groups, elites, or reference groups. The approach put forward here is not incompatible with the study of group politics, but is primarily concerned with the framework within which the data of group relations will eventually have to be placed. If the political act is to be seen as an act of steering, as Karl Deutsch has suggested, the selection from among alternate possible directions of value allocation through tendency conflict may be a promising way of thinking about the steering process for Soviet society. It may also serve to focus attention on human action, as opposed to system needs, as a central concept in the study of the Soviet system. In regard to our more immediate purposes, a tendency analysis of Soviet policy-making offers the possibility of locating intermediate activity within a broader system of behavior, and of maximizing the use of available data. Ultimately, however, the utility of a model is assessed by its application and comparison with others.

CHAPTER XI ~ BY H. GORDON SKILLING

Group Conflict in Soviet Politics
Some Conclusions

THIS FINAL chapter will attempt to draw conclusions not only from
the essays of the contributors to this volume but also from other books
and articles which have employed an interest group analysis, or an ap-
proximation thereof, or which have dealt with specific groups in Soviet
politics.[1] It will also discuss some further applications of interest group
analysis and evaluate some of the criticisms of this approach.

Characteristics of Group Activity

The groups we have been examining in this book, although substantial in size, form a relatively small proportion of the total population. We may roughly estimate the numbers involved as 100,000 to

---

[1] I shall refrain from explicitly referring to the findings of our contributors.
Citations will be limited to other books and articles used in preparing this final
chapter. See in particular Alexander Dallin and Alan F. Westin (eds.), *Politics in
the Soviet Union: 7 Cases* (New York, 1966); Peter H. Juviler and Henry
W. Morton (eds.), *Soviet Policy-making: Studies of Communism in Transition*
(New York, 1967); Philip D. Stewart, *Political Power in the Soviet Union* (Indi-
anapolis and New York, 1968); Ghita Ionescu, *The Politics of the European
Communist States* (London, 1967); Wolfgang Leonhard, "Politics and Ideology
in the Post-Khrushchev Era," in Alexander Dallin and Thomas B. Larson (eds.),
Soviet Politics Since Khrushchev (Englewood Cliffs, 1968), Chap. 3; Sidney
I. Ploss, "Interest Groups," in Allen Kassof (ed.), *Prospects for Soviet Society*
(New York, 1968); H. Gordon Skilling, "The Party, Opposition, and Interest
Groups in Communist Politics: Fifty Years of Continuity and Change," in Kurt
London (ed.), *The Soviet Union, A Half-Century of Communism* (Baltimore,
1968), pp. 119-149; Frederick C. Barghoorn, "Prospects for Soviet Political De-
velopment: Evolution, Decay, or Revolution?" *ibid.*, pp. 77-117; Milton Lodge,
"'Groupism' in the Post-Stalin Period," *Midwest Journal of Political Science*,
XII, No. 3 (August 1968), 330-351; Milton Lodge, "Soviet Elite Participatory
Attitudes in the Post-Stalin Period," *American Political Science Review*, LXII, No.
3 (September 1968), 827-839; Philip D. Stewart, "Soviet Interest Groups and the
Policy Process: The Repeal of Production Education," *World Politics*, XXII, No.
1 (October 1969), 29-50; Joel J. Schwartz and William R. Keech, "Group In-
fluence and the Policy Process in the Soviet Union," *American Political Science
Review*, LXII, No. 3 (September 1968), 840-851.

379

200,000 *apparatchiki*, 100,000 managers in heavy industry, several 100,000 military officers, perhaps the same number of security police, 100,000 lawyers, 300,000 economists (including planners and statisticians), and 6,000 writers (members of the Writers' Union).

These elite groups belong to what the Soviet Union calls the "intelligentsia," or alternately, persons engaged in "mental labor." They form only a small part of this "stratum" (*sloi*) of the population to which 20,000,000 persons, according to the Soviet census of 1959, belonged.[2] Conscious that this category includes persons such as lower officials and service personnel not properly belonging to the intelligentsia, some Soviet scholars have defined the intelligentsia more narrowly as "those professionally engaged in highly qualified mental labor requiring specialized secondary or higher education" and constituting the chief source of livelihood. This still embraces a huge number of persons, approximately 15,700,000, including the technical-economic intelligentsia (about 5 million), the scientific and cultural intelligentsia (approximately 5 million), and the leading workers in state, party and other apparatuses, including the army and security forces, and the managers (about 2.4 million).[3] Boris Meissner has estimated that of these vast numbers, a smaller group of more influential persons may be discerned, numbering some 400,000 top bureaucrats, the "power elite" proper; some 1,700,000 economic managers, the elite of the economic and technical intelligentsia; and an undefined number of the "prestige elite"—writers, scientists, artists, etc.[4]

It can be seen that the groups studied in this book represent a relatively small part of the Soviet intelligentsia, however defined. Of these gross numbers, needless to say, only a fraction actively participates in public affairs. This is the section of society sometimes known as "the informed public" (*obshchestvennost*), which "participates in public life and represents public opinion."[5] We are, therefore, dealing with a narrow elite of leading persons who claim to speak for their associates and for the broader masses. As V. O. Key, Jr., has pointed out with reference to the USA, the correct image of pluralism may be not a

[2] Nicholas De Witt, *Education and Professional Employment in the USSR* (Washington, D. C., 1961), pp. 481-484.

[3] See Ts. A. Stepanyan and V. S. Semyonov, *Klassy, sotsialnye sloi i gruppy v SSSR* (Moscow, 1968), pp. 135-136, 162ff. The figures are those estimated by Boris Meissner, "The Power Elite and Intelligentsia in Soviet Society," in London (ed.), *op.cit.*, esp. pp. 159-162, 173.

[4] Meissner, *ibid.*, p. 162.

[5] Juviler, in Juviler and Morton (eds.), *op.cit.*, p. 45.

society divided into massive groups, but rather one in which pluralistic interactions occur among "leadership echelons."[6] In these circumstances pressure politics is "a politics among the activists," with the masses playing no active role in the groups to which they belong.[7] Under Soviet conditions, in the absence of genuine elections and with severe limits on freedom of association, assembly, and expression, the restricted or "elite" character of group activity is even more pronounced.

GROUP DIFFERENCES

Our evidence demonstrates that although political groups in the Soviet Union have some features in common, they also differ profoundly from each other (as well as from groups in other societies), both in their character and in their modes of activity. There is a wide variation in their degree of legitimacy, or of their toleration by the authorities, with some groups, such as the police, military, and *apparatchiki* accepted, of necessity, in practice; others, such as the economists and lawyers, frequently employed in a consultative fashion; and others, such as liberal writers, or opinion groups in general, often severely condemned. In a somewhat similar way there is a span of differentiation as to the actual autonomy of group action, with some escaping from political control to some degree and others being severely circumscribed. The resources at the disposal of groups range from the coercive powers of the police and the army to the purely persuasive influence of economists, writers, and lawyers. The latter is based mainly on an expertise with which the regime cannot dispense, or in the case of the writers, on the quality of their writings and their popular appeal. Their methods are equally diverse, taking the form of words or action, in private or in public. Access to places of power and their contact with the informed public also vary significantly. The groups pursue contrasting ends, including purposes deemed to embody the public interest, or more restricted self-oriented interests or values, and embracing both the positive objective of influencing public policy and the negative one of vetoing or blocking authoritative actions. The aims may be primarily economic, or political, or of still other character. The groups are diverse also in the degree of their inclusiveness and cohesiveness, and of internal differentiation. There is much dissimilarity in the extent of internal interaction; some groups, such as the liberal writers, are extremely conscious of the identity of their interests and have frequent contacts

[6] *Public Opinion and American Democracy* (New York, 1967), p. 530, n. 9.
[7] *Ibid.*, pp. 507-509, 526-527, 537.

381

with each other, while others, such as the managers, function largely on their own with relatively few direct mutual communications. All these contrasting attributes change over time so that it is difficult to generalize even about one group. Although an examination of all of these aspects of group politics is manifestly impossible, some of them deserve further comment.

As noted in our opening chapters, political groups in the Soviet Union are seldom organized, and *if* organized, are dominated by functionaries who are usually not elected and not responsive to the wishes of their constituents. Among the intellectual groups, the economists do not have an association of their own and have not proposed one; the lawyers have been unable to secure authorization for a professional organization; the writers have a union, but one which at best serves only the material interests of its members and does not protect or defend their freedom of expression. In the case of the intellectual groups, a tiny fraction of the lawyers, economists, educators, and others are grouped together in academic institutes whose facilities provide them with a basis of operation as well as a livelihood. The more bureaucratic groups, including the professional people employed in government departments, the military, the police, and the *apparatchiki*, function within these government or party institutions, which also offer them an arena of activity. The managers occupy a curious twilight zone, since they have no association of their own and are yet able to function through the ministries of which they are employees. No doubt any group, whether occupational or opinion, benefits from having a platform for its activities and is hampered by the severe restrictions, or the absolute ban, on the forming of associations. They may, however, use the agencies and organizations to which they belong, at least in a limited degree, for the presentation of their attitudes and claims and may in some circumstances be able effectively to exploit these institutions for their purposes. Whether organized or not, group action usually takes the form of the statements or deeds of a few outstanding individuals, who arrogate to themselves the authority to express group interests and are not selected by or authorized to act for the group. In fact, however, their initiatives may be subsequently endorsed by other group members in their own statements or actions. Nor is it excluded, for example, that a small circle of leaders may plan their moves jointly, as presumably do the signers of manifestoes or letters, or the participants in technical conferences, or those cooperating in a "family circle" in a locality.

382

GROUP INTERESTS AND THE PUBLIC INTEREST

The evidence indicates that perhaps all groups pursue both narrow group interests and values *and* broader public interests and values, as well as articulating the interests and values of other social groups. The police and military, for instance, seek to defend their own vested interests inherent in the privileged economic and social position occupied and to achieve the goals of autonomy from party control and a significant role in policy-making. They are also linked with the interests of the system as a whole, which makes them a close ally of the party apparatus. In addition, they have their "professional interests," arising out of the expert character of their functions, and "ideological interests" based on their special views of public policy. In many cases, such as the interests of the military in a high military budget or the promotion of heavy industry, it is impossible to separate what is a "selfish" interest reflecting their own position in society and a concern for national strength and security as they conceive them. In a somewhat similar way, the *apparatchiki* have their vested personal interests in status, income, and other privileges, but also narrower interests identified with their sphere of work or the geographical region of their activity. The pursuit of funds for agriculture or for their own oblast redounds to their personal benefit as successful "operators," but is also in the broader interest of those directly benefited by such allocations. In addition, it may be assumed, the *apparatchiki* have not only a general interest in the maintenance of the system as a whole, but also one in its more effective operation and in the winning of public support for it. The managers' concerns with operational autonomy, professional standards, and maximization of personal income, may be regarded as self-centered demands, but they are also an expression of their conception of the public interest.

When we turn to the intellectual groups, and to the opinion groups generally, the serving of the public interest seems to predominate, although the personal aspect is not absent. All of these groups are bound together by "professional" standards or by a common "ideological" bent, and in their actions and words, they seek to promote the interests of society as they interpret them. The common professional status of the lawyers, linked by the values and the standards of their craft and their training, is presumably characteristic also of the economists and writers, and of other scholars. Within such groups, deep differences of opinion are manifested, reflecting diverse concepts of the public inter-

383

est, whether in respect of legal change, economic reform, or literary freedom. Although these appear on the surface to be "public" concerns, they are usually also linked with the interest of the members of a particular group in enhancing their own status as scholars or creative artists, and in reaping the advantages which flow to them from a certain direction of public policy. For a "liberal" writer, for example, the abolition of censorship, although preeminently pursued in the interest of society as a whole, also guarantees him the right to express himself freely and hence in a very real sense the right to an assured income and a respected status. For him, "truth" is not merely one of the highest social values but a matter of "life or death." Conversely, for the "conservative" writer, the maintenance of censorship and of the party's literary dogmas makes it possible for him, perhaps with mediocre talent, to enjoy the perquisites of a successful literary producer. It is difficult, moreover, to believe that the more mundane matters of salary, social status, etc., are not important considerations for these groups, as is the case of their colleagues in other countries, and that they do not urge their organizations, such as the Writers' Union, or the Union of Educational and Scientific Workers, to protect these interests.

GROUP COHESIVENESS AND DIFFERENTIATION

Occupational groups manifest both substantial cohesiveness and marked internal differentiation. Although our contributors vary considerably in their emphasis on one or the other, their data provide evidence that in almost all groups there is, at the same time, some community of interest on certain issues and sharp clashes of opinion on others. The balance of unity and disunity varies according to the group and changes with the issue involved, so that general conclusions are difficult to draw. Separate comments on each of the seven groups seem, therefore, desirable.

In the case of the *apparatchiki*, contrary to common assumptions, there is a great deal of conflict of interest and opinion. Both at the top and the lower levels there are potential cleavages based on differences of age, ethnic affiliation, education and experience, place of work, and department of employment. Actual cleavages *between* the specialized branches of the central and local secretariats, as well as *within* branches, and conflicts between central and local party organizations, are clearly documented. The high degree of specialization of obkom secretaries, as between agriculture and industry, as well as of specialized party officials in various fields, and their vigorous defense of their own sphere and of their own locality are demonstrated. There is a strong presumption, then, that the party apparatus is not monolithic, but represents a complex of interests, divided no doubt on other issues as well as on those relating to industry and agriculture. This does not exclude some common interests among *apparatchiki*, taking the form, for instance, of a united front at the local level or of a general adherence to certain doctrines such as the one-party system. There is also presumed to be a common interest not only in defending the topmost leader but also in seeking to influence him and his policy. Not excluded is the possibility that the *apparatchiki* might at some stage show a common interest in curbing the enormous power which the General Secretary holds over their fate.

The military exhibits a similar amalgam of a high sense of solidarity in general and pronounced divergencies on specific issues. The officer group is described as closely knit, with its own sense of identity and its own values and interests, a kind of exclusive caste competing with other groups for status, resources, and influence.[8] It is united in defense of its ideological and institutional interests and of its privileged status in society. At the same time, it is not monolithic on all issues, but is riven by differences between individual services, between political workers and military professionals, old-style commanders and technical experts of the new breed, young and old, "Stalingrad" and "Muscovite" cliques from World War II, etc. Cutting across inter-service boundaries there are also profound differences of opinion on resource allocation, the use of war as an instrument of policy, and many aspects of military strategy.[9]

The security police are depicted as a much more unified group, enjoying, like the military, a highly privileged economic and social status, possessing a common education and training, and having a "sense of professional and organizational identity." Perhaps because of the paucity of information on this powerful "police community," little evidence is available on potential divergence within the security police. The counterbalancing of MVD and KGB is noted, and presumably hidden friction

[8] Cf. Thomas Wolfe's statement of the military's "self-awareness as a group with a professionally autonomous identity and its own sets of interests and values." "The Military," in Kassof (ed.), *op.cit.*, p. 121.

[9] Cf. Wolfe, *ibid.*, pp. 123-140, and his other studies, "Soviet Military Policy After Khrushchev," in Dallin and Larson (eds.), *op.cit.*, Chap. 5; "Soviet Military Policy at the Fifty-Year Mark," in London (ed.), *op.cit.*, pp. 247ff.

may exist between various departments of the KGB, such as those responsible for domestic and foreign operations respectively. There are hints also of differences between younger and better educated members of this profession and the older veterans. One may speculate concerning actual or potential differences of opinion among the security police on the changing role of terror and on legal reform, with the younger members perhaps taking a different attitude from those who served during periods of terror and were personally involved in the crimes of those times.

The managers, or at least those in heavy industry, are described as having common interests which have remained basically unchanged since the Stalin era. There are suggestions that there may be important differences between heavy and light industry managers, and other generational, or branch and regional divisions, within the management group. There is also an apparent ambiguity in the desire of the managers for greater directorial autonomy and their opposition to economic reforms moving in that direction. This ambivalence is presumably a reflection of the central conflict discerned within the managerial group between the entrenched production-oriented engineers, who are fearful of economic reform, and the new class of "businessmen" managers, who favor it.

Although assuming varied forms, a corresponding counterpoise of common and different interests is evident within the intellectual groups. The jurists are divided into many occupational subcategories, such as the advocates, the jurisconsults, the procurators, the judges, the law teachers, and the legal scholars, each of which has a certain unified attitude. They share, however, "common concerns and distinct attitudes" and above all are linked together by professional standards. These links are formed by the overlapping of their work, the mobility between groups, their common education, and the common body of literature used. They are all "jurists," who "interact with each other" and who "share certain values which are implicit in their role as jurists." This does not mean that they have the same opinions on major questions. There are "liberals" and "conservatives" on some issues; there is also a distinct difference of approach between the legal scholars and the practical workers, with the former usually favoring legal reforms more strongly than the latter.

The economists, like the jurists, presumably share some common professional standards and values and have a community of outlook in this respect. They are, however, not homogeneous but sharply split into rival "opinion groups," which reflect in some degree differences in age, mathematical training or lack of it, and institutional affiliation. Much depends on the generation, with significant distinctions between the few remaining pre-revolutionary scholars, the "hacks" of the Stalinist period, and the post-revolutionary group (born in 1917 or after). Younger economists with mathematical training are likely to support economic reform; older ones, who lack such training, oppose it. Economists at certain institutions, such as the Siberian Section of the Academy or the Central Mathematical Economics Institute, are likely to be "innovative"; those at the Institute of Economics, conservative. Although a "liberal-conservative" dichotomy is observable, the economists generally divide into a greater number of subtly varying groupings on a given issue.

Finally, among the writers, common interests seem to be marginal and opinion groups decisive. Occupational subgroups might presumably be distinguished and examined, such as the editors of publishing houses, the editors of newspapers and literary journals, the professors and research scholars, the critics, even perhaps the censors, each with special concerns and interests of his own. No doubt the differences between the writers of Moscow, Leningrad, and the provinces, and between the younger and older writers, are not without importance. The overriding division, however, is between "liberals" and "conservatives," whatever their specific occupation or affiliation may be, with presumably various nuances of opinion between these extremes. No doubt all writers share some concern to uphold literary standards, and the genuine artists, "liberal" or "conservative," will on occasion make common cause for such considerations. Writers are, however, more likely to polarize, with the "liberals" espousing the cause of high artistic standards and of freedom of expression, and the "conservatives" defending the duty of the writer to serve the party and its line of policy.

GROUP ALLIANCES

The crisscrossing coalitions of political groups were evident in the case studies of other authors as well as in the analyses of our contributors. In the shaping of the 1958 educational reform, for instance, a loose grouping of teachers, administrators of the RSFSR Ministry of Education, higher educational and scientific personnel, factory managers, and even some party functionaries opposed the polytechnical aspects of

Khrushchev's proposal.[10] In the fight over the reorganization of the Academy of Sciences, there were four general groupings, including the theoreticians or pure scientists, ranged against the engineers, the representatives of union-republic and other local research institutions, and some university professors.[11] In the discussion of the antiparasite laws, lawyers, judges, and procurators opposed the draft decrees, and government officials, political activists, and some ordinary workers supported them.[12] In the debate on the family law, the reformers included most lawyers and legislators, the Supreme Soviet legislative committees, most judges, the press, including *Izvestia*, the officials of Zags, who were mostly women, as well as pedagogues, doctors, and various other officials. The main opponent was the party *apparat*, supported by a legal scholar and the head of the Central Statistical Administration. There were, it was reported, "groupings of reformist and conservative opinion cutting across bureaucratic and professional lines."[13] The linkage of the party functionaries with other groupings, such as the state bureaucrats, at the national level, on the basis of common functional interests, or at the local level, with administrators, for common local purposes, form the main theme of the study of the *apparatchiki* in our volume. More specific alliances of party and police; of party and army against the police; of economists and scientists; of jurists and managers; of writers and scientists; of the more "modernizing" military with economists, scientists, and managers; or of other military officers with heavy industry managers; or of economists and managers have been mentioned by our contributors.

A phenomenon of great potential importance is the emergence of broad alliances of persons from many occupational groups, such as the writers, natural scientists, social scientists, mathematicians, creative artists, workers in the humanities, engineers—and even an occasional military officer, farm leader, or worker—in petitions for legal reform, or in protests against limitations on freedom, or against what they regard as legal injustices such as the Daniel-Sinyavsky trial, and even in statements on political issues such as the invasion of Czechoslovakia.[14] Even more

[10] Schwartz and Keech, *op.cit.*, pp. 843-844.

[11] Loren R. Graham, "Reorganization of the U.S.S.R. Academy of Sciences," in Juviler and Morton (eds.), *op.cit.*, pp. 138ff.

[12] Marianne Armstrong, "The Campaign Against Parasites," *ibid.*, p. 168.

[13] Juviler, "Family Reforms on the Road to Communism," *ibid.*, pp. 45-50, 54.

[14] See below for further discussion. Cf. also Chap. VIII, above. For a collection of such documents, see the two special numbers of *Problems of Communism*, entitled "In Quest of Justice," XVII, No. 4 (July-August 1968), and XVII, No. 5

pregnant with possibilities for the future is the mutual interaction, and informal cooperation, of particular groups across the frontiers within the communist world, and even with those in noncommunist countries, as evidenced, for instance, by the protest of some foreign communist parties against the Daniel-Sinyavsky imprisonment, or the appeals by Soviet dissenters to these parties or to the United Nations.[15]

METHODS OF GROUP ACTION

Most groups, whether based on institutions and associations or acting in a loose and informal manner, are likely to employ a variety of informal and noninstitutionalized methods for the defense of their interests and the pursuit of their ends. In general, groups may be classified according to whether their methods are coercive or persuasive, or a cross between the two. Indeed, these elements are so intimately interlocked that both are usually present, with coercion helping to persuade and persuasion often having coercive aspects, as in propaganda.[16]

The security police rely heavily on coercion or the potentiality of co-ercion to attain their objectives, but they also employ instruments of persuasion, especially propaganda, to promote a favorable image of the security forces and a public acceptance of the necessity for strict police methods. The military, although not normally able to use their over-whelming force in domestic struggles, possesses a potential coercive power that may weigh heavily in the balance, but relies also on the written or the spoken word to defend its interests. The party *apparatchiki* and other bureaucrats employ coercive measures, too, in the form of penalties, "administrative" measures, or obligations imposed on members and non-members, but use propaganda to mobilize the public, to win general allegiance, and to gain support for specific policies.

At the other extreme, the intellectual groups are for the most part dependent exclusively on their powers of persuasion, and this in a context of established official doctrine and strict limits on free expression. What

---

(September-October 1968). For similar appeals and protests in the Ukraine, see *The Chornovil Papers*, compiled by V. Chornovil (New York and Toronto, 1968).

[15] This subject deserves more consideration in future research. See my chapter, "Group Conflict and Political Change" in the book edited by Chalmers Johnson, *Change in Communist Systems* (Stanford, 1970). Cf. Griffiths, Chap. x, above.

[16] See my analysis of this problem in relationship to communist politics in general in *The Governments of Communist East Europe* (New York, 1966), pp. 13-17, and Chap. 12.

is said and written in public is no doubt but a small part of the total discussion, much of which goes on behind closed doors and in the privacy of homes. Even silence may in a given situation convey a hidden meaning.[17] Increasingly, dissenters and protesters send petitions, usually not published, to the legal and political authorities or the newspapers and circulate secret manifestoes from hand to hand among friends and associates.[18] Self-publication (*samizdat*) of magazines, novels and poems, and political tracts has become a widely used procedure.

As in the West, a major objective of all groups is to influence policy through "persuasion," by "partisan analysis," as Lindblom has put it, which seeks to win over the policy-maker by providing information and analysis concerning a technical problem and by convincing him that the policy desired by the group squares with his own philosophy.[19] Another prime goal, again as in the West, is to impinge on public opinion, creating a mood favorable to the objectives of the group and preparing the ground for broader campaigns to influence the authorities. These "pressures" and "counterpressures," as they might well be called, whether based on reasoning, organization, propaganda, compulsion, or violence, play a role in Soviet group politics which is comparable in kind, if different in form, to their role in group politics elsewhere.

Group Influence

At the outset the point must be made that "influence" or "effectiveness" is not a criterion of the existence or nonexistence of a group. In every society there may be interest groups which are unable to exert a meaningful influence on the course of public policy. For instance, Soviet lawyers have tried for years, in vain, to secure the recognition of the "presumption of innocence" or the presence of counsel during pre-trial investigation. Moreover, the action of groups may produce unanticipated consequences, including even the very opposite of the group's objectives. Thus the "liberal" Soviet writers, seeking to expand the area of free expression, have provoked increased repression. Such failures demonstrate not that groups and group conflict do not exist, but only that some groups lack the strength to be influential. Indeed, by very definition, group

---

[17] Cf. the remarks of Leonid Ilyichev (*Pravda*, March 8, 1963); "After all, silence also means something, also expresses some point of view."

[18] See "In Quest of Justice."

[19] Charles E. Lindblom, *The Policy-Making Process* (Englewood Cliffs, 1968), pp. 65-66.

390

conflict assumes that some groups may win, others lose, in their rivalry for influence.

It should also be noted that the role of groups in politics is not limited to their direct influence on specific policies or decisions. An examination of group conflict in any society must include within its purview the part played by a group or groups in politics in general, including their impact on public opinion and the long-run climate of thinking, for example, with respect to economic reform. As a Czech scholar, in private conversation, spoke of his own research, the important thing was "to articulate the problem and to set forth the alternative solutions," even if the immediate results might not be great. Similarly, it has been argued, the task of the "liberal" writers lies less in the drafting of resolutions on specific current questions, and more in the exposition of the idea of freedom in their creative works. The student of group conflict should, therefore, be concerned not merely with the impact of specific "claims" or "demands" of groups but also with their more general attitudes on public affairs and the effect of these on the secular evolution of society.

In this volume it has been assumed from the outset that the major power of decision-making rests in the hands of a few top leaders and that the making of policy is not the automatic result of the pressures and counterpressures of rival groups. Decisions *may* be made by the ruling elite, on their own initiative, without reference to group pressures, or in defiance of the attitudes expressed by important groups. Leaders *may* also manipulate the elite groups, using them in their own struggles for power and controversies over policy. Yet the evidence presented in this book and elsewhere suggests that sometimes the decisions of the rulers are taken as a result of the influence of groups and in a milieu of competing and conflicting tendencies. Leaders may "respond" on occasion to the threats and the arguments of rival groups, favoring one over another, or seeking a compromise between their interests.

Group conflicts may or may not be linked directly with the "factional politics" at the topmost level of the Soviet political pyramid.[20] In some

---

[20] This is the term used by Sidney Ploss, in his "Interest Groups" (Kassof [ed.], *op.cit.*, Chap. 4). This chapter was devoted primarily to "those conflicts of self-interest in the body of the nation which have become the stuff of factional politics in the CPSU" (p. 78). These interests, he wrote, are "ultimately philosophic, with rival ideas about how to govern the society and conduct foreign relations being championed by non-associational groups which recruit followers in all the centres of administrative power" (*ibid.*). His chapter dealt with the "functional groups" of the party, state economic, military, and police apparatuses, and the "conflicting ideological, sectional, generational, and personal interests" within

cases the connection between interest groups and factional struggles is clear and may even result in the ouster of individuals, including the top leader, at the highest level. The military have been closely associated with such factional politics and contributed to the ouster of Malenkov and perhaps of Khrushchev.[21] The police, likewise, were directly involved in leadership conflicts and may have had something to do with Khrushchev's removal. In these and other issues the leaders often took the initiative and manipulated these powerful groups in the interests of their struggle for power.[22] Top leaders sometimes intervened in favor of certain groups and exploited them and the issues involved for their own ends. Khrushchev, for instance, catered to the "liberal" writers for a time in the interests of his own political aims. Khrushchev, too, in seeking specific reforms, literally goaded the economists into discussion of economic change, initiated the discussion of the revisions of the legal codes and of the Academy of Sciences, and launched the antiparasite laws and the military reforms.

There is, however, a substantial area in which political groups may themselves take the initiative. No doubt they are better able to do this at a time of collective leadership and especially when that leadership is divided or in deep crisis.[23] There are occasions when, without an invitation or even a "green light" from on high, and perhaps even against the wishes of the leadership, groups may bring forward questions for discussion and advance proposals for action. This was particularly the case of the educators in their campaign to dilute Khrushchev's original project of educational reform, and again in their resistance to his policy of promoting production education.[24] It was also true of the resistance of the lawyers to the draft antiparasite laws and to the laws eventually enacted. The military opposed crucial reforms launched by Khrushchev. In a more positive manner, liberal writers have raised the issue of the abolition of censorship, lawyers and others have proposed reforms in the family law, and the military have brought forward alternative ideas of military strategy. In such cases, as Philip Stewart has argued in his study of educational policy, groups have played important roles in identifying problem

---

them (p. 85) and with the resulting "intra-party battles over practical political issues," mainly at the top leadership level (p. 78).

[21] Cf. Raymond L. Garthoff, "Khrushchev and the Military," in Dallin and Westin (eds.), op.cit., pp. 247-248, 253.

[22] This was also the conclusion of Schwartz and Keech in their case study on educational reform (op.cit., p. 845).

[23] Ibid., pp. 847-849.   [24] Ibid., and also Stewart, "Soviet Interest Groups."

GROUP CONFLICT IN SOVIET POLITICS

areas, making proposals, building public support, arousing interest among the policy-makers, and communicating directly with them.[25]

Group action and influence do not necessarily involve, therefore, direct access to the topmost decision-makers. Only the official groups have such a channel of contact, through the Politburo itself. The security police has usually been represented directly in this body, and at one time, the military had such a spokesman in the person of Marshal Zhukov. The party *apparatchiki* have always had several of "their own," including the general or first secretary, in the top organ, although not in all cases expressing an apparatus standpoint. The managers may also be considered to have such representatives, at present in the person of Alexei Kosygin. In the Central Committee, the representation of the *apparatchiki* and of the state bureaucracy has always been high; that of the military, substantial; that of the security police and managers, more limited; and that of the intelligentsia, such as the writers, economists, or lawyers, no more than nominal. The military has a crucial channel of approach to the top in the Higher Military Council.[26] Such "elite representation" of political groups at the highest level is perhaps an index of their relative importance, but it is not an accurate measure of their influence, potential or actual, in the policy process.

More important is the informal access of the military, the police, and the *apparatchiki* to the top leaders, to the *apparat* departments, and the ministries. Managers, too, have a line of contact to their own ministries, and through the oblast secretaries, to the central party authorities. Some scholars, such as the scientists, may employ the channel of the Presidium of the Academy of Sciences, or government agencies dealing with science and technology. Other specialists, including the scientists, economists, and lawyers, are called in for consultation on government and party committees of all kinds, as well as commissions of the Supreme Soviets, and thus secure access to the decision-making process.

All groups, without exception, seek to use the media of communications and to influence the views of the leaders, higher circles, and the public at large through such debate and controversy. Although in some cases such public discussion may be prompted by the leadership, in other cases it occurs spontaneously and in spite of restrictions. In this way, groups may, without having direct access to the policy-makers, affect the climate of opinion and perhaps pave the way for eventual action.

[25] Stewart, *ibid.*   [26] Wolfe, in Kassof (ed.), *op.cit.*, p. 116.

393

A final judgment on the actual influence of groups on specific policies cannot at this time be rendered. Some scholars, in discussing the group approach, have doubted the influence of groups or the possibility of measuring it. Case studies in this volume and elsewhere have indicated, however, that some groups have had a measure of success in achieving their aims. The military was shown to have been able at times to defend its autonomy and its views on military strategy and to force the dilution of Khrushchev's first set of reforms, although failing to block his second campaign.[27] The security police was perhaps able to hinder Khrushchev's program of cultural relations abroad and to impose restrictions on literary freedom. The party *apparat* prevented the adoption of the proposed family reform which had been worked out after long discussions among many groups.[28] The scientists succeeded in carrying through the desired reorganization of the Academy of Sciences and in excluding the engineers from this body.[29] The lawyers were shown as exerting some influence on the drafting of the legal codes and in improving the antiparasite laws and in causing their eventual demise.[30] The economists were able to affect government decisions concerning success criteria and price formation. A coalition of forces secured changes in the educational act of 1958 as compared with Khrushchev's original project[31] and actually reversed his proposal of "production education."[32] It is clear, of course, that on most issues there are rival coalitions of forces facing each other—including vested interests seeking to preserve the *status quo* and innovative forces striving for change—and that the resolution of such conflicts may lead to the victory of some groups, the failure of others, or to a compromise of opposing viewpoints.

Interest Groups and Political Change

Western discussions of the future of Soviet society have painted a somewhat simplified picture of the contending political groups and their attitudes toward the *status quo* and reform. Some groups, such as the party *apparatchiki*, police, or the army, have been described, without reservation, as conservative; others, such as the managers, and the intellectuals generally, as innovative. A struggle between a conservative or

[27] Cf. Garthoff, *ibid.*, pp. 256-259, 272.
[28] Juviler, in Juviler and Morton (eds.), *op.cit.*, pp. 47-48.
[29] Graham, *ibid.*
[30] Armstrong, *ibid.*, p. 180. Cf. John N. Hazard, "Social Control Through Law," in Dallin and Westin (eds.), *op.cit.*, p. 221.
[31] Schwartz and Keech, *op.cit.*   [32] Stewart, "Soviet Interest Groups."

reactionary party apparatus and a reform-minded intelligentsia has been adopted as a useful model of analysis.[33] As a matter of fact, the evidence of this book demonstrates that every occupational group is divided into opinion groups and that "reformists" and "conservatives" are to be found in all of them except perhaps the security police. Moreover, there is a wide spectrum of opinion within each group, ranging from reactionary to radical, through many intermediate degrees, so that a simple "liberal-conservative" dichotomy is not adequate.[34] It is also significant that the composition of most of the groups has changed greatly since the Stalin era and will undergo further shifts in future, so that their attitudes are not static.

The *apparatchiki*, as the major ruling force, are usually considered as the group most dedicated to the maintenance of the *status quo*. Certainly they represent the key factor in the political process, with direct access to the inner sanctum of decision-making, the Politburo.[35] In general, they are devoted to the basic principles of Soviet society, such as the one-party system and the leading role of the party. Yet, as a younger group, they are not necessarily more "conservative" than other groups such as the state bureaucracy, the managers, or the army. The new generation of *apparatchiki*, moreover, is better educated and has more specialized training and experience. They are not necessarily to be regarded as enemies of all reform, even in such matters as legal reform or literary freedom. Although it is difficult to discern, there is presumably a spread of opinion and a wide range of attitudes on specific issues. For instance, lower-level *apparatchiki* may favor a decentralization of economic management. In close contact with the people of their own regions, they may also favor greater investment in agriculture or more emphasis on the production of consumers' goods. Even the ideological workers have practical concerns about education and employment that may make them less doctrinaire than is usually presumed.

The security police are described as being the most ardent supporters of the *status quo*, including the one-party system and Marxist-Leninist ideology, as well as, of course, the security system itself, and most likely

[33] See Boris Meissner, in London (ed.), *op.cit.*, pp. 153-181, and his "Totalitarian Rule and Social Change," *Problems of Communism*, xv, No. 6 (November-December 1966), 56-61. Cf. Frederick C. Barghoorn, *Politics in the USSR* (Boston and Toronto, 1966), pp. 216-217.

[34] See Boris Meissner, "Totalitarian Rule and Social Change in the Soviet Union," *Modern World*, v (1967), 93 and n. 31.

[35] Cf. Jeremy R. Azrael, "The Party and Society," in Kassof (ed.), *op.cit.*, esp. pp. 66-70.

to resist basic changes. They are fearful of dissent and of Western influence and play a prominent role in the repression of the reformers, especially among the intellectuals. They are regarded by most of the reform-minded groups as the arch-reactionary defenders of the *status quo*. On certain issues of reform under Khrushchev, especially those connected with de-Stalinization, this led them to adopt an oppositional standpoint. Yet the police may not be entirely monolithic and may differ in their attitudes, even toward the use of terror and the guarantee of legality. Their ranks have undergone significant changes since Stalin, so that the younger and better educated elements may represent a segment of higher quality than their predecessors.

The military are described as essentially "conservative," favoring the *status quo* and opposing modernizing tendencies, such as an orientation of economic policy toward the consumer or a greater freedom of expression by writers and artists. Their ideology tends to be "patriotic" and "militaristic" and to frown on currents of pacificism among the youth in the ranks.[36] In some respect, as an older and more professional group, they may adopt an even more conservative stance than the *apparatchiki*. There is a kind of "cohesive brotherhood at the upper elite levels," resulting from the interpenetration of party and the military, and the association of the military, scientists, and industrial managers, forming what might be called a "military-industrial-scientific complex" of primarily conservative tendency.[37] Yet there are, among the officers, younger, technically trained persons who may find common interests with the more progressive scientists and managers and may favor modernizing tendencies in the economy, as well as in military strategy. Moreover, the military's attitude to police terror has been a negative one, thus placing it, on that issue, in the ranks of the reform-minded.

The industrial managers occupy an ambivalent position, largely as a result of their shifting place in the economy and the changing composition of their ranks. Many of them, accustomed to the old ways of centralized planning, are oriented to the achievement of quantity production and are trained in engineering; they form, especially in heavy industry, an element of conservatism in Soviet life. Yet there are younger managers, perhaps especially in light industry, schooled in "business," who favor an economy oriented more to the market and the consumer, and who support a wider autonomy for managers as a whole. During and after

[36] Cf. Wolfe, *ibid.*, p. 134.   [37] *Ibid.*, pp. 126-127.

the Stalin era, the managers have been drawn much more from white-collar families and have a higher educational level, although still mainly in engineering. The growth of a professionalism of a new kind may bring them into informal alliance with the reform-minded economists and other more progressive elements.

The intellectuals, and especially the creative cultural elite, are normally thought of as being in the van of reform. It should not be forgotten, however, that within all the intellectual groups—writers, economists, lawyers, scientists—there are profound differences of view and many segments which are highly conservative. All lawyers are not for legal reform; all economists do not advocate economic reform; all writers are not concerned with greater freedom of expression. Generational differences may play an important, although not decisive, role in this respect, and the young writers, economists, lawyers, and scientists may represent a strong force for reform. The succession of generations among the economists will, for instance, bring the innovators to the fore. In all groups the passage of time will bring about the demise of old Stalinists. Differences may also be discerned between the more progressive theorists or scholars and the less reformist practical workers. Vested interests or official affiliations may, however, often counteract professional values.

In general, it may be assumed that the strongest reform elements may be found among the cultural intelligentsia and, to a lesser extent, among the scientific and technical intelligentsia. The widely circulated memorandum of the physicist, Academician Andrei D. Sakharov, and the support of many scientists and mathematicians for petitions for reform and letters of protest testify to the presence of a reform orientation among natural scientists.[38] A statement drafted by members of the Estonian technical intelligentsia, opposing "neo-Stalinism" and demanding a moral renewal and political democracy, suggests that even among engineers and technical specialists there exists a desire for reform, going beyond Sakharov, who was sharply criticized.[39] An alliance may be

[38] For text of the Sakharov statement, see *New York Times*, July 22, 1968. For other documents, see "In Quest of Justice." See also complaints as to the political attitudes of the scientists and the technical intelligentsia in *Kommunist*, No. 18 (December 1968), pp. 36-45. Only 17 of 79 leading scientists at the Physical Chemistry Institute in Obninsk participated in political work, it was said. Cf. references to similar complaints in the Soviet press in the *New York Times*, September 12, 1968; December 14, 23, 1968; February 23, 1969.

[39] The text was given in *Frankfurter Allgemeine Zeitung*, December 18, 1968.

emerging between what have been called the "truth-seeking" and the "efficiency-seeking" intelligentsia which would provide a strong force pressing for reform.[40] Most significant, too, is the fact that the demands of the reformers, whether writers, scientists, or engineers, are not limited to narrow professional goals but embrace far-reaching change in the economic and political order, such as the limitation of the power of the KGB or the *apparat*; radical economic reforms; a democratization of the political system, including a legally established opposition and a multi-party system; the end of censorship; changes in Soviet foreign policy.[41] Often their claims are, however, based on the provisions of the constitution and existing statutes and urge, for instance, the implementation of the civil rights proclaimed in these laws.

The possible combinations and permutations of the future are almost unlimited and hence unpredictable. One can assume the existence of a reactionary grouping drawn from some members of the police, the *apparat*, the army, and cultural bureaucrats, with the support of *Komsomol* leaders, implementing a neo-Stalinist policy. One can speculate also as to a moderately conservative alliance of some of the military, the *apparat*, the managers, state administrators, and more conservative scholars and creative intellectuals. One can conceive of a more reform-oriented grouping of the technical, cultural, and scientific intelligentsia, the "moderate modernizers" to use Leonhard's term,[42] with some support within the apparatus and the managerial strata, and perhaps among the nationalities and religious groups. Less imaginable at present is a grouping of radical reformers, seeking fundamental alteration in the system itself and even resorting to violent or revolutionary means. In no case, of course, would the groups be the sole motive force for "change" or "no change," as the initiative and the responses of the top leadership would play a significant, if not crucial, role, in the course of events. Moreover, the attitude of the broader social masses, such as the workers and peasants, and the nationalities, at present largely inarticulate and impotent, may perhaps decisively affect the final outcome.

[40] James H. Billington, "The Intellectuals," in Kassof (ed.), *op.cit.*, esp. pp. 463-464, 468-470. Cf. also Sidney Monas on the rise of the intelligentsia, in "Engineers or Martyrs: Dissent and the Intelligentsia," *Problems of Communism*, XVII. No. 5 (September-October 1968), 3, 5.

[41] See in particular the statements of Professor Sakharov and the Estonian technical intelligentsia cited above.

[42] Leonhard, in Dallin and Larson (eds.), *op.cit.*, pp. 42, 69.

Past, Present, and Future

It was during the Khrushchev period that the visibility of conflict in Soviet politics became so great as to awaken serious dissatisfaction, among Western scholars, with the totalitarian model and to stimulate the use of group analysis. Retrospectively, it became evident that this approach was appropriate for any period of Soviet history, including the Stalinist phase, as well as for other communist states. Even under Stalin, there was a sharp conflict of groups and tendencies, although in forms reflecting the more autocratic and terroristic nature of Soviet politics at that time and in a manner less easily observable. As terror declined, the possibility of the articulation of group interests and group values widened, and many groups achieved a certain degree of autonomy and even of *de facto* legitimacy. After the fall of Khrushchev, the rise of what has been called neo-Stalinism[43] set narrower limits to the activity of groups, although not restoring the Stalinist system in its full form. It may well be argued, therefore, that Soviet politics has always been characterized by group conflict, but that the conflict has differed in successive periods in the relative importance and influence of particular groups, in the size and composition of the groups themselves, in their style and methods of action, in the degree of opportunity for overt articulation, and in their ability to exert an influence on the course of politics. In the same way the role of groups in different communist countries at successive periods of their development has gone through various phases of evolution and has differed substantially at each stage.[44]

Although our contributors have concentrated on the post-Stalin period, their essays have also discussed at least briefly the different situation existing under Stalin. The defense of group interests and group values was at that time rendered extremely difficult by the reign of terror and the constant campaign of propaganda. Even powerful groups

[43] This term was used by Sakharov in his memorandum, and by the statement of the Estonian technical intelligentsia cited above.

[44] For an effort at comparative analysis of group politics in communist countries, see my "Group Conflict and Political Change" in Johnson (ed.), *op.cit.* Five categories were proposed: i. quasi-totalitarian, ii. consultative authoritarian, iii. pluralistic authoritarian, iv. democratizing and pluralistic authoritarian, and v. anarchic authoritarian. This scheme of analysis (with the omission of the last category) was applied to Czechoslovakia at different stages of development in my "Leadership and Group Conflict in Czechoslovakia," in R. Barry Farrell (ed.), *Political Leadership in Eastern Europe and the Soviet Union* (Chicago, 1970).

such as the *apparatchiki* and the military were subordinated to the supreme dictator and were unable to express their interests effectively. The *apparatchiki* were deprived of their central function of "authoritarian mobilization."[45] The military was reduced to a "client" relationship, without having a part even in the determination of military doctrine and strategy.[46] The fulcrum of power passed to the security police,[47] and, to a lesser degree, to the state bureaucracy. The managers, although curbed in their own sphere of jurisdiction, had, through the ministerial system, some limited opportunity to articulate their interests. Intellectuals were almost powerless, their ranks purged, their freedom of expression abolished, their disciplines rendered stagnant. Law and economics were more or less destroyed; literature suffered a terrible decline. The articulation of viewpoints was by invitation only, in the case of indispensable experts such as the military or the economists, and if it was attempted in a more spontaneous manner, fraught with the gravest danger. A few brave souls sought in devious ways to carry on their creative work, and even to express veiled dissidence, or by silence, to suggest a position at variance with the official line.

Under Khrushchev, as we have noted, the balance of power shifted substantially, with the restoration of the dominant role of the party *apparat*, the consequent decline of the security police, and the rise in influence of other occupational groups, including the intelligentsia.[48] At least in the initial stage the *apparatchiki* became once again the dominant factor in politics. The security police retained great power and prestige, second only to the *apparat*, in Barghoorn's judgment, but were restricted in their capacity for independent action. The military regained much of its influence and for a time, during the Zhukov period, possessed wide authority. Later it lost ground but retained great potentiality in its near monopoly of the means of violence. The industrial managers gained greater autonomy of action in their own sphere, but lost direct access to the centers of power as a result of Khrushchev's reorganizations of party and management. Above all, the intellectual groups, in spite of party controls, achieved a new position in society,

---

[45] Cf. Azrael, in Kassof (ed.), *op.cit.*, p. 63.

[46] Cf. Roman Kolkowicz, "Heresy Enshrined: Idea and Reality of the Red Army," in London (ed.,), *op.cit.*, pp. 236-237; Garthoff, in Dallin and Westin (eds.), *op.cit.*, pp. 246-247.

[47] Cf. Martin Jänicke, "Monopolismus und Pluralismus im kommunistischen Herrschaftssystem," *Zeitschrift für Politik*, XIV (1967), 151-153.

[48] *Ibid.*, pp. 153-154.

sometimes enjoying a significant consultative role in policy-making and sometimes expressing oppositional views or issuing protests. Great tension continued to exist between the *apparatchiki* and the creative arts and the scholarly professions, but the absence of terror liberated the latter from the all-pervading fear which had rendered action impossible under Stalin. This in turn reduced the power of the *apparat*.

This simplified summary obscures the fact of the ebb and flow of the relative power of political groups in different periods. As long as Lenin lived, the leeway for group action had been wide and the intensity of group conflict was high. Even under Stalin, the approach to total control was a gradual one, and indeed was never complete. There were also periods of relaxation in the Stalin period, as, for instance, during the war years. Under Khrushchev there were many zigs and zags in the relative influence of groups, as official policy veered in one direction and then another. After the fall of the ebullient dictator, further shifts have occurred, including a surge forward by the security police, a rise in the power of the *apparat*, and some decline in the role of the intellectual groups.

Nonetheless the authoritative Soviet attitude to the role of groups remained unchanged after the fall of Khrushchev. Kirill Mazurov, speaking on the occasion of the anniversary celebrations in 1968, reasserted the doctrine of the leading role of the working class and its spokesman, the Communist Party, and declared: "Therefore, in the Soviet state there is not, and there cannot be, any social group which would have the privilege of evaluating its own activity otherwise than from the viewpoint of the aims and political interests of the working class."[49] A month later, Lukyanov, a commentator in *Pravda*, writing under the title, "Socialism and Political Freedom," denounced the notion of "absolute freedom," which he defined as "the unlimited possibilities for a person or group [*kollektiv*] to act in society as they see fit." He rejected the "pluralist model of socialism," "with its struggle

[49] *Pravda*, November 7, 1968. In an earlier article, even the progressive Rumyantsev, then editor-in-chief of *Pravda*, while approving "the presence of different schools and tendencies, different styles and genres competing with each other," and advocating "the free expression and collision of opinions," had declared that the party would reject "groupism" (*gruppovshchina*) as "incompatible with the spirit of creative competition in science and art" (*ibid.*, February 21, 1965). Cf. other attacks on groups in the literary world, especially on those around *Novy mir* and *Oktyabr*, in *Pravda*, January 27, 1967. Cf. an attack on lawyers who put group interests above the public interest, in *Kommunist*, No. 12 (August 1964), p. 71.

401

H. GORDON SKILLING

of parties, with its parliaments and oppositions," and with its attempt "to pit the mass organizations against each other." "Not the 'free play of forces' but the intelligent delineation of functions for common, co-ordinated work under the leadership of the Communist Party . . . this is the basic principle of development of all mass organizations under socialism, the chief guarantee of the unity of the socialist society."[50] At least in official doctrine, then, there was to be no place for group activity or group conflict in Soviet politics.

In the West, however, there has been much speculation about the future evolution of the Soviet political system and among other things, the potentialities of interest group activity and the pluralistic tendencies which this represents.[51] Some have talked of the rise of a "managerial elite," or a "revolt of the intellectuals," of the emergence of military rule or the restoration of a police state, and of resistance by the "power elite" or the "*apparatchiki*." Much importance has been attached to the tension between the *apparatchiki* and the intelligentsia, with differing degrees of optimism as to the possibility of an increase in the influence and power of the latter and the ability of the former to adapt to the new conditions of Soviet society.[52] It has been argued that continued domination by the party apparatus will bring about a degeneration of the Soviet system, and that only an institutionalization of group repre-sentation can avert this process of decline.[53]

The analysis of Soviet interest groups is still in its infancy. Prediction

[50] *Pravda*, December 4, 1968.
[51] See in particular the article by Z. Brzezinski, "The Soviet Political System: Transformation or Degeneration?" *Problems of Communism*, xv, No. 1 (January-February 1966), 1-15, and the series of articles under the general heading "Whither Russia?" in succeeding issues of this journal during 1966 and 1967, especially that by Wolfgang Leonhard, "Notes on an Agonizing Diagnosis," *ibid.*, xv, No. 4 (July-August 1966), 36-42. See the especially interesting chapters by Frederick C. Barghoorn, "Prospects for Soviet Political Development," in London (ed.), *op.cit.*, and "Factional, Segmental and Subversive Opposition in Soviet Politics," in Robert A. Dahl (ed.), *Regimes and Oppositions* (to be pub-lished by Yale University Press). Cf. his earlier chapter, "Soviet Russia: Ortho-doxy and Adaptiveness," in Lucian W. Pye and Sidney Verba (eds.), *Political Culture and Political Development* (Princeton, 1965), Chap. 11. Cf. Kassof's conclusion, *op.cit.*, pp. 498-501.
[52] See Barghoorn, *Soviet Politics*, pp. 44-46, 82-83, 216; Barghoorn, "Soviet Russia: Orthodoxy and Adaptiveness," pp. 508-510; Brzezinski and Huntington, *Political Power: USA/USSR* (New York, 1964), pp. 415-416; Meissner, "Totali-tarian Rule and Social Change," *Problems of Communism*, pp. 59-61; Kassof (ed.), *op.cit.*, pp. 497-498; Jänicke, *op.cit.*, pp. 156-158.
[53] Brzezinski, "The Soviet Political System," *loc.cit.* The author suggested that the Central Committee might be made "an institutionalized arena for the media-tion of group interests."

402

of the future of group conflict depends not only on increasing knowledge of this aspect of Soviet political life, but also on a satisfactory explanation of the reasons for the advance of interest groups—in other words on certain assumptions concerning the dynamics of Soviet political development. It is possible at this stage only to hazard some general speculations as to *why* interest groups have risen to prominence. In some writings there has been an explicit assumption that their development has been a more-or-less inevitable by-product of modernization, and especially the increasing complexity of a modern economy, the rising educational level of the Soviet population, and the growing body of experts and professional specialists. This has brought with it a decline in the utility of coercion and a disfunctionality of *apparat* rule, a growing pragmatism and a decline in ideology, and a stress on functionalism and professionalism.[54]

No doubt there *are* social and economic forces at work which encourage interest group activity in the USSR. It seems clear, however, that this latter development has been the consequence of certain conscious decisions of individual leaders and other participants in Soviet political life, decisions which were not necessarily predetermined and which might be reversed in the future. The rise of group activity under Khrushchev was, in the first place, the result of an initiative from above, representing an effort by Stalin's successor to make the political system more rational in its process of decision-making and more responsive to the actual needs and demands of the people, especially of the influential elites. Under Stalin, policy decisions were in most cases transmitted to the population in a predominantly one-way flow of information and were imposed upon them by coercive means. Khrushchev, seeking to enhance the role of persuasion and to reduce that of coercion, sought in effect to establish more of a two-way flow of information, through consultation with certain sectors of the population. This included advisory participation by individual experts in the making of policy and, in a kind of extended consultative system, the encouragement of wide-ranging debate on alternative policies, conducted primarily by specialists. No doubt this development was in part dictated by the changing conditions of Soviet life. Nonetheless, it was a purposeful act of leadership, designed to remove some of the defects of the system and hence to prevent its disintegration or breakdown. However, the consultative

[54] Cf. Schwartz and Keech, *op.cit.*, pp. 849-851. On communist states in Eastern Europe, see Ionescu, *op.cit.*, pp. 81-85, 165-166, 273ff.

403

process was not embodied in institutional form and was restricted to the elite sectors of Soviet society. Moreover, the activity of groups continued to be regarded as illegitimate and to be hemmed in by many restrictions, increasingly so under Khrushchev's successors.

At the same time, the rise of interest groups was also the product of actions from below, particularly by the specialized elite groups, which took full advantage of the new opportunities created by the lessening of coercion and the atmosphere of intellectual and political relaxation associated with de-Stalinization. Professing loyalty to the communist system, but seeking to reform it, the professional groups often went beyond the role of invited consultants and acted as spokesmen of alternative policies, thus implicitly challenging the leading role of the party in decision-making. Sometimes the groups manifested an autonomy of action that overstepped the bounds set by the party and openly expressed opposition to policies initiated by the leaders. This in turn forced the latter to seek to regain control of the deliberations and to circumscribe group conflict. Increased repression in turn generated more radical opposition, which was sometimes, in Barghoorn's term, "subversive" in character.[55] A kind of seesaw of regime initiative and counterinitiative by groups therefore occurred, with gains and setbacks experienced by both sides. Still largely excluded from this informal give-and-take, and even more from formal participation in policy-making, were the larger social groups, such as workers, peasants, or nationalities.

It is, therefore, difficult to forecast the evolution of group activity in the Soviet Union. Soviet Russia is not a society with a long tradition of associational activity and wide freedom of discussion. On the contrary, Russian traditions, as well as communist theory and practice, have in the main been hostile to the idea of independent interest groups and have set strict limits to their activity. Yet the traditional role of the intelligentsia, especially of the writers, as the "conscience of the nation" and as a source of reforming and revolutionary ideas, must not be ignored.[56] During the Stalin period there was carried through a purposeful destruction of all bodies capable of resisting or even of slowing down the process of rapid political and economic development, and society was largely atomized into isolated individuals, dissuaded by terror from coming together for the defense of their interests. The very success of Soviet economic and social development under Stalin, how-

[55] Dahl (ed.), *op.cit.*
[56] Billington, in Kassof (ed.), *op.cit.*, pp. 453-457.

404

ever, undermined this totalitarian structure and, especially in the more relaxed environment of his successor, bred conditions conducive to a reconstitution of groups and of the process of group activity.

The emergence of a complex and differentiated society and the greater latitude for group activity in the post-Stalin period has made it unlikely, although not impossible, that the progress already achieved will be entirely reversed. Nonetheless, the rise of group activity has been and will no doubt continue to be slow and erratic and may suffer setbacks, as has already happened under Khrushchev's successors. It is not inevitable that the process will develop inexorably in the direction of a pluralist society, or a fully democratic one. Nor is it preordained that certain groups such as the managers or the creative intellectuals, or for that matter the *apparatchiki*, the police, or the military, will necessarily play the predominant role and decisively mold the shape and course of Soviet life.

There is, moreover, no assurance that interest group activity, in itself, will benefit the Soviet people. Much, if not everything, will depend on *which* groups predominate and *what* attitudes they take on the reform of the *status quo*. Nevertheless, the growing confidence of the specialized intellectual groups and their recent taste of greater freedom, as well as their indispensability in a modernized society, suggest that these groups may enjoy a certain scope for the expression of their views and the pressing of their claims. Whether their example will be contagious and will infect broader social groups; whether the latter will successfully strive to exert greater influence; whether existing social organizations, and others yet to be formed, will be more responsive to group attitudes; whether some form of group representation in a reformed electoral system will be developed—none of these can be foretold at present. Whether any of these developments occur, and in what form, will depend on the willingness and the desire of the leaders to encourage a more genuine expression of group interest, on the degree of insistence by the groups themselves, and on the interplay of these two factors in Soviet development.

Viability of the Interest Group Approach

Turning back to the question of method with which this volume began, we proceed now to discuss certain other ways in which the interest group approach can be implemented, or in fact has already been applied.

We conclude by considering certain fundamental criticisms of this approach and by drawing some conclusions.

ADDITIONAL APPLICATIONS OF THE METHOD

Our volume has not by any means exhausted the possibilities of using an interest group approach in the study of the Soviet political system. We have left untouched a number of crucially important aspects of group conflict. For one thing, there are many other elite groups within the Soviet intelligentsia as a whole which deserve study as much as those included in this book. This is undoubtedly true of the scientists and the educators, which have been analyzed elsewhere by other authors.[57] Although the amassing of data might be more difficult, research could be conducted concerning other categories of the technical and economic intelligentsia, such as engineers or agronomists, or of the scientific and cultural intelligentsia, such as artists or journalists. Similarly, it would be possible to analyze the attitudes and claims of groups such as state officials, both at the center and in the entire system of soviets; collective and state farm chairmen; managers in other sectors of industry and trade; and functionaries of mass associations.

Some critics have regretted our reluctance to cast the net of our investigations more widely to include some or all of the broader social categories of Soviet society. It must be admitted that attention has been concentrated, both in our own volume and in other studies, on elite interest groups. As noted earlier, we have taken the view that the opportunities for political articulation, at the present stage of Soviet development, are much less for the broader groups than for the elite groups and that evidence of group conflict of this kind is therefore more difficult to secure. The broader groups, while they do not possess the "power" of the official groups nor the "influence" of the intellectual groups, may have some means of articulating their interests and demands on society, for instance, the nationalities through the union-republic institutions and the republican party organizations; the workers, through the trade-unions; the peasants, through the raikom and obkom party secretaries, or the local soviets; the women and youth, through their associations and their newspapers; and regional groupings through lower party and soviet organs. There is certainly no logical reason for

[57] On the scientists, see Graham, *loc.cit.*; Alexander Vucinich, "Science," in Kassof (ed.), *op.cit.*, Chap. 12. On the educators, see Richard Little, "The Academy of Pedagogical Sciences—Its Political Role," *Soviet Studies*, XIX, No. 3 (January 1968), 387-397.

excluding from interest group analysis such broader categoric aggregates, and research in this area might be productive. Some evidence has been presented by other scholars that such groups and the conflicting opinion groups within their ranks have found means of expressing their interests and opinions and pressing them on policy-makers.[58]

Another possible target of research, already suggested by the foregoing, is the organized associations active in Soviet public life. This would include not only those with massive membership, such as the trade-unions or the *Komsomol*, but also the creative unions and the many other smaller organizations, such as the Association for the Protection of Nature or the Association for the Maintenance of Historical Monuments. One of our contributors dealt with an organized interest group, the Writers' Union, and concluded that it did not fulfill the purpose of representing the interests of its members. Further research concerning other associational groups might provide evidence as to whether these groups resemble those in other political systems or differ profoundly from them, and whether they are becoming significant elements of the Soviet political process.

We have also imposed another limitation on ourselves by focusing on group conflict at the center of the Soviet political system and at the all-union level. The clash of interest groups is, of course, likely to be duplicated at lower levels, away from Moscow, as at least one of our contributors, in discussing the *apparatchiki*, has demonstrated. In a book written seven years ago, the veteran analyst of Soviet politics, Merle Fainsod, examined in detail the conflicting tensions and pressures at work in the Smolensk oblast.[59] Although he did not employ the concept of interest groups, Fainsod gave abundant evidence of the conflicts of the oblast party organization with various social groups, and with other institutional agencies such as the police, the military, the soviet

---

[58] On the nationalities, in addition to the Chornovil Papers cited above, see Vernon V. Aspaturian, "The Non-Russian Nationalities," in Kassof (ed.), *op.cit.*, Chap. 7, esp. pp. 168-173, where he discussed the unsuccessful resistance of the non-Russian nationalities to the educational reforms in 1959. See also Y. Bilinsky, *The Second Soviet Republic: The Ukraine After World War II* (New Brunswick, 1964), esp. Chap. 8. On the youth, and the expression of their interests through literature, see Peter Viereck, "The Mob Within the Heart: A New Russian Revolution," in Juviler and Morton (eds.), *op.cit.*, pp. 101-102, 109. On women, as "a significant but not decisive grouping" in the discussions of family law reform, see Juviler, in Juviler and Morton (eds.), *op.cit.*, pp. 47, 55. On religious groups, see B. R. Bociurkiw, "Religion and Soviet Society," *Survey*, No. 60 (July 1966), pp. 62-71.

[59] *Smolensk Under Soviet Rule* (New York, 1963).

407

organs, etc. He also discussed the conflicts within the obkom organization, between different departments, and with the raion organizations below and the central organs above. He stressed the presence of local alliances, or "family circles," which linked together agencies and groups at the oblast, raion, or collective farm level, in order to defend local interests against the next higher level of authority.[60] Another study at the oblast level, in Stalingrad, was conducted by Philip Stewart, who examined what he called "institutional" interest groups and offered other concepts useful for group analysis in general.[61]

Our book has concentrated on individual groups, and the character and role of each one in certain relevant aspects of the political process. Another fruitful approach would be to examine specific issues of public policy and the part played by conflicting interest groups in their discussion and resolution. Some case studies have in fact been included by our contributors in their chapters on the military, the economists, and the lawyers and have been attempted by other authors.[62] As suggested by both Hough and Griffiths, such an approach, examining not one group in relative isolation, but the cluster of groups or "interest complex" in a given arena of controversy, would clarify the range of relevant groups, the alliances for and against particular solutions, and the degree of success or failure attained by individual groups or coalitions. It would be possible for each case to construct a specific model of group activity and policy-making in the Soviet context. Research based on a series of models of this kind might bring out more clearly the essential features of Soviet policy-making and the role of groups therein.

Our contributors, without exception, have employed traditional methods of research and have eschewed a behavioral approach. Milton Lodge has used mathematical behaviorism in several studies of Soviet "elites," making a detailed statistical analysis of five major groups, namely the central party *apparatchiki*, the central economic bureaucrats,

---

[60] *Ibid.*, pp. 85, 107, 111, 270-273.

[61] *Political Power in the Soviet Union.* His attention was devoted primarily to the party secretaries, the heads of the soviets, the Komsomol, and the leaders of some major industries, and to a lesser extent to the weaker literary, scientific, educational, and engineering groups, and to their "potential influence" through representation and participation in the party obkom structure.

[62] Schwartz and Keech, *op.cit.*, and Stewart, "Soviet Interest Groups." Cf. also Little, *op.cit.*; Graham, *op.cit.*; Juviler, in Juviler and Morton (eds.), Chap. 2; and Armstrong, *ibid.*, Chap. 7.

the military, the literary intelligentsia, and the legal profession.[63] This involved a systematic selection of data from the leading articles in certain newspapers which were deemed to express the attitudes of the specific elites, during a period extending from 1952 to 1965. Lodge concluded that the five categories each possessed some degree of group self-consciousness and shared certain values on policy issues; that the groups were pressing for a greater degree of influence in policy-making and that elite participation did in fact greatly increase over the period, thus intensifying conflict between the party and the other groups. The study suffers, however, from a major weakness in that it neglects the possibility of differences of attitude within each elite. In the case of the literary elite, this is compounded by the use of two newspapers of sharply opposed orientation, *Oktyabr* and *Novy mir*, as the source of "the attitude" of the group. Although much may be learned from a computer analysis of this kind, one should guard against the illusion that its findings are more "scientific" than those provided by the traditional method of carefully weighing important articles and speeches from a wide variety of sources.[64]

THE BALANCE OF OPINION

In the many discussions conducted during the preparation of this volume, and referred to in the preface, a wide array of opinion was expressed on the relevance of the interest group approach to Soviet politics. On the one hand there were skeptics who argued that this approach distorted the reality of politics in the USSR by minimizing the dominant role of the party and exaggerating the part played by groups. On the other hand, there were critics who believed that the method was valid and productive and should be carried to its logical conclusion by being applied to other groups in Soviet society. Finally, there was a third reaction,

[63] See the articles by Lodge, cited in n. 1, above.

[64] A somewhat similar content analysis of newspapers and journals which were assumed to represent six Soviet and American elites that exert influence on decision-makers was published by Robert C. Angell and J. David Singer, "Social Values and Foreign Policy Attitudes of Soviet and American Elites," *Journal of Conflict Resolution*, VIII (December 1964), 329-491. The six Soviet elites were the military, scientific, cultural, labor, government-party, and economic. The results of this massive statistical analysis were meager and revealed little significant information about differences among Soviet elites. More meaningful results were achieved by Vera Dunham, in an article included in the Angell and Singer report, in which she used literary sources to identify differences of view within the cultural elite and to detect the influences exerted by them on the political elite.

expressed by one of the editors, Franklyn Griffiths, who recognized the conflict of interests and opinions as central to Soviet politics, but preferred to treat this in terms of "tendencies of articulation," as set forth in his chapter above.

The response of the skeptics reflected their feeling that the Soviet system was so different from Western pluralistic societies that an analysis using a concept derived primarily from the American or Western political experience was inappropriate. It was argued that Soviet political culture, indeed Russian culture throughout the centuries, was hostile to pluralism in any shape or form. Soviet official ideology not only repudiated *gruppovshchina* (groupism) but set rigid confines within which opinions could be expressed. There were many institutional limitations on freedom of expression, especially censorship, and on freedom of association, which hampered the articulation of group interests and made research on the subject difficult, if not impossible. The relative weaknesses of mass organizations and of representative bodies in the Soviet Union, and the unorganized character of whatever group activity occurred, were regarded as serious impediments to effective group action. Above all, the overwhelming predominance of the party apparatus, and the means available to it for the control of other entities and associations, prevented the emergence of groups that had any degree of autonomy of action. Hence like-minded persons possessed no formal ways of expressing their interests and attitudes and could not organize themselves in a meaningful way. The articulation of interests could therefore at best be esoteric and Aesopian, and the resulting effects might be better described as representing "trends of opinion" or "informal groupings." These considerations led to doubts whether such groups as might be discerned could have any substantial effect on policy-making. In sum, the essential conditions of pluralism, in the form of some degree of group integration and means of mutual communication and some degree of autonomy, were absent.[65]

The more positive reaction to the interest group approach recognized the existence of diverse groups and tendencies and the crucial significance of conflict among them in the Soviet political process, thus providing a partial response to the skeptics. Arguing that group conflict

[65] See Andrew C. Janos, "Group Politics in Communist Society: A Second Look at the Pluralistic Model," in Samuel P. Huntington and Clement H. Moore (eds.), *Authoritarian Politics in Modern Society: The Dynamics of One-Party Systems* (New York, 1970), pp. 437-450.

410

existed even under Stalin, these critics observed that in the post-Stalin period the opportunities for group action greatly expanded and that both new groups and new techniques of expression had emerged. Admitting the limiting factors of party primacy and institutional controls, they stressed the widened possibilities of group articulation, partly with the encouragement, and partly in defiance, of the supreme political authorities. The party apparatus no longer possessed the apparently absolute powers of the past and was itself divided, so that its all-embracing control over other groups was diluted, and its function was increasingly that of an arbiter, or even a mediator, between competing groups. The leadership was more and more dependent on expert advice and had to choose between conflicting views of specialist groups.[66] Moreover groups, in various degrees, sometimes escaped from the party's power and defended their own interests and attitudes with some measure of independence. While interest group action was often informal and unorganized, this did not, it was thought, militate against the usefulness of group analysis. Moreover, groups were able to use institutions and organizations as arenas of discussion and as bases of operation, and in some cases to establish control of them. Party ideology was a constricting factor, but it did not prevent the assertion of differing viewpoints, each claiming to be the correct interpretation of official doctrine. Similarly, while professing obedience to party policy, groups could present diverse and dissenting views as to the correct meaning of the party line. Communications were overt as well as esoteric, so that research on this subject, although often difficult, was not impossible for the Western scholar.

Griffiths, in his chapter, offered cogent criticisms of the "group approach" as exemplified by the work of David Truman. He expressed doubt as to the utility of the concept of the aggregate or reified "political interest group." He argued that this concept could be applied only with difficulty to Soviet politics inasmuch as the aggregate nature of the group eludes precise definition, as does its impact on policy. He found Bentley a valuable starting point for developing a mode of analysis which used the concept of "tendency of articulation" and focused on the streams or tendencies of activity within the system as a whole rather than on the inter-relations of groups as subsystems. While stressing conflict as an essential feature of Soviet politics, Griffiths emphasized,

[66] Cf. Jerry F. Hough, "Reforms in Government and Administration," in Dallin and Larson (eds.), *op.cit.*, pp. 37-38.

as he put it, "issues rather than groups," and "the process of tendency conflict on these issues rather than the conflict of structures invested with purposes and power of their own."[67]

Griffiths' alternative approach includes a number of suggestive conceptions of value in interpreting Soviet politics. Without ignoring the significant differences between the two approaches, this editor does not, however, find the two completely incompatible or mutually exclusive. Although Truman's analysis was taken as my point of departure, many reservations were made as to its applicability to the Soviet political scene and his concepts were adjusted accordingly. In particular, group conflict was not treated as the central or even the predominant feature of Soviet politics, nor was it assumed that the groups as subsystems were dominant in the political process. The analysis emphasized, moreover, not the structured or organized character of groups but rather the empirically determined patterns of action which may characterize either a whole occupational group or an opinion group within an occupational category. This was not entirely removed from the approach of Bentley, who, of course, was also an exponent of an *interest group* analysis. Nor was it far from the concept of the "analytical group" discussed by Griffiths. I was more inclined, however, to accept as a reality the interaction within the individual Soviet group, or between groups, since members are presumably well aware of the actions and ideas of others and mutually influence each other.

The term "tendencies of articulation" is especially valuable in directing attention to the common streams of action outside the framework of the occupational group. My approach, although recognizing the differentiation within an occupational group and the existence of opinion groups that cut across occupational lines, ran the risk of creating the impression that groups were to be identified exclusively or mainly with occupations. The use of the alternate somewhat abstract concept proposed by Griffiths, however, may be no less free of problems than the use of the concept of "the interest group." Nor would there be any less difficulty in estimating the influence on policy. In practice, therefore, to refer to "groups" and "group alliances" may in fact be a useful way to make more concrete otherwise diffuse "tendencies of articulation." In turn, tendency conflict analysis may provide a framework for interpreting interrelations within and among groups.

[67] See Chap. x, p. 372 above.

The other contributors to this volume accepted the validity of the concept of "interest groups" and its value as a tool of research. Most of them warned of the great differences between interest groups in the Soviet and noncommunist systems but concluded that the term could be usefully adapted to Soviet conditions. In their own analysis, however, they defined the term differently and employed it in varying ways. Some tended to adopt a version closer to Truman; others, one that was derived from Bentley. Some laid the greatest stress on the common interests of an occupational group; others emphasized the importance of conflicting opinion groups within the occupational categories. We did not regard it as desirable, even if it were possible, to insist on a unified approach binding on all contributors and have resisted the temptation, in this concluding chapter, to question assumptions or concepts which do not conform to those proposed in the opening chapters.

The conclusions set forth above are those that may be drawn from the data on group activity presented in the individual chapters. In this editor's opinion, these confirm many of the hypotheses concerning the character of interest groups and their relevance in the Soviet political process, on which the volume was originally based. Far from creating, as some have argued, a chaos of unstructured facts, the interest group approach provides a useful method of organizing some of the data of Soviet politics. These findings may also be valuable in making the analysis of tendency articulations by intermediate actors proposed by my coeditor. Unlike the latter analysis, however, the interest group concept does not offer a complete model of the Soviet political system or of the process of decision-making within that system. I do not assume, as already noted, that political interest groups are the principal feature of Soviet politics, or that these groups are the dominant factors in the political process. They are, however, an important element, the neglect of which makes the picture of Soviet politics incomplete and distorted, and the inclusion of which renders it richer and more authentic. To that degree, in my view, the volume has amply demonstrated the utility of the interest group approach to Soviet politics.

During the past two years there has been an increasing readiness among Western scholars to recognize the existence of "interest groups" and their importance in Soviet politics.[68] As indicated by the literature

[68] Juviler and Morton (*op.cit.*, pp. v-ix, 9-13) referred to "pluralistic pressures" and "opinion groups," and of the "latent opposition," amorphous and unorganized, of peasants, workers, nationalities, religious groups, and the younger

413

cited in this chapter, the interest group approach has already attracted a number of practitioners in the field of Soviet studies. We are, however, under no illusion that this approach will be generally accepted as appropriate for the study of Soviet society. In the Soviet Union, interest group analysis, as applied to the United States, has been subjected to forceful criticism, and there is no evidence of a willingness to consider its possible usefulness for the study of communist systems.[69] In the West

---

generation, and of "loyal opposition" of ministerial bureaucrats, planners, scientists, managers, military leaders, technical experts, social scientists, and cultural authorities (pp. 8-9). Kassof (*op.cit.*) wrote of "the absence of professional, occupational, regional or ethnic groupings with a meaningful degree or organization" (p. 7) and of the difficulties under which interest groups operate, but noted the "cross-pressures generated by the increasingly complex and vocal 'constituencies' that arise in a society dependent upon the services of indispensable functional groups—managers, scientists, military professionals, and the like." He argued that "the arena for the interplay of interest groups, though still modest, has expanded significantly" (p. 498) and predicted "some increases in individual and group autonomy" (p. 501). Dan Jacobs, "The Politburo in the First and Fifth Decades of Soviet Power," in London (ed.), *op.cit.*, described the Politburo as "a mediator of interests, a resolver of externally based demands," and referred to the youth, intelligentsia, industry and government bureaucracy as conducting assaults on it (pp. 59, 71). Dallin and Westin wrote of the conflicts between "segments of the Soviet bureaucracy," "the myth of a homogeneous ruling party," and "strains at the lower levels" between various groups. They noted that "the circle of participants in Soviet politics has expanded significantly" and that "something like 'interest groups'" have begun to crystallize (*op.cit.*, pp. x-xi). David Lane, in a brief review article, "Socialist Pluralism," *Political Studies*, XVI (February 1968), 102-105, wrote: "The crux of the analysis of political power in the U.S.S.R. is the interrelationship between these groups. The party as a vertically articulated unit, the 'vanguard' of Leninist theory, no longer is apposite to a relatively stable, heterogeneous, industrial society." Milton Lodge, in "'Groupism'" (p. 351), described the party as "not a monolith but rather a competitive political arena in which the specialist elites (commanding knowledge, skills, and technical expertise as political resources) come in conflict with the overriding interest of the *apparatchiki* in maintaining its privileged position in the political system" (p. 351). In his "Soviet Elite" (p. 839), Lodge writes: "The conception of the Soviet political system as a monolith is a myth." He believes that "the Party is not omnipotent," and that "Party-Specialist elite interdependence, not Party dominance, characterizes Party-elite relations." "New models of Soviet politics are obviously needed" (p. 839).

[69] See the well-informed exposition and criticism of American literature on *zainteresovannye gruppy* by V. G. Kalensky, *Politicheskaya nauka v S SH A* (Moscow, 1969), pp. 29-41. Contrast *Osnovy nauchnovo kommunizma* (3rd ed., Moscow, 1968) for a brief and orthodox discussion of "groups" or "working collectives" in Soviet society. The "collective" is there defined as "a group of people, who find themselves in immediate intercourse with each other, who perform definite industrial, scientific-technical or other tasks in the interests of society, and who are bound together by a common aim, and a disciplined and reciprocal responsibility." There is no discussion of the political role of such groups except as a means of linking the personal and the social interest and guaranteeing personal freedom (pp. 504-505).

414

some scholars continue to prefer what seems to us to be the outdated model of totalitarianism. Early proponents of this concept, such as Hannah Arendt and Carl Friedrich, have defended its enduring value.[70] Other scholars have, however, in varying degree, criticized the usefulness of the totalitarian concept.[71] Some specialists find other conceptual schemes derived from Western political science, such as systems analysis, the organizational or bureaucratic models, the processes of communication or participation, the concepts of development or of the elite, more suitable for the Soviet context.[72] There is no virtue at this point in engaging in controversy about these alternatives. The value of combining relevant models in the interpretation of Soviet politics has in any case been argued with cogency.[73] No doubt in some cases various

[70] See Carl J. Friedrich, "Totalitarianism: Recent Trends," *Problems of Communism*, XVII, No. 3 (May-June 1968), 32-43. See also the new edition, revised by Friedrich, of Friedrich and Brzezinski, *Totalitarian Dictatorship and Autocracy* (2nd ed., Cambridge, Mass., 1965) and that of Hannah Arendt, *The Origins of Totalitarianism* (3rd ed., New York, 1966), both of which were reviewed at length by Robert Burrowes, "Totalitarianism: The Revised Standard Version," *World Politics*, XXI, No. 2 (January 1969), 272-294. For a defense of the totalitarian concept, see also the review of Friedrich's revised edition by Hugh Seton-Watson, in *Government and Opposition*, II, No. 1 (January 1967), 153-159, and his review article of books by Barghoorn, Meyer, and Azrael, "Totalitarianism Reconsidered," *Problems of Communism*, XVI, No. 4 (July-August 1967), 53-58. For a critical appraisal of the totalitarian concept, see Frederick J. Fleron, Jr., "Soviet Area Studies and the Social Sciences: Some Methodological Problems in Communist Studies," *Soviet Studies*, XIX, No. 3 (January 1968), 326-329, 338, reprinted in Fleron (ed.), *Communist Studies and the Social Sciences, Essays on Methodology and Empirical Theory* (Chicago, 1969), pp. 1-33.

See also Friedrich's review of Ionescu's book, *op.cit.*, in *Government and Opposition*, III, No. 2 (Spring 1968). In his original book and its later revision, as well as his more recent defenses of the concept of totalitarianism, Friedrich did not directly concern himself with interest groups, although implying that the totality of control rendered them either weak or nonexistent. In this review, Friedrich admitted that every society was to some degree pluralistic and argued that his concept of totalitarianism had taken these pluralisms ("islands of separateness") into account. Noting that the groups "permitted" by the apparatus had "an *esprit de corps*" and "a life of their own," he nonetheless argued that the totalitarian syndrome involved "a near monopoly of all effective organization devoid of almost all independent individual or group initiative" (pp. 253-254).

[71] In addition to the articles by Burrowes and Fleron cited above, see also Juviler and Morton (eds.), *op.cit.*, p. vi; Dallin and Westin (eds.), *op.cit.*, p. ix; Ionescu, *op.cit.*, p. 13. Lodge, "Soviet Elite," p. 839; Lane, *op.cit.*

[72] See the symposium by John A. Armstrong, Alfred G. Meyer, John H. Kautsky, Dan N. Jacobs, and Robert S. Sharlet, "Comparative Politics and Communist Systems," *Slavic Review*, XXVI, No. 1 (March 1967), 1-28. Fleron's *Communist Studies and the Social Sciences* contains reprints of articles which present a number of alternative methods, concepts, and models for the study of Soviet politics.

[73] See Alex Inkeles, "Models and Issues in the Analysis of Soviet Society," *Survey*, No. 60 (July 1966), pp. 3-17. Arguing that there is no such thing as a

models are mutually exclusive or basically contradictory, but in other cases they may usefully supplement each other. Each scholar, following his own preferred route, will no doubt contribute something to our deeper understanding of the Soviet political system. It is our view that the interest group approach, or the tendency analysis, can perform precisely such a function in the common enterprise of Soviet and communist studies.

---

right or wrong model but only "richer and poorer ones," Inkeles wrote: "All have a piece of the truth, but it is rare that any *one* model is really adequate to the analysis of a richly complex concrete historical case" (p. 3). While not rejecting the totalitarian model entirely, he subjects it to severe criticism.

LIST OF CONTRIBUTORS

H. GORDON SKILLING. Professor of Political Science, University of Toronto. Author of: *Communism National and International—Eastern Europe After Stalin* (Toronto, 1964); *The Governments of Communist East Europe* (New York, 1965).

JERRY F. HOUGH. Professor of Political Science, University of Toronto. Author of: *The Soviet Prefects: The Local Party Organs in Industrial Decision-Making* (Cambridge, Mass., 1969).

FREDERICK C. BARGHOORN. Professor of Political Science, Yale University. Author of: *Soviet Russian Nationalism* (New York, 1956); *Soviet Foreign Propaganda* (Princeton, 1964); *Politics in the USSR* (Boston, 1966).

ROMAN KOLKOWICZ. Professor of Political Science, University of California, Los Angeles. Author of: *The Soviet Military and the Communist Party* (Princeton, 1967). Editor of: *The Warsaw Pact* (Arlington, Va., 1969); *Soviet Strategies of Arms Control* (New York, 1970).

JOHN P. HARDT. Professorial Lecturer in Economics, Institute for Sino-Soviet Studies, the George Washington University and Head of the Strategic Studies Department, Research Analysis Corporation, McLean, Virginia. Author of: "Soviet Economic Development and Doctrinal Alternatives," in V. Treml (ed.), *The Development of the Soviet Economy: Plan and Performance* (New York, 1968); "Choices Facing the Soviet Planner," in M. Kaser, *Soviet Affairs*, No. 4, *St. Antony's Papers*, No. 19 (Oxford, 1966). Editor of: *Mathematics and Computers in Soviet Planning* (New Haven, 1966).

THEODORE FRANKEL. Editor-in-chief, *Problems of Communism*, Washington, D.C. Author of: "Methodology and Soviet Domestic Policy," *Canadian Slavic Studies*, *I*, No. 4 (Winter 1967); "Soviet Reforms: A Tentative Appraisal," *Problems of Communism*, *XVI*, No. 3 (May-June 1967); "Art, Politics and the Soviet Writer," *Commentary*, 41, No. 5 (May 1966).

RICHARD W. JUDY. Professor of Economics, University of Toronto. Author of: "Information, Control, and Soviet Economic Management," in *Mathematics and Computers in Soviet Economic Planning*

(New Haven, London, 1967); "The Measure of the Technological Gap Between the Soviet Union, Eastern Europe and the West: The Case of Computer Technology," in *East-West Trade and the Transfer of Technology* (New York, 1970).

ERNEST J. SIMMONS. Formerly Professor of Russian Literature at the Russian Institute, and Chairman of the Department of Slavic Languages, Columbia University. Author of: *Pushkin* (Cambridge, Mass., 1937); *Dostoevsky, the Making of a Novelist* (Oxford, 1940); *Leo Tolstoy* (Boston, 1946); *Russian Fiction and Soviet Ideology* (New York, 1958); *Chekhov* (Boston, 1962).

DONALD D. BARRY. Associate Professor of Government, Lehigh University. Author of: "The Specialist in Soviet Policy-Making: The Adoption of a Law," *Soviet Studies* (October 1964); "The USSR Supreme Court: Recent Developments," *Soviet Studies* (April 1969). Editor of: *Governmental Tort Liability in Eastern Europe* (Leiden, 1970).

HAROLD J. BERMAN. Professor of Law, Harvard Law School. Author of: *Justice in the USSR* (rev. ed., New York, 1963); *Soviet Criminal Law and Procedure: The RSFSR Codes* (Cambridge, Mass., 1966); *The Nature and Functions of Law* (2nd ed., with William R. Greiner, Brooklyn, 1966).

FRANKLYN GRIFFITHS. Associate Professor of Political Science, University of Toronto. Coauthor (with Lincoln P. Bloomfield and Walter C. Clemens, Jr.) of *Khrushchev and the Arms Race* (Cambridge, Mass., 1966); author of various articles on Soviet and Canadian foreign policy.

418

INDEX

Hungary, 120n, 274, 276
Huntington, Samuel P., 12, 47,
68-69, 340

individuals, as reified entities, 345n;
in bargaining over political
expectations, 368; in informal
groups, 342, reference groups,
348, reified groups, 343; in patterns
of interaction, 347; in tendencies
of activity, 353; reasons for
uniformity of behavior, 362-363;
role in articulating group
interests, 382
industrial enterprise directors, *see*
industrial managers
industrial managers, 11, 20n, 75-76,
236, 237, 292, 316, 350, 405;
access to decision-making, 173,
186-189, 202-203, 393; as a group,
9n, 33, 34, 171-173, 175, 176,
182, 186-187, 192, 194, 203-208,
366, 382; attitudes to economic
reform, 171-172, 196, 198-199,
227, 394, 396-397; conflicts among,
172, 173, 176, 206, 386; conflict
with other institutions, 172, 173;
defined, 175-177; education, 177,
178, 181, 185, 192-193, 198-200,
206n; group interests and public
interest, 383; interests shared
with ministries, 202; number,
175-178 *passim*, 177n, 178n, 192,
192n, 380; party control, 172, 184,
188-189, 202, 400; party
membership, 176, 178, 181;
political background, 177-181
passim; purges, 178, 179, 181,
188, 194; social background, 177,
179-181, 192; tenure, 179, 181-182,
194
    articulation of interests: at
conferences, 186-187, 201; by
bargaining with ministries, 187;
through members of ruling elite,
188; through technical journals,
201, 201n
    common interests, 183, 187,
386; autonomy of operation, 183-
184, 194-198; personal income and
status, 185-186, 200, 204;
professionalism, 184-185, 198-200,
205
Inkeles, Alex, 5, 10n, 415-416n
Institute for the Study of Crime, 312n
Institute of Soviet Legislation, 312n

Institute of State and Law, Academy
of Sciences, 312n, 314
Institute of the National Economy
(Moscow), 238 (table 1), 242,
246 (table 3)
institutional interest groups,
408, 408n
intellectual dissent, and KGB, 97,
115, 119
interest, defined, 27-28, 28n
interest complex, 408
interest group analysis, and its
application to the Soviet Union,
11, 23, 31, 38, 47-49, 133-134,
292-293, 335-336, 340-351, 354-357,
405-416, 414n; alternative
approach, 412-416, 415n.
See also chapter X
interest groups, 24-29, 31-33,
31n, 338, 339, 339n, 381-382
    access to decision-making, 39-42,
393; actions taken on own initiative,
392-393; as pattern of interaction,
339, 339n; as reified entities, 338,
340-341, 343-345, 354, 411; as
specialists, 10, 10n, 34, 34n;
attitudes to change, 173, 394-398;
cohesion and differentiation,
384-387; influence on policy-making,
44-45, 344, 390-391, 394, 401;
interaction of members, 31-32,
31n, 32n; media used, 42-44, 393;
mobility within, 32; potential
influence, 344, 344n, 408; use of
coercion and persuasion, 389-390
    activity, 38-40, 44; anomic, 44;
bargaining, 368, 368n; coercion
as method, 389, 403; increase in,
403-405; lack of organization, 382;
official policy towards, 44, 399-404,
401n; persuasion, as method, 366,
389-390, 403; private expression,
43-44; Western speculation about,
402, 402n. *See also* elites,
individuals
    alliances, 26, 387-389; in
appropriation process, 61-64
passim, 77, 81-82; in debate on
economics, 231-245; party and police
against the military, 98. *See also*
cross-group linkage, heavy industry,
resource allocation
    conflict, 8-10, 9n, 399; among
top leaders, 35-36, 391-392;
impact upon opinion, 391; in

423

military by party, 98. *See also*
the specific chapters
Politburo, 40, 258, 316, 393,
395; as mediator of interests, 414n
political economy, draft textbook, 222n
Political Power: USA/USSR by
Brzezinski and Huntington, 340
Ponomarev, B. N., 84n
Pool, Ithiel de Sola, 345
Poskrebyshev, A. N., 114n, 117
Pound, Roscoe, 294, 295
Powell, G. B., 39, 89, 91, 188
Powers, Francis, 309
Pravda, 43, 104, 115n, 127, 184,
221, 222, 234, 235, 254, 263,
264, 269, 272, 275, 276, 284, 401
Právny obzor, 13
Preobrazhensky, Y. A., 185
price formation, 240-241; discussion
after *1955*, 241-242; discussion and
compromise, *1962, 1963*, 242-247;
discussion in *1930's*, 219; in *1951*,
220n; reform of July *1967*, 245.
See also economists
private associations, *see* pressure
groups
The Process of Government by
Bentley, 337; as bond between
groups, 207; tendency analysis,
351-357
procuracy, fear of MGB under Stalin,
117; functions, 311; in tsarist
Russia, 298n, 311; post-*1917*, 298,
298n; opposition to legal scholars'
proposals on right to counsel, 329;
role in hearing complaints of
citizens, 332
Procurator General of USSR, 311, 321
professionalism, and conflicts cutting
across institutional lines, 208
*Progress, Coexistence, and
Intellectual Freedom* by Sakharov,
285
Proletcult, congress of, 254
propaganda, as instrument of
persuasion, 389
public protests against trials of
writers, 278-280
purges, 179, 188, 273-274; of
economists, 216, 219, 220; of
managers, 178-179, 181, 188, 194;
of secret police, 105; of writers, 261
Pysin, Konstantin, 58, 59

RAPP (Russian Association of
Proletarian Writers), 255-256

ratchet principle in planning, 62
Red Army, *see* military
Red Directors, 177-179 *passim*, 183,
187, 192
Richman, Barry, 198
Rigby, T. H., 9
Roberts, Henry L., 372n
Romashkin, P. S., 316n
Rome, 279
Rosenau, James, 362
Rudenko, R. A., 311, 311n, 316
Rudkovsky, A., 201n
Rudnev, K., 197
Rumania, 120n, 276
Rumyantsev, A. M., 210-211, 210n,
212, 275, 367, 401n
Russian tradition, absence of pluralism,
410; hostile to concept of
independent groups, 404; use of
police, 99-100

Sakharov, Andrei D., 399n;
memorandum of, 285, 397
Salinger, J. D., 276
samizdat, 277, 283, 288, 390
Sartre, Jean-Paul, 281
Savinkov, Nikolai I., 118, 118n
Schwartz, Joel, 340, 344
Schwartz, Solomon M., 179
Scientific Council on the Application
of Mathematics and Computers in
Economic Research and Planning,
243, 243n
Scientific Council on Economic
Accounting and Material Stimulation,
and economic reform, 236-237
Scientific Council on Problems of
Price Formation, conferences,
1962, 1963, 242-243, 243 (table 2)
scientists, 11, 24, 122, 122n, 129,
138; access to power, 393; allied
with optimality group of
economists, 244; and improved
criteria in enterprises, 227-228;
and Liberman proposals, 238
(table 1); attitudes to change, 397;
classified by subgroups, 25-26;
criticism of economists, 229-231
passim; influence on policy, 394
Secret Service (USA), 93
security agencies, 154, 172, 183, 301,
309, 341, 350, 405; access to power,
393; and factional struggles of top
leaders, 98, 114n, 392; and
intellectual dissent, 97, 115, 115n,
120-121; as a group, 9, 9n, 20n,

BOOKS WRITTEN UNDER THE AUSPICES OF THE
CENTRE FOR RUSSIAN AND EAST EUROPEAN STUDIES,
UNIVERSITY OF TORONTO

Peter Brock and H. Gordon Skilling (eds.), *The Czech Renascence of the Nineteenth Century* (University of Toronto Press, 1970).

James R. Gibson, *Feeding the Russian Fur Trade* (University of Wisconsin Press, 1969).

Brenton Barr, *The Soviet Wood-Processing Industry* (University of Toronto Press, 1970).

George S. N. Luckyj, *Between Gogol' and Ševčenko* (Harvard Series in Ukrainian Studies, Wilhelm Fink Verlag, Munich, forthcoming).